Time

- Gateway to Immortality

Wilbur Wright

Wright Books
Southampton

First published in Great Britain by

Wright Books
The Shrubs
Allington Lane
Southampton SO3 3HP

Printed by Hobbs the Printers, Millbrook, Southampton, from Camera-Ready Copy as supplied. Set in Times Roman.

ISBN Number 0 9512547 3 1

This book is dedicated to
the 33rd Aircraft Apprentice Entry
R.A.F. Halton 1936–1938

CONTENTS

Introduction			Page 3
Chapter 1		Precognition	11
	2	Time, Space and Dimension	50
	3	Dreams	100
	4	Inspiration and the Time Shunt	132
	5	What Kind of Universe ?	153
	6	The Enigma of Identical Twins	183
	7	Probability, Synchronicity, Destiny	194
	8	Mind and Consciousness	218
	Index		
	Bibliography		

LIST OF ILLUSTRATIONS

		Page
1.	Dunne's Time Mechanism	55
2.	Ouspensky's View of Time	66
3.	Earth Duration—Extension—Space 1	73
4.	Earth Duration—Extention—Space 2	74
5.	Space 2 Dimensions	75
6.	Flatland	78
7.	Lineland	79
8.	Euclid's Fifth Postulate	80
9.	Riemannian Geometry	81
10.	Rotation of Cylinder	82
11.	Mobius Strip Universe	83
12.	Bentov—Subjective/Objective Time	84
13.	—Effects of Rotation	85
14.	—Superliminal Velocities	86
15.	Levels of Consciousness	89
16.	Levels of Consciousness—Menzones	90
17.	Image Production	125
18.	The Time Shunt	140
19.	Curved Space 2 Dimensions	160
20.	Thomas Young Experiment—2 Slits Open	166
21.	Diffusion Pattern—1 Slit Open	167
22.	Anticipated Pattern, Both Slits Open	167
23.	Actual Pattern, Both Slits Open	167
24.	Space-Time Distortion	170
25.	Radical Expansion from a Single Discontinuity	171
26.	Galactic Distortion at High Velocities	176
27.	Human Duration-Extension	178
28.	Probabilities and Possibilities	200
29.	The Human Brain	223
30.	Neuron—Diagrammatic	225
31.	Magnetic Induced Coherent State	242
32.	Limb Regeneration in Salamander	255

GLOSSARY

AD	Anno Domini
AVM	Air Vice Marshal
BC	Before Christ
BE	Bose Einstein
CO	Commanding Officer
DG	Dyzygotic (twins)
DNA	Deoxyribonucleic Acid
ECG	Electro-encephalograph
EMF	Electro-Magnetic Field
EMG	Electro-magnetic
FTF	Fixed Time Field
FTL	Faster than Light
GI	Government Issue
KE	Kinetic Energy
kps	Kilometres per second
kph	Kilometres per hour
MZ	Monozygotic (twins)
MP	Military Police
mph	Miles Per Hour
mps	Miles Per Second
PC,PCG	Precognition
PCE	Precognitive Experience
PF	Probability Field
PM	Present Moment
R.A.F.	Royal Air Force
RNA	Ribonucleic Acid
RNZAF	Royal New Zealand Air Force
St.	Saint
STBD.	Starboard
ST	Space-Time
STC	Space-Time Continuum
UFO	Unidentified Flying Object

FOREWORD

This is, in my opinion, the most important book on Time since J.W. Dunne's last book *`Intrusions'* appeared in 1950. This was my opinion even when I read it in an earlier and much clumsier version called *`Immortality and the I Ching'*. Now, in this expanded and revised text, I have no doubt that it will take it's place beside Tyrrell's *`Personality of Man'* and Rhine's *`Reach of the Mind'* as a classic of 20th century parapsychology.

My acquaintance with this remarkable man was a matter of pure chance. My literary agent rang me some time in the mid-80s to say that he had met a writer named Wilbur Wright at a literary party, and that Wilbur had asked if I might be interested in looking at a typescript on the subject of Time. My first reaction was to groan : I receive, on average, two unsolicited typescripts every week, and have learned that the best thing is to put them in the post the same day - otherwise they get mislaid, and I find myself having to respond apologetically to increasingly indignant letters from their authors. But when my agent assured me that Mr. Wright seemed to be a normal and sane person - and that, moreover, he was a successful novelist - I decided that it was probably worth taking the risk of being saddled with some gigantic and incomprehensible work full of mathematical diagrams.

In fact, *Immortality and the I Ching* was a small, neatly-bound book and proved to be as easy to read as it was to hold. There was something reassuring about its personal tone and its lack of abstract words. He explained that between 1946 and 1954 he had three times dreamed the winners of major races - and this in spite of the fact that he did not have the slightest interest in horse racing. This had made it obvious to him that there is something wrong about our commonsense idea of Time. It must mean, in fact, that there is some sense in which future events have already taken place. This flies in the face of our most basic experience of Time - that it is a kind of one-way street. Dunne's famous*`Experiment with Time'* (1927) had pointed out that when we say that Time `flies' or that it drags, we must be measuring it against some other sort of Time. And presumably there must be some other time by which we measure this second sort, and so on *ad infinitum*. Dunne's `Serial Time' seemed to posit a kind of multiple universe in which everything than can happen *does* happen. And this somehow offends our sense of economy, since it demands an infinite number of you's and me's. Wilbur Wright was suggesting something rather less bewildering - a universe in which all events exist as *possibilities*, but which are `actualised' one at a time.

Now, what makes his idea so fascinating is that he is no abstract theorist with the mind of a jigsaw-puzzle enthusiast. He is a practical man - and, considering his achievments as a writer, a remarkably modest one - who has been driven to brood on the problem through personal experience. When I asked him what had first drawn his attention to the problem, he told me it was the experience of his fellow fighter-pilot Doug Worley, who dreamt of his own death in action the next day (the story will be found in the introduction to this book, so I shall not repeat it.) His own dreams of winners in subsequent years confirmed his sense of what `Professor' Joad called `the undoubted queerness of Time'.

When Bernard Shaw was frequenting the British Museum Reading Room as a young man, be became acquainted with a strange character called Thomas Tyler, an expert on ancient Middle Eastern languages and on the sonnets of Shakespeare (Shaw describes him in his preface to *The Dark Lady of the Sonnets*.) Tyler had had a number of these `premonition' experiences which Wilbur Wright describes in the opening chapter of this book - `I have been here before' - which led him to consider that Nietzsche was correct, and that universal history repeats itself over and over again, like some popular film that goes on for endless performances. This led Tyler to assume that free will is an illusion. He made his own translation of the Book of Ecclesiastes, and preached a total and nihilistic pessimism.

Shaw sees to have accepted the `I have been here before' experience, but argued that the Life Force has merely hit upon the device of the clockmaker's pendulum to give life the chance to evolve.

Wilbur Wright also declines to allow his observations to decline into pessimism. He cites, for example, the case of `Lady Z', who dreamed that her coachman fell off his box and landed on his head. The next day, when she observed her coachman slumped forward, she called a policeman who caught the man before he fell off the box. The same point arises in a story cited by Louisa Rhine, of how a young mother dreamed of a camping trip in which she left her baby unattended by a stream, and the baby drowned. When, weeks later, she was on a camping trip and suddenly recognised the scene of her dream, she tucked the baby under her arm when she returned to the tent to collect the soap - and so, we must assume, averted the tragedy.

Now, in this respect, Wright's theory of Time has an element in common with that of P.D. Ouspensky, whose novel `*The Strange Life of Ian Osokin*' is based on his own `I have been here before' experiences. But although Ouspensky, like Nietzsche and Tyler, accepted them as proof of `eternal reoccurrence', he declined to believe that each swing of the pendulum *has* to be identical. We *can* alter events. Life is not a film but a play, in which the actor can give a dull or a brilliant performance of the same part. And, little by little, the events themselves will change with each swing of the pendulum.

Wilbur Wright goes a step further. While we can predict exactly where the earth will be in X years from now, we cannot predict where human beings will be, because human beings have the ability to move about, to some extent, within the `Probability Field'.

Now, this is an extremely important consequence that immediately carries Wright beyond the limits of the Time theories of Dunne and Ouspensky. Precognition certainly exists; but it is not precognition of something that must and *will* happen. It is more like consulting a railway timetable, which tells us that a train is due to run at a certain time, but not what will happen to it. Which is why, to some extent, it is possible to change what will happen.

My own favourite illustration is a story told by Brian Inglis in `*The Power of Dreams*'. A girl woke up imagining that she was in bed with a male colleague - a colleague to whom she was not remotely attracted. But later that day, after an office party, she ended up with the colleague in a `necking situation' in a car, and he begged her to let him go back to her flat. About to agree, she remembered her `dream' and refused. It struck her later that she might well have ended up pregnant - these were the days of inadequate contraception - and that her dream had been a kind of warning.

What strikes me as so important here is that it underlines one of the basic problems of human existence - our tendency to live `mechanically', taking life for granted. The girl might have found her job rather boring. But the thought of a shotgun wedding - or an abortion - must have made her suddenly recognise that compared to an unwanted pregnancy, the most boring office job is a cause for rejoicing.

This, for me, is the most important problem of human existence : that crises `awaken' us to the delightfulness of `normal' everyday life, and that if we were not so stupid, we would be able to awaken ourselves, so that boredom would become an impossibility.

This is why Wilbur Wright's book produced in me that curious sensation that G.K.Chesterton called `absurd good news'. There is a great deal in his theory that I do not understand, and a great deal on which I feel I must simply suspend judgement. But as I read this book for the second time, I found that my scalp prickled again and again with the kind of excitement that A.E. Houseman says he experiences as he reads poetry. Consider, for example, this passage from the author's `Summation' on page 149 :

> *`There are two basic categories of human inspiration : the involuntary input usually encountered in altered states of consciousness, and voluntary inspiration appearing as a flash of intuition leading to the solution of a problem with which the conscious mind has been grappling fruitlessly.*
>
> *`All the evidence suggests that inspiration emanates from a source outside the body in our 3-D universe.*

`That source is the migratory omnipresent element of the human personality which has its own duration-extension in Space 2.'

Now having read that remarkable Chapter Four several times, I *think* I understand what he is saying. Yet in a sense, precise understanding hardly seems to matter. What excites me is that, like Hegel, Wilbur Wright is an inspired thinker who has constructed his `system' on certain basic insights. And, like Hegel, he is a kind of visionary who is permanently thwarted by the inadequacy of human language. These insights have produced in him a fundamental conviction of *meaning*, the notion that life is not a mechanical dance of atoms, or a Hardyesque tragedy, but some kind of magnificent revelation that we are capable, in certain moments, of grasping and transforming. By writing *`Time - Gateway to Immortality'*, I believe that Wilbur Wright has staked his own claim to the kind of immortality that will be conferred by readers in the future.

Colin Wilson
Gorran Haven

Trigger Mechanism

This photograph of the `old hands' of No. 3 Fighter Squadron on a German airfield early in 1945, includes (left to right, back row) : Hassal, Pierre Clostermann, Walker, Peter West, the Commanding Officer Bruce Cole, and Macintyre. Front row - Gordon Duff, Doug Worley, Wilbur Wright and Torpy. It is reproduced with his kind permission from Pierre Clostermann's book `*The Big Show*', Corgi Paperback 1965.

It was the precognitive death dream of Doug Worley, and its implications, that sparked off the author's search for a Time Mechanism which ended 46 years later with the publication of this book.

AUTHOR'S NOTE AND ACKNOWLEDGEMENTS

In 2 Kings you will find this : `*Behold - the half was not told me'* - and therein lies the problem. The minimum qualifications to write a book on the origins of the universe, and to postulate a new theory on the way in which the Time mechanism works, should include first class University degrees in metaphysics and mathematics : I have neither, and only an ex-R.A.F. Halton aircraft engineering apprentice would have the unmitigated gall and audacity to attempt the task.

Further, when the time came after 30 years of research to set down my findings, I learned that I had contracted a Class 1 `nasty' in the bone marrow, which reduces significantly the time remaining to get this work into print.

My sole justification is that when I read a number of books by `experts' I found they were written in the characteristic scientific jargon, while remaining incomprehensible to the layman. But this should not debar laymen from having their own ideas, even if they lack the ability to prove anything mathematically. The `proof' barrier can sometimes be breached by the use of common sense - if there are a number of explanations for a phenomenon, the one which seems to make most sense is usually correct, and this is called Occam's Razor.

Seemingly, the only way to obtain a book on the subject of Time and the Universe that I could understand without the need for mathematics, was to write it myself. And if, in the process, I come up with even a single concept acceptable to the experts (albeit reluctantly and grudgingly) I will consider the time and effort well spent. G. Spencer Brown wrote in `Laws of Form' :

`Discoveries of any great moment in mathematics and other disciplines, once they are discovered, are seen to be extremely simple and obvious, and make everybody, including their discoverer, appear foolish for not having discovered them before.'

The Bibliography includes many sources and authors who have generously given permission to quote from their work. Other more remote references have proved near-impossible to trace and where I have quoted without the customary permission because of lack of time, may I express at once my gratitude and apologies : such a lapse is, I suggest, forgivable in the context of a book which will, God willing, be a source of reference and comfort to mankind for many years to come.

Wilbur Wright
Southampton

INTRODUCTION

I may have stumbled quite fortuitously onto the secret of Time.

* * *

This, I hasten to confess, was not the initial object of the exercise. Having invested in a tiny word processor, I began to record and cross-reference data I had accumulated for more than thirty years on the para-normal, with particular reference to precognition. I had no intention of digressing into strange backwaters like reincarnation, immortality, survival after death and the *modus operandi* of the universe, but I was drawn extremely reluctantly into these difficult areas.

Several important discoveries have been made by comparative morons, unqualified and totally-inexperienced researchers with the sole redeeming ability of recognising common-sense when they encountered it. They were aware - or hoped - that somewhere behind their ideas there was almost certainly a mathematical proof of some kind, but it was left to others to work out the sums. It was their fundamental conception, that spark of inspiration which opened up the floodgates. Thomas Kuhn[1] points out that significant scientific breakthroughs are rarely accepted when they are first announced. A scientist making such a breakthrough, even a Galileo, Copernicus or William Harvey, will be ignored or even ostracised. Shakespeare had the right of it :

> *`I have no spur to prick the sides of my intent, but only vaulting ambition, which o'erleaps itself and falls on the other'. . .*

Everyone experiences that compulsive desire to find answers to ancient mysteries. We raise up our eyes to the starry vault and wonder `How ?' and much more intriguingly `Why ?' Few possess the time and means to explore *terra incognita* and all become victims of the deadfalls and man-traps abounding along the way, because of the endless convoluted complexity of the landscape. By some scientific version of Parkinson's Law, this complexity increases exponentially with each new discovery, giving impetus to efforts to expand computer memory storage space to record mankind's current knowledge. Parallel processing may provide a viable solution.

Most researchers specialise in a single subject, or facet of a subject, and not by choice. The spectrum of knowledge is now so vast that no single mind can assimilate a billionth part of it. Researchers become locked ever more deeply into a spiral of confinement and specialisation, and I was angered and frustrated by the sheer exclusiveness of the scientific establishment.

Was it possible to write about Time, space and destiny in a way that amateurs like myself could understand ? All I knew for certain was that I could find few such books. My natural curiosity applied the spur.

Inevitably, there are errors herein. I have made assumptions and developed postulates that many cosmologists will reject out of hand. But a concept making sense surely deserves and demands exploration. Further, the idea must fit into the general scheme of things. If a piece of a jigsaw puzzle has the same colour and configuration as the area surrounding the hole, if shape, size and orientation appear to be viable, reason suggests the piece will fit. And by fitting the piece experimentally into the hole, one gains additional data about the surrounding areas, further evaluating the suitability of the piece. Does it accord with the picture's design and structure ? Does it enhance our conception of the complete picture itself ?

My nebulous idea of the way that Time might work seemed revolutionary but not wholly original. P.D. Ouspensky[13] had gone down a similar road but at some point took a wrong turning; admittedly, it led him into areas of great potential, related human intelligence and its place in the universe. But I was after the secret of the Time Mechanism itself - and the primary requirement was that it must fit our world view of Time. I found common denominators and major connections in reincarnation, telepathy, inspiration, quantum physics and the phenomenon of *deja vu*, the feeling that one has experienced an event before.

Now, the most extraordinary development occurred.

As a hide-bound atheist, it seemed to me grossly unfair that personal immortality depended on believing unquestionably that on the Day of Judgment all graves would open up, and the dead would stand in line before the Almighty to be judged. Irreverent ? Perhaps. Blasphemous ? Probably. But this is how it was sold to me. Believers surviving this inquisition went to Heaven : the others went the other way into the hottest of Hells.

I could not accept that. It was buying a pig in a poke : if it was untrue, you would never know because you were dead. In my view, you kept on going until you stopped. And once you stopped, you went to sleep and you never woke up. Period.

But I was uneasy : if I was right, survival of the human personality after death was a natural non-religious function of the universe. I didn't like that idea, and fought bitterly to find some other explanation - but there was no getting away from it : this human spark would not be extinguished by death.

A more disturbing realisation was that this gigantic, awesome and incredible universe could not have come into existence by sheer chance. And that, to a hardened atheist, was a more bitter pill than the first ! Yet the harder I researched, the more inevitable it looked. The odds against chance were astronomical - something like 10^{645} power against it occurring spontaneously.

I was being sucked down into a maelstrom of concepts which terrified me. The problem was just where to stop, but if each step was clearly sign-posted, I had to go along with the current.

Proof of my Fixed Time Field thesis was essential, and I found it in four specific areas. First, the phenomenon of precognition. Second, inspiration. Third, quantum mental physics. Fourth, in life histories of identical twins separated at an early age. Each category has a number of subdivisions providing further corroboration, and remarkably, in every case the evidence fits neatly into its ordained place : no exceptions, wild cards, anomalies, inconsistencies. The reactions of most experts were identical - an ill-concealed incredulity that a damned amateur without qualifications managed to work it out for himself, and a sense of deep irritation in failing to recognise that which had stared them in the face.

Others have been more generous. Colin Wilson[2] says :

> *'Wilbur Wright was understandably obsessed by this problem of dream precognition, and in the early 1980's decided to undertake the kind of exhaustive study of parapsychology and modern physics that might provide him with the answer. The results of his study challenge comparison with Dunne and Ouspensky, and establish him as one of the major time theorists of the twentieth century'.*

I began accumulating data as long ago as 1934; a childhood belief in the existence of magic developed into the belief that nothing was impossible. It was all a matter of time : in 1934 the atomic bomb was science-fiction, but 11 years later the first bomb hit Hiroshima. In 1939, no one believed man would ever walk on the moon : a scant twenty years later the first man went into orbit.

Ergo - given the right time and environment, magic works, and we have to rationalise our thinking to cope with new concepts. UFO incidents have been recorded for thousands of years, and many believe in the existence of an older advanced civilisation somewhere in our universe. It was assumed that they had watched us for millennia, avoiding contact with a brutally warlike species bent on conquering the cosmos. But if mankind eventually develops time-travel, future observers could appear in the present day, later returning to their own singular time. Those with the ability to see instantaneously the solution to a problem in a mind-boggling feat of intuition have achieved such rationalisation : Einstein himself was the classic example.

Developing parameters for an environment in which magic works is not impossible : I may throw a coin in the air and achieve a thousand 'heads' in a row — but I might have to wait a very long time to see it happen again. It is a matter of trying long enough, and in an apparently eternal universe there is time enough.

A peculiar 'white noise' distorts the mass of paranormal material I accumulated. Case history is voluminous and fascinating; for years I concentrated on the effects, rather than the causes. I accumulated endless examples of precognition, telepathy and the rest, and read Charles Fort avidly because he was the first 'Reporter of Extraordinary Events' (excluding the Biblical prophets). Fort was the first to ask `Why ?'; while he could provide no real answers, he did much to define the problems.

But I failed to ask the fundamental question - not `*Does precognition work*' but `*How* does it work ?' Vast case history answers the first question categorically : few human beings have not undergone a precognitive experience. Yet who pauses to ponder how such a thing could happen ?

In 1945, I was guilty of that omission, but could no longer avoid the issue after a pilot on my fighter squadron dreamt that he would die the next day. Doug Worley was not the first, nor the last, to experience foreknowledge of this kind. It happens all too frequently in wartime when all our dreams are filled with blood and terror and the fear of death. In combat, fears are magnified and exaggerated; in bomber and fighter squadrons I found myself studying the behaviour of men under constant threat of violent death. I made a unique personal discovery - that all courage is rooted in mimicry. I flew with men outwardly cool and supremely confident, fearless in the face of danger, and I modelled my behaviour on theirs. Only after the war ended I realised that each had been as scared as I, but they coped with an impossible situation by aping everyone else, displaying a kind of `ersatz' courage indistinguishable from the real thing.

So we flew our three or four missions a day, and the names on the Operations Roster changed as pilots were lost, or completed their tours of operations, replaced by fresh-faced young men who learned the Great Secret in due course: that sooner or later everyone runs out of luck. Doug Worley's dream of death triggered a curiosity as strong today as it was in March 1945. He was a friend of three years standing, an eternity in wartime when a pilot's life expectancy was measured in days, not months. We had trained and marched, drank and womanised together, and Doug was a solid realist, a true extrovert who loved fighting his war; as the end approached and we harried the Luftwaffe from the skies, he worried constantly that the party would end prematurely, just when he was beginning to enjoy himself.

Doug came to me one morning with a small bundle of private possessions. He was pale but composed; as he lit a cigarette his fingers were steady.

"See my family get this stuff, will you ? I have a feeling I am due for the chop today."

"Balls," I said rudely. "We all get that feeling at times."

"Not like this," Doug shook his head decisively. "I wasn't really dreaming. Sort of half-awake, half-asleep. I was taxying along a runway very fast and the whole tail was on fire."

I spoke to the CO, who tried but failed to convince Worley that he was battle-happy, needed a rest. He suggested Doug took a day or two off, but without success; in the end Worley convinced us both by his matter-of-fact attitude. He was not frightened or worried - if anything we sensed a feeling of relief that all the uncertainty and the hassle was over. That day, he said, he could go out and have a ball, because he would not have to `sweat it out'. . .he *knew* what was coming. The sole disturbing factor was the involvement of fire, something we all feared obsessively.

Up to that time, our job was medium-level fighter sweeps and ground-strafing the enemy transport and armour flowing northwards to Flensberg; the shattered Luftwaffe was operating spasmodically in pairs and fours and it was only a matter of time. Yet some fame-seeking bird-brain in 2nd TAF decided we should attack the German airfields themselves. That same day, eight Tempests made a low-level attack on the airfield at the southern end of Lake Schwerin.

In post-war Lübeck I met Herr Schwab, a Luftwaffe flak gunner who had been based at Schwerin : the crews were aroused at 4 am to prepare for a low-level R.A.F. raid. There must have been a mole in our Intelligence Corps, for they knew we were coming : we ran into massed 88mm radar-predicted guns set at zero trajectory. Three of us came out alive but damaged, but Doug Worley was not among them. I last saw him out on my starboard wingtip, 20 feet above the runway, red flames streaming back from the cockpit. Deliberately he turned a few degrees to starboard and flew into the open mouth of a hangar which exploded, destroying nine German aircraft inside.

Doug Worley received no decoration, posthumously or otherwise. It wasn't our turn for the gongs that month. But afterwards, I became obsessed with the phenomenon itself. *How could Doug Worley have foreseen his own death in a dream, unless it was a fixed, immutable and observable event up there in the future ?* More - what kind of a universe could accommodate the acquisition of knowledge of events which had yet to occur ? Most worrying was the sense of inevitability about Doug's death. He rejected any idea of being grounded - he could be knocked down by a passing petrol tanker, and if he was due for the chop, he preferred to meet it doing the job he loved. When a man is locked into some irreversible process of destiny, there is a therapeutic feedback : all the worry and uncertainty was gone when he awoke from the dream. Doug went, exactly as he had seen in his dream - but he went a happy man.

Any viable explanation would be found in the way Time itself worked. (I use here `Time' for the generic subject, and `time' in reference to duration). But I derived minimal results from my research into Time : for something which governs most of our waking lives and which we treat with careless familiarity, we know almost nothing of the Time function. We experience it subjectively, measure it objectively, but have no more idea how it works than Aristotle twenty-five centuries ago.

This was both depressing and encouraging. We tend to assume all the major discoveries have been made, all natural laws discovered - but most of the really big secrets remain intact - how the universe came into existence, how gravitation works, the Time enigma itself. Doug Worley's death-preview presented a fundamental paradox, a universe in which all events yet to happen have an observable existence in future time. Further, our subconscious minds can apparently witness such events *and* transmit the data to the conscious mind on waking ! Evidently, the domain in which future events had been previewed was outside our 3-dimensional universe, implying the existence of a parallel or co-existent universe, or perhaps additional dimensions to our own.

Such ideas contradict all our ideas on causality (the principle that every event is the result or consequence of some prior event or decision). Two points relevant to the Worley case :

1. The very act of `pre-viewing' events seems to make some kind of avoiding action possible, by avoiding flying that day - in which case the pre-viewed event might not happen - but then how could it be previewed in the first place ?

2. Alternatively, a previewed event might not occur inevitably, but a `new' event generated by the avoiding action might well do so ! The act of pre-viewing, therefore, may be part of the process of inevitability.

Some paradox ! Future events may exist potentially in many versions : an observed version is not necessarily that which will occur. It `may' happen, introducing additional complications of probability and possibility - but herein lay a clue. I knew of a domain in which probability and possibility rule - quantum physics and the world of the atom.

The Law of Causality, cited frequently in discussing the paranormal, could well be termed the `First Law of Commonsense' : e.g. a trigger must be pulled before the gun fires and before the bullet leaves the barrel. Were this not so, life in the Old West would have been even more hazardous ! The concept of Destiny disquieted me. In wartime, the idea of a predetermined inevitable future undermined my confidence much more than other distractions sporting black crosses. We believe we are sole controllers of our own destiny, that such unique entities as human beings cannot terminate irrevocably in death. Many take out insurance - religious beliefs, and they are entitled to do so. For me, any discussion of Time must encompass survival after death, immortality and reincarnation.

There is a subtle difference : an `immortal' once born never dies, but a `reincarnated' personality must first experience physical death. Christian ethos promises eternal life in `Heaven', a Timeless domain outside the material universe. Buddhism and Hinduism, however, embrace `cyclic reincarnation' until the soul ascends to the perfect numinous level.

A `timeless zone' is in itself contradictory. How can a surviving and `thinking' entity capable of sensing duration (time-lapse in the physical universe) exist in a Timeless realm ? Existence is a derivative of change, which occurs during a period of duration, itself a product of motion. No Time exists in a static universe, regardless of the absence or presence of an entity capable of recognising it.

We seek constantly to penetrate the veil of the future : sometimes knowledge comes involuntarily, and at others it is encouraged by use of artifacts. Precognition is either voluntary or involuntary, but the sheer unpredictability of the process defeats us - predictably ! Yet it has occurred so frequently in all parts of the world since the beginning of recorded history. Few human beings have not undergone a precognitive experience, the strength and impact of which depends the sensitivity of the subject. PCEs range from simple `hunches' or indefinable fleeting premonitions, to fully-fledged precognitive dreams recalled clearly on waking.

Deliberate exercise of a precognitive ability involving financial benefits for an unscrupulous operator opens the door to charlatans, fraudsters and confidence men. For that reason I exclude all PCEs involving cash transactions, but this still left thousands of genuine cases of precognition. Creed, nationality or colour appear to be irrelevant : aboriginals who have never read a book report the same phenomena as civilised educated people. The Zulus called precognition *`opening the gates of distance'.*

But paradoxes proliferate : for example, a normal well-balanced person about to fly abroad awakes with a stark `memory' of personal involvement in a dream-disaster. An airliner crashes with heavy loss of life and the dreamer recalls an urgent `voice' saying : *`Don't take the trip !'* A normal reaction would be *`Oh, well - it was only a dream...'* and forget it. But not this time : the dreamer heeds the warning, cancels the trip and reads of a terrible disaster next day. Sometimes the dream is forgotten on awakening and the dreamer is left with only a nagging worry or premonition he can't put into words.

The phenomemon generates a multitude of questions. Somehow, `someone' has acquired knowledge of an event yet to happen. But how ? What is this unknown entity and what are its motives ? Where and how does it exist and how does it make contact with the sleeping mind ? Why has it chosen this particular dreamer ? Can it be the sleeper's own subconscious mind ? If so, why does it communicate only in sleep, or altered states of consciousness ? Specifically, why use as a channel of communication dreams ? They are notoriously ephemeral, illogical, riddled with imagination, symbolism and fantasy, incorporating an automatic built-in forgetting process.

I began to hypothesize. All PCEs occur in alternative states of consciousness - narcosis, hypnotism, sleep, day-dreaming, religious ecstasy. The human brain incorporates an interface between human consciousness and some co-existent universe. Part or all of the human personality appears to cross that interface at will - and the early part of this book uses that hypothesis for simplicity. The true explanation is complicated, necessitating this oblique approach. Further, that entity - let us call it the `self' - can observe events in this co-existent universe and transmit the data to the conscious mind on waking. Since all past and future events exist in that domain, it is Timeless. The origin and characteristics of the `self' and the nature of consciousness are of supreme importance in the search for that interface : much depends on the duality or singularity of the self. If singular, it is capable of existence in both universes. If dual, one aspect of it is migratory during altered states of consciousness.

This is an extraordinary concept. Yet the concept of duality fits into our hypothesis very neatly, when we consider conscious and subconscious minds. (I use `*subconscious*' in the context of mental activity on more than one level or state : `*unconscious*' refers to complete cessation of mentation in anaesthesia or following a severe head blow). Further, it melds with the physiological structure of the two lateral brain lobes (right and left) and frontal and occipital lobes. The left `conscious' lobe is predominant in waking life, whilst the right `subconscious' is the source of intuition and imagination.

The interface between conscious and subconscious minds corresponds to the frontier between the two universes. One is Timeless - but how can we define that ? All past and present events exist permanently, and all future events potentially in the co-existent universe, which I call the Fixed Time Field. (Abbr. FTF). Past events have immutable reality, achieved as each Present Moment elapses, thereafter existing in our memories and records. In the FTF all past events are displayed in a cosmic Bayeux tapestry, but future events have no such permanency. Ahead of the Present Moment there is only a Probability Field in which events exist only potentially, in a range of variations.

The FTF is `timeless', without motion, a static star-bright rigid continuum, a domain of pure thought in which all radiation is in wave function, as is human consciousness. When a human `self' penetrates the FTF, it is not limited by velocity or distance : it is omnipresent throughout the co-existent universe, as an entity travelling at infinite speed will exist simultaneously at all points along its track. There is no duration, no Time, making Dunne's concept of a Serial Time and Serial Universes redundant.

Now I was in really deep water ! Trying to make sense of precognition was burden enough, yet I could not fault in my reasoning thus far : connections clearly existed between PCEs, the state of consciousness in which they occurred, the physiological nature of the brain and the structure of the cosmos itself.

Deep within the atom, we find a level of discontinuity beyond which familiar natural laws no longer apply. Matter ceases to be solid. Rather it is open space inhabited by subatomic particles orbiting atomic nuclei, which may not even be real as we understand reality : existing as `probabilities', Time does not appear to exist, and we have to describe certain characteristics of particles in terms of a `strangeness factor'. But Time is the common denominator of all precognitive experiences, and an in-depth examination of precognition is our next step.

* * *

CHAPTER ONE

PRECOGNITION

`From a theoretical point of view the promonitory cases . . . are the most extraordinary'.

Dr.D.J.West (Psychical Research Today, Duckworth, 1954)

`If there is one extrasensory phenomenon which challenges materialistic thought most outrageously, that effect is precognition. For if precognition is a fact, either the law of cause and effect is violated, or else we live in a deterministic universe. Despite its seeming impossibility, the phenomenon of prediction and precognition has been known since the most ancient times in every culture'.

Gowan : `Operations of Increasing Order' 1980

`Precognition is the most puzzling, perhaps, of all psychic phenomena'.

Prof. H.H. Price

`Precognition — much the most puzzling, perhaps, of all ostensibly paranormal phenomena'.

Prof. C.D. Broad

`It is difficult either to ignore the evidence, or to believe it'.

Aristotle

`To make contact with that which does not yet exist is, for many, a contradiction in terms, a philosophical paradox, an outrage — or it even may. . .come under the category of "impossibility". . .

Gardner Murphy : `The Challenge of Psychical Research'

`Foreknowledge of the future. . .would involve the shattering of the whole scientific fabric. If the things reported happened, we must set to work to create a new heaven and a new earth. . .'

F.Podmore - Journal of the SPR, 1908

CONTENTS

1. General World View
2. The Scientific Approach
3. Aspects of Precognition
4. Biblical Prophecies
5. Michel de Nostradame
6. The Oracles
7. Involuntary Precognition
8. Types of Precognitive Experience
9. The Indefinite Future
10. Some Personal Experiences
11. Racing Certainties
12. Some Classic Precognitive Experiences

SUMMATION

1

PRECOGNITION

1. General World View.

`Second sight', the ability to pull aside for a brief moment the veil of the future, is deeply-rooted in mankind, featured in every country and race from the beginning of recorded history. In 2000 BC the Chinese produced the *I Ching* or Book of Changes, a working predictory system in use even today, whilst the Greeks - Aristotle and the Peripatetic School in Athens - were familiar with the phenomenon. Indeed the Oracles, including the famous Olympus soothsayer at Delphi were as well-used as railway timetables are today (sometimes with a higher degree of accuracy !). In an age when science was contemplative rather than mechanical, belief in precognition flourished, but with industrialisation and our increasing awareness of ourselves and the universe, the old belief in magic faded.

Our conscious (left-lobe) mind, part of the human personality, processes input data from our senses : sight, hearing, touch, smell and taste. Additional inputs originate in memory, experience, instincts and imagination, contributing to our complex everyday thought-processes. But this is only the tip of the iceberg. When *homo sapiens* made his debut, he found an apparent dichotomy of existence. When awake, his mind was occupied with daily problems of survival and safety; if he thought at all about death and the Beyond, it was in terms of a full-stop to existence.

Somehow, the animals he killed had lost the spark of life and lay inanimate waiting for his stone knife. Nothing in that dead carcase remained of life or consciousness, which would respond to the prick of an arrowhead even in sleep, a state he found most perplexing. Some part of him apparently never slept, alerting him to imminent danger.

Queerly, his body went on functioning during sleep. His heart kept beating, his lungs pumping, and if he became cold, his hands pulled the furs higher - all this, without waking.

Sleep, obviously, was different to death - a gateway to an extraordinary world of colourful adventure, terror and joy inhabited by strange people, personalised dreams in which he was a participant or spectator. Shamans, medicine men, witch doctors and soothsayers used dreams for predictions and prophecies. Logical enough to early man : this was a place of magic; further, one's dreams often contained visions of the future. Unsurprisingly, belief in precognitive experiences burgeoned - until the researches, theories, postulates and proofs of scientists told us that precognition was impossible.

So it is - to those who disbelieve in magic. Information we absorb via normal senses contributes to our world-view of reality, and we are disturbed on encountering things which go far beyond reason. We believe in our senses : if we glimpse something which seems alien to our reality, we reject it instantly and seek an explanation fitting normal experience - a rejection which can be powerful and long-lasting, as I can testify.

Returning from leave in 1940 to my Lincolnshire bomber station, I had no cigarettes but knew there was a supply in my locker in the hangar. The squadrons were not operating that night : all was dark and quiet under a starry frosty sky. At midnight I entered the hangar crew room in darkness, first checking the blackouts were in position - and realised I was not alone. Someone was groping in a steel locker not far from mine and I recognised Stoker, a mid-upper gunner on McIntyre's Hampden crew who normally flew with the turret open for optimum visibility. Clad in black flying boots, uniform trousers, tunic and Irwin jacket, he was rummaging urgently in his flying clothing locker.

I said : "Hey, Stoke - what're you doing ?"

Avoiding my eyes, he said irritably: "Can't find my bloody gloves."

"Hard luck. Turn the lights out, will you ?" I found my cigarettes and so to bed. At breakfast, after an absence of a week, I asked my neighbour what had happened while I was away. "Oh, the usual. Very dodgy night before last. They went to the Dortmund Ems Canal to drop mines. McIntyre ran into heavy flak and bought it over the target."

"My God," I said. "Stoker was damned lucky, not going."

"Stoker ? Oh, he went in with the rest ! There was a ruckus before they left - someone had nicked his flying gloves. He went without them in the end, and it was a damned cold night. He was moaning all the way to the transport bus."

"You mean," I said slowly, "he bought it too ?"

"That's what I said, innit ? Mac took a direct hit at low level and they went straight in. The mine went off. They had no chance at all."

I went back to my room. Two days later the shakes began; I went to the Doc. who gave me a stiff sedative and asked me to write down exactly what had happened. This I did, on the back of some Daily Routine Orders, but the shakes went on. The MO took me off duty for three days, told me to forget about it, but many weeks passed before life became normal again. Why ? In my eyes, Stoker had appeared perfectly normal, had opened his locker door - meaning he was `solid', as far as that goes. He heard me, spoke to me, and what really terrified me was this : how many more of these things are walking around in our world, indistinguishable from living persons ?

It was not so much meeting a ghost, but rather trying to reconcile that with everyday reality, in which impossible things did not happen.

Many case histories are on file and some apparitions have been photographed. Brian Inglis[21] provides an example showing a group of newly-graduated naval ratings : one of their friends had been accidentally killed two days before graduation, but his face is clearly visible peering at the camera between two ratings in the back row. Extraordinarily, the back row of men were standing on wooden forms : to appear as he did at head level *behind* them, the dead rating must have been standing in clear air. None of the group were aware of his presence.

The reply of a person asked if he believes in the paranormal, specifically precognition, will be conditioned by his own experiences. If he or a relative has had a PCE, he will say so, whilst the more sceptical are very forthright. They will demand proof and evidence. They will query the source's viability and predictably be unwilling to become involved. `Seeing is believing' - meaning themselves : they are not prepared to accept what others have seen.

Society is divided into believers and nonbelievers, most of the former being originally in the other camp. Many people reject the whole subject as nonsense, even heresy because of its incompatibility with God's teachings. The Church as a general rule frowns on all paranormal manifestations, especially those promoted by the Spiritualist movement - yet happily confirms miracles based on hearsay evidence from people who should know better.

The problem lies in persuading people to accept evidence of phenomena which do not fit in with our scheme of things, yet most people believe that dowsers can find underground water, using no more than a hazel twig. The idea of a man walking on the Moon was derided, but in the Sixties, millions of us watched Neil Armstrong take that *`one small step for Man...'* The truth is we cannot say truthfully that `It's impossible'. Only that `It's impossible, at this time'.

Precognition is a difficult pill to swallow, particularly for the scientific establishment, since it appears to contravene the Law of Causality itself— that the cause must in all cases precede the effect.

John Gowan [22] also quotes from `*Adventures in the Supernormal'* by E. Garrett, Paperback Library 1949 :

`*There is an element of surprise and adventure about the experience of precognition which would appear to free itself from all conscious direction, even from personality itself, for when any action becomes automatic and effortless, it ceases to evoke consciousness. One enters into a place of participation which has no connection in time and space with conscious direction, or conscious telepathic communication. The experience remains as* "real" *as any other and suggests that there must be a timeless and spaceless communication between our intuitive selves and the great eternal laws of nature.*

Garrett and many others, vaguely aware of the connection between paranormal phenomena and the six dimensions of the Fixed Time Field, were never able to determine or identify it. He mentions twice the timelessness aspect of Space 2, stressing the involuntary nature of precognition and the dissociation from conscious thought which characterises it. I remember clearly the surprised feeling in a lucid precognitive dream.

John C. Gowan writes :

`*If there is one extrasensory phenomenon which challenges materialistic thought most outrageously, that effect is precognition. For if precognition is a fact, either the law of cause and effect is violated, or else we live in a deterministic universe. Despite its seeming impossibility, the phenomenon of precognition and prediction has been known since the most ancient times in every culture.'*

Professor H.H. Price : `*Precognition is the most puzzling, perhaps, of all psychic phenomena'.*

Professor C.D.Broad [23] : `*Precognition - much the most puzzling perhaps, of ostensibly paranormal phenomena. . .'*

Aristotle wrote : `*It is difficult either to ignore the evidence, or to believe it. . .'*

And Gardner Murphy : `*To make contact with that which does not yet exist is, for many, a contradiction in terms, a philosophical paradox, an outrage— or it may even come under the category of impossibility. . .'*

F.Podmore wrote :

`*Foreknowledge of the future... would involve the shattering of the whole scientific fabric.If the things reported happened, we must set to work to create a new heaven and a new Earth.'*

Professor E.R.Dodds wrote :

`*Modern theories on precognition (a) try to evade the paradox by* *juggling with the Time concept itself; (b) try to re-interpret the phenomenon in terms of subconscious inference from super-normally acquired knowledge of the present, or (c) reversing the ostensibly `causal' relationship treating a PCG experience as being in some psychokinetic manner the cause of the subsequent event.* And he continues : *Of all ostensible supernormal phenomena, precognition has been accepted in virtually all societies, from the most primitive to the most sophisticated, the most widely-accepted in popular belief and also in the belief of educated men. Yet of all such phenomena, it is probably the one of which it is hardest to give any rational account. . . How can an event as yet non-existent, causally determine an event in present time ?'*

I think Dodds missed the point completely. PCG is a totally illogical phenomenon, with no rational explanation possible using traditional methods of assessment. Like Broad, he fails to commit himself to full belief in PCG, using the word `ostensibly' to cover his bets. I began my own work by defining three parameters which encapsulate both problem and solution, postulating that PCG does occur :

A. To determine a Time mechanism accommodating the existence of potential future events in a form permitting them to be observed by the human mind.

B. To evolve a paradigm of a structured universe which would accommodate a Time mechanism as defined in A.

C. To identify the mechanism by means of which a human mind is enabled to observe and report such future events to a waking conscious mind in the present moment.

To regard PCG with suspicion and misgivings when almost everything we do is based on predictions of future events seems contradictory. We must take care not to confuse precognition with prediction. G.N.M. Tyrrell[24] said that prediction, *per se*, concerned natural events - inferences based on observations of past events which assume that natural laws govern their occurrence, such as almanacs, rail timetables and weather forecasting; such predictions are usually based on human intentions and planned programmes.

Tyrrell defines a PCE variously as :

* A prediction made from subconscious observation of certain facts, drawing conclusions expressed as a prediction.

* A subconscious yearning or an intention to do something, appearing

as a prediction.

* A subconscious desire to fulfill a prediction by verbalising it, that is to say, `wishful thinking'.

* A form of telepathic communication.

But there is no comparison between guessing about future events expected with some degree of probability, and foreseeing events with no apparent reference to the present. True precognition (expressed verbally or in writing beforehand) is not prediction based upon Present Moment knowledge, but foreknowledge of an event which has been `seen to happen' beforehand. Because of the unpredictable and variable nature of human events, we should avoid confusing precognition in any way with a human prediction which may be unfulfilled. Premonitions usually are.

Precognition is `knowing' : prediction is `guessing'. While paying homage to Dr. Rhine[25], Soal and others, I suspect they were barking up the wrong tree, experimenting with prediction, rather than precognition. Their subjects were asked to predict which of a selection of 5 cards would be turned over, in a pack of 25 - in effect guessing at the format of a single future event with only five variations - the shape of the image on a card. This contains an inescapable element of chance : the normal expectation would be 5 correct guesses in 25, and higher scores would be logical variations in a long sequence, later balanced by some abnormally low scores. I have not been able to identify any research into the ultimate scores in very long runs, but I suspect that in a million tests, the abnormal higher scores would be almost exactly balanced by the lower.

To constitute a true test of precognition, subjects would be asked to describe some imminent event, one of much greater complexity than a simple card design. Many would invent the most extraordinary events imaginable : an airliner crashing into a skyscraper, an earthquake devastating San Francisco or an alien spaceship landing on the East Lawn at the White House.

Yet the element of chance always intrudes : there are as many guesses as card experimenters. Once in a while a subject may guess correctly at an image generated in his subconscious, but true precognition must always involve acquisition of knowledge of future events from a source outside the subject's conscious mind. This may stem from a deliberate attempt to gain knowledge, using such artifacts as crystal balls or cards, the process always involving opening the mind to input of data from sources other than our five senses.

This difference between prediction and precognition is crucial to understanding the process involved, but a traditional interchangeability between the two exists : foreknowledge of a future event may be obtained exercising precognitive abilities on a basis of present-day knowledge..

2. The Scientific Approach

The Rhine and Soal experiments began in the Thirties. Whilst Dr. J.B. and Mrs. Louisa Rhine at Duke University, Durham NC became convinced they possessed clear evidence of both telepathy and precognition, S.G. Soal in England was repeating their experiments between 1934-1939 with little success, so much so that he believed they were either frauds or totally deluded.

During that period, at Cambridge University, Whately Carington obtained some strange results in experiments with telepathy, by opening a dictionary at random and drawing a picture of the first encountered noun he could illustrate graphically. The drawing was locked in his study overnight while all over Britain, volunteers tried to guess the selected object, sending their dated sketches to Carington for assessment.

He found little or no evidence of telepathy, but something else - a pattern of time displacement in the accurately-dated submissions, covering a period of several days after and before the experiment ! Contacting Soal, Whately Carington suggested re-examining unproductive results for such a time displacement. Doing so reluctantly, Soal was astonished to discover similar trends : one subject, a photographer named Basil Shackleton, made scores significantly above chance expectation.

For three decades research was in the doldrums : whilst precognition under laboratory conditions had been confirmed, there were no clues as to how the process worked. Instead, a great impetus was given to collecting examples of PCG in human society, which continues to the present day. This phase was extended in the early Sixties when Karlis Osis and J. Fahler[26] found that hypnosis enhanced precognitive ability. Later that decade, Gertrude Schmeidler of City College, New York, established a link between the quality of PCG results and personality characteristics of the subjects.

No reasonable person, surely, will deny that PCG does occur, and frequently. We tacitly accept it but dislike talking about it, until someone asks directly if we believe in PCG - whereupon most people agree, even if they have not experienced it themselves. Paraphrasing the TV advertisement: *'I can't see into the future- but I know a man who can...'* Whilst my personal experiences leave me in no doubt, I accept that some people are less than sensitive to PCG. My collection of well-documented PCEs form only a minute fraction of the total cases on record : it seems probable that most human beings have undergone a PCE of some kind. That it may have been subsequently ignored, forgotten, denied or derided does not detract from its reality. Understandably, people have a deep-seated fear of anything paranormal contravening our natural laws, for we live in a world in which Magic does not happen, no matter how skilled the TV illusionist. Baffled, fascinated but unafraid, we watch apparent miracles comfortably aware they are but theatrical sleight of hand. When some extraordinary event occurs, we rationalise it via the arid and stale arguments of imagination and coincidence.

This attitude persists even after startlingly-real precognitive dreams of incredible clarity, recalled in full on waking, when the previewed incident occurs exactly as it did in the PC dream. Our minds, conditioned to a world-view of normality and comforting reality, simply refuse to accept the evidence.

By instantly forgetting dreams on waking (`oneirolysis') the problem is exacerbated. Who knows how many PCG dreams viewed by the sleeper are lost in this way ? Dunne[6] himself, recognising the problem in `*Experiment With Time*' developed a method of recording dreams by keeping a pencil and paper by his bed. Waking at any time, he wrote down what he could recall of each dream, re-reading the notes several weeks later. To prevent automatic rejection of PCG dreams, he read his notes as *applying to events which had actually occurred in the interim period.* Fortunately, tape recorders make the task much easier, and I have recorded dreams for twenty-five years. I seem to have four or five significant and unmistakable PCG dreams each year, mainly pre-views of trivial events, but one in a hundred or so involves a traumatic incident involving some person other than myself.

PCG dreams are the commonest form of PCE but the rarest to be recalled in detail, for the reasons I have explained. PCEs include day-dreams, sleeping dreams, hypnotic and drug-induced trances, self-induced trances, episodes of religious ecstasy sometimes induced by lack of food, sensory deprivation and self-flagellation and altered states of consciousness. They may be involuntary or deliberately induced, dependent upon the motivation of the subject.

So unpredictable is the future that many suffer an irrational fear of events to come; pessimism is defined as `*the tendency to expect the worst and see the worst in all things*'. Understandably, many of us harbour a craving to know what Fate holds for us : indeed, we are willing to part with hard-earned cash to find out. The astonishing conclusion is that we must automatically assume that (a) future events are predetermined, and (b) they exist in some form which allows them to be pre-viewed !

This has been so throughout recorded history, yet we assume that events happen simply by chance in a particular version perceived in the Present Moment. Even in prehistoric times, human beings experienced precognitive dreams and premonitions - it seems to be an inherent faculty of homo sapiens. Further, the ability to see into the future is strong in a few individuals; the early witch-doctors and shamans, whilst performing gruesome rites with bones and chicken entrails, knew that they possessed some extraordinary faculty. With belief in PCG endemic in every culture and land, all these people cannot be foolish and misguided.

3. Aspects of Precognition.

To summarise, we have delineated the boundaries between prediction and precognition. We may now list some fundamental facts about the latter :

PRECOGNITION

VOLUNTARY	INVOLUNTARY
* Prediction based on known facts.	* Dream.
* Deliberate attempt to use paranormal faculties to view future event.	* Premonition.
* Use of artifacts : crystal ball, cards, I Ching, palm-reading etc.	* Day-dream.
	* Visual or audio
	* Self-hypnosis
	* Hunch.

The use of artifacts to induce PCG experiences is well-documented. Some 4000 years ago the Chinese developed the *I Ching* (The Book of Changes) a form of written binary computer based on a universal paradigm in which future events exist in multiple versions. In some strange way the operator (person consulting the *I Ching*) obtains an insight into the trend of future events, on which he can base a present-time decision to ensure the most beneficial version will achieve reality. The system functions on a quantum mind relationship between the operator and potential events in Space 2, the *I Ching* acting as a catalyst.

Lyall Watson[27] lists similar but less sophisticated items used by primitive people - divining sticks, bundles of bones, sand trays, fowl entrails, ouija boards, tea leaves, fungi of hallucigenic species, incessant drumming and human sacrifice - most of which are now redundant.

4. Biblical Prophecies.

The dividing line between prediction and precognition, and between involuntary and voluntary PCG, is very finely drawn. We do not know how the Biblical prophets obtained their data. Both Old and New Testaments are filled with prophecies - it was arguably the most active and productive industry of those far-off times. But was Divine intervention responsible for those queer prophecies ? Or were they voluntary PCEs ?

Many Biblical prophecies were manipulative in character : the acceptance of some future Messiah's divinity could be assured by laying a foundation of prophecy many years earlier. Like miracles, they were prearranged in many cases. For example, the provision of the ass on which Jesus rode into Jerusalem that fateful Easter time. At Passover most people walk to the Holy City and the great temple : only a presumptive Messiah would ride an ass, the most common form of transport. When He arrived at Bethany, He sent two disciples to a nearby horse-dealer where, He said, they would find an ass tethered to a tree waiting for them. This they did, and returned proclaiming yet another miracle. But months earlier on another visit to the Temple, Jesus had instructed other disciples to purchase the ass and arrange for its stabling. The dealer was instructed to tie the animal to a nearby tree on a specific date, from whence its owner would collect it.

Coincidence ? Perhaps. Take again our first example. Two hundred years before Christ, prophet Zechariah predicted that the Messiah to come would enter Jerusalem riding upon an ass, indicating that He was above worldly customs and confirming His divinity. Christ, a learned student of the Scriptures, knew of this and many similar prophecies; in many cases we find Him deliberately manipulating events to fulfill a `prophecy' which could have been a simple device by an earlier holy man to impart authenticity to Jesus' claims to divinity. Theological students may rise in protest, but there is extensive evidence for this thesis. Psalm 22, Verse 18 says *`They will pierce his hands and feet'*. The trial of Jesus displays hard evidence that he engineered his own crucifixion, which would fulfill many early prophecies. Verse 7 says *`The chief priests and scribes will mock him'* and this occurred. Psalm 22 mentions *`vinegar mixed with gall'*, administered by Joseph of Arimathea. Exodus 12, Verse 46 predicted that the legs of the two crucified robbers would be broken, but not those of Christ. (In such circumstances this was an act of mercy: bereft of support, victims quickly suffocated and died). Zechariah 12, Verse 10, predicts that the Messiah's side would be pierced with a lance - and this occurred. There are more than 20 such established prophecies in the life and death of Christ, far more than mere coincidence : the evidence of manipulation is overwhelming. The validity of Biblical prophecies must be questioned seriously, as deliberate ploys to lay a foundation of authenticity for some future Messiah. After all, it is not difficult to manipulate a real event to match a prophecy.

The Old Testament abounds with prophets. Queen Jezebel (Kings I) employed no less than 850. Moses had but one, who passed on accurately God's warning of the Seven Plagues about to be visited upon Egypt.

5. Michel de Nostredame.

Best known by his Latinised surname, Nostradamus was born at noon on December 14 1503 (old calendar, the Gregorian version being issued in 1582) in St.Remy de Provence to parents of simple lineage. By his ninth birthday, his family had converted from Judaism to Catholicism, but the influence of prophecy-ridden Jewish scriptures cannot be totally discounted. His grandfather taught him something of Latin, Greek, Hebrew, mathematics and what the boy himself called `Celestial Science' - astrology, of which the primary thesis is that a person's future can be calculated using positions and movements of stars and planets, and this could be the partial source of his predictions, for I believe that PCG dreams played little or no part in their generation. His prognostications are enveloped in vagueness, generalisation, symbology and in many cases impervious to verification or translation - common characteristics of all astrological predictions.

He began writing his Almanac in 1550, his famous Prognostications in 1554. The latter work is now world-famous and interested readers are recommended to the Erika Cheetham version (Corgi,1975). The Prognostications cover almost 500 years, exceptional among prophetic writers, including the notorious prediction that the world will end in a great Final War in 1999. After the Gulf War, I suggest this now appears far less outlandish and improbable than it did in the 16th Century.

The ten parts of the book are called `Centuries' (no connection with dates) comprising ten groups or `centuries' of 100 `quatrains' in blank verse or prose, a grand total of 1000 predictions. Many are too obscure in content and meaning to be understood, especially after 500 years, but certain predictions are astoundingly accurate. Here is a famous example.

The Dreyfuss Case.

Alfred Dreyfuss, a Jewish-French Army officer, was condemned in 1894 for treason - selling military secrets to the Germans, France's traditional enemy, on the evidence of so-called `intercepted letters'. Publicly degraded, he was sent to Devil's Island penal colony for life. He was recalled four years later to face re-trial : rife anti-Semitic feelings in Paris ensured he was again found guilty - but with mitigating circumstances. He was pardoned 10 days later by President M. Loubet, after the letters were proved to be forgeries.

Now, the Minister called upon to review the case in 1899 had found Dreyfuss guilty for the second time, a M. Waldeck Rousseau who (with more than a dozen close political friends) was heavily biassed against the prisoner. Many assumed, correctly or not, that Rousseau was the author of the forged letters. Nostradamus' prediction (Century 1-7) reads :

> *`Arrived too late, the act had been done. The wind was against them - letters intercepted on their way. The conspirators were fourteen of a party. By Rousseau shall these enterprises be undertaken.'*

There seems little doubt that in some queer way Nostradamus had observing this drama, or perhaps a newspaper report, in its entirety. In his quatrain we find every important element in the story, including the name of the culprit Rousseau - 400 years before the man was even born !

In Century 2-24 Nostradamus describes Hister (Hitler) : `*The child of Germany observes no law'*, and in Quatrain 2-62, there is a reference to the 100-Hour Gulf War : `Maybus will then soon die and there will come a dreadful destruction of people and animals'. `Maybus' - synonym for John Major and George Bush : after their union `dies', devastation sweeps Iraq.

Remarkably, Nostradamus describes in Century 1-2 his method of divination :

`Sitting alone at night in secret study; it is placed on the brass tripod. A slight flame comes out of the emptiness and makes successful that which should not be believed in vain'.

And again :

`The wand in the hand is placed in the middle of the tripod's legs. With water he sprinkles both the hem of his garment and his foot. A voice, fear; he trembles in his robes. Divine splendour; the god sits nearby'.

The method was practiced by Iambicus in the 4th century. A reprint of his book *De Mysteris Egyptorum* was published in the city of Lyons in 1547, at the time of his visit there. Nostradamus (then 34 years old and widely travelled) almost certainly read it and began writing his Prognostications seven years later. What was his method ?

Studying privately the forbidden books on magic, he placed a bowl of water on the tripod and lighting a small flame, peered into it. Probably he used the bowl as present-day fortune-tellers employ a crystal ball to focus concentration, but Nostradamus undoubtedly had the psychic ability to conjure up images. He even heard a voice, adding to the visual effect, and was constantly afraid whilst the gift had possession of him - a classic example of induced altered state of consciousness. Nostradamus clearly establishes contact with his self in Space 2, which observes events far into the future. The voice phenomenon is common among people who undergo PCEs. Many of the Prognostications involve other countries and nationalities, but overseas events are often reported in the French Press. To an all-seeing self in Space 2, all printed material (and possibly spoken words) are accessible, as I can testify personally.

In Nostradamus' time, this was sheer magic - and we may have to revise that word ! Collins' English Dictionary defines it as *`the art that, by use of spells, supposedly invokes supernatural powers to influence events'.* I am now producing something unique, previously unwritten, using a word processor and electronic programme enabling me to produce written English language on a black screen like a piece of polished marble. This, not so long ago, would have been described as `magic' : one is reminded of the Ark of the Covenant, on one side of which was an opaque panel. When a person stared at the panel, his name appeared in writing. . .

6. The Oracles.

These were a wholly Greek pre-Christian phenomenon, reputedly the replies of a god or an inspired priest to enquiries about future events. More probably, the voice of someone possessing some paranormal abilities and a reputation for being at once abstruse and obtuse, especially in confrontation with the pompous, privileged and pretentious personages of the period. Here are some examples :

Croesus (King of Lydia, 560-640 BC).

Outlining a projected war to the Delphic Oracle, he was told *`When Croesus passes over the River Halyus he will overthrow the strength of an empire'*. It would be (the Oracle omitted to say) his own empire. . .

Pyrrus (King of Epirus 306-272 BC).

When he was about to wage war on Rome, the Oracle told him : *`I say, Pyrrus, that you the Romans can conquer'* - an ambiguous statement he lived to regret.

Philip (King of Macedonia 359-336 BC)

When he asked the Oracle if the Persian expedition would be successful, the reply was : *`The ready victim for death before the altar stands'*. But the victim was Philip himself...

Oedipus (Son of Laius, King of Thebes).

Warned by the Oracles that he would be killed by his own newborn son, Laius had Oedipus abandoned in remote country to perish. Found and adopted, the boy suspected his adoptive family were not his real parents, eventually consulting an Oracle. He was told that he would murder his father and marry his own mother (note the corroborative element between two Oracles). The boy was shocked and moved to Thebes. But en route Oedipus met a stranger (his father) and killed him in a fight. In Thebes, he met his real mother Jocasta, but unaware of her identity, he married her. At this point Oedipus, now the King, summoned the blind soothsayer Tirewsias to name his father's murderer.

The precognitive element is clearly identifiable. The Oracles, well informed on local events and the affairs of ruling families, utilised the information obtained (whatever the method) to exercise a traditional sadistic streak. Yet other examples display uncanny accuracy and fine details which defy explanation :

Croesus, King of Lydia.

This apocryphal story was recorded by Herodatus at a time when Croesus, threatened by the Persians, was concerned by the Oracles' tendencies towards ambiguity and symbolism. He ordered seven of the best-known to participate in a test of their abilities. One hundred days after the messenger departed carrying his instructions, he would ask each of the Oracles *`What is King Croesus doing now ?'*

The only correct answer came from the Delphic Oracle :

`I can count the `sands, and I can measure the ocean; I have ears for the silent and know what the dumb man meaneth. Lo ! On my sense there striketh the smell of a shell-covered tortoise. . . Boiling now on a fire, with the flesh of a lamb in a cauldron. Brass is the vessel below, and brass the cove above it.'

Designing this test, Croesus chose circumstances so bizarre that a solution by imagination or guesswork was near-impossible, yet the Delphic Oracle described them with extraordinary accuracy. The people behind the Oracle may have bribed palace servants to gain access to the secret, but Croesus, alert to trickery, would take due precautions.

Ancient Greece had more than its share of soothsayers : Cassandra, perhaps the most famous, foresaw the fall of Troy, the famous Wooden Horse and the slaying of herself and Agamemnon by Clytemnestra. The Sibyl, another seer, was notorious for her terrifying frenzies of clairvoyancy. Virgil records :

`Her hair rose on her head, her colour changed
Her breasts heaved, she fell into a trance
She seemed to grow, she spoke in no mortal voice
Out of a cave a hundred voices
Poured out the Sibyl's prophetic answers.'

In Rome, too, the voice of the seer was heard with dread and respect. Who can forget those terrible words from Shakespeare's *`Julius Caesar'* :

`Beware the Ides of March. . .'

7. Involuntary Precognition.

Knowledge of a future event is `given' to the subject unbidden, without warning and at any time of day or night, in any of a number of ways. The subject is unprepared, astonished and often terrified by the episode, with elements of confusion, symbolism and needless complexity. In some episodes the subject dismisses the premonition as a figment of his imagination, or forgets it at once. There is invariable automatic and instant rejection by the mind, when faced with the impossible.

I recall watching Neil Armstrong and other astronauts `bouncing' around on the Moon : my mind rejected the picture out of hand, coming up with the tentative explanation that the astronauts' boots were fitted with springs ! The effect reminded me of early Hollywood cartoons.

In PCEs we acquire knowledge of future events in various ways :

* Dreams (sleeping state, subconscious mind functioning).

* Daydreams (hypnagogic state).
* Hypnotic trance.
* Drug-induced altered states of consciousness.
* `Flash' of intuition.
* Hunch or premonition
* A sound message, audible only to the subject, often clear and distinct as if someone is speaking directly into the subject's ear. The message may be implanted directly into the subject's neural receptors, transmitter nerves and ganglions. The recipient is unable to distinguish simulated from real sounds.
* A combined visual-audio manifestation.
* Assorted but often remarkable side-effects including unusual aromas and sometimes a brilliant white light which surrounds a visual image or symbol.

8. Types of Precognitive Experience (PCE).

Since the majority of cases which involve deliberate attempts to foresee the future are of a fraudulent nature, intentionally or otherwise, and a number of cases in which there could be telepathic communication between the operator and the subject, by means of which the former may gain knowledge of future actions contemplated by the latter, I shall concentrate on the involuntary experience.

Analysing recorded examples of PCEs, a pattern begins to emerge. Since some subjects are more sensitive than others, PCEs will have greater impact and occur to them much more frequently. They recall PCG dreams in greater detail, possibly because of superior connections between right and left brain lobes. Most PCG dreams are personalised : the events portrayed involve only the dreamer, his circle of acquaintances and family. The strangers we encounter have an anonymous ephemeral existence : they are forgotten as readily as other details of the dream.

The `time scan' of dreams or PCEs is limited to the lifetime of the subject : I know of only two examples in which the dream environment is set in the distant past or future - Mother Shipton and Nostradamus. This is logical : the distant future will always appear incomprehensible; to a dreamer in Nelson's time `seeing' a person sitting in front of a radar screen watching the trajectory of a Space Shuttle, the scene would be incomprehensible , and I believe some of Nostradamus's predictions were vague and ambiguous simply because he could not understand what he had `seen' in the future. Most of his material, we know, did not come from dreams. There are people who seem to have lived previous lives, sometimes far back in history, but such experiences are related to hypnotic age regression experiments, not dreams. Danah Zohar[20] shows a relationship between the accuracy of a PCG experience and the time lapse before the pre-observed event occurs : the shorter the lapse period, the more accurate the pre-viewed event.

Interestingly, of the huge volume of recorded PCG dreams, a significant proportion feature incidents of extreme triviality, and this is predictable if we accept the idea that our self exists in both Space 1 and Space 2 with access to the future : much of what it sees will be every-day humdrum events. In life, weeks and months may go by with nothing disturbing the even tenure of existence; the exploratory range of PCG dreams rarely extends more than a few weeks into the future and trivial events will feature largely in our dreams. Frequently, we fail to recognise them as precognitive in content : if I dream that I dropped a teacup when drying, it may be a memory of the last time it happened - or a preview of the next !

It is only with dreams with extraordinary impact that the autonomous `forget' instruction is bypassed. This makes sense : if we remembered in every detail every incident in every dream, memory banks will soon overload : in the process many PCG dreams are lost beyond recall.

Here we should define precognition (acquisition of knowledge of some future event which has yet to happen) and `prediction' (an inferential guess at a probable outcome of events based on one's current knowledge of circumstances) but there can never be a finely-drawn line between the two. Indeed, many people in the prediction business such as bookmakers, touts, gamblers, fortune-tellers and clairvoyants may possess a degree of paranormal ability (which they would deny vehemently !). Weather forecasters, insurance experts and stock market operators base predictions wholly on stored data, past experience and analysis of trends, with no paranormal connotation. For example, we may predict that by noon tomorrow we shall be in Oxford Street London - but only because we know that a suitable train leaves at 9.15 ! This prediction contains a high degree of probability, but a prediction with a 100% probability of becoming reality is impossible by definition, if one ignores the effect of Time. For instance, I can predict that I am about to type the word `future' and that prediction has been totally fulfilled because there was no time for an external effect to prevent me. But in predicting I will make a telephone call to Spain in thirty minutes, the probability is significantly reduced because many things can happen to prevent me making the call.

A prediction, therefore, should not be confused with a PCE. All PCEs fall into two categories: those which achieve reality and those which do not, and this opens the door to some staggering paradoxes. . .

9. The Indefinite Future.

If I dream of breaking a leg in falling from a ladder when cleaning windows two results are possible. One, I disregard the dream, subsequently fall off the ladder and rationalise this as coincidence. Two, I heed the warning, avoid falling and the dream is not fulfilled. But in that case how could I have foreseen the accident ?

The mainline event (i.e. the cleaning of windows) must exist in a number of variations :

* I abandon window-cleaning : no accident occurs.
* I climb the ladder, with no accident occurring.
* I climb, fall off and escape without injury.
* I climb, fall off and break a leg as previewed.
* I fall off the ladder and die from injuries received.

Further sub-variations exist in regard to the degree of injury, but the inherent paradox remains : how can one pre-view an event which never occurs ? Here are some case histories in this category.

The Shepherd Case (cf George Behe).

In February 1912 American businessman Mr.B.O. Shepherd visited England, planning to return in mid-April on the *Titanic*'s maiden voyage - every man's dream at the time. He booked passage eight weeks prior to sailing date, but back home in Hemingford Nebraska, his wife saw the *Titanic* sinking in a terrifying dream. She wrote to Shepherd at once imploring him to use some other ship, following up with a cable repeating her plea. Luckily for him, her husband was impressed, believed her and cancelled his passage. The mainline event - the sinking - was inevitable but human beings can foresee and avoid a minor secondary event such as personal involvement in the greater disaster. The escape or fatal involvement of a few hundred human beings would have no effect on the ultimate fate of the *Titanic* - that was part of Destiny.

The Battle Case (cf George Behe).

This was not a full-blown PCG dream, but a very strong premonition which was probably the residual effect of a half-forgotten dream. Mr. C.S. Battle from Vancouver B.C. was visiting friends in London early in 1912, before sailing home. They urged him to delay and enjoy the famous *Titanic*'s maiden voyage. Indeed there was no reason not to do so, but Battle had a strange premonition of disaster and deliberately re-booked on the *Olympic*, sailing a week before the *Titanic*.

Battle was quite happy to sail on the *Olympic* : his subconscious mind had correctly identified the *Titanic* as the source of danger. Clearly this was no casual passing perception of `some' possible ship-wreck : the ship was identified.

The Adelman Case (cf George Behe).

Another premonition-type PCE involved a Seattle musician Frank Adelman and his wife. While in London, they made reservations on the *Titanic* but Mrs. Adelman experienced a strong sudden premonition involving the ship : telling her husband, she insisted he postponed their departure, and changed to a later ship. Finally, after long discussion, he flipped a coin - and lost. They did not sail on the *Titanic*. Many researchers miss a vital connotation here : evidence suggests that psychokinesis (moving material objects by act of will) is possible. In her disturbed state, could Mrs. Adelman have influenced the fall of the coin ?

The Robert Morris Case.

Robert Morris, whose son largely financed the American War of Independence and was in the group which framed the American Constitution, was an agent for a Liverpool shipping firm. Whilst awaiting the arrival of the *SS Liverpool* at Oxford, Maryland, Morris Snr. dreamed that he was killed by a round from a ship's cannon, a salute fired in his honour. He cancelled the ship visit in order to avoid the threat. But Captain Mathews of the *Liverpool*, advised of his guest's strange dream, thought Morris was superstitious and foolish. Morris said `Call it superstition if you like, but our family is reputed to have the gift or curse of receiving premonitions of impending disaster.' The Captain convinced him that no cannon would be fired, and reassured, Morris consented to join the shipboard party. But during the festivities, Mathews told him the crew, unable to pay the traditional compliment and fire a salute, were upset. Morris said uneasily : `Oh, very well- but do not fire the salute until I or someone else gives the signal.'

Mathews said he would go ashore with Morris when the time came and would give the signal himself when they were well clear of the ship. He ordered the gunner not to fire until he raised his hand, but as they were being rowed ashore, a fly alighted on the Captain's nose and he raised his hand to brush the insect away. The gunner assumed this to be the signal and fired the salute : the wadding from one of the guns embedded itself in Morris's arm above the elbow, breaking the bone and creating an infection which eventually killed him.

From a determinist viewpoint, we have serious difficulties here. First, had Morris not dreamed as he did, he would have gone unsuspecting to his death. Second, the accident might have occurred in a number of versions but the mainline event - his death - was extremely probable. Third, had the Captain been unaware of the dream, he would not have promised Morris a safe return to shore - in which event Morris would probably have cancelled his visit at once. Fourth, we must ask why the gun was not pointed safely out to sea. Could it have been a British plan to assassinate Morris ? Fifth, the dream, the Captain's knowledge of it and the accident all appear to have been part and parcel of the mainline event; a fatalist might suggest that Robert Morris's death, like that of Doug Worley, was inevitable.

The case has been quoted by many writers, most of whom appear to have missed the crucial point : how could Robert Morris, whilst asleep, preview an event which had yet to happen ? More pertinently, from where did the warning emanate ? And if, as seems extremely probable,

Morris's death was inevitable, why was the warning issued at all ? Is it possible that Morris could only recall on waking that part of the sequence which involved his death ? What part in this process was played by the fly which settled on the Captain's nose ? The fly could not be aware of its role in the accident : its intervention was purely fortuitous whilst being part of the mainline event.

Obviously, Morris's self in Space 2 previewed a real future event in a single dominant version, thereafter inserting a warning into the dream sequence. There may have been other versions which it ignored, selecting the worst to use in the dream, but I believe the Probability Field around Morris was extremely strong, permitting only the one version to occur.

This leads us into uncharted waters : the Field also interfered with satellite events to ensure the inevitable, such as Morris telling the Captain of the dream (precipitating the latter's promise not to fire unless all was well), Morris's resulting decision to make the visit, the crew's complaint about the lack of a salute, and finally the arrival of the fly which generated the Captain's false signal ! Morris's injuries themselves bear the mark of intervention : the shell wadding may have killed him outright, but he escapes that - only to die from an infected wound.

The degree of probability of each human future event is governed by the number of event-versions built into Space 2 ahead of the Present Moment, whilst preknowledge of the *mainline event* enables the subject to take possible avoiding action, if other alternatives exist.

Such action is successful only when the subject is strong enough to overcome the local Probability Field.

The Ward Case (cf George Behe).

Unusually, a small child received a PCE warning. Little Jack Ward's father was an experienced ship's steward who had been shipwrecked five times. A native of Southampton, Ward's first White Star Line assignment was the *Titanic*. One day his son said he should not sail because `the ship was going to roll over'. Naturally, Mr. Ward ignored the warning and sailed on April 12 1912.

Mrs. Ward waited outside the Company offices for two days with other relatives of the crew, hoping against hope; on April 17, the strain was too much and she broke down, but Jackie was confident his father was alive : three nights in a row he dreamed his parents had `gone to the pictures' (visited a movie theatre). On the morning of April 19, the little boy ran into the local newspaper office waving a piece of paper.

He said excitedly : `I've a cable from my Dad ! He's saved !'. But Jackie had already had the news, in three repetitive precognitive dreams. Children often exhibit strong paranormal abilities, which fade later in life - one of the penalties of living in a highly-materialistic society.

The Case of Lady Z.

Quoted by H.A.C.Dobbs in 1965. Lady Z dreamed that when she was in her coach near Piccadilly, her coachman fell off his seat onto his head, crushing his hat. Next day, wishing to go to Woolwich, she ordered a 10 am start, whilst hoping for an excuse to go by train. Her coachman demurred, saying he could not be ready until 11 a.m but they arrived at Woolwich without incident. Returning, as they neared Piccadilly, she noted that other drivers were staring at her coachman : he was leaning back as if the horses were pulling violently. Turning into Down Street she remembered her dream, jumped out and called a policeman, who caught her driver as he swayed and fell off the box. Lacking any warning, the coachman would have fallen and been injured— as she had seen in her dream. A clear case of successful intervention.

Saltmarsh recognised the possibility of a variable future and was motivated by Russian researchers V.A. Folk, N.S. Krylov and L.A. Khalfin[28] to investigate the time-energy uncertainty relationship of the Heisenberg Uncertainty Principle, introducing a complex Time and energy paradigm (Soviet Journal of Experimental and Theoretical Physics,1947). H.A.R. Hobbs wrote :

> `*The essence of the theory I have been putting forward is that time is a complex variable, not just a simple variable. According to the principle of quantum (particle) theory, such an assumption implies that energy is also a complex variable, since time and energy are complementary quantities in the sense of Heisenberg's Uncertainty Principle. This is exactly the position taken up by the School of Rus sian Scientists. I conceive of virtual interactions which have physical effects between particles of real rest mass (such as protons, electrons and molecules of ordinary matter) and particles of imaginary mass.* (Wave function ? Auth.) *Such interactions will be perfectly frictionless and it will therefore be possible for two human brains to exchange particles of imaginary mass without the magnitude of such interactions being in any way attenuated by spatial separation or distance. In these interactions between brains and particles of imaginary rest mass, which I will call psitrons, travelling without any form of attenuation through friction or resistance in the intervening space, you have the physical mechanism required for ostensible precognition. These will be available to give a causal explanation of the direct acquaintance with the objective probabilities of events still in the future.'*

Heisenberg's Uncertainty Principle is crucial to quantum (particle) physics. At subatomic level, where matter appears to lose its solidity, four basic forces operate.

1. **Gravity.**

2. **The Strong Nuclear Force.** Billions of times stronger than gravity, it holds together the atomic nucleus composed of neutrons and protons, which are composed of particles called quarks. The electrons orbiting the nucleus are kept in place by the third force :

3. **Electromagnetism.** Finally—

4. **The Weaker Nuclear Force**, which causes the decay found in certain elements like uranium.

Of the four, electromagnetism governs the characteristics and orbit of subatomic particles, and is the most promising source of contact between human brain cells and the self (which is an electromagnetic field surrounding the body and brain) and the potential wave-function indeterminacy ahead of the Present Moment. Let us look again at electrons.

In 1900, German physicist Max Planck was studying black body radiation i.e emissions produced by colourless black bodies when heated, by virtue of the energy added. It had been assumed that electrons (elementary particles orbiting an atomic nucleus) emitted energy until exhausted, but Planck discovered that oscillating radiating bodies emit and absorb energy only in specific amounts. This is equivalent to saying that heating water results in temperature rises of only 10 degrees at a time ! It was a radical discovery.

Electrons, Planck found, radiated energy in `spurts', their remaining energy falling to successive finite levels until they were exhausted. The energy loss or gain took the form of tiny `chunks', the size of which could be calculated by using a constant (a specified unchanging number). Further, low energy `chunks' such as those from the red end of the light spectrum are smaller than white (high energy) chunks.

But subatomic particles are not specifically particles or waves. Instead, we encounter a confused blend of states called a `wave packet'. We can measure the spin and mass properties of a particle individually, but we cannot determine both at the same time : the act of viewing itself introduces uncertainty, and this Probability Factor or Field is, I believe, identical to that which determines which of a number of versions of potential future events will achieve reality. In the context of a huge universe it would appear that the personal fates of individual human beings have little consequence - yet this is precisely the case ! In some queer way the destiny of each sentient being is an integral factor, an essential component in the functioning of the universe.

The following cases are quoted from Danah Zohar [20].

The Susan Anthony Case.

In the late Nineties, Miss Anthony's doctor suggested that she should move from Philadelphia to Atlantic City for health reasons. Soon after arriving, she had a vivid dream, in which she was being burned alive in a fire involving a number of seaside hotels. Next morning, she told her niece of the dream, saying `We must pack at once, go back to Philadelphia,' and they left Atlantic City immediately. Next day, their hotel and ten others, with miles of the timber boardwalk, were destroyed by fire. There was heavy loss of life.

In such a disaster the mainline event is clearly fixed and immutable, involving inanimate matter and structures. The presence or absence of a few human beings would have no significant effect. Miss Anthony received her warning in a single dream emanating from her own self functioning in Space 2, which had observed the impending disaster. But with what motivation ? Was it a self-survival mechanism like that which awakens wild animals at the approach of danger ? Do animals foresee imminent danger in PCG dreams, as we do ourselves ?

The Mr.Brighton Case.

An incident recorded in a British SPR report before the first World War. Mr. Brighton, asleep aboard a yacht at anchor in fog, dreamt that a voice warned him he was about to be run down by another vessel. Awaking, he went on deck to check, but everything seemed normal. He dreamed again, re-checked and once more found nothing untoward, but he was now seriously concerned. Climbing the mast, he saw above the fog another craft bearing down on him, shouted to the captain of this vessel who put his helm over and avoided a collision.

The case is well known, but H.F. Saltmarsh pointed out that an experienced seaman like Brighton may have noted subconsciously sounds made by an approaching vessel. But could this have occurred twice, generating two identical versions of the dream ? Improbable, at least.

The Marian Warren Case.

In April 1973 Mrs. Warren with more than 100 other Somerset housewives had booked a day trip to Switzerland in a chartered Vanguard airliner. Three weeks before departure, she dreamed that she saw the aeroplane come over some trees and crash into the snow. She saw the bodies of her friends being laid out, and extremely upset, she cancelled her booking, accepting only a 50% refund. She told one close friend about her dream, but no one else because : *`I thought no one would believe me'*. The aircraft did crash, with heavy loss of life.

This is a common factor in PCEs. Normal well-balanced people are loath to repeat PCG dream experiences to others, partly because a risk of ridicule and because we dream every night of normally trivial imaginary events which at times take on the mantle of nightmare. Most such dreams do not come true - or if they do, we never know, having forgotten the dream on waking. So viable documentary and/or eyewitness proof of foreknowledge of an event is essential, to verify precognition.

In 1966, at the time of the Aberfan disaster in Wales, London psychiatrist J.C. Barker accumulated material on premonitions by people who had died at the precise time predicted. Some, he believed, literally frightened themselves to death as the day and moment approached.

But Barker was uneasy about the uncertainty of precognition and premonitions. If such warnings were common, why had they not been used to prevent disasters and save lives ? He asked Peter Fairley, science editor of the London Evening Standard to publish an appeal for examples of premonition and disaster. Other newspapers collaborated; Barker received 76 replies, 16 of which he later discarded. To evaluate the data, he used criteria previously established by parapsychologist G.W. Lambert[31] :

* Was a precognitive experience recorded or reported to other persons before the event ?
* Was the time interval between PCE and event short enough to indicate a close relationship between them ?
* Was the event something unlikely to happen at that time ?
* Was it an event which would be literally fulfilled and not merely foreshadowed in symbols ?
* Were the details in the PCE identical with those of the disaster ?
* Was the subject unstable or emotionally reliable, sincere and believable ? Did he allow bias and fantasy to creep into his narrative ?

A Central Premonitions Bureau was set up in London and New York, but can modern society accommodate such disaster warnings ? So many premonitions of the Aberfan disaster (a moving mountain of coal slurry engulfed an entire village school) were received that it should have been possible to institute an official Coal Board check of all slagheaps near the village. But official Government departments responsible for spending taxpayers' money could never justify expenditure on a wild-goose chase generated by children wrapped in nightmares. Aberfan is an excellent example of a virtually inevitable mainline future catastrophe involving inanimate material in motion : our social structure ensured that intervention was impossible.

Some ground rules are becoming evident. Of many major catastrophes previewed in PCEs, I have been unable to identify any instances in which a potential disaster has been averted, for obvious reasons. If an aircraft engineer dreams of making a major servicing error on a Jumbo jet scheduled to leave next day with 400 people on board, he may hurry back to the job and check his work. A potential disaster may have been averted, but can we really prove it ? The culprit would avoid reporting the dream, in case men in white coats offered him a room with padded walls - for being so stupid as to report the incident. Of such is the fabric of our society.

The Arthur W.Osborn[29] Cases.

Osborn quotes two `evasive action' examples, one involving a son visiting his family on holiday in Hobart, Tasmania. Before leaving for Kingston, his mother had a premonition that he would have an accident and warned him to drive carefully. Halfway home, he recalled the warning and slowed down to 25 mph. Seconds later the car skidded on an ice patch (the only one encountered during the journey) and colliding with the embankment slid into the ditch. Had he been travelling at normal speed, he would have been killed.

This typical PCE was not in dream format but just as effective - yet Osborn missed a most important point. *What made the young man remember his mother's warning at the critical moment ? What prompted his subconscious mind to recall it then ?* A telepathic warning from his mother ? He may have had his own measure of precognitive ability.

In the second example, a music-teacher was standing behind a pupil seated at the piano. Suddenly the sheet music seemed to vanish and he saw a portion of the road along which he would drive later that day. He seemed to see a car come round a bend on the wrong side of the road at high speed, heading straight for him. Then the vision vanished. Approaching the same bend later, he recalled the vision and without volition pulled over to the side of the road. As he did so, a car came round the bend very fast on the wrong side, just as he had foreseen it.

The subject was not in an altered state of consciousness, but was concentrating on the pupil's performance. His self in Space 2 apparently previewed the potential accident on the previous night, but failed to get through the warning in a dream. This, the music teacher had forgotten, but his subconscious mind saw its opportunity and produced a visual warning at a time when his conscious mind was wholly preoccupied with the student. See the chapter on Inspiration and the Time Shunt.

J.B. Priestley (`*Men and Time, Aldus 1964*) studied such cases, which he labelled FIP - `*Future Influencing Present'*. Dunne believed implicitly that the future was variable, that events might be avoided by Present-Moment decisions.

Goddard - The Man in Someone Else's Dream.

Eventually made into a film starring Michael Redgrave *(`The Day my Number Came Up')*, this case is famous - for the wrong reasons. It is not an example of intervention, but of misinterpretation of the dream. Much of what follows is quoted from `Premonitions' by Herbert B. Greenhouse[4].

In 1946 Air Vice Marshal Sir Victor Goddard, RNZAF, was about to leave Shanghai for Tokyo. He attended a farewell celebration given by the British Consul-General, at which he overheard an English officer named Dewing describing a dream from the previous night. Unaware that Goddard was listening, Dewing told a friend : `*Too bad about Goddard. He died last night in a crash - in my dream.*' Noting that the AVM had heard the remark, Dewing apologised profusely and agreed to describe the dream in detail. He had seen `*A rocky shingle shore. . . a snowstorm during an evening flight. . .the plane was flying over mountains short of fuel. . .a crash.*' The plane was an R.A.F. Dakota carrying three civilians including a girl, as well as the Service passengers.

In fact Goddard was due to fly in a Dakota `*Sister Anne*' with all-military occupants, but events began to develop ominously. First, the civilian Consul-General received orders for Tokyo and was assigned a seat. Then Seymour Berry, a British civilian journalist, was given a lift to Tokyo by the pilot. Finally, a Tokyo official in need of a secretary signalled Shanghai requesting the Consul-General, to bring one with him - a girl named Dorita Breakspear. *Two additional men - and now a girl, all civilians.*

These seat allocations had all emanated externally from three different sources and it seemed impossible they could have been predicted accurately. Air Vice Marshal Goddard, naturally, was becoming uneasy. To tell the truth, so was I, reading the account. The Douglas Dakota, according to Herbert Greenhouse, took off from Shanghai at 06.30 am and was still flying 9 hours later, having gone up as high as 19,000 feet. No Dakota in my experience could fly so long in such conditions.

At 3.30 p.m., flying in driving snow, they located a small Japanese coastal village with towering mountains inland. Short of fuel, they crash-landed successfully on the shingle beach, fulfilling all the significant elements of the dream - except for one. Goddard survived unhurt.

Seeking some degree of correlation, we find that seven major items appear in both the PCG dream and real events, and this is far too high a proportion to be attributed to coincidence :

1. The rocky shingle-covered shoreline.
2. The snowstorm.
3. The time (evening).
4. Over mountains in cloud.
5. The three additional civilian passengers, including a girl.
6. The crash-landing short of fuel.
7. Correct identification of aircraft.

Admittedly, a snowstorm was predictable in the winter of 1946 - and Japan is a mountainous country. Far East Transport Command used the Dakota extensively, plus a few Curtis Commandos and Avro Yorks : Dewing was on solid ground predicting a Dakota. Shanghai-Tokyo was a long haul and given an early take-off, it would be early evening when they began to run short of fuel,given long-range tanks.

Remarkably, the dreamer Dewing was not involved with the trip himself; his dream was not a personal warning. Second, it involved someone he knew (Goddard) and thirdly, Goddard survived. Obviously, Dewing had seen something in his dream, but not the event-version which achieved reality next day. I believe that his self, in sleep, had previewed not the actual crash but *his conversation next morning describing the dream to Goddard !*

10. Some Personal Experiences.

Whilst serving at R.A.F. Hemswell, Lincolnshire in 1940, I became a subject in another person's PCG dream. An air gunner friend Stoker came to me on Derby Day and said that he had dreamed the previous night that he met me in the hangar under the wing of a bomber and told me the name of the winner of the Derby. We were standing at the time under the wing of a Hampden bomber, as he had dreamed - and he told me the horse's name. As things turned out, the horse did not win ! During a post-war period I had three unmistakable precognitive dream experiences, all connected with horse racing. Repetitive dreams, they followed a common format : each time I am standing in a race-course grandstand (I have never attended a race meeting in my life) watching events. Some shadowy figure stands beside me and conversation is almost ritualistic : I ask my companion : *`What won the big race'* and he obliges with the name of a horse. My response is invariably : *`There's no such horse running—'* to which he replies *`Well, it won anyway !'*

There the dream ends abruptly. The dreams occurred between 1946 and 1954, the horses and years involved being Airborne (1946); Arctic Prince (1948) and Nahar (1954). In the subsequent 36 years there have been no reoccurrences, and I do not believe there will be any more. These things go in cycles and I have had my chance. Foreknowledge did me little good : the period coincided with a stage in my career in which I had no interest in horse-racing - only in flying aeroplanes as well as I could. But the way the sequence ended was in itself remarkable - a lucid dream in which I became aware that I was dreaming. Immediately the dream began I turned to my shadowy companion and said: *`Oh, no ! Not you again !'*

His precise reply does not come to mind, and he supplied me with a horse's name `Radar' for the Cambridgeshire Handicap next day. That, presumably, was as close as he could get to the name of the winner `Nahar', and I was left with an impression of rueful apology on his part, combined with a sense of affront. He was, I was given to understand, *`only doing his job'* and *`hadn't come here to be insulted'...* That impression is still with me today, and I must have upset him - he never appeared again.

Why he bothered in the first place, I cannot tell. I have no interest whatsoever in horse racing - none of the horses know which will win, let alone the jockey, trainer and owner. Was it a deliberate attempt to make me rich by proxy ? If so, who was my generous advisor ? I like to think it might have been my father, dead these forty years, who would happily bet a week's wages on which raindrop would reach a window ledge first. But in all three cases, I spread the news around the squadron, and after Arctic Prince won in 1948, the local bookie arrived to ask me where I got my information !

The Red Airliner.

Dream symbolism can be at once obscure and impressive. When I was working in Devon in 1972, I dreamed I saw an airliner crossing from right to left at high speed and extremely low level over a crowded airfield, skimming the heads of the people in front of me. A piece of the aircraft fell away and instantly it dived into the crowd and exploded on impact. The whole dream was in full colour yet passed in absolute silence, which seemed contradictory : I expected the spectators to be screaming loudly, and to hear the explosion itself. I awoke in a cold sweat with the image still clear in my mind - a memory of an airliner painted brilliant pillar-box red.

Now, no airliners are red, a colour associated with danger. Very impressed, next morning I described the dream to my secretary and office manager. Seventeen years had elapsed since my last PCG dream. Some weeks later I saw on TV the Russian Concordski crash at the Paris Air Show - in total silence, until the news reader began describing the accident. It duplicated my dream exactly - except that the aircraft was painted silver-grey, not red. Eventually I realised that this was the only way my Dream Constructor could tell me it was a `red' (i.e. Soviet) aircraft.

The Snake Dream.

Snakes have always terrified me, but not in this dream, in which I was in deep jungle undergrowth, staring down at a small clearing near my feet across which an enormous snake was moving. It was no more than three feet away, yet I watched it calmly until it vanished from sight. I told my wife about it next morning; she shares not only my interest in precognition but my abhorrence of reptiles. That evening we were watching a David Attenborough nature programme about the Amazon Basin fauna, during which the cameraman focussed downwards on a 30-foot long anaconda flowing through a break in the vegetation. We stared at each other and said simultaneously `Snap !'

The paradoxical lack of fear was explained : I was watching a film, not a real snake, and my dreaming mind knew it. But it raised a further issue : this trivial incident was a five-second film extract shown 24 hours in the future - so why had it been used ? It was this haphazard selection process, with most PCG dreams involving unimportant transient events, that motivated an in-depth study of the dream process itself, in the general context of Time research.

11. Racing Certainties.

The Williams Case

Many PCG dreams involve horse-racing tips but others go unreported because they are forgotten on waking, or for fear of being ridiculed. The mechanics of the process are invariably amusing and fascinating, displaying an aura of sardonic amusement on the part of the dream-making entity. Writer G.N.M. Tyrrell[24] relates : Mr. J.H. Williams of Dulwich awoke on May 31 1933, after dreaming that he listened to a broadcast commentary announcing the first four placings in the Derby, to be run that day. (Such dreams often occur shortly before the event). He recalled the names Hyperion and King Salmon, but forgot third and fourth placings. Now, Mr. Williams totally abhorred gambling and took very badly to this violation of his principles. In his dream, he listened on earphones (standard equipment in those primitive days of `cat's whisker' radios) to an old wireless set which strangely was out of order at the time. Nevertheless Williams described his dream to three friends who signed confirmatory statements, after which he had the set repaired and began to listen, the second time, to a race commentary being broadcast for the first time !

Williams' dream-maker had abstracted a scene not from the race itself, but from his own immediate future in which he was listening to the broadcast. Did that entity know the radio was unserviceable, but that the dream would prompt Williams to have it repaired ? This implies calculated premeditation, and we must question the entity's motives : why select the Derby in the first place, since Williams disliked gambling ? If an external entity, was it playing a joke on him ? If it was William's own self, it may have betrayed some secret yearnings to have a flutter...

The Godley Case.

Colin Wilson quotes the case of Mr. John Godley (later Lord Kilbracken) who awoke on March 8 1946 with the names of two horses he had seen in a newspaper in a dream. One was Bindle, the second Juladdin. Calling on a friend Richard Freeman to check the press, they learned that Bindle was running in the 1 pm race at Plumpton, Juladdin at Wetherby. They backed the two horses to win, netting more than £100 - a substantial sum at that time. In a similar PCG dream some weeks later, Godley dreamed of calling his broker from a small and stuffy telephone box, asking for a tip for the last race. He was told `Mentores, at 5 to 1'. Next day, he rang from a confined and undoubtedly stuffy call box in the Randolph Hotel : the conversation duplicated the dream - and the horse won !

The source of information in both cases was not the race itself but events concomitant with it. The first dream involved reading a newspaper, which Godley did later to check the runners; the second used a future Godley event (the telephone call) to convey the information. That it was a dud tip does not affect the main issue, merely confirming the existence of an indeterminate future. Yet there is a strange connotation of some Time loop : Godley read the newspaper only because he had dreamed he would look at it. He telephoned only because his dreaming mind had seen him making the call ! Godley had a firm recollection of that claustrophobic call box, whilst he spoke to a broker whose voice his sleeping mind reproduced faultlessly - previewing an event as yet several hours in the future.

12. Some Classic Precognitive Experiences.

The *Titanic* Cases.

All major natural or human disasters feature warning dreams and premonitions, and the 1912 loss of the *Titanic* was no exception, probably because of the vast publicity. Its size and opulence (by far the largest and most luxurious ship of its day) dominated the Press; carrying 2,200 crew and passengers, it was inevitable that some would undergo a PCE involving the ship. In fact, there was an unprecedented avalanche of so-called `psychic' reports. George M.Behe quotes a 1912 commentary in the Milwaukee Journal :

`JUST MISSED IT' CLUB FOLLOWS SEA WRECK.

> *To Date only About 6,000 Were to Take* Titanic *but Changed Their Minds. It's certain that two boats the size of the* Titanic *could not carry the crowds that "just missed taking" the lost ship. To date some 3,478 Americans, 2,950 Britons and 476 scattered, all more or less prominent people, have entered the "just-missed-it" club. It appears that 4,965 of these had engaged passage but had cancelled their reservations before the* Titanic *sailed. Of this number, 899 had premonitions of disaster. The rest were in Paris and couldn't break away. Of the balance, 732 are glad they were not aboard at the time, as they would surely have come home on the* Titanic. . .'

Despite a tongue-in-cheek approach, the article had some basis in fact. It is a sad reflection on society that there are those who will always try to cash in on tragedy for a fleeting moment of self-importance, such as the modern-day curse of idiots making hoax fire and bomb calls, and others who plague families of kidnap victims with vindictive and groundless threats. In fact, most of the *Titanic* cancellations arose from prosaic and logical foundations : their escapes from tragedy were simple and lucky coincidences. Here are some examples of genuine precognition of the *Titanic* disaster :

The Frauenthal Case (cf George Behe).

A classic example of repetitive PCG dreams, in which the Dream-Producer seems determined to get a message through by hook or by crook. New York lawyer Isaac C. Frauenthal arrived in France in March 1912 for the wedding of his brother Henry : planning to travel home together in the *Titanic* they arrived in Southampton on April 12 to board the ship.

After sailing, Isaac told his friends he had a dream before departure, of being aboard a big steamship which suddenly crashed into something and began to go down. He saw the gradual settling of the ship, heard the cries of frightened passengers. At first, he said, he regarded it as a nightmare, but the dream occurred again the following night.

On the night of April 14, Isaac was reading in bed when he heard a long drawn-out `rubbing noise'. He woke his brother, who said it wasn't serious, but Isaac had other ideas. Remembering his dream, he went on deck and overheard Captain Smith advising John Jacob Astor to waken his wife, in readiness to take to the lifeboats. Isaac convinced his brother and they made for the boat deck. Mrs. Henry Frauenthal was put into one of the boats but threatened to jump overboard unless they both joined her. On impulse, the brothers jumped down into the boat, and all three survived.

The details remembered on waking leave no doubt that in some strange way Isaac's dreaming mind observed an event as yet five days in the future. It succeeded in getting a warning through - but how many victims of disaster may have had similar warning dreams, but forgot them on waking ? We shall never know. . .

The Mr.Middleton Story.

Quoted by Andrew Mackenzie[5] it is one of many on record involving the *SS Titanic.* The famous vessel, 882.5 feet long and weighing 46,328 gross tons, struck an iceberg south of Newfoundland and sank with the loss of 1,502 lives on April 14 1912. An English businessman J. Connon Middleton booked a passage on March 23, and a week later he dreamt of seeing the ship floating on the sea keel upwards, passengers and crew swimming for their lives.

Next night, the dream was repeated. He related afterwards feeling `*uncomfortable, depressed and very despondent'.* Four days after the first dream, Middleton cancelled his passage, largely because a cable from America suggested that for business reasons he should postpone sailing. After cancelling his booking, he told his own family and several close friends about his dream, which they subsequently confirmed. Strangely, two of them, when interviewed for a report in the Journal of the SPR, said that Middleton had seen himself as `*floating in the air just above the wreck'.*

This dream has some very unusual aspects. Whilst Middleton in some queer way previewed the event, he did not `see' the version which became reality. The *Titanic* did not turn turtle but went down slowly by the bows until she slid almost vertically under the waves. Further, Middleton took the dream as a personal warning : even without the cable from America, he would have cancelled his ticket. Most remarkable was his memory of *`floating in the air above the wreck'*. If our ideas about activities in Space 2 are correct, Middleton's self observed one of a number of possible variations in the *Titanic's* duration-extension.

When the advancing Present Moment had reached Mr. Middleton's pre-departure spatial location, the disaster was 10 days ahead of him, part of the amorphous wave-function Probability Field, observable by his self.

This infers that, even in the wave-function flux of the duration extension ahead of the moving Present Moment, Space 2 entities can view some, and probably all the many possible event-variations, rather like watching a bank of TV monitors each displaying an individual event version.

This appears to corroborate my own view that repetitive dream sequences involves re-runs of the original, rather than the creation of new dream-stories, the self having selected the same event-version each time. No other thesis can explain the near-identical formats and subject material found in such sequences.

The Mr.Macdonald Story.

Colin Macdonald, a 33-year old marine engineer with experience of Atlantic crossings, was offered the post of second engineer on the *Titanic*'s maiden voyage. Careerwise, it was an excellent opportunity, but Macdonald had a bad feeling about the job. Offered the position three times, he consistently declined it, but the man who took his place, Mr. Hesketh, lost his life. It is unclear whether this was a PCG dream - it may have been a thrice-repeated premonition in Macdonald's mind even before the job offered. I include the case as a repetitious dream Macdonald forgot on awaking, leaving him with a typically vague premonition of a terrible catastrophe.

The Hanson Story (G.Behe).

Peter C. Hanson and his wife Jennie of Racine, Wisconsin planned to visit his family in Denmark, having saved the necessary funds and sold his business. But Jennie shocked her brother in Racine when saying goodbye. *`I dread taking this trip to Denmark. I have a feeling I will never return alive. I just know the boat will sink or something awful will happen to me, going over or coming back. If you ever find my body...'*. She went into details on the funeral arrangements she wanted, including burial clothes and flowers.

Astonished, her brother Thomas treated her forebodings humorously and the couple sailed for Scandinavia on February 14 1912.

When arranging passage home in April, Hanson's brother decided to accompany them and all three booked on the *Titanic*. After the collision, Peter Hanson put his wife into a lifeboat saying `Jennie, you'd better go so one of us can tell the story back home'. He stepped back and both men went to their deaths with the great ship.

Mrs. Hanson's PCE may have been a precognitive dream like most PCEs. She could sense only dimly a looming tragedy involving a ship, suggesting that she may have forgotten the rest of the dream sequence. Interestingly, Jennie assumed automatically that she was doomed to die alone, because she made no provisions for Peter's funeral - in her dream she may have observed a version of the disaster incorporating her death, but a different variant became real as we have seen.

The Ryan Case (cf George Behe).

Eugene Ryan from Athlone boarded the *Titanic* at Queenstown with friends, to whom he described a bad dream about the ship. Bertha Mulvihill recalled the incident : `A boy named Eugene Ryan from my town was with us. When we left Queenstown, he told us he had dreamt that the *Titanic* was going to sink. Every night at sea he told us of the dream. On Sunday night, just before we retired, he told us the *Titanic* would sink that night - he had plainly seen the ship in collision with an iceberg.'

No Eugene Ryan survived the sinking, or was in the steerage passenger list, but Miss Mulvihill may have been referring to Eugene Daly from Athlone, who did survive but never referred to premonitions.

Mr.Stead and the *Titanic*.

When well-known journalist W.T.Stead lost his life in the *Titanic*. the incident is seen as a classic `time shunt' (Page 139). Mr. Stead had obtained foreknowledge of the disaster in several different ways and his death was significant to the Spiritualist movement, which sought to gain publicity from the disaster. With others, he had formed `Julia's Bureau' dabbling in communications with the dead. Stead regularly visited fortunetellers and clairvoyants, two of whom warned him specifically of the dangers of travelling on water. In 1911, Count Louis Hamon (real name William John Warner) told Stead in a letter that the critical months would be July, October, December and April. (Such predictions are rarely precise : these months cover the four seasons of the year). Hamon added that travel would be particularly dangerous during the month of April 1912. Whilst this seems to be a *bona fide* case of PCG, there were some doubts about Hamon's evidence after the *SS Titanic* was lost.

When Stead consulted palmist/clairvoyant W. de Kerlor in September 1911, he was planning a trip to Russia but the psychic said he would be going to America instead. `*I can see only a picture of a huge black ship, of which I see the back portion - and where the name of the ship should be written there is a wreath of immortelles. . .I can see only half the ship; that symbol may mean by the time the ship is completed - when one will be able to see it in its whole length - it is perhaps then that you will go on your journey.'*

Construction of the *Titanic* by Harland & Wolff began in 1909 in Belfast, Northern Ireland. By September 1911 the ship had been launched but much fitting-out remained ; de Kerlor was correct in saying that the ship was only half-completed. Later that year de Kerlor had a dream in which he saw himself as W.T. Stead in the midst of a catastrophe at sea. *`Thousands of bodies and people struggling to survive. . .I could hear their cries for help'.*

Finally, in October 1911, American May de Witt Hopkins met Stead in Paris. Afterwards she wrote to a friend Miss Scatcherd describing an audio-PCE in which she `heard' a voice talking about Stead. It said of the journalist : *`The time is soon coming when he will be called home... after his return to England. In the first of the next half year - in six months'.* After a pause the voice said : *`His time has come; his career is ended'.*

The Story of the `Titan'.

This is an odd case of pseudo-precognition based on extrapolation. In 1898, fourteen years before the *Titanic* sailed into the mists of history, author Morgan Robertson wrote a novel called *`The Wreck of the Titan* about the loss of a new liner on her maiden voyage after colliding with an iceberg. The case is frequently quoted because of the many correspondences between the vessels, but there are strong grounds for discounting it as a PCE. Like the real liner, *Titan* was supposedly unsinkable, of comparable dimensions, carrying 24 lifeboats which were insufficient for the number of people on board. (Due to an outdated Board of Trade regulation, all ships exceeding 10,000 tons were required to carry 16 lifeboats, and the *Titanic* designers met only that requirement, whilst providing four Engelhardt collapsible boats. There was room for just 1,178 people in the boats - and the *Titanic* carried 2,200 souls. The safety limit should have been at least 35 62-seat lifeboats : Robertson's *Titan* carried 3,000 people, with 24 lifeboats available. The connotation is obvious : Robertson knew the regulations of the day).

Strikingly, both incidents involved an iceberg, but whilst the *Titanic* struck submerged ice a glancing blow, *Titan* rode up over a sloping ice-field to stop almost wholly out of the water, before rolling over. Notably, the impact occurred on the starboard side in each case.

But Behe points out that Robertson was basically extrapolating his current knowledge of Transatlantic liners in 1898 to visualise how a future 1912 giant might look. Extending the ship length, he could calculate the probable tonnage, and thus the passenger capacity, as I might design a 2013AD imaginary hypersonic Jumbo jet carrying 1000 people from London to Sydney in three hours.

Correspondences between the two ships, nonetheless, are very striking :

	Titanic	*Titan*
Persons aboard	2,207	3,000
Lifeboats	20	24
Tonnage	66,000	75,000
Length	882	800
Propellers	3	3
Speed on impact	23	25
Point of impact	Stbd. Side	Stbd. Side
Object hit	Iceberg	Iceberg

The third correspondence between the ships was the choice of name `*Titan*'. Behe says this was entirely predictable : Robertson sought a name for the largest ship ever built, and the Thesaurus provides some possible candidates : Gigantic, Colossal, Gargantuan, Monstrous, Titanic. Semantically, there is only one runner : `Gigantic' is perhaps a little over the top, but `Titanic' sounds right. In fact, Robertson chose `*Titan*'- but could as easily have gone for `*Titanic*'.

In the June 1962 SPR Journal, G.W. Lambert suggested that inference, rather than precognition, accounted for most of the correspondences. Robertson was familiar with the shipping world, and once sure of the size of the ship, the rest was simple deduction. I agree with this view.

The Dream of Abraham Lincoln.

Arguably the most-publicised precognitive dream ever recorded involved President Abraham Lincoln in 1865, fulfilling all but one of the paramount requirements listed on P.35 :

1. The details were reported to others before the event.
2. The time interval between dream and event was short.
3. Whilst Lincoln was the first President to be assassinated after William H. Harrison in 1841, it was by no means an improbable event. He was a troubled man : as the Civil reached its final stages, he was hated by the South, disliked by many in the North and had received many abusive and threatening letters.
4. The dream event was fulfilled in every detail.
5. Lincoln was normally a reliable stable person, not given to flights of imagination.

The story begins in March 1865 when, talking to his biographer Ward Hill Laman, Lincoln described a recent dream in extraordinary detail, which disturbed him so much that he did not sleep for the rest of the night and was concerned for some considerable time after that. Some researchers suggest it was not so much an example of precognition, as the product of a subconscious mind worrying about Lincoln's problems at the time, but I take a different view, risking a charge of being biased. So many correspondences with actual events followed that the odds against the dream happening by chance are astronomical.

> `*About ten days ago,'* Lincoln said, `*I retired very late. Soon I began to dream. There seemed to be a deathlike stillness about me. Then I heard subdued sobs, as if a number of people were weeping. I thought I had left my bed and wandered down-stairs from room to room; no living person was in sight, but the same mournful sound of distress met me as I passed along. . .It was light in all the rooms, but where were all the people who were grieving as if their hearts would break ? I was puzzled and alarmed. Determined to find the cause of a state of affairs so mysterious and so shocking, I kept on until I arrived at the East Room which I entered. There I met with a sickening surprise. Before me was a catafalque upon which rested a corpse wrapped in funeral vestments. Around it were stationed soldiers acting as guards and there was a throng of people, some gazing mournfully upon the corpse whose face was covered, others weeping pitifully.* "Who is dead in the White House ?" *I demanded of one of the soldiers.* "The President. . . He was killed by an assassin." *Then came a loud burst of grief from the crowd, which awoke me from my dream.'*

Some days later, Lincoln also told his wife about the dream, adding `*Somehow, the thing has got possession of me, and like Banquo's ghost, it will not down'.* Two other events on the last day of Lincoln's life bear the same stamp of precognition : at a Cabinet meeting attended by General Grant, Secretary of War Stanton and others awaiting news of a final victory, Lincoln said slowly: `*Gentlemen, something extraordinary is going to happen, and that soon. . .I had a dream, and I have had the same dream three times. . . I am on a great broad rolling river, and I am in a boat. . . and I drift. . .and I drift.'*

Later that day, President Lincoln said to his bodyguard William Crook : `*Crook - do you know, I believe there are men who would want to take my life.'* After a pause, he added : `*And I have no doubt they will do it.'*

The episode generates many questions. Lincoln was prone to premonitions and hunches, and the war and political situations at that time were critical. He was a man of deep perception and imagination and knew he was a possible target; this may have manifested itself in dreams and forebodings. Lincoln had the repetitive dream about the river three times. The death-dream sequence itself appears to be semi-lucid : Lincoln was able to think logically as he wandered through the White House. Significantly, what he described was an accurate presentation of the lying-in-state which followed - but what of the soldier to whom he spoke ?

Such dreams are often symbolic : the constructor-entity may resort to various devices to convey meanings or information, as in my own dream of the Red Airliner. Whilst the main event was accurately described, there were complications in conveying the details to Lincoln's dreaming mind, which the dream constructor solved neatly by having him talk to a soldier on guard. Such ploys are common - see Godley's dream of his bookmaker telling him a horse's name, and my own mysterious companion at the race course.

The dream would mean nothing to Lincoln until the identity of the corpse was revealed by the guard - that was an essential factor. Evidence shows that Lincoln told a considerable number of people about his dream before he was assassinated, including biographer Ward Hill Lamon, Mrs. Lincoln and those present at the final White House Cabinet meeting. There seems little doubt that Lincoln's self pre-viewed his own death : it is eerie and disturbing to realise that during the period of mourning and unseen by the mourners, that entity from ten days in the past was observing its own lying-in-state.

+ + +

SUMMATION

* Sheer volume of authentic case history, occurring in every era of recorded history, forces us to accept, however reluctantly, that precognition does occur.

* Almost all human beings undergo PCEs, whether or not they recall or understand them. PCEs take many forms.

* They can be voluntary or involuntary. The former, by their deliberate intent, may be suspect and involve use of artifacts.

* Foreknowledge of a future event appears to contravene the Law of Causality, but this applies only in Space 1. All PCEs therefore are generated in Space 2.

* PCG dreams are almost wholly products of past memories and imagination extracted from Space 1 neural storage circuits but the exceptions contain data from future events in Space 2.

* PCG dreams are almost without exception about trivia.

* A `previewed' event may not necessarily happen. An alternate version may be generated by a present-time decision/action, or occur by

chance in terms of a Probability Field in Space 2.

* Insensate objects including celestial bodies follow a fixed and predetermined track through Space 1 following the gravity contours imposed by Space 2.

* Sentient creatures with the ability to move possess a power of choice in regard to imminent future events, governed by the Probability Field in Space 2. But mainstream events in the future of such creatures are variable by chance, for the same reason.

* Most PCEs feature a short interval between PCE and event but there are exceptions, such as Nostradamus's predictions.

* Accuracy of deliberate predictions decreases with interval.

* The world view of precognition is that it contravenes natural laws and is therefore impossible. Science regards those laws as inviolable but is hidebound to a Space 1 viewpoint. Given evidence confirming PCG, the tendency is to discount this evidence.

* While many writers discuss precognition, few if any offer an explanation of the mechanism involved.

* The phenomenon of precognition is no phenomenon. In Collins' English Dictionary it is defined as : *'Anything that can be perceived as an occurrence or fact by the senses'*. Presumably, our five normal Space 1 senses.

* The precognition mechanism therefore is a Space 2 construct and its explanation will be found in the Fixed Time Field in Space 2.

* Most PCEs occur in dreams.

+ + +

CHAPTER TWO

TIME, SPACE AND DIMENSION

`I believe that the gravitational distortion of space and time predicted in Einstein's general theory of relativity provides a possible scientific explanation of precognition,retrocognition, clairvoyance and astral projection, provided we accept the additional postulates that individual consciousness can alter the biogravitational field of a living organism and that the biogravitational field distorts the local subjective space-time of the conscious observer. . .I conjecture that distortions can be manipulated in such a way that the rate of time flow at the location of the participator does not match the corresponding rate of time flow at the object being observed and influenced. . .the differential in the time flows of participator and object in principle can be so adjusted that the participator working within his local light cone `sees' into the probable future or past of the object (that is, he samples universe layers)'.

Space-Time and Beyond (Bob Tobin)

`However successful the theory of a five-dimensional world may be, it is difficult to ignore a voice which whispers *"At the back of your mind, you know that a fourth dimension is all nonsense"*. I fancy that that voice must have often had a busy time in the past history of physics. What nonsense to say that this solid table on which I am writing is a collection of electrons moving at prodigious speeds in empty spaces, which relatively to electronic dimensions are as wide as the spaces between the planets in the solar system ! What nonsense to say that the thin air is trying to crush my body with a load of 14 lbs to the square inch ! What nonsense that the star-cluster, which I see through the telescope obviously there now, is a glimpse into a past age 50,000 years ago ! Let us not be beguiled by this voice. It is discredited'.

Sir Arthur Eddington : Space, Time and Gravitation.

`O call back yesterday, bid time return. . .'

William Shakespeare `Richard III'

CONTENTS

1. The Imponderables
2. Dunne - the Pathfinder
3. The Paradox of Time
4. The Dichotomy of Time
5. The Riddle of the Dimensions
6. Euclidean and Riemannian Space
7. The Effects of Rotation
8. Nature of the Present Moment
9. The Variable Future
10. My World View of Time
11. Physical Time Travel
12. Mental Time Travel

SUMMATION

2

TIME, SPACE AND DIMENSION

1. The Imponderables.

Time is the great enigma - the Mystery of Mysteries, an indefinable and incomprehensible phenomenon surrounding and permeating every aspect of our lives. It regulates our activities, determines our priorities. Time - over which we have no control whatsoever. . . In `Birthday Poem' W.H.Auden wrote :

`*Oh let not Time deceive you. . .you cannot conquer Time. . .*'

Speculation focuses on four fundamental questions.

Is Time real or unreal ?
Does it move only in one direction ?
Is it reversible ?
Does Time have an end or a beginning ?

Henri Bergson[3] based his whole philosophy on the concept that outer or chronological (objective) time is unreal : reality can only be found in our inner sense of duration (subjective time). This real time, Bergson believed, has nothing to do with Space : `we must reject the ever-present temptation to "spatialise" our thoughts about Time'. He published `Time and Free Will' in 1912 - the same year the *Titanic* went down. . .

Time is a constant irritant, an itch we cannot scratch, yet we can neither define it nor explain it. We cannot see or touch it. We confirm its existence subjectively by visible changes, objectively by measuring devices - clocks. Deeply enmeshed in the Time concept are the twin enigmas of destiny and survival; our every thought and decision is oriented towards self-preservation and the maximum possible time on Earth. The Law of Causality directly affects our survival prospects : every Present-Time action and/or decision has future repercussions, trivial or important. We try to improve the odds on survival, learning the wisdom of waiting until the right time to cross the road, avoiding cliff edges and refraining from kissing the strong-man's wife. Long life, like road safety, is `no accident' - you have to work at it.

These responses to the causal effects of Time originated with *homo erectus.* Blessed or cursed with limited tenure on Earth, and faced with the dangers and terrors of his prehistoric world, he experienced deep-rooted insecurity. For all he knew, death was the end of everything : his life was in his own hands, and if he couldn't hack it he was doomed - unless he got help. This was unlikely, from other human beings or animals who regarded him as a free lunch, and mankind craved for an external source of support and possible salvation.

That stimulus left its mark in all religions, but to `*Homo sap*', life devolved into a few basic problems : How long will I live ? What happens when I die ? What will happen to me tomorrow ? How can I find out ? Forewarned, can I avert the danger ? Out of the woodwork crawled creatures who asked : `*How much is it worth to find out ?*'- the soothsayers, prophets, clairvoyants, mediums, fortune-tellers and astrologists with crystal balls and horoscopes, Tarot cards and tea-leaves, African witch-doctors with their rattling bones and Haitian voodoo-men with filthy rituals. Naive people will always pay good money to hear what they *want* to hear, not what they should be told, for Mother Time does not give up her secrets easily.

So what is `Time' ? After two millennia we have only a partial answer - `time' is a measurable interval between two events. By another name `duration', it can be measured mechanically in the absence of a human mind. Clocks do not indicate a period of duration has elapsed - they identify the Present Moment in time. We recall the previous time-check to calculate mentally how long a period of duration has elapsed. Queerly, clocks never register the precise Present Moment. No matter how precise the presentation, we need time to assimilate the data - by which time a new PM is being indicated.

How long does the PM last ? Reason suggests that, however brief a period we sense, the PM must occur in the middle of a short period of duration, during which we observe our surroundings and assimilate the knowledge mentally. The `*specious present*' is an infinitely-short interval, for every whole period can be halved, *ad infinitum*. The succeeding PM starts when the current 3-dimensional frame of reference changes in the slightest degree, so that our physical perception of the PM involves scanning an endless changing montage of frames of reference at a certain rate.

So we have to revise all preconceptions about the nature of Time. Certain natural rhythms govern our minds, providing continuity and occasionally some predictable patterns. We know day follows night, and night day. Summer precedes autumn, and is itself preceded by spring, generating the concept of sequence and order.

Saltmarsh suggested that the `now' of the PM is spread out, so that a specific PM becomes the `specious moment'. It may be of short duration for the conscious mind and much longer for the subconscious, distorted by different states of mind. Yet still we do not know how Time works. Remarkably few, if any writers on precognition make a connection between precognition and Time. Herbert B. Greenhouse devotes half a page out of 300+ to the subject. Andrew Mackenzie[5] does not even include the word `Time' in his index.

2. John William Dunne[6] - the Pathfinder.

Dunne, a brilliant aeronautical engineer, was an early researcher into precognitive dreams and a Time mechanism to accommodate such experiences. He noted that whilst some of his dreams seemed to contain references to future events, his mind automatically rejected them, since they seemed to contradict natural laws which he, as an engineer, had been trained to accept. Dunne's dreams are cited frequently; he became something of a celebrity, a pathfinder and a cult figure in the search for a true Time mechanism. One significant example involved a dream in which he `saw' newspaper headlines about events which had not yet happened, including a report on the Cape to Cairo Daily Telegraph Expedition of 1901. A year later Dunne dreamed of reading a newspaper headline about an island volcanic eruption :

VOLCANO DISASTER IN MARTINIQUE'

which was soon followed by the incident proper.

In some dreams Dunne was a participant : in one sequence he was floating in an oddly-shaped canoe upon water of extraordinary clarity. He recorded the details using a special procedure; years later he made a flight in an early dirigible airship. Passengers occupied a light-alloy gondola suspended below the gas bag, and Dunne had no difficulty in recognising the odd `canoe-shape' of his dream. The `glass-clear water' was, of course, the air itself. He devised an experiment involving recording his dreams each time he awoke, checking them later against subsequent events, but he encountered a fundamental problem. Whenever he established a connection between a current event and some past dream, his mind sought to account for it by coincidence or self-deception.

His solution was elegantly simple : in Present Time, when reading through his dream reports, Dunne taught himself to regard them as simple accounts made *after the events occurred*, in diary form. At once he began to identify unmistakable correlations between earlier dreams and current events, becoming convinced that the only viable explanation would be found in the Time mechanism itself.

Dunne's theories, introduced in his books `*Experiment with Time*' (1927),`*Serial Time*' and `*Nothing Dies*' have long since been discounted, but they triggered an upsurge of Time research in the first half of the 20th century. Part IV of `*Experiment in Time*' is headed `Temporal Endurance and Temporal flow, and I reproduce in Fig.1 Dunne's diagram of a possible Time mechanism.

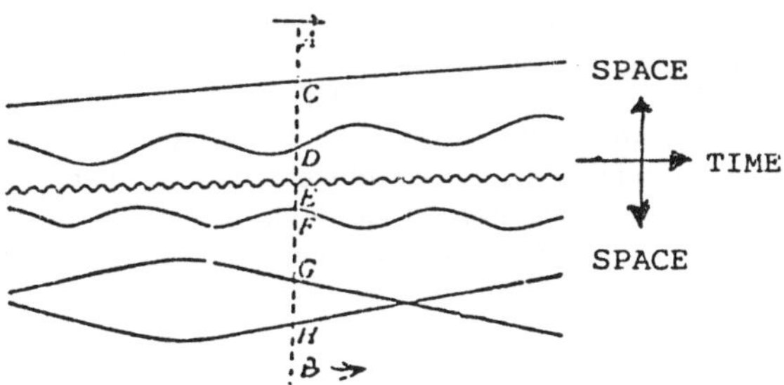

Note that world-line intersection points C,D,E,F,G and H `move' as the Present Moment A - B traverses the Time dimension T.

Fig. 1

Line AB is a three-dimensional frame of reference perceived by an Observer 1 in ordinary Space at a specific Present Moment. Passing through all such frames of reference are `world lines', such that any frame of reference is different to its predecessor due to the angular and irregular variations in world lines. The 3-dimensional frame of reference AB moves with the Present Moment along the Time dimension T, but there is an inconsistency in the label `TIME'; this is simple duration. Also, the title `Temporal Flow' is contradictory : to Dunne, Time is generated by motion of the Present Moment through the Time dimension - yet he speaks of `flow'! This is the age-old enigma we have been unable to resolve. In 1934, Dunne stated the current world-view of Time :

1. *Time has length, divisible into past, present and future.*
2. *This length extends into a direction different to all three of the linear dimensions of this universe.* (This is a bald statement which may

be unacceptable to many readers for no other reason than it sounds impossible, yet it provides an important clue to an arrangement of *six* dimensions).

3. *Neither the past nor future is observable : the future because it has not yet happened, the past because it has gone, existing only in memory. All observable phemonena, therefore, exist in a field situated in a unique `instant' in the Time length - the Present Moment.*
4. *This `present' field of observation traverses in some queer fashion along the Time length, so that events which are first in the future become Present, and then Past. Thus the past is constantly growing and Dunne refers to this movement as the `Passage of Time'.*

Dunne himself refuted (3) above, demonstrating that the future can be observed (albeit haphazardly and involuntarily) but two fundamental errors undermined all his subsequent work. First, he confused Time with duration, ignoring the `rate of movement' of the PM which identified his `TIME' line as duration. Second, whilst suggesting that a moving PM encounters future events, he could not abandon his `flow' of Time, suggesting that while an Observer moves `through' Time, he *experiences* Time as a flow. But this, beyond question, is subjective duration. Whilst coming incredibly close to a real solution, Dunne like so many other Time theorists was defeated by historic language and semantic anachronisms.

3. The Paradox of Time.

The problem was neatly summed up by the philosopher Aurelius Augustinus, Bishop of Hippo, a millennium and a half ago. *"What, then"*, he asked, *"is Time ? If someone asks me, I know. If I wish to explain it to someone who asks, I know not."* J.T.Fraser[7] quotes amusingly the French mathematician Louis Poinsot who, when asked *"What is Time ?"* would ask of the questioner : *"Do you know ?"* If the answer was `*Yes*', he would say : *"Very well - let us talk about it."* If it was `*No*' he would say : *"Very well - let us talk about something else."* The difficulty is to think lucidly about the unthinkable.

Newton's concept of Time is remarkably clear :

> *`Absolute true and mathematical time, of itself and from its own nature, flows equably without relation to anything external, and by another name is called `duration'; relative, apparent and common time is some sensible and external (whether accurate or inaccurate) measure of duration by means of motion, which is commonly used instead of true time, such as an hour, a day, a month, a year'.*

This is at once glibly persuasive and arguably misleading. Yet Isaac Newton was groping intuitively in the correct direction; he talks of two `times' (absolute and common) instead of `Time' and `duration' : both are duration under different labels and there is no mention of a Time mechanism. Aristotle understood the relevance of motion in creating duration :

`We apprehend Time only when we have marked motion'.

Like Newton, Aristotle confused duration with `Time'. Motion, then, is related to duration, which itself is an aspect of Time. But motion in what direction ? And at what velocity ? Does it really matter? Real motion may occur in an infinite number of directions within a three-dimensional continuum, and this opens yet another can of worms - dimensions.

Albert Einstein (1879-1955) first established the relationship, the `relativity' between space, time and motion. Remarkably, the Chinese some 4000 years ago had similar ideas. Why has it taken us so long find a viable Time mechanism ?

Five factors were relevant before Einstein appeared :

First, `duration' (the only manifestation of time we can observe) was confused with true Time. Isaac Newton, Dunne, Aristotle and countless others fell into this insidious trap.

Second, our senses tell us we experience Time as a`flow', bringing events down to us from the Future into the Present Moment. There, they achieve reality and fade into the Past, existing only in memories and records of mankind. (An odd dichotomy exists : many writers regard it as a progress from the past, through the Present Moment and on into the future. It is all a matter of view-point).

Third, an insidious and misleading terminology has crept into our language to support the fallacy of a `Time-flow'. We speak of `time passing' and the `passage of time'; subjectively we sense irregularities in the `rate of time flow' - that `time is dragging' or `flashing past'. The Rev. Richard Jago wrote in the 18th Century :

`With leaden foot time creeps along... While Delia is away'.

Fourth, unidirectionality or the `arrow' of Time : `now' must always precede `then'.

Fifth, the Law of Causality states than an effect cannot precede its cause.

But we are speaking of duration, not `time'. After an objective (measured) interval of 1 hour between events A and B, we say that `an hour of time has passed', but this is semantically incorrect. We should say that `an interval of 1 hour separates events A and B' - but this is too clumsy and pedantic. If twenty subjects are asked to guess the length of a duration period, we will find twenty different answers, because subjective assessment is biassed and distorted by our mental state at the time.

Samuel Goudsmit and Robert Claiborne[8] wrote `*Time... stands still, slips away from us or flies past us. We can save time or lose it, spend time or waste it...even beat it or kill it. But what we cannot do is define it'.* Absolutely right : the writers should have started by defining time (duration) and Time (the great mechanism which drives the universe). I encountered this basic fallacy in most reference books. But if we wish to be precise we can define `interval' as `duration in time' or simply duration. If we wish to identify a particular PM in a period of duration, we call this `epoch'. It is also a spatial location on the time-track of a moving body. And there is `sequence' - the order in which events occur.

These factors have an extraordinary effect on our world-view of Time as `flow'. If we listen to an approaching car, we know it will soon pass us in a future Present Moment. Time, it seems, brings that event to us from the future. As the car passes out of sight, it remains only as a memory. Accordingly, we perceive ourselves as motionless in a moving universe, in which Time flows past us in a never-ending stream.

Predictably we find in Time literature many analogies to water in motion. From Isaac Watts' classic hymn :

`*Time, like an ever-rolling stream, bears all its sons away'.*

But to me, this `flow' theory was always a non-starter. I was an aircraft pilot for 25 years, and learned to calculate the distance covered in a specific time at a given speed, thus :

$$\text{DISTANCE} = \text{VELOCITY} \times \text{TIME}$$

where Distance may be in miles, Velocity in miles per hour, and `Time' in hours. By transposition :

$$\text{TIME} = \frac{\text{DISTANCE}}{\text{VELOCITY}}$$

But `TIME' here is clearly duration, measured in hours. Flying some 200 miles at a speed of 200 mph, flight `duration' is 1 hour, but this tells us nothing about Time itself. While Aristotle identified correctly the relationship between time and motion, he was no innovator : the contemporary Mohist school held that :

`*Movement in space requires duration. . . Distances left behind by a moving object constitute space. . . The changes in position of a moving body such as the Sun or Moon awaken the concept of Time'.*

Whilst we sit in our peaceful garden apparently at rest, the surface of the Earth is rotating at about 0.44 kps, while we orbit around the Sun at 30.4 kps. The solar system itself rotates around the galactic hub once every 200 million years. Like all others in the expanding universe, our galaxy is moving at high velocity towards the periphery. In fact, our solar system is travelling towards a point midway between Hercules and Lyra, at a staggering speed of 268.8 kps - yet the total resultant velocity through intergalactic space is still only a tiny fraction of the speed of light C, i.e. 300,000 kps.

Little wonder that we developed a distorted view of Time. In his famous analogy of a flame, Heraclitus suggested that Time involved instant replacement of the flame by another identical to the first, but Parmenides would have none of this : nothing, he said, could come out of nothing. Zeno used his remarkable paradox of motion to show (to his own satisfaction at least) that motion is change, change is time. He used the now-famous example of the race-track : the end of the track can never be reached, for no one can traverse an infinite series of points in finite time. Whatever distance is left to run, the runner must first cover half of it before entering the second half - which again must be divided and so on, *ad infinitum.* When Diogenes the Cynic first heard this argument he emulated the example of a certain famous pig, got up and slowly walked away ! As they say in America - it figures. . .

Heraclitus believed that everything in the universe is in a state of flux. In Plato's Theætetus, we find a quote from his master's writings : *`You cannot step twice into the same river, for fresh waters are ever flowing in upon you'*. But Heraclitus' real views come down to us almost solely by quotations, and we find considerable controversy in the writings of the ancient Greeks. The Monists held that *`there could be no motion without a void'*, but their view of a void was a `plenum' (a volume occupied by matter). As Bertrand Russell pointed out, they were wrong in believing there could be no motion in such a continuum. I believe that the Stoics and Greek philosophers spent a great deal too much time in esoteric and frequently pointless arguments, unable to see the wood for the trees, and while this may smack of heresy to the purists, I have no personal difficulty in recognising Time and subjective/objective duration. William of Ockham, who died *circa* 1349, developed the maxim we now know as Occam's Razor : `In explaining something assumptions must not be needlessly multiplied'.

Well, I am all for simplicity. I would hesitate to denigrate the work of the pioneers in eliminating many sidetracks, diversions and wild goose chases in the search for Time. Further problems arise in the endless search for definitions of terms which seem to me to be self-explanatory. For example, the Void. Space. To most laymen, it is the volume separating two or more solid objects. If no air is present it is a vacuum, and lacking any material, it is a void. Space is freely observed by simply looking at the Moon, separated from us by Space which reason tells us must be endless. If an `end' is postulated, we may well ask `What lies beyond ?'. We are told that Space is curved, that if we go far enough we may come back to our starting point. Fair enough : we can use the analogy of a Mobius Strip with a three-dimensional cross-section. Staying within the strip, we would arrive back at our start line - but what lies outside the Strip itself ?

Aristotle had his own views. *`The theory,'* he says in Physics 208b, *`that the void exists involves the existence of place : for one would define void as space bereft of body'.* Very true. Space may be a void (without matter) or a plenum containing material objects. Such objects occupy a location in Space, yet if all matter ceased to exist, that location must still exist. The major problem lies in developing a system of coordinates to identify a location in Space.

Einstein helps us. He said that distance is between events and not between things, and involves Time as well as space. But whilst he omitted to tell us how Time works, men were probing the enigma centuries ago. Timæus wrote :

> *`When the father and creator saw the creature which he had made moving and living, the created image of the eternal gods, he rejoiced; and as this was eternal, he sought to make the universe eternal, so far as might be. Now, the nature of the ideal being was everlasting, but to bestow this as tribute in its fullness upon a living creature was impossible. Wherefore he resolved to have a moving image of eternity, and when he set in order the heaven, he made this image eternal but moving, according to number, while eternity itself rests in unity, and this image we call Time'.*

It is said that Friar Bacon made a brazen head : if he heard the head speak he would succeed in the work in hand, and if not he would fail. A man named Miles was set to watch the head, and while Bacon was sleeping the head uttered these words : `Time is'. Half an hour afterwards it said `Time was', and after half of another hour, it said `Time's past', fell down and broke into pieces.'The story is apocryphal, but illustrates how easily man falls into the twin traps of regarding Time as a flow, confusing duration with Time. Yet Timæus was close to the truth with his `moving image of Time'.

St.Augustine was a far-sighted man but he could not see past the `flow' barrier. He believed that neither past nor future exist, but only the present : it is only a moment and time can only be measured when it is passing. *`The only way out of such contradictions,* he said, *is to say that past and future can only be thought of as present : `past' must be identified with memory, and `future' with expectation, both memory and expectation being `present' facts.' To say that there are three times : past, present and future - is a loose way of speaking'.*

But Augustine knew this solved nothing. *`My soul yearns to know* *this most entangled enigma. . .'* he said pensively - and I know exactly how he felt.

Most modern writers fall victim to the Time paradox. David Loye[9] describes the experiments made by Wilder Penfield in the course of brain research. Penfield could evoke illusions of passing time by stimulating the right brain lobe of a subject. Again, we see the fundamental error of confusing duration with time; Penfield was investigating variations in the brain's ability to assess time lapse - i.e. duration. Loye points out that we identify time sense normally with the left lobe, rather than the right. *`How,* he asks, *can we reconcile this apparent contradiction ?*

In our dreams, daydreams and trances we have no perception of duration : our conscious mind in the left brain lobe notes change and motion, perceiving this as duration. We can assess lapse of time accurately only by reference to measuring devices such as clocks : Penfield, apparently, stimulated the right brain lobe to open, temporarily, the physical link between right and left lobes and between subconscious and conscious minds. Such a connection may occur in mentally-disturbed patients who `hear' voices in their head - the inter-lobe link is permanently open. Patients `hear' voices of dream-characters. The frontal brain lobe is also involved, as we shall see in a later chapter.

Sigmund Freud had similar views. *`There is nothing in the Id that corresponds to the idea of time,'* he wrote. (Id - the mass of primitive instincts and energies forming part of the subconscious mind). *`There is no recognition of the passage of time. . . and no alteration in its mental processes produced by the passage of time'.*

For `time' read `duration' ! The world-view of Time incorporates a linearity regardless of whether we consider Time as a flow of events past us, or events created by the movement of matter through space-time. Ornstein [7] writes of this effect: *`During each day our consciousness flows in and out of linearity. . .Each night we dream and enter a world in which the linear sequence of time has much less meaning. Events in the dream space seem fluid'.*

According to David Loye, this other world exists within the right brain lobe, but an interesting side-issue emerges. All dreams, generated in the same region, have movement. Dream sequences of still-life or static landscapes would be of little interest. Accordingly, the dream-constructing mechanism in the right lobe possesses an intrinsic perception of duration, clarifying to some extent how the mind may function. A conscious mind perceives duration objectively, and experiences it subjectively - but not in sleep, in which we have no perception at all of duration in the physical world. But this subconscious perception of duration is exercised in dream sequences generated in the right lobe. Duration-awareness would seem to be an attribute of the migratory self, helping us to assess its activities in the Fixed Time Field. It perceives and remembers not only a `still picture' of an individual frame of reference in its duration-extension but movement in montages extracted from many adjacent Present Moments constitute events.

Can the self differentiate between `past' events and future events which have yet to happen ? We shall see. Loye in my view was mistaken in believing that the linear `time' we experience consciously/subjectively does not appear to exist in the dream state - in other words, two different `times'. In discussing the birth of space and time, he writes :

> *`At first, there must have been no time as we know it. There would have been a state of motion in which there was neither space nor time'.*

This view is upheld by Stephen Hawking and Roger Penrose.[11] It is axiomatic that without motion there can be no duration, no interval. Given a `state of motion' there must be duration, which itself requires space and moving bodies. Loye suggest that as organisms evolved they developed a time sense from their perception of movement, which he calls `spatial time' (but which must necessarily function in the left brain lobe : it is, in fact, perception of duration). Finally, he postulated a third `time' produced by the development of bi-lobular brains in mammals, which he calls `Serial time'. He is referring in every case to the perception of duration.

Nor is Loye unique in that respect : Wolfgang Kohler[12] wrote : *`Experienced time has certain characteristics in common with experienced space. . .'* We know this to be true - we perceive duration by movement through space, and one complements the other. There is an odd passage in Kohler's work emphasising the dichotomy of Time and the effects of language bias in complicating our perception. He writes :

> *`In English we may have something `before' or `behind' us both in the spatial and temporal meanings. We look `forward' in space as in time, and death approaches in time just as somebody approaches in space'.*

There are major anomalies here. `Looking forward in space' infers looking in the direction of motion, and our orientation to the line of motion is irrelevant : movement of the Earth, Sun and Galaxy continue regardless. It is quite impossible to gaze up into the sky and determine our direction of motion. Second, Kohler writes of `death approaching in time', as if we remain stationary and future events come to us. Death is a potential future event embedded in the FTF somewhere along a duration-line : take Abraham Lincoln's famous dream of seeing his own corpse lying in state on a bier in the White House. Third, I cannot accept Kohler's final statement that `something approaches us in space.' In a universe where all matter is in motion, we can never know precisely the spatial relationship of two bodies : the effect is the same if a stationary body `A' is being approached by moving body `B', or vice versa. Or, indeed, when both A and B approach each other in space.

Precise definition in metaphysics is crucial. P.D.Ouspensky[13] began with basics : a man's life is taken as a line from birth to death :

1854..1904

Where he was before 1854 and after 1904 is unknown. But we meet immediate problems of definition : does `life' mean existence in the physical body ? Does the self enter the body at birth, or did it exist before the act of conception ? Does it survive after death of the body ? According to Ouspensky science deals solely with man's body and the world-view that the body does not exist before conception or after dissolution into basic elements on death. But philosophy regards such confinements as unanswerable and consequently naive.

Well, that is possible. The possibility of existence before birth and after death, Ouspensky writes, is closely connected with the mystery of Time - and Time guards its own secrets well. He begins with a world-view of Time as :

Before + Now + After

....

But the same applies to existence before birth and after death, viz :

Before................Now................After
Before birth........Life........After death

Here, says Ouspensky, we make our fundamental mistake - that `time' in the sense of `before, now and after' is the product of our lives, our being, our perception. But he made the characteristic and common error of confusing subjective perception of duration with Time, recognising the fact but making little progress towards a solution. *`We use `Time"*, he says, *`without understanding its true meaning.'* And that is absolutely right. *`We take eternity to be an infinite extension of time,'* he continues, *`while really "eternity" means another dimension of Time'.* True : infinite duration, measured objectively, is `eternity'.

Here Ouspensky falters. Instead of probing the idea of `another dimension of Time' he drifts away into realms of reincarnation, transmigration of souls and the cyclic universe. Nietzsche and the Pythagoreans eschewed the idea of eternal reoccurrence, without the benefit of modern metaphysics and cosmology to hypothesise *how* it could happen. Nietzsche and Ouspensky came close to a breakthrough in arguing that repetition could not be proved on our plane (our own 3-dimensional universe) with Time being the Fourth Dimension. Repetition, he said, requires five dimensions, i.e. an entirely new `space-time eternity'.

I believe it requires six - three each in our own universe and in the

FTF. But the fundamental `cyclical' thesis is found in all periods of history. Aristotle's pupil Eudemus wrote a major work *`Physics'* of which no trace remains, except in later commentaries by philosophers such as Simplicus :

> *`Some accept and others deny that time repeats itself. Repetition is understood in different senses. One kind may be in the natural order of things like repetitions of summers and winters and the movement of the heavenly bodies and phenomena produced by them, such as solstices and equinoxes. But if we are to believe the Pythagoreans there is another kind of repetition.*
> *`That means I shall talk to you and sit exactly like this : everything will be the same as it is now, and time, as it can be supposed, will be the same'.*

My own ideas follow this line very closely. If a second universe coexisted with our own empty universe before the Big Bang, containing templates of all the potential events in the eons to come, that arrangement will *still* exist after all the material in our expanding universe has reached light velocity and conversion into pure energy. Assuming this eternal blueprint in the FTF matrix exists, and another Big Bang occurs, precisely the same sequence of events will materialise (ignoring minor modifications in main-line events imposed by human actions).

Remarkably, Hinduism and Buddhism are centred on this concept of a repetitive universe, and we encounter yet another mystery - *deja vu* (French : already seen) defined as *`the experience of viewing a new situation as if it had already occurred'*. Does a reborn human self surviving physical death of the body carry some memories of its previous life on Earth ? And if reborn into a replica of its pre-Big Bang body, would it possess memories of previous events ?

We shall put forward a much simpler and logical explanation in due course. But readers interested in the phenomenon should read Alexis Tolstoy describing in idyllic detail his life in rural Russia, walking by lake and dam and watching the labourers sitting on the grass. In the final verse, he writes :

> *`And the Jew,with his beard,walked by,*
> *And the weir made just such a noise,*
> *All this has happened before*
> *Only I cannot tell when.'*

And in `Sudden Light' by D.G.Rossetti :

> *`I have been here before,*
> *But when or how I cannot tell :*
> *I know the grass beyond the door,*

The sweet keen smell,
The sighing sound, the lights around the shore.
You have been mine before -
How long ago I may not know :
But just when at that swallow's soar
Your neck turned so,
Some veil did fall - I knew it all of yore.

Then, now - perchance again !...
O round mine eyes your tresses shake !
Shall we not lie as we have lain
Thus for love's sake,
And sleep, and wake, yet never break the chain ?'

Ouspensky quotes a variant to the last stanza :

`Has this been this before
And shall not thus time's eddying flight
Still with our lives our love restore
In death's despite
And day and night yield one delight once more ?'

Ouspensky's work features the interminable confusion of Time and duration, yet clearly he is groping at the locked portals of truth :

`The idea of time as the fourth dimension does not contradict the ordinary view of life, so long as we take time as a straight line. The idea only brings with it a sense of greater preordination, of greater inevitability. But the idea of time as a curve of the fourth dimension entirely changes our conception of life. If we clearly understand the meaning of this curvature, how the curve of the fourth dimension is transformed into the curves of the fifth and sixth dimensions, our view of things and ourselves cannot remain any longer what they were.'

His definition of these dimensions is uncertain and abstruse.

`If dimensions are considered to be straight lines, a fifth dimension is perpendicular to the line of the fourth and intersecting it. That is, a line passing through every moment of time, the line of the infinite existence of a moment'.

Now, this at first sight seems analogous to our own thesis on dimensions. Ouspensky takes duration as `time', the fourth dimension, but omits to mention that it is also observable in our own universe. The fifth dimension, which he does not name but which is analogous to our own

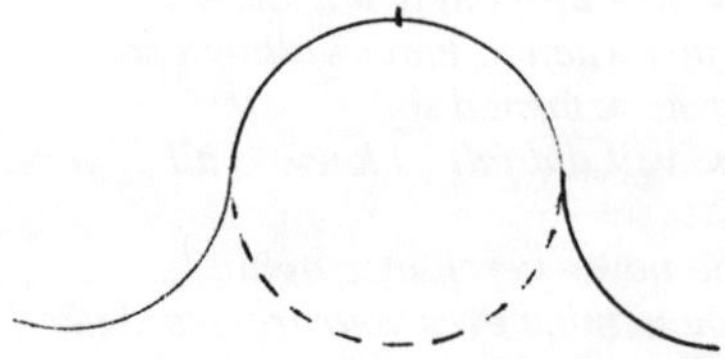

Extrapolating the idea of the curvature of dimensions into waves, i.e. undulatory vibrations, every wave comprises a complete circle. Imagining life is a wave, we obtain this figure in which the point of birth coincides with the point of birth - a reference to a cyclic universe.

Fig. 2

`extension' dimension, is perpendicular to the fourth - duration. But then he writes `*It is a line which passes through every moment of time, the line of the infinite existence of a moment'.* And here he appears to lose the thread of his argument. He does not name fourth or fifth dimensions, presumably perpendicular to each other and therefore in a flat plane. It is but one small step to envisage the sixth as perpendicular to both the others.

But here Ouspensky charges into an arid cul de sac, writing about `*undulatory vibrations'*, suggesting that `*a wave always comprises a complete circle.*

If we imagine life as a wave, Ouspensky suggests, the point of death coincides with the point of birth. From this point, I believe his arguments lose viability, because there is no real attempt to produce a workable Time mechanism which embraces all the postulates he makes. Further, there is the persistent difficulty of confusing Time with duration, and most of all, no connection at all with the paranormal phenomena (including precognition) which connect duration with the Time Mechanism. Ouspensky continues :

> `*Life in itself is `time' for man. For man, there is not and cannot be any other time outside the time of his life. Man is his life. His life is his time'.*

And again :

> `*If I die today, tomorrow will not exist for me'.*

This is true - if `I' cease to exist in any form after today. But if the self on death migrates to a continuum in which every day, from the Big Bang to final dissolution of the universe, exists eternally and simultaneously, then all of our tomorrows exist for us. Dead or alive. It is not for me to say that persons who died many yesterdays ago can communicate with us in our own `today', but millions so believe. And if they are correct, all our tomorrows exist eternally.

Yet I feel that Ouspensky sensed the existencc of the Time structure which eluded him always :

> *`The three-dimensionality of Time is completely analogous to the three-dimensionality of space'.*

So near. . .and yet so far. But there is sound evidence of the existence of some kind of internal clock. Many people have the ability to wake up at a specific time after briefing the subconscious mind accordingly before falling asleep. Occasionally I listen to programmes in the BBC World Service during the night in Britain; without external help I wake up seconds before the programme starts, in time to switch on the radio.

Modification of the speed of our organic processes by reducing the ambient temperature causes a corresponding fluctuation in our time perception. I have experienced an extraordinary effect at times when I am half-asleep, half-awake on dark extremely cold mornings. I am anxious to know the time but reluctant to expose my arm to check my wristwatch. I conjure up a vision of a clock-face before my closed eyes, and presently I detect a faint ghostly impression of hands indicating the time. It is usually correct within a minute or so but the hands waver uncontrollably.

Such effects are admissible if we accept the concept of a migratory `self' working outside our ordinary `Space 1'. In the FTF it can view all past and future events, and is aware of the `time', i.e. the spatio-temporal position of the moving Present Moment. Instructed to wake up at a given time, the self re-enters the left lobe at the required time and we wake up.

In defining the `future' we encounter serious difficulties. J.B. Priestley[14] suggests three options. First, it may be a zero, a blank, a nothingness because it has not yet come into existence. Second, it is fixed, predetermined and complete, waiting for us to discover it. Third, it is neither nothing nor fixed and immutable - it is variable and half-shaped, partially created, offering a number of possibilities which may soon become actual events. Priestley was tortured by his inability to see a way out of this maze. He wrote :

> *`...honesty compels me to admit that if events on a large scale are already determined and so inevitable, being part of a fixed future, and if as we certainly believe that precognition can be experienced in dreams, then there is something I ought to be able to explain - and I can't'.*

Dunne, he points out, insisted that we could change the future, and we shall prove that this is perfectly true. But Priestley was unable to cope with the paradox of precognition, lacking a viable Time mechanism. We can tackle the problem by suggesting that there are five possible futures :

Inevitable.	Symbolised by motions of celestial bodies and seasons.
Predictable.	Planetary movements.
Guessable.	Inferential trends based on current knowledge.
Possible.	Range of variations of potential events.
Probable.	The version most likely to become real.

The Probable Future wild card, in considering any human-related event, infers that we can influence an event so that a particular version achieves reality. But how can this be possible ?

\+ + +

A practical solution seemed as distant as ever. Faced with phenomena we find difficult to explain, it is convenient to make a `model' incorporating the data accumulated to date. The model will change and develop with the increasing expertise available, providing viable data is used. Otherwise GIGO rules : *`Garbage in, Garbage out'* !

Two significant developments occurred this century. The first was a trend towards logical/mathematical theses after Albert Einstein gave us a new insight into the nature of Time, specifically the problem of defining `simultaneity' and `succession' from the viewpoints of two separate observers, and particularly on the effect of their movement at different velocities (one travelling at very high speed) in their perception of the Present Moment.

For my part, I saw the Present Moment as a moving discontinuity, a travelling `life-wave' with velocity equivalent to our normal quantified speed through space.

The second and the most important aspect was the changing ambient climate in regard to the acceptance of paranormal phenomena by the scientific establishment. J.B.Priestley quotes one important philosopher :

> *`In my view there can be no direct connection between (a) the status of Time in modern physics and (b) questions about precognition and parapsychology. There may an indirect (sociological) connection in that the more open-minded the community of physicists becomes about (a), the more rooted may be their opposition to all thought about (b)'.*

As Priestley himself says: *`If a man, with his theory at stake, makes up his mind not to be shown that queer things are happening, little can be done except to make a face at him and a rude noise...'*

And he quotes another anonymous pundit :

'I do not consider that theories of Time could have any useful part to play in this. Nature is a flux to us, and this we atomise into isolated events. In order to compensate for the isolation, we introduce Causality and Determinism. How far this itself is demanded by nature as a necessary part of our thinking, I cannot say. They require that isolated events be arranged or ordered in a rational pattern, and our ordinary mundane macroscopic experience enables us to do this ordering via two abstractions of the events. So we do ordering in space, and ordering in time. Thereafter, to take 'Time' as something in itself, a self-subsistent entity analogous to Matter-Space-Time events from which Time has been abstracted is a piece of mental acrobatics'.

An experienced skin diver once described the problems of scuba diving for a specific objective in water thick with plankton as searching a fog-bound football pitch at night for a pea from the referee's whistle. The simile is apt when reading such views as those above. . . To define order in space and time, we cannot avoid reference to duration : in moving, we encounter first one object then another, and the time lapse is duration. The order in which we encounter the objects provides sequence. Yet again, we find the age-old trap of confusion.

I found some corroboration for the FTF in the work of Oxford nuclear physicist D.H.Wilkinson[56] who believed it possible that there might be independent but interacting universes analogous to the Fixed Time Field :

'Perhaps there do exist universes interpenetrating with our own; perhaps of a high complexity, perhaps containing their own forms of awareness, constructed out of particles and other interactions than those which we now know, but awaiting discovery through some common but elusive interaction that we have yet to spot'.

That interaction, I suggest, is the postulated interface between the self and the universe at quantum level, introduced by Danah Zohar[19], based on the work of Professor Herbert Fröhlich of Liverpool University in the Seventies. At that time, it was widely thought that consciousness may result from the brain taking on, in some strange way the properties of a superconductor.

Gary Zukav[15] writing in 1979, also arrived at a similar hypothesis :

'If, at the quantum level, the flow of time has no meaning, and if consciousness is fundamentally a similar process, and if we can become aware of these processes within ourselves, then it is also conceivable that we can experience timelessness.'

The particles forming our physical bodies are in two categories : first, *fermions*, which include electrons, protons and neutrons and endow matter with its familiar solidity. Second, *bosons*, which are particles of relationships such as photons, virtual photons, the plus and minus *w* particles and the neutral *z* particles which produce radioactive decay. Quantum physics provide the foundation upon which we can construct the Fixed Time Field thesis, and establish the absolute necessity of the human observer in our convoluted universe.

All the matter in our Fixed Time Field universe exists in particle-function (in the `past' components of duration-extensions which grow constantly behind the moving Present Moment) and in wave-function ahead of the PM moving discontinuity. Every individual particle, whether in particle or wave form, has a duration-extension from the moment of its creation into the far distant future and its eventual demise. Transmission of information along the duration-extension occurs by particle interaction, precisely as the discharged photon in the Thomas experiment is able to pass through two slits in a screen at the same time and exhibit interference patterns seen only when wave functions interact. All particles ahead of the advancing Present Moment exhibit wave-function characteristics and exist as probabilities, thus providing a framework for the variable format of future events.

Dunne's contemporary J.B.Priestley harboured an increasing suspicion that the former's Serial Time concept was suspect and constructed his own thesis of three Times : `Passing Time' (which he failed to recognise as duration); `Time 2' involving a slow and contemplative perception, and `Time 3', the imaginative creative `speeded-up' Time. Trying to match this concept to Dunne's `Time 2' (the time-lapse rate of the moving Present Moment) he became bogged down in the subjective perception of duration, distorted by the subject's state of mind.

Almost without exception, Time writers concentrate on subjective perception of duration by human observers, and I found no relevance in Bergson's *`Time and Free Will'*. In *`Time as Succession and the Problem of Duration'*, Friedrich Kummel was another victim of the Time/duration confusion. There were no clues to a Time mechanism in *`Time and Synchronicity in Analytical Psychology'* by M.L. von Franz[44] , who was preoccupied with subjective effects of duration, but I found some authors working close to the periphery of Time itself. Inevitably they took wrong turnings into frustrating cul de sacs.

I read Jung on *`Synchronicity'*, and *`The Time Sense in Psychiatry'* by Jost A.M. Meerloo; *`Subjective Time'* by John Cohen and *`The Voices of Time'* by J.T. Fraser. I went back again and again to *`Time'* by Goudsmit and Claiborne; *`Timewarps'* by John Gribbin and countless others - but none of them told me how Time works. Plainly, there was some validity in Dunne's reasoning, marred by frequent inconsistencies in his postulates. Specifically, he suggested a `time flow' and that I could not accept.

Change was a major factor. In a totally static universe, there is no change - and no Time. Dunne, presenting his moving `frame of reference', evolved an extraordinary explanation of the `rate' of movement, but his `Time line' was simple duration. His key to Fig. 1 should read :

SPACE

----------> DURATION

SPACE

How did he explain this anomaly ? Evading the concept of potential future events awaiting the arrival of a moving observer, he suggested that to measure the time-lapse rate of the travelling Present Moment, a secondary `Time 2' would be necessary. This led him into the unproductive labyrinth of Serial Time and Serial Universes, but he avoided neatly the inference of an infinitely-large number of adjacent Present Moments by postulating `world-lines' which are sadly reminiscent of the Victorian `flip books' of still photographs, each slightly different to the next and producing a semblance of motion. But the only `time' involved is that required to flip through the book - and that constitutes duration.

Dunne came very close to the idea of a `duration-extension' of a moving body like the Earth in our three-dimensional universe, viewed from outside, in the form of a cylindrical construct extending from the time when the Earth condensed from the interstellar dust into the far-distant future. Any cross-section represents an epoch in the Earth's history. But Dunne fell at the last hurdle, asking :

> *`Why should we extend these world-lines beyond the moving observational field ? Why do we not assume that the world-lines are simply "growing with time" ?'*

Dunne' approach, which had promised so much, had become much too unwieldy and confused to retain any viability : it had a cult following for almost fifty years, only to be overtaken by the advancing wave of progress. But we should not undervalue his contribution.

4. The Dichotomy of Time.

Despite my failure to develop a working model of the Time mechanism, I was making progress. I had learned a great deal, and had eliminated (to my own satisfaction at least) most of the old theories. I was convinced that all future events existed in potential but variable form somewhere outside our familiar universe; reason suggested that this realm coexisted with our own reality. But what kind of universal paradigm could accommodate such an arrangement ?

What I am about to suggest is not new. Other writers have hinted at it, fought through the foothill thickets without seeing clearly the shape of the mountain peak beyond. Some failed because of a deeply-rooted antipathy to the paranormal, failing to perceive that natural laws would have to be extended to accommodate Magic. All too many (with the truth virtually staring them in the face), evaded the challenge and went off at some unproductive tangent. Ouspensky came closest, perhaps, in studying death and eternal reoccurrence of life - Time, he suggested, may be finite in the material universe, and may be the fourth dimension : Time, he suggests, is a curve of that dimension, which contains future events.

Dimensions form an essential part of the structure of Time. Here, I must introduce to the reader the concept of the Fixed Time Field, by means of some common analogies. For simplicity, I shall use `Space 1' for our own universe and `Space 2' for the FTF (Fixed Time Field).

Analogy 1 - The Flowing Stream.

Assume that a blind man is standing knee-deep in a stream representing a `flow' of Time, facing upstream towards the `future'. Floating leaves drift downstream towards him, representing future Time events. Approaching the blind man, each is a potential `impact event' if its random course brings it into contact with his legs. He will become aware of that event's existence, but knows nothing of many other potential events which drift past without achieving reality. No impact event can be repeated by the same leaf at any other time.

Blind and unaware of any impending impact, he can take no avoiding action. He can, however, step aside voluntarily, a random decision without motive, causing the original leaf to miss his leg; it remains a potential impact event and never achieves reality. Another leaf may make a contact indistinguishable from any others. The `leaf-impact' scenario, *per se,* is one of a number of self-contained future event versions. Similarly, our blind man may step forward upstream, initiating a fresh range of versions with a different `Present Moment' identification.

In real life, our random daily decisions may determine which `event version' achieves reality, and this is the fundamental basis of the Law of Causality. (Remember - we have assumed that Time is a flow of events past a stationary observer). Normally it is irrelevant which leaf makes contact, but a heavy log approaching from upstream is a different matter. The blind man is unaware of the danger - but on the bank his twin brother, who has no sensory defects and sees the danger, shouts a warning - *but our blind man is also deaf...*

Extrapolating the analogy, the person on the bank may not be the blind man's brother but a bystander, prepared to wade into the stream and save the blind man - provided the cash incentive is adequate...

This is a reasonably accurate presentation of a world-view of Time as a `flow'. The blind man's location in the stream represents a stationary Present Moment past which future events flow in succession. It encapsulates possibility, probability and determinism, and our inability to observe the future via our normal senses. The `wild card' man on the bank `outside' the blind man's universe may view events upstream in the future, but not the past leaf impact events which exist only in the blind man's memory.

The analogy is completed by assuming that the blind man represents the conscious mind, and the man on the bank is the subconscious mind, with direct and instantaneous contact between the two via the inter-lobe link. Details of future events may be transmitted to the conscious mind on waking up.

Analogy 2 - The Static Lake.

Our blind man is now wading slowly forward across a shallow knee-deep lake, encountering leaves scattered on the surface, whilst the log floats motionless in his direct path. Advancing at the same rate as our stream flowed, the impact-touch of leaves feels identical : each leaf is another potential impact event, and his location represents the Present Moment, moving forward with him through space and duration. Individual leaf-impact events may be :

* *Moving leaf A strikes leg B with kinetic energy (KE) `X'.*
* *Moving leg B strikes stationary leaf A with KE `X'*
* *A and B, both in motion, make impact with total KE `X'.*

Our blind man cannot tell which analogy is operative. (The third example is equivalent to wading up a sluggish stream at a rate producing identical impacts to the other examples). Similarly, our inefficient senses are unable to distinguish whether Time is a flow, a stationary field of pot-

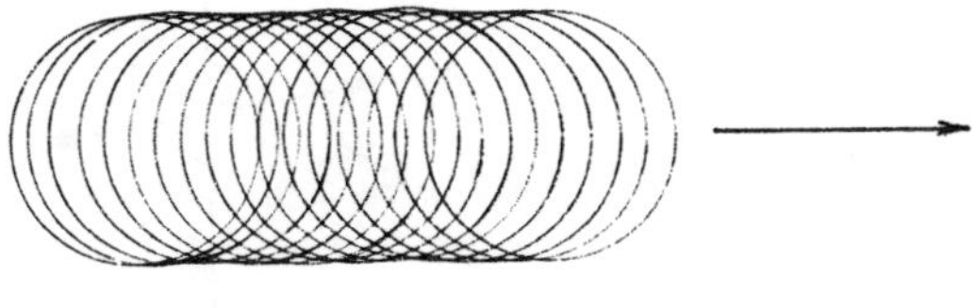

Earth's Duration-Extension

Fig. 3

ential events, or a combination of both ! Incapable of identifying Time as such, we seize upon the only aspect we can observe - duration - and assume that it *is* 'Time'.

Which analogy is correct ? Well, motion through space generates duration and is part of the Time mechanism itself. Moving objects create duration, following a singular linear dimension in 3-D space regardless and outside of our three normal dimensions. Duration is a manifestation of a universe co-existent with our own.

5. The Riddle of the Dimensions.

Plato said : '*There can be no Time in a static universe...*'. It is difficult, in a continually expanding moving universe, to conceive an object absolutely stationary in relation to all other bodies. Such an objective assessment is possible only *outside* Space 1, our 3-dimensional universe. But what would an hypothetical observer see in Space 2 ? (See Fig. 3).

The Earth, occupying every millisecond a new location in Space 1, would appear as the cylindrical extension described previously, formed by an infinite number of Present Moments. Each PM constitutes a spatial location : every cross-section corresponds to a specific epoch, such as the first millisecond of 1492. Another, further along Earth's duration extension, may be 15.00 hours Basic Galactic Time January 1st 2792 when we welcome to Earth the first Galactic Federation Ambassador.

The Solar System will be an extraordinary construct. The Sun would be an endless bar of fire reaching far back into Space and Time to the moment of the Big Bang, and onwards into a future we cannot imagine. Around it, the planets (orbiting the Sun in the plane of the ecliptic tilted at 67 degrees to the Sun's direction of motion) would appear as a beautiful

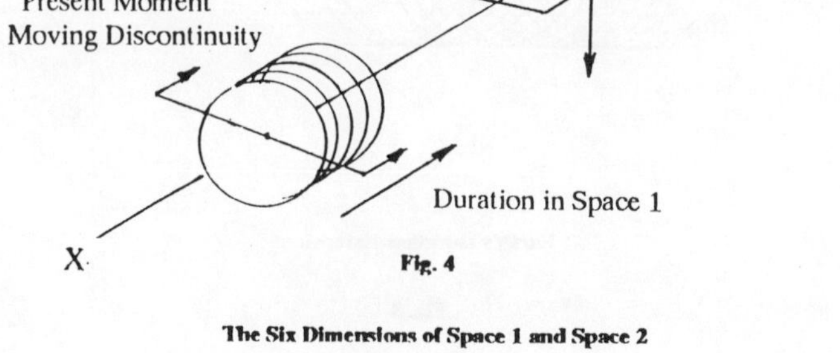

Fig. 4

The Six Dimensions of Space 1 and Space 2

multi-coloured array of spiral lines. Had that angle been 90 degrees, the effect would be annular extensions around the Sun fire-cylinder.

I doubt seriously if any human mind could view such a stupendous display and remain quite sane. A total non-believer myself, I can understand the *need* to believe in the existence of some Supreme Designer, when faced with the stark incandescence of the Solid Universe.

In Fig. 4, the moving Earth follows a linear duration-dimension X-X which exists not only in our physical universe, Space 1, but also in the Space 2 where our observer is located ! This one simple fact unlocks the mystery of Time.

\+ + +

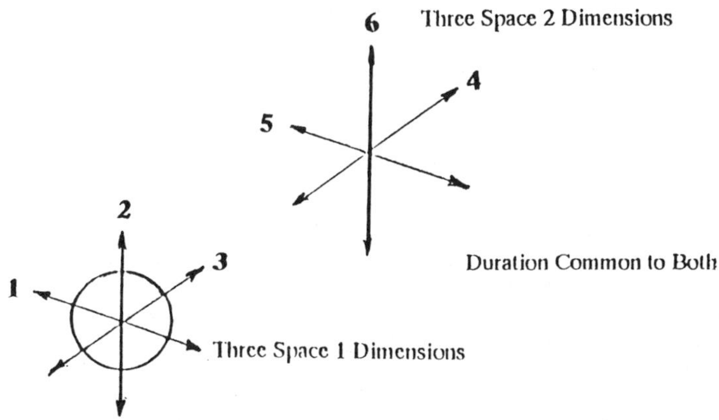

Fig. 5

In the past, Time has been regarded as the Fourth Dimension, and this turns out to be perfectly true, but logically there must also be the Fifth and Sixth Dimensions in Space 2 as shown above.

The fifth, which I have named `extension', is located at right angles to the fourth (duration), corresponding to a flat surface in our universe. To complete the construct, the sixth dimension is at right angles to both fourth and fifth, and I named it `form', since it forms the familiar three-dimension construct with length, width and height. Fig. 5 shows that the duration axis in Space 1 is also the first dimension in Space 2, and fourth in the series of six.

However, the duration-line is not straight. Einstein shows us that

Space-Time is curved by the effects of gravity, but this does not affect our Space 2 dimension-structure : no matter which way, or how much, the duration-axis is curved, the form and extension axes may still be shown at right angles to it *even though they too are curved in Space-Time !* The curvature will be so slight that to all intents and purposes all angles are 90 degrees, as they would be in regions of zero gravity.

Can we relate Present Moments to this paradigm ? Whilst each corresponds to a Dunne `field of observation' in our universe, there is no `Time' in a motionless universe devoid of intelligent entities. Our very perception of the Time mechanism makes it real, the PM manifesting itself only in our consciousness. Our own perceived Present Moment carries us along our duration-extension from birth to death in Space 2, as we move through Space 1. We all experience the PM simultaneously at each instant and it will be seen by any Space 2 observer as a moving discontinuity or `*life-wave'* travelling along the duration-extension.

Its rate of movement corresponds to the Earth's combined space velocity, which may be calculated accurately, but is only a minute fraction of light velocity C (186,000 miles per second). We encounter extraordinary effects on the PM of travellers in hypothetical interstellar spaceships moving at near-light velocity C, suggesting a universal or standard PM perceived at relatively small fractions of C. Literally, a spaceship clock will indicate elapsed time much more slowly than an Earthly observer, because distance shrinks at high velocity. Taking Earth to be on the periphery of the spherical expanding shell of the travelling PM discontinuity, and a starship heading away from Earth at near-C velocity, the effect is that of a bulge on the surface of the shell, enabling the ship to reach a given distance from the shell much sooner than we on Earth. This is Time dilation - see P. 91.

We experience duration as a manifestation of additional but unseen dimensions, forcing us to extend our enquiries to embrace Space as well as Time. (Again, we use `Space' as the generic subject, and `space' in terms of real spatial separation). Much of what follows is quoted with the kind permission of Mr. John Randall[16] .

6. Euclidean and Riemannian Space.

We live in a 3-dimensional and sequential universe featuring a logical progression from 1 dimension (line) to 2 (square) and 3 (cube) in the simplest terms. Euclid's Theorems show that each additional dimension must be at right angles to the preceding one, and also to each other. All material objects have 3 dimensions (length, width and height), and we use various numerical systems to describe them.

This is a progressive and expanding system characteristic of Nature which tends to continue, control and extrapolate any successful process. We are incapable of imagining a fourth dimension at right angles to all three of our familiar ones, but whilst it is theoretically possible to construct a tesseract, the 4-dimensional equivalent of a cube, it is not a concept with which we can feel comfortable. More sensibly, in extending a 3-dimensional system, we may regard one additional dimension as the first in an adjacent but identical 3-dimensional system ! Natural laws prevent two objects from occupying the same space simultaneously, but there is nothing in the rules against occupying two spaces at the same time ! For example, the co-existent dimensional structures in Spaces 1 and 2 occupy the same volume of void, and we can accept this scenario with equanimity. Consider a cubic metre of space on a sunny beach. Passing through that cube of air at any given time is the whole light spectrum, observable by passing white light through a prism. There is a continuous change of frequency from red (long) through orange, yellow, green, blue,indigo and violet (short). Similarly, there is a wide electromagnetic band of radiation from infra-red (with a longer wavelength than light but shorter than radio-waves) to the ultra-violet (with a wavelength shorter than light but longer than X-rays). Further, the cube is permeated by a range of radio and TV transmissions and cosmic rays from outer space.

Each co-exists with the rest by reason of differing wavelength characteristics and the same principle will apply in a pair of co-existent universes. Our failure to identify a Space 2 frequency is not really surprising, since no one has ever been there to take a reading. The very existence of Space 2 must be hypothetical until some mathematician does his sums, but we know that all matter has both wave and particle function characteristics, and waves have pitch and frequency - all variables.

Basically, three coordinates will describe any Space 1 object. A line needs but one : length. A square, two : length and width. And a cube all three : length, width and height. But this fails to describe a object adequately, for it ignores Time. An object, even a human being, may be non-existent at one moment and extant in the next, at the moment of conception. Some seventy years later, that existence may terminate in death. No object can be described comprehensively without specifying two coordinates : its period of existence and the epoch of origin.

Take the analogy of a novel, in which pages represent years. A new-born human being appears on Page 25, and departs life on Page 95 at the age of 70. It is insufficient to say that the human lived for 70 years: we must say `from -' quoting a date.

As in Fig. 2, objects have three conventional spatial dimensions, the intersection of which moves along a linear axis corresponding to a Space 1 dimension, creating duration and forming a duration-extension in Space 2. By extrapolation to form further axes at right angles to `duration' - (`extension' and `form') the three-dimensional continuum of Space 2 is established, i.e. an orderly progression system from 1 to 6 dimensions.

Does it end there ? Let us quote, as did John Randall, the work of Edwin A. Abbott, who postulated in the late 19th century `Flatland', a community confined to the 2-dimensional surface on which they live. They cannot imagine a solid 3-dimensional object, believing that no other

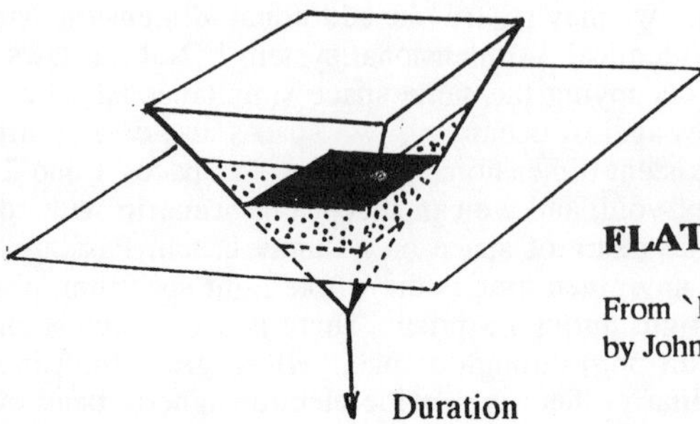

FLATLAND

From `Psychokinesis'
by John Randall

Fig. 6

world or dimension exists. But to us, in a 3-dimensional world, Flatland is merely a series of moving lines on a flat surface with only two dimensions - Length and Width.

Suppose we pass a solid object like an inverted black pyramid, with a central band of yellow, through the 2-D plane of Flatland (Fig.6). What would the Flat inhabitants see ?

Initially a point appears, a black square 2-dimensional body which expands in two directions at the same time (a most unnatural process in Flatland !) until it changes colour to yellow. At this point, Flatland scientists may draw some initial conclusions :

One : There must be dimensions additional to their familiar two. They are aware of duration, even in their limited environment, and measuring the rate of penetration against expansion of the square, they postulate the existence and movement of a three-dimensional body shaped like a pyramid of unknown size.

Two : Any expanding 2-dimensional square must be a manifestation of a 3-dimensional universe coexistent with their own flat domain.

Three : Steps one and two became possible only when they saw the vital connection between duration and a third dimension.

Similarly, a 1-dimensional civilisation living on a straight line observing penetration by an expanding object (Fig.7) will recognise the penetration-rate (duration) as confirmation of at least one additional dimension. The actual shape of the object is immaterial - the angular penetration could be a square as shown, or a triangle. Nor is it necessarily a 2-dimensional object (it could be, for example, a cube or prism) but such

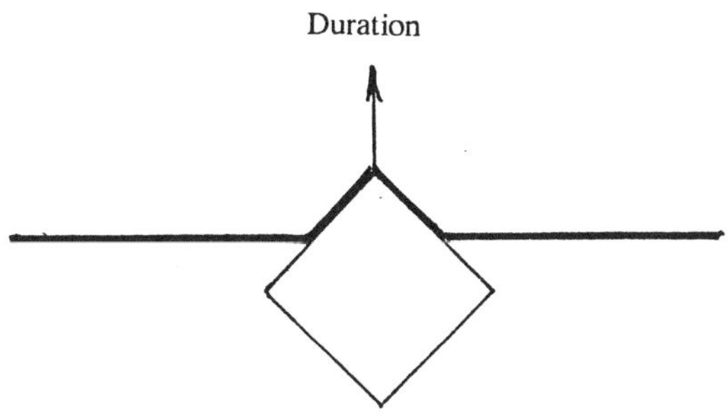

From `Psychokinesis'
by John Randall

LINEWORLD

Fig. 7

a concept would be beyond the comprehension of Lineworld scientists. To complicate their problems still further, we could make the object move along the line while penetrating it, or even rotate !

Significantly, this process may be applied to a multi-dimensional universe like our own : we see and recognise duration, and by natural geometric progression we recognise it as a manifestation of additional dimensions :

1 dimension	=	Lineworld.
1 + duration	=	2 or more dimensions.
2 dimensions	=	Flatland.
2 + duration	=	3 or more dimensions.
3 dimensions	=	Our 3-D Universe.
3 + duration	=	4 or more dimensions.
4 + 2	=	Fixed Time Field.

I was tempted at this stage to extrapolate the sequence to determine how many dimensions are accessible from 6-dimensional co-existing Space 1/Space 2 ! But enough is enough, for the moment. All calculations thus far have been based on Euclidean geometry. The great 3rd century Alexandrian mathematician set out a group of mathematical proofs of theorems or theses in a unique system of three-dimensional geometry taught in many schools. Similarly, Pythagoras taught that in a triangle containing a right angle, the square on the hypotenuse is equal to the sum of the squares on the other two sides. Each postulate such as *`The sum of angles contained in a triangle is always 180 degrees'* is accompanied by a proof.

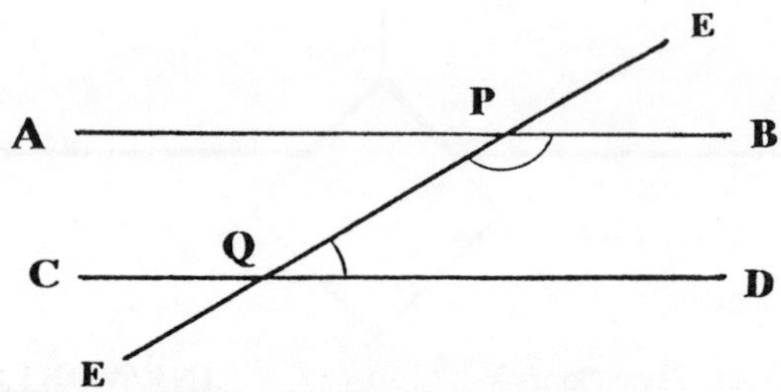

From `Psychokinesis'
(J.L.Randall)

Fig. 8

But by the 19th century, mathematicians were questioning the validity of many of Euclid's theorems, especially his Fifth Postulate (Fig.8). which states : if angles QPB and PQD add up to less than 180 degrees, the lines APB and CQD will meet if extended on that side. Certainly, on flat surfaces, this was true, and it could be proven, albeit with some difficulty. Mathematicians including Gauss (1777-1855) attacked the problem by assuming the postulate was untrue, eventually creating an entirely different geometrical system in which the Fifth Postulate was invalid.

In Euclidean geometry, only one line can be drawn through a given point parallel to an adjacent straight line. Lobatchewsky, Bolyei and Riemann postulated that a number of lines could be drawn through that point ! Whilst this suggestion appears to run contrary to commonsense, we must remind ourselves that `commonsense' functions only in our non-magical Newtonian universe. In non-Euclidean geometry, similar remarkable things can happen : in Riemann's spherical geometry drawn on the surface of a globe there are no parallel lines at all, and the angles of a triangle total *more* than 180 degrees ! (Fig.9).

All this reminds us that we may place far too much reliance in natural laws. To paraphrase Mr. Abraham Lincoln's speech at Clinton in 1858 :

`Some laws work all the time, all laws work part of the time, but all laws don't work all of the time'.

This is especially true of dimensions; forty years ago J.B.Priestley wrote :

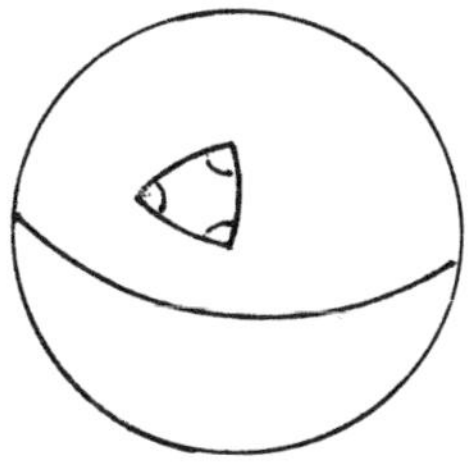

Riemann Geometry on Curved Surface
Angles total more than 180 degrees

Fig. 9

`The wildest theory of fantastic dimensions seemed to me to have a little more sense to it than the conventional view of Time - which nearly everyone I knew accepted without question.'

He was a contemporary of Dunne at a time when the `flow' postulate was widely accepted, in the lack of an alternative explanation, but I do believe that Priestley sensed in some odd fashion the existence of some continuum in which future events exist in potential, a co-existent three-dimensional domain, and strove to develop the concept into words. He wrote :

`We experience things in Time because our `Now' so to speak goes steadily forward, as if we were travelling through a dark land-scape with a searchlight. We invent Time to explain change and succession.'

This is very close to our description of a moving Present Moment, and Priestley had clearly discarded the `flow' theory as unviable. The PM goes steadily forward - but through what ? He stopped short of filling his `dark landscape' with potential future events - yet it was such an obvious deduction. If we do not wait for events to come to us, we must encounter events as we move forward through Time. Many researchers were stalled here, unable to explain why some events previewed in a PCE fail to occur, perhaps because of some `avoiding action'. It raised awkward questions in regard to probability, possibility and destiny, impossible to answer in the lack of a fundamentally viable Time mechanism - but the Fixed Time Field thesis appears to satisfy this requirement.

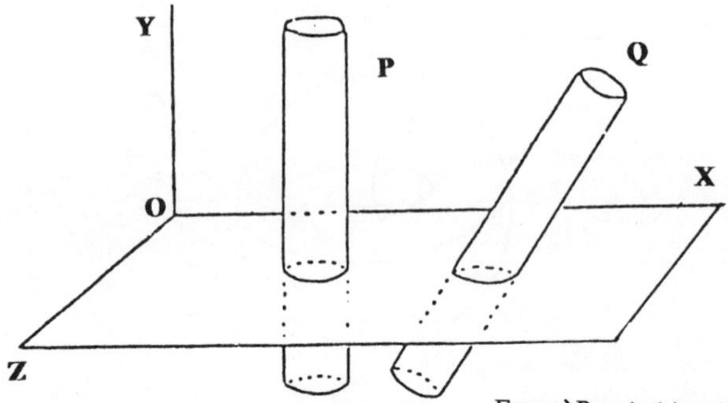

From `Psychokinesis'
by John Randall

Fig. 10

7. The Effects of Rotation.

Randall introduces an odd twist into his analogy. What, he suggests, would be the effect on the Flatlanders of inserting an inverted pyramid vertically into the flat terrain from a third dimension ? Given the clue of duration, the Flatland scientists would recognise a three-dimensional pyramidal body of finite size, since the square penetration area decreased steadily until it disappeared. In a more complicated version, a cylinder is inserted half-way, and then rotated ! (Fig. 10).

The Flatlanders see first a 1-dimensional object, a circle of constant diameter revealing no indication of penetration or length of the object, or other dimensions. But if we in the 3-dimensional world rotate the cylinder from the vertical, the circle becomes an elipse - to the Flatlanders, an extraordinary distortion of a hitherto solid body ! Randall suggests we may experience similar effects in seances or altered states of consciousness; no one can explain why the human body is capable of amazing feats in times of great stress. For example, a person trapped under a heavy vehicle is rescued by a friend lifting the truck unaided long enough for the victim to escape.

Two personal examples. In 1961, our car was forced off the road by a reckless driver; we came to rest on our near side at the foot of a steep slope. Opening the upper (driver's side) door to climb out, I heard an ominous crackling noise resembling a fire. Kneeling on the car wing, I reached down, grasped my wife's coat with one hand and effortlessly lifted her bodily from the car. At the time my wife weighed 121 pounds. Later, the most I could lift one-handed at arm's length was 12.5 pounds.

The second extraordinary example occurred on a Cambridgeshire airfield in 1941. A Stirling bomber crashed on take-off, slid through the boundary fence over a railway line into a field before catching fire. The sole survivor, a Canadian pilot Flt.Lt. Smith, was wearing a thick flying

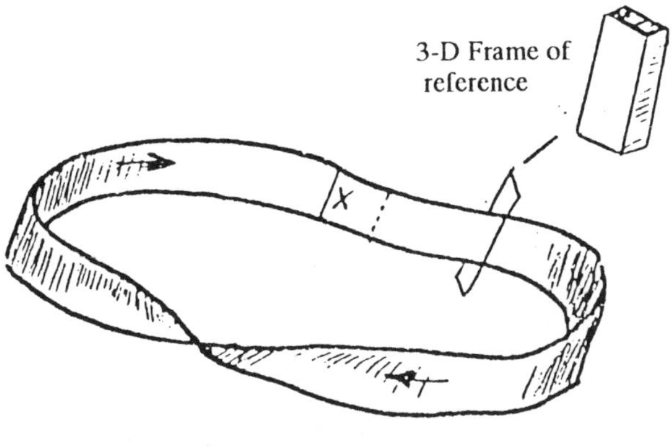

Fig. 11

The Mobius Strip Universe

suit, was six foot two inches in height and weighed 200 pounds. With the ircraft ablaze from the cockpit aft, he escaped through a triangular hinged 12" `clear-vision' panel in the front windscreen. Next day Smith tried to repeat the feat, wearing similar clothes, but succeeded only in getting his head and forearm through the panel. Faced with certain death, he had distorted his body to less than half its normal width.

Had he distorted his body outside normal space-time, as the Flatland cylinder was rotated ? There were other connections with rotation. In the FTF the fifth and sixth dimensions resulted from rotating a single dimension through 90 degrees. With the Mobius Strip - a length of paper joined into a loop after rotating one end through 180 degrees (Fig.11) - tracing a pencil line from one point all the way round the strip, brings one back to the starting point ! And if one takes scissors to cut along the pencil line, the end result is not two loops but a single strip twice as long !

Finally, I quote Itzhak Bentov [17], on objective/subjective Time and the limiting factor of C, the velocity of light. Refer to Figs.12 and 13.

A photon (light wave/particle) travels at about 300,000 kps. Bentov uses the Dunne postulate of a Present Moment `X' encapsulated in a 3-dimensional field of reference, represented by a horizontal line AXB traversing up a vertical `duration' line (Fig.12). Above AXB is future Time; beneath it, past Time. Above `X', intervals of 1 second are marked, up to 3 seconds, and intervals of 100,000 kps are marked along AXB up to 300,000 kps. From each mark, horizontal and vertical lines are drawn, their intersections connected by a radial line which represents C (light velocity) at 300,000 kps.

By extending and duplicating the radian in the left semi-circle the circle is divided into four quadrants : future and past, separated by the

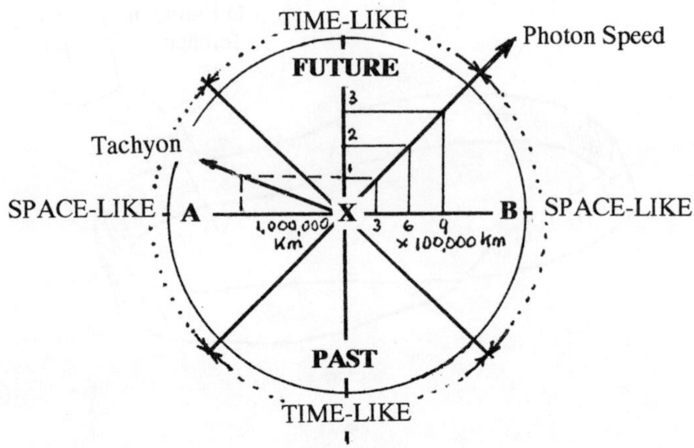

Fig.12

two spatial sectors. All potential future events are `time-oriented' within the limits of C, and all past events are inside the enclosed Time sector.

Physicists postulate the existence of a tachyon - a faster-than-light particle. Bentov shows a tachyon travelling at 1 million kps (about 3C) in the north-west quadrant as a horizontal 1-second line intersecting a vertical 1,000,000 kps line. The faster the tachyon goes the shorter the duration until reaching a value of zero, making that quadrant wholly spatial. No Time element is present.

As `X' moves up the duration line simulating movement through space, we experience subjective measurable `time lapse' duration. Ignoring emotional distortions of subjective time lapse, we experience true duration. Here, I introduce the concept of `instantaneity', meaning that any object moving at infinite velocity along a duration line will effectively occupy all locations along the line at the same time and be `omnipresent'. Similarly, by expanding consciousness to occupy all space simultaneously, we would become `omniscient', a good definition of which is *`having unlimited understanding'*. In Fig. 12 subjective and objective Time coincide; spatial sectors are similarly objective and subjective.

Objective and subjective Time rarely coincide. Subjective appreciation of Time is coloured and distorted by mental attitudes : we may think that Time is `dragging' or `flashing by' compared with clock time. Bentov suggests that in altered states of consciousness, our subjective space-time coordinates separate from the measured objective coordinates, rotating the vertical subjective time axis in Fig.13 (dotted line AXB) clockwise round the common centre 'X'. In Fig. 14 the axis AXB has been rotated through an angle <>. If we draw again a horizontal 1-second line to meet the newly-rotated axis AXB at W, we find that the distance X-W is equivalent

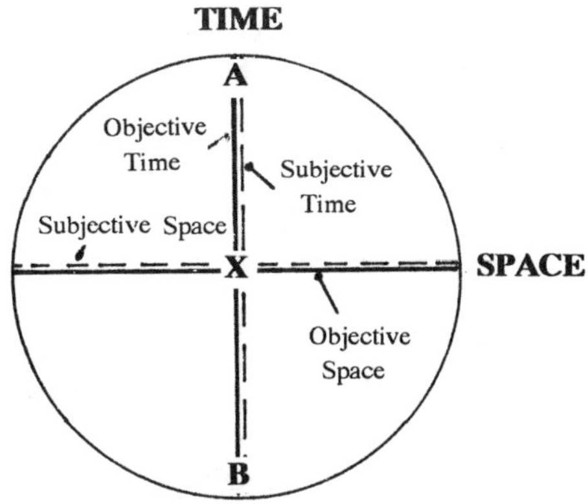

Fig.13

to 4 seconds of subjective time.

Full 90-degree rotation results in a wholly `subjective' Time realm totally dissociated from our own duration-oriented universe. Is this Space 2 ? Apparently not. There is no `Time' or motion in Space 2 - only the duration-extensions of moving bodies in Space 1. Is motion possible in Space 2 ? No - except for the advancing `life-wave' of the Present Moment, it is a static domain of wave-function or matter particles. Thought is a quantum-type wave function independent of space or time : we can imagine standing on the Moon beside the Lunar Lander, and instantly we are there - mentally at least. Physical travel would require the use of magic - but magic is simply manifestations of modified natural laws such as teleportation - instantaneous personal transition between two spatial locations by effort of will alone.

The effects of rotation seem germane to our inquiry. Gyroscopes - heavy-rimmed discs rotating at high speed - seem to defy natural laws, and when standing on a flat surface with the axis at a pronounced angle will not fall over - the principle of gyroscopic rigidity. Also, application of a lateral force to the top of the disc will not push a gyroscope over : instead, the application point precesses round the wheel in some queer fashion through 90 degrees in the direction of rotation - the principle of gyroscopic precession. Scientists have shown experimentally a significant measurable loss of weight in a two-gyroscope system, which itself is rotating whilst the gyros mounted on pivoted arms rise and fall ! Anti-gravity ? Watch this space. . .

We perceive a series of ephemeral 3-dimensional frames of reference, each in a Present Moment. An instamatic photograph would not visibly differ in any way from one taken a microsecond later, but perhaps

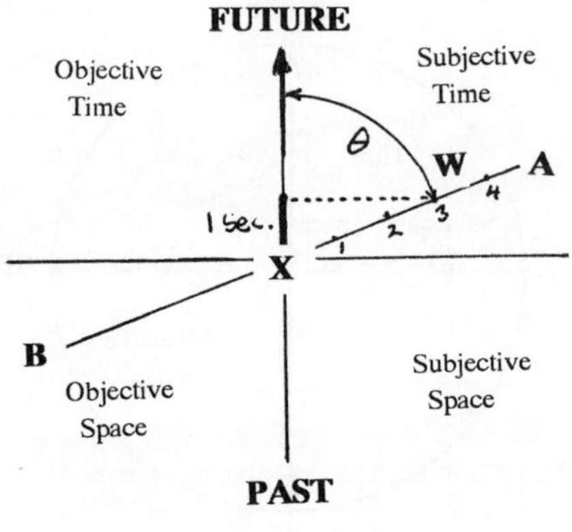

Fig. 14

after 10,000 prints we see a microscopic change in the position of a bee's wing in mid-stroke. The brain compares frame against frame until movement is confirmed, passing the information to the conscious mind whilst updating the image constantly : the succession of events enables us to perceive duration. Note that each successive reference frame and instant epoch corresponds to a spatial location on our duration-track. We perceive subjective duration but not each Present Moment - only a montage of successive PMs.

Before we are born, our parents share their Present Moment as they journey together through Space and Time with every other living entity on Earth. After birth, we experience the Present Moment with everyone else, rather like boarding a train filled with people : we share their sequential views of the world along the line, but the train never reaches the terminus. People board the train (are born) replacing those who have died, whose bodies are stored somewhere on the train until nature takes its course. Newcomers use the same `train time' (Present Moment) as everyone else and the train is a moving discontinuity on the line into the future.

When did it start the trip ? At the time of the Big Bang there was duration, inherent in the form of high-speed subatomic particle motion, but unperceived until some *homo erectus* noted that certain animals came to the river to drink when the Sun was in a particular quadrant of the sky : this would be an excellent time to lie in wait next day. Only sentient beings recognise a Present Moment. Eons were to pass before the Chinese (the first to understand the existence of a Time mechanism behind the duration experience) evolved a world-view of Time similar to my own. Four thousand years ago, they wrote a book named the *I Ching*. What, you ask, is so important about that ?

The *I Ching* performs as a binary computer, scanning future events. A present-time decision indicated by the book will usually ensure that the most beneficial version of a future event will achieve reality.

Incredible ? Perhaps. But true : that book is still used in many parts of the world by those who know its secret. You may take my word for it : I am one of them. For more than 20 years I have taken no important decision without consulting the Book of Changes.

To summarise : bodies and entities in Space 1 create duration, a linear axis on which any spatial location is also an objective Time location or epoch. As objects transit spatio-temporal locations, living creatures experience a Present Moment, a near-instantaneous presentation of an observed frame of reference. Each PM is of infinitely-short duration : we sense a great number during the period the brain acquires, assesses, analyses and accepts the data presented. Because mental processes are comparatively slow, we perceive only a single continuous Present Moment.

8. The Variable Future.

The duration axis, one of our six spatial dimensions, is not necessarily a straight line. A Space 2 observer perceives the Earth's duration-extension as a cylinder, any cross-section of which represents a single epochal frame of reference. The Earth's spatial location in 2091 can be calculated accurately : transit of that location is a potential future event which will achieve reality when we reach it. Because movement of celestial bodies is predictable, the *probability* of the event is very high, for the mass, momentum and inertia of the Earth, undeflected by air resistance, ensure that we will reach our 2091 spatial destination safely.

This principle does not and cannot apply to future events involving sentient creatures capable of independent movement. Mankind possesses total and random freedom of movement in Space 1.

Human future events, therefore, exist potentially in a range of versions, some of which finally achieve reality at random, whilst others result from human choice - hopefully, we try to influence which version of an event *may* occur. We cannot change the future *ad lib* to suit ourselves, but in some obscure way, core or mainstream events awaiting us are predetermined in general context *but variable in minor detail.* We can choose which bus we take, but everyone makes the ride, and here we encounter additional imponderables - probability, possibility and destiny. Still more disturbing : who or what has planned these events in such extraordinary detail ?

To answer that question, we must go back to the origin of the universe, at the moment of the Big Bang, and also to Chapter 5 of this book.

9. My World-View of Time.

Mankind has always been fascinated and baffled by the enigma of

Time, and I am no exception. I have outlined my thesis of a Fixed Time Field containing future events in potential, accessible to the human self in altered states of consciousness where it observes versions of future events. That data passes to the conscious waking mind via the *corpus callosum* between left and right brain lobes.

I encountered some widely-divergent world-views of the `self'. Stan Gooch[18] suggests that in the beginning `Spirit' (analogous to Jung's `universal consciousness' ?) existed in a non-spatial/ non-temporal realm. There was also `Space' described as an inanimate set of conditions, in contrast to the `animate' Spirit. I found this a little too esoteric : at the Big Bang, no life existed and any `spirit' presence must have been Godlike in nature. When in due course *homo sapiens* appeared, any direct connection between him and any `Spirit' existing in the void hardly seems possible.

We are in deep waters here. The predetermined events embedded in the FTF could not have come into existence independently : a Designer of some kind is essential. Since the FTF existed within the empty void *before* the Big Bang, the Designer too must be eternal (with no identifiable time or place of origin) as well as being omnipresent and omniscient in Space 1, Space 2 and all other realms.

But Gooch's `No-Time No-Space', similar in many ways to the FTF, is inhabited by human `self' entities released in altered states of consciousness. There is one inconsistency : motionless Space 2 is clearly Timeless, a solid and static domain in which only mental exploration is possible. But is it `Spaceless' ? Obviously not. It is a three-dimensional continuum like our own. The Sun and planets may be in the form of solid bars and spirals but there is space between them, space corresponding precisely to that in Space 1. Duration-extensions occupy part of the Space 2 continuum, which may not be the only domain co-existent with Space 1. Such realms should not be confused with `levels of consciousness' - conditions of varying mental activity. We may conveniently describe them diagrammatically (Fig. 15) and Gooch's `realm of the Spirit' may be the numinous level. He goes on :

> *`The Spirit's penetration into the spatial realm signified the beginning of creation, from which emerged a paradigm consisting of elements of both Space and the spiritual aspects of our conscious life.'*

This is fundamentally flawed in my view. No one seriously believes that we are the only sentient race in the universe, and spiritual attitudes will certainly differ in the thousands of galactic civilisations which exist. Only a thousand years ago, Aztecs and Mayas regarded the Sun as a deity, making human sacrifices in which hearts were torn from living victims. We cannot discount the enormous interval between the Big Bang and the first appearance of *homo sapiens*. The age of the universe is approximately 20 billion years, according to Alan Sandage, an American astronomer. *Homo erectus* appeared about 3 million years ago; Neandearthal

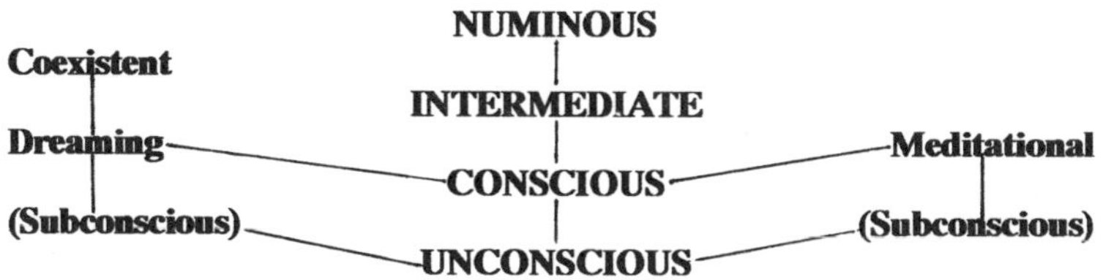

Fig. 15

Levels of Consciousness - Menzones

Man 250 thousand years ago, *homo sapiens* soon afterwards. In terms of a 10,000-year-old universe, man emerged in the last 0.0001 seconds.

Early Man dreamed as we do today, dreams probably recurrent nightmares of death, starvation and terror. With Christianity, the Bible and its prophets we perceived the precognitive content of dreams and speculated about their source. The FTF-associated dream-world invariably features images specific to our physical world - people, places, sounds, and colours with which we are familiar, and it should not be confused with the numinous*.

What precisely do we mean by `spirit' ? Generalised terminology describes the mind as *`the faculty of original or creative thought, a non-material system functioning in the electrochemical neuron networks of the brain'*. Using the airliner analogy, the human body is the aircraft with automatic or autonomous systems. The mind is the pilot, responsible for analysing and processing the data presented and initiating programmes designed to ensure safe operation and survival. But the mind can only function objectively when there is guidance from a still higher entity capable of assessing the ethics and humanitarian aspects of decisions. That entity is the self (sometimes called the `soul' or `spirit'). In our analogy it represents the ground controller who directs and guides the pilot safely onto the runway. We should be quite clear in our minds of the difference between mind and self.

The mind operates in the conscious (left lobe) and subconscious (right lobe) modes, presenting two options. Is the mind dual in nature, operating separately and independently in each mode or a single observ-

---

* Defined as a realm of eternal spiritual existence totally divorced from all materialistic universes.

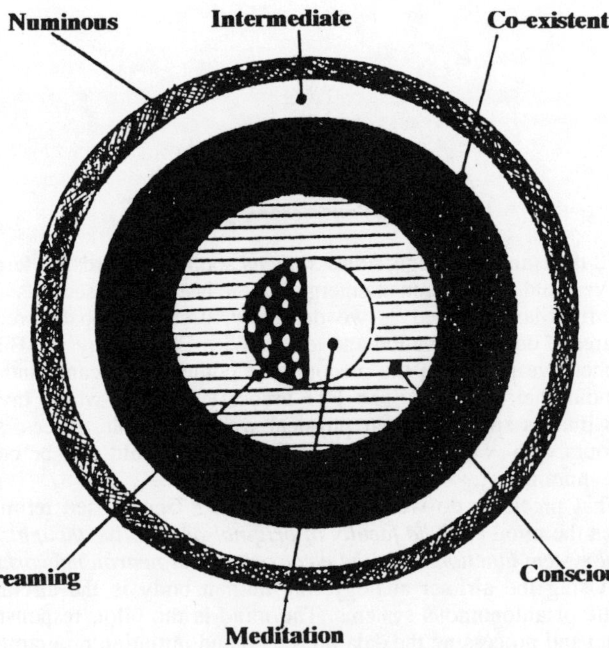

Fig. 16

Levels of Consciousness - Menzones

ing entity functioning in Space 2 in altered states of consciousness ?

Even more significant : which (if any) part of the self survives physical death of the body ? If so, in which consciousness level or temporal/spatial domain ? Much depends on the ultimate solution of this problem, and I believe that the solution will be found in the Time mechanism. Remarkably, Gooch subscribes to the idea of a *`forward movement through Time',* apparently discarding the flow theory. I believe he envisaged something like the FTF without recognising its significance. Yet in *`The Paranormal* (P. 210) he says : *`Although the passage of normal time* (i.e.duration - Author) *slows down for an organism travelling at very high speeds, Time still goes forward'.*

What does Gooch mean ? *`Passage of time'* suggests a flow. Does he refer to the passage of an object through Space/Time - or the passage of Time itself past a stationary observer ? The statement is in the context of time dilation, but the *rate of duration* does not slow down for a high-velocity observer, who sees nothing abnormal in his ship's clock : rather distance itself shrinks, enabling his Present Moment to reach a more distant spatial location in the same elapsed time. We show here a low-velocity spaceship *ALPHA* travelling from X to Y along (for the sake of simplicity) a straight line 1 million km long at a speed of 10,000 kilometres per hour, taking 100 hours. Below it, a second spaceship *BRAVO* is travelling at 500,000 kph. Its mass is increased enormously, distorting the curvature of Space-Time still further : whilst the length of the arc is still 1 million km, the distance between X and Y has effectively shrunk to only 100,000 km, and *BRAVO* will reach Y in 2 hours. This is the classic example of Time dilation.

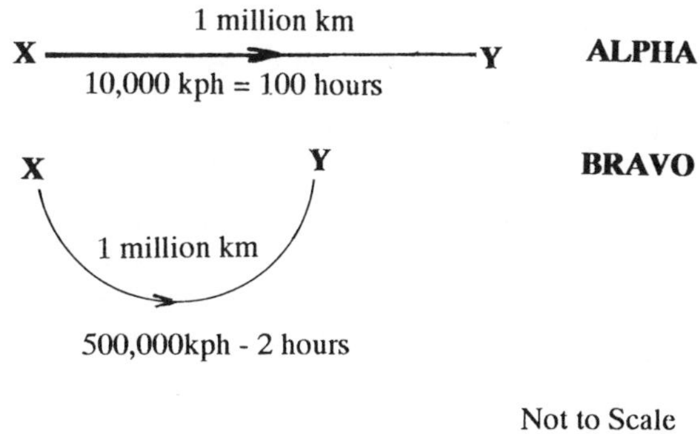

Gooch writes of high-velocity travel and time dilation, suggesting movement through Space, but it is all very confusing - and how can Time go forward ? Does he mean duration ? The truth is that neither Time nor duration constitute objects capable of moving through space. Duration is a measurement of time and forms only part of the Time mechanism proper.

But it is possible that Gooch is referring to the `universal clock' which measures our slow progress along the Space 1 duration axis - i.e. our net resultant velocity through space.

Definitions form major obstacles in the way of complete understanding, and in all too many works on Time we find a fundamental confusion of `duration' with Time. Gooch is correct in saying that Time is irreversible : in associating movement with duration, no specific *direction* of motion is involved. It is irrelevant which way we move, whether we sit facing the engine or away from it : journey interval is always the same. The roots of duration are found in physical change.

Many find entropy a difficult concept. All physical processes feature a `downward' trend, heat flowing from a hotter object to a cooler one, whilst air in high-pressure meteorological systems flows towards low-pressure areas. Mixing two different substances in solution, the tendency is towards a homogeneous single mixture. In all cases, an original state of high order (with clear-cut differences in states) degenerates into a low-order compromise : hot gas mixed with cool gas initiates a tendency towards a uniform temperature system in which all particles move about at random with no tendency to flow in any one direction.

The temperature, pressure or colouration level of any mixed high-entropy (final state) system is irrelevant. The real criterion is that total order must always decrease and end in absolute disorder. But by definition this is impossible in a constantly-changing universe.

This is extremely relevant : when we seek the conditions necessary for the human self to function in some other continuum, we find a well-defined discontinuity resembling that encountered in the quantum world of subatomic particles where matter is no longer solid : natural laws no longer apply. Similarly, when a human personality experiences altered levels of consciousness such as hypnosis, drug-induced trance or religious ecstasy, a consciousness-discontinuity occurs, where natural laws no longer apply. It is a state of near-absolute order.

Entropy, therefore, features in any process of change, which is a function of time lapse and duration. It should not be confused or compromised in the process of mankind's evolution, improvement and advancing knowledge. Who can deny that, within a few centuries, there may be no fresh pure air anywhere on Earth, that our children's children will be breathing the same oily polluted sludge from the Arctic to the Falklands and from Hamilton, Scotland to Hamilton, New Zealand ? Entropy is entropy, even by another name such as genocidal neglect.

10. Physical Time Travel.

Beloved of science-fiction writers, true time travel is conventionally a journey from the far-distant Future (when we are sufficiently advanced to develop the necessary technology) to the Past. It could, of course, be a journey back to the Present Moment, which generates some interesting speculations ! For example, a time traveller arriving in 1991 will experience our advancing Present Moment and accompany us towards the future. In theory, he should have been born at some date after 2091, to avoid returning to an Earth where he already has existence - the classic Time paradox.

Hypothetical Time travel is multi-directional - either back into the Past or forward into the Future. Can it be achieved by travelling at infinite speed through our 3-D universe to the spatial location of the Earth in, say, 1791 ? What will our Time and Space ship crew see ? Setting out in 1991, instantaneous transit will bring the ship to the correct (but empty) spatial point, still in the ship's year 1991. Because of Time dilation, a slower ship travelling at Earth speed would take 200 years to arrive - and find its date clock registering 2191. But one fact emerges clearly : a Time traveller from the Present to the Future would find only the solid matter of Earth in a duration-extension. He would see the Present Moment progressing wave-like along the great cylinder, but there would be no sign of sentient creatures ahead of the PM : only an opaque haze of matter particles in wave-function mode, variable events waiting to achieve reality.

Fiction writers use the concept of `hyperspace', supposedly a characteristic of the curved nature of Space-Time. The following analogy is useful : consider one side of a sheet of paper to be 3-dimensional Space, and fold it once. A pencil thrust through the paper will emerge into the original side. The traversed distance is extremely small and crossed easily, compared to the distance between the two penetration points when the paper is unfolded. `Hyperspace' is the inside of the folded sheet of paper, co-existent with our own universe on the outside of the paper, which may be of near-infinite thinness.

There is corroboration of these basic facts in the General Theory of Relativity. Strangely, for such a hypothetical journey one does not need a starship at all, or to travel at near-light speed. All we need is a means of exiting from Space 1 - but in what domain would we find ourselves ?

It will be the Fixed Time Field in Space 2, but problems arise. If a ship carrying passengers could enter Space 2 from the Earth, it would do so at a precise point on the duration-extension equivalent to that date. From that instant our PM would advance into the future, leaving the stationary ship behind in what is now the Past. This is in a solid-state continuum in which motion is theoretically possible, such that the ship could move `forward' alongside the duration-extension following or even passing the moving Present Moment (which moves at comparatively low velocity), creating its own PM. The crew could observe future events and perhaps even re-enter the duration-extension at some future date !

Conversely, the ship might travel back along the Earth's extension cylinder far into the past and emerge for surveillance. Would the Time travellers be able to land and make contact ? This is a debatable point, and I think further speculation would be unproductive - except to ask : `What about UFOs. . . ?' Any future-time space-ship arriving via Space 2 might be non-material in character. Interestingly, most UFO reports involve lights or luminous shapes, and no material physical evidence, wreckage, debris, remains of occupants have ever been produced. Further, UFOs appear to defy our Space 1 natural laws of conservation of energy, inertia and momentum, and they vanish without trace.

A celestial body's future track ahead of the Present Moment is not necessarily fixed. In regions of strong and fluctuating gravity fields, it may be variable; one version involves divergence from its direct spatial path, while a second potential track follows the original path. The governing factor is the strength of the gravity field and the body's distance from its epicentre, for example, a black hole. At a specific spatio-temporal location the cylindrical duration-extension will lose its fixed and immutable character, dividing into two co-existent probability fields containing all the wave-function subatomic particles which will form the final realised spatial track. At some point the wave-function indeterminate body will condense within the gravity template to emerge as the definitive version. This sounds very complicated, but in essence it is no more difficult than pouring molten metal into one or other of a pair of moulds.

All other future events along the `unused' `Time-line' will remain potential in nature. The PM moving discontinuity will continue until it reaches the next nexus point when once more, one system or another will achieve reality. The net effect is a number of future possible tracks, not to be confused with the theory of serial or parallel universes favoured by Dunne and others which generate far more questions than they answer. Moreover, we have reached this point in our thesis by the application of commonsense and logical deduction.

11. Mental Time Travel.

The sentient self may travel into a future containing indeterminate and nebulous human events, often in multiple versions, located potentially ahead of the Present Moment, whilst the conscious mind must await the arrival of the PM to learn which version will achieve reality. However, the Probability Field ahead of the PM tends to ensure that the most probable version of an event will occur, and in some way this may be observable by the self. This would explain why most precognitive events do occur, except when the subject takes positive avoiding action.

How is it possible for the self to view such events ? The explanation is fairly simple : it has a duration-extension similar to that of every particle, cell, molecule, human being or planet, which extends into the future ahead of the Present Moment as far as the spatio-temporal location corresponding to the death of the subject. Over that duration-length in Space 2, therefore, the self is omnipresent, able to view any and all cross-sections instantaneously. And it can insert information into its conscious mind at any point along the extension.

The future death-event, of course, remains only a probability. Ah, you may say, we all have to die some time ! But it is not impossible that some future scientist will identify and isolate the aging virus or disease, or perhaps evolve a way of replacing *all* the degenerating body cells, not just a favoured few. Death then becomes a possibility, rather than a probability. The adventurous roaming self is not restricted to its own duration-extension : seers such as Nostradamus and Old Mother Shipton were able to preview events far beyond their own life-times.

The self does not suddenly emerge into Space 2. It functions in Spaces 1 and 2 simultaneously. But the process of involuntary emergence into a totally different continuum is not unknown and numerous examples are on record. The actress Susannah York experienced just such a transition when she was walking along a country lane - an interlude she described as a transcendental revelation.

Assuming the year is 1991, the self can extract information on events in 2001 because in effect, it exists and is present at both these dates *and all others along that person's duration-extension.*

Any confused reader should not lose heart : a detailed and viable explanation of this process will come in due course. In fact this book is a kind of time-machine in its own right : instead of one page a day systematically, we can shift forward a hundred pages and read a page we would encounter in the normal way in three months time. And queerly, on re-reading that future page, we experience the sensation that we have already done this once before, but can't remember where or when. . .

\+ + +

Our Time mechanism functioning in coexistent Space 2 permits the human personality to observe future events in altered states of consciousness, and to confirm this, we have begun by demonstrating beyond doubt that PCG has occurred throughout recorded human history. Next, we must show that the human self functions in Space 2, and finally, identify the means by which the Space 2 data is transmitted to the Space 1 conscious mind.

A human subject falls asleep but is not necessarily dreaming. The self exists omnisciently in Space 2, and in the left (conscious) lobe which it vacates and enters the right lobe, leaving the physical body to its autonomous systems. The self exists at all locations along its duration-extension as a body-mind EMF, whilst mind is a wave-function distillate generated within a background consciousness created by molecular vibration in the neural dipoles (vibrating molecules in the cell walls of living tissue in the brain), a system of high order. The self is `aware' in the right lobe, with access to stored memories and Space 2 potential future events and Past events. In sleeping mode it has no awareness of Time or duration in Space 1, but it perceives duration in the dream sequences it observes. Occasionally the dreaming self/mind becomes fully aware of its joint identity - i.e. the self becomes dominant - resulting in a lucid dream. Mind and self recognise the dream process, retaining the ability to change dream content by introducing Space 2 data, or awake when it wishes.

What might the self observe in Space 2 ?

The immediate object of attention will be the duration-extension of the Earth, like some enormous slightly-curved cylinder, formed by innumerable adjacent frames of PMs stretching back into the Past, where all events have achieved reality and cannot be changed. The moving PM discontinuity will be seen as a `Life Wave' advancing into the Future - but ahead of it there is only a roiling mass of particles in wave-function mode within a Probability Field, awaiting transformation into Reality. The Probability Field, in determining which of the possible versions of an event may achieve reality, ensures that no version exceeds the bounds of possibility, i.e. that the natural limitations of Space 1 will still apply. A slightly-defective Field permits impossible events to occur - Magic.

The wave-function Probability Field in Space 2 collapses progressively as the PM discontinuity passes along the duration-extension, resulting in a permanently-growing Past - a solid particle-mode cylinder encapsulating immutably for all time the events which have occurred.

The reader may find this a strange idea, because we are unaware of the activities of our self in Space 2. Indeed, it is difficult to imagine why it does what it does - what motivates it. This may help :

At the precise moment your conscious mind is reading these words, your subconscious self may be looking over your shoulder, having shifted its focus of attention forward from your sleeping body back in 1988 ! Doubtless it did not report what it sees to your conscious mind when you woke up : our lives feature so many trivial irrelevant actions and events that it is neither logistically possible nor desirable to remember them. The brain, therefore, operates an efficient filtering mechanism to prevent useless information reaching our conscious mind in the moment of waking. We forget most dreams very quickly. If you are wondering why it is so difficult to recall dream details, it is because they are located in the right brain lobe behind a barrier which opens ephemerally only in the hypnagogic state. The forgetting process is `oneirolysis'.

But there are exceptions. Should the self in Space 2 observe a future event threatening its human body, it may compose a dream warning so strident that we recall it on waking. The warning may also get through during altered consciousness states as a premonition, a hunch or even a verbal warning `heard' only by the recipient.

SUMMATION

We can now list the conclusions drawn in this chapter :

(a) Time does not `pass', *per se*. Rather, we experience it as the realisation of a series of potential future events integrated into a Fixed Time Field (Space 2) and observed within an ephemeral montage of

Present Moments as we move through duration and Space 1.

(b) What we perceive subjectively is duration, not `Time', measurable objectively, and there is a `Rate of Duration' (the rate at which the Present Moment moves along the duration-extension in Space 2) which is equivalent to our total resultant velocity through space.

(c) The Time mechanism incorporates the six spatial dimensions of Space 1 and Space 2.

(d) All sentient beings on Earth experience the same PM, geared to our comparatively low spatial velocity. At the high velocities near C, Time Dilation occurs. The travellers in a high-velocity spaceship experience a similar `rate of PM perceptions' but because space-time distances literally shrink, less time appears to pass.

(e) Sentient beings at birth are caught up in the same Present Moment experienced by others born previously. On death, an Earth entity's body continues to move spatially until cremated or dissolution occurs, but the connection between the self's Space 2 nonmaterial extension and its Space 1 body is severed : the Space 2 entity continues to exist. The self's Space 2 duration-extension extends from its original conception to final dissolution or re-entry into a new foetus.

(f) There is evidence to suggest that all new-born persons may have a full duration-extension in potential, but life may be terminated at any time by accident or adverse probability. In other words, premature death is possible at any time, dependent upon the successive event-versions which achieve reality.

(g) These versions may be either inimical or beneficial to the subject person : we rationalise their realisations in terms of good luck or bad, ascribing the event-selection to chance. In fact, we allow random forces to determine the great majority of decisions effecting our future lives.

(h) Each Present Moment, a brief perception of a 3-D frame of reference equivalent to a spatial and chronological location, passes too quickly for human senses to recognise or assess. The PM montage we perceive persists long enough for the brain to scan the changing presentation and pass the information to the mind, and for the latter to analyse and assess the meaning. We note in the process movement and change taking place in a short period of duration, while the body (apparently) does not move. The impression gained is that of a constant flow of event-pictures past us, or a `flow of Time'.

(i) The transit of the solid matter of the Earth and our bodies through a future-event space location is one catalyst changing potentiality into reality. Another is human intervention to collapse the wave function.

j) Celestial bodies under the natural laws of momentum and inertia in-invariably reach their predetermined spatial locations, being incapable of voluntary movement. However, sentient beings have such a capability : by their actions and decisions, they may determine which of a range of potential future events will achieve reality - the Law of Causality in operation. But where a future event is pre-viewed and the subject takes `avoiding action', another version will achieve reality. This may not be a direct contravention of Causality - see the section on `Time-shunt'.

(k) The Fixed Time Field in Space 2 is a three-dimensional continuum co-existing with our own. We can recognise only one aspect in Space 1 : the duration axis along our motion path. It is also the first of the three dimensions in Space 2.

(l) In common with hypothetical one and two-dimensional domains, any recognisable aspect of duration indicates the existence of additional spatial dimensions in some co-existent continuum.

(m) There is no `Time' in Space 2 but there is space, endowed by the duration, form and extension dimensions. No `Time' is possible since there is no moving matter in Space 2. It is a stationary solid universe frequented only by non-material `self' entities originating in sentient beings in Space 1.

(n) As a three-D observer can function `outside' the 2-D world of Flatland and `see' both the two dimensions of Flatland and the three of our own universe, so a non-physical migrant observer from Space 1 can `see', in addition to our three spatial dimensions (by selecting PM cross-sections) the three dimensions in Space 2.

(o) Whilst human choice can influence which version of a future event achieves reality, the underlying `main-line' event will always occur in one form or another, but compatible with the predetermined `script'. Such choices are confined and bounded by `probability' and `possibility' limitations, by means of a Probability Field. `Impossible' events occur when there is a temporary aberration in the Probability Field.

(p) Connection of the subconscious mind in Space 2 with the conscious mind in Space 1 involving the transmission of observed data occurs as a result of an altered state of consciousness. Examples of such states are sleep, daydreaming, hypnosis, drugs or otherwise induced states of trance and religious ecstasy.

(q) Transference of knowledge of any future event obtained during such contacts is called Precognition. The interface between Space 1 and Space 2 is located in the area of the *corpus callosum* (literally tough body linking the left and right brain lobes, probably in the limbic, thalamus and hypothalamus areas). (See Chapter 8)

(r) Certain aspects of `rotation' may have a degree of relevance in regard to Time and dimensions, especially in relation to the properties of gyroscopes.

(s) The characteristics of the Fixed Time Field generate many questions of great importance to mankind, including destiny, determinism, synchronicity, probability, possibility, the viability of the Law of Causality and the survival of the human personality after physical death.

\+ + +

CHAPTER THREE

DREAMS

`We are the music-makers. . .
We are the dreamers of dreams. . .'

Arthur O'Shaughnessy 1844-1881

`If you can dream - and not make dreams your master. . .'

Rudyard Kipling 1865-1936

`There are more things in heaven and earth, Horatio, than are dreamt of in your philosophy. . .'

William Shakespeare 1564-1616

`Dreams, as everyone knows, may be confused, intelligible or positively nonsensical, what they say may contradict all we know of reality, and we behave in them like insane people since, so long as we are dreaming, we attribute objective reality to the contents of the dream'. . .

Sigmund Freud 1856-1939

`We are such stuff as dreams are made of, and our little life is rounded with a sleep. . .'

William Shakespeare

`So I awoke, and behold it was a dream. . .'

John Bunyan 1628-1688

`He was part of my dream, of course - but then I was part of his dream too !'

Lewis Carroll 1832-1898

`Weary with toil, I haste me to my bed
The dear repose for limbs with travel tired;
But then begins a journey in my head
To work my mind, when body's work expired. . .'

William Shakespeare - Sonnets

CONTENTS

1. General World View
2. A World of our Own
3. The Legacy of Misdirection
4. The Purpose of Dreams
5. The Dream Producer
6. Jung and the Id.
7. The Collective Unconscious
8. Jungian Dreams
9. Channels of Communication
10. The Content of Dreams
11. The Quality of Imagery
12. How Long does a Dream Last ?
13. Dream Programming
14. Menzones
15. Dream Production
16. Sources of Dream Data
17. Disaster Premonitions

SUMMATION

3

DREAMS

1. General World View

For our purposes, dream research may be categorised under :

(a) The cause and purpose of dreams.
(b) The image generation mechanism involved.
(c) The paradox of precognitive dreams.

The history of dream research contains too many flawed theories, dead ends, frustrating cul-de-sacs resulting from unjustified speculation, dogmatic belief in individual hobbyhorses and unwarranted conclusions drawn from sketchy or fragmentary evidence, and when I suggest that Freud and Jung were willingly caught up in a flood of self-deception, I know I shall be setting the cat among the pigeons with a vengeance. Here is a brief outline of theories presented by early researchers.

Sigmund Freud[32] (1856-1939)

An Austrian psychiatrist, he was the originator of psychoanalysis based on free association of ideas and analysis of dreams, stressing the importance of infantile sexuality later in life, and developed the Oedipus

Complex, an emotional construct involving the desire of a child (usually the male) to possess sexually the parent of the opposite sex. He published in 1899 `*The Interpretation of Dreams'* advocating the therapeutic use of dreams in treating mental disorders.

I cannot support Freud's ideas that dreams contain clues which are important or even vital to the dreamer's state of well-being - or that they provide clues to his mental state at the time of the dream. In my view our predominantly-visual dreams at best are dual-purpose : to provide a form of `do-it-yourself therapy' to counteract the strains and hardships of daily life, and secondly, to provide an emergency channel of communication between our conscious and subconscious minds. But before I am condemned out of hand for such heresy, let me say this : I believe firmly that an autonomous `Dream Producer' system functioning in the right brain lobe produces a continuous programme of dream scenarios. To supply his incessant demands for dream material, he draws on past memories of experienced events, some previews of future events, the multiplicity of emotions of the personality and mind itself, and lastly a leavening of imagination. No subject is barred, no source too insignificant, for the demand for new dream scenarios is enormous. No dream, *per se,* is constructed specifically to convey a message of distress to some hovering psychiatrist or analyst.

It is reasonable to assume that such a Dream Producer may use almost any material, whatever the source - but inclusion of that material does not infer that the dream is a reflection of some disturbed state of mind or disorder in the dreaming subject. Material selection is a random process : if a dreamer wakes and recalls a sequence of being locked in a cupboard, this is not a confirmation that he is suffering from claustrophobia. The Dream Producer may have stumbled on a childhood experience, recalled some TV programme or newspaper item about a child being trapped in a scrap refrigerator - or simply used imagination.

It is totally unjustified, in my view, to draw any conclusions about the meaning of dreams, in which the symbolism often encountered is the work of the Dream Producer, if he cannot locate a relevant memory trace or run down the precise reference he needs. (See my own dream of the Red Airliner). Further, the dream-remembering process is so imprecise, haphazard, random and diverse as to be the most unreliable and questionable channel of communication one can imagine. There is no guarantee that any dream will be recalled, of the half-dozen or so we experience each night, nor that it will be remembered accurately and *in toto.*A half-remembered dream is worse than no dream at all, if one is relying for analysis on accurate reporting.

Since Freud emerged on the psychiatric scene in 1899, the analysis of dreams (and the therapeutic uses to which the findings are applied) has played a significant part in the treatment of mental disorders, but I remain unconvinced : it seems to me that once an analyst identifies the problem correctly (i.e. without resorting to dream analysis) the prime mover in any subsequent improvement in symptoms is the patient himself, providing he is shown the problem, using a process of autosuggestion. That some of his dreams may contain data resembling the patient's symptoms is purely coincidental, but all too often the psychoanalyst pounces upon the `evidence' and suggest a line of treatment. The identification of a patient's problem may be achieved without recourse to ephemeral dreams : most care organisations such as Samaritans confirm that with well-planned and sympathetic questioning, the root problem is usually forthcoming. It is true, of course, that many patients display symptoms of some deep-hidden neurosis which can be relieved once the problem is identified, preferably by word-association tests or hypnosis which provide far better methods of in-depth investigation than dreams.

Finally, if we can show conclusively that the basic purpose of dreams has little or nothing to do with psychoanalysis and the treatment of neuroses, the whole Freudian background comes into proper perspective. I accept unreservedly that this assessment of Freud's work may be perhaps simplified and unrealistic. I am no psychiatrist, and whilst psychoanalysis is a recognised form of therapy it is by no means an exact science, for so much depends on the integrity of the analyst himself. And whilst many experiments have been performed to test Freud's theories, all the evidence is subjective and open to doubt. Symbolism is a classic example. The Nobel Prize winner J.P. Medawar suggested that *`the content of dreams may be entirely devoid of meaning'.*

In 1890 Freud, at the age of 34, began to study hysteria symptoms; with a colleague Dr Joseph Breuer, he used hypnosis and suggested that hysterical patients were recalling painful episodes which occurred many years previously : Freud theorised that hysteria, obsessions, phobias, various types of hallucination and delusions were basically barriers erected by patients against intolerable and harrowing memories. Freud turned his attention to neurosis and at this stage, for no definable reason, he began linking the subject to dreams. This was a by-product of `free association' sessions in which he encouraged patients to talk freely about themselves : in the process, many referred to dreams they had experienced, and thus the connection was made.

His first patient was himself, and he dreamed of childhood experiences (a golden lode of inspiration for the Dream Producer) which elicited sad or happy memories as might be expected. Where Freud erred disastrously, in my view, was to *associate such past memories with a present state of mind* - and from a purely logical standpoint there is no connection whatsoever but coincidence. For the Dream Producer in Freud's mind might have chosen any one of a thousand other subjects for his scenarios : for example, it is wholly irrational to believe, after dreaming about an attack by a savage dog, that one was frightened by a dog in childhood - the dog was but one of a million possible subjects available to the Dream Producer. And from this mundane foundation grew the entire pseudo-science of psychoanalysis, which seems to me to be on the same level as astrology.

Predictably, Sigmund Freud, in applying conventional scientific methods of research to dreams, ran into serious problems. He took us down a long and diversionary sidetrack into a cul-de-sac from which we have not as yet fully extricated ourselves. Charles Mycroft[34] points out that our dreams are insubstantial creations with ephemeral existence which cannot be categorised in the true sense of the word `phenomena' (which is another way of describing `events of which the mind takes note'). A dream is an image, not an event. Freud made a fundamental error in categorising dreams as `phenomena', enabling him to employ traditional scientific method and formulate certain laws applicable to the dream process. As a further complication he identified some dreams as `abnormal psychical phenomena' analogous to some neurotic disorders, and this opened a veritable Pandora's Box of troubles ! It also made quite a few psychiatrists very rich. Freud's logic is fiendishly unassailable :

Item : Dreams are universal experiences common to all.
Item : They are also abnormal psychic phenomena.
Item : All of us dreamers, *per se*, are abnormal mentally !

It is impossible to convey fully the subsequent confusion thus visited upon us. It was a basic corollary of his `abnormality' thesis that, because imagination is an element of all dream structures, it is itself abnormal. And this in turn renders every imaginative creation suspect.

We have come a long way from Freud. It requires a dedicated act of faith to believe that all dreams are sexually-oriented, revealing complex interactions within the brain. First, there is the inherent difficulty that dream analysis requires a dreamer and an external assessor (usually a psychiatrist) for a full assessment. Second, all dreams by their very nature are notoriously ephemeral, incomplete, illogical and partially or completely forgotten on waking ! A less reliable channel of communication could hardly be envisaged. Third, patients' accounts of dream stories are usually confused, randomised and frequently composed of trivia, as we have seen in Chapter 1 : the things most easily forgotten are the things we want to forget, and one of the brain's functions is to filter out all unimportant trivia in our dreams which might clog the memory storage system. Fourth, the dreamer cannot go back and re-run the dream himself : apart from the repetitive variety (which have a specific purpose) dreams are strictly one-night stands.

Carl Gustav Jung[33] (1875-1961)

Swiss psychologist Jung's inability to accept Freud's emphasis on the sexual instinct ended their earlier collaboration. Jung was the founder of analytical psychology, developing the concept of the `collective unconscious' (CU), its archetypes and identifying the concept of extrovert and introvert psychological types. He based his CU concept on the universality of symbols in every country and society - but is it not equally feasible to say that every human mind (and its Dream Producer) functions everywhere in exactly the same way ? And that when assembling a dream scenario and lacking the precise idea, reference or description, the DP will often use a symbol to complete the picture ? The bottom line is not homogeneous world-wide symbolism, but the *modus operandi* of the dream-producing mechanism.

Jung differed extensively from Freud in his attitude towards dream theories. Norman MacKenzie [35] lists four categories which illustrate this point :

(a) Dream Causation

Earlier researchers were divided between psychological and physiological theories, yet neither provides a complete answer to the primary question : whether dreams are part of the physiological processes of the brain, perhaps as a form of therapy, or whether they are generated specifically to provide an outside agency (i.e. a psychoanalyst) with clues as to the cause of certain mental disorders. *In this respect it is noteworthy that dreams have been around quite a lot longer than psychoanalysts.*

(b) Associated Phenomena

Including somnabulism, sleep-talking and the deeper insight into dreams provided by hypnosis.

(c) Types of Dream Experience

Including lucid, recurrent dreams, nightmares. Researcher J. Abercrombie resorted to categorising dreams as tools to be used in identifying the part they played in the mental or physical life of the dreamer. In some, he suggested, dreamers were able to solve problems or find lost objects. In creative dreams, problems, solutions or revelations were presented to the dreamer. There were precognitive and postcognitive dreams, and others containing information on distant but current events, the first and last of which may be classified as paranormal.

(d) Dream Symbolism

It was from this category that Freud drew most of his material, from actual content of dreams. Mackenzie points out that certain themes are common to many dreams, such as the sensation of flying and of incarceration, teeth extraction, swimming, being naked and personal bereavement.

But is there anything unusual about the selection of such material by the Dream Producer ? Forced to include extensively the trivia of everyday life in dream scenarios, he will select joyfully the more sensational events and the dreamer's reaction to them, which will remain sharply in focus on waking. Moreover, such events (singular or inclusive) are experienced by every human being, and predictably encountered by most analysts. Freud reduced such images to a series of simple sexual forms, a view which was rejected by Jung rightly, in my view. Freud assumed far too much from his own fragmentary ideas and his views were accepted for a time solely because he was the first to put forward such ideas.

2. A World of our Own

Why do we dream ? What *are* dreams ? No one knows for certain. Some researchers hold the view that dreams are but a print-out of brain processing of the day's data input, but the dream content suggests otherwise, e.g. items from past memories and imagination, linking such concepts together in the form of scenarios. A small number of dreams are precognitive, incorporating data from future events. Confusion regarding the purpose of dreams arises from the incoherent and meaningless presentation, because the brain processing system functions on a random basis, with haphazard mixing of data input. This is at best an arbitrary conclusion : more probably dreams are occasionally incoherent because of deficiencies in the dream-construction process. The history of dreams and dream research is not relevant to our researches : we are interested primarily in the nature of dreams and how they are produced, in our search for the elusive interface between the human self and Space 2. Not all dreams are meaningless; some, in the precognitive category, carry specific messages.

3. The Legacy of Misdirection.

I support unreservedly Charles Mycroft in his thesis that our dreams are not simply images we observe but experiences we create for ourselves. Especially for ourselves - because we are present in our dreams, sometimes as an observer, at other times as a participant. We may be accompanied by friends we recognise, or strangers we do not know at all, but we retain self-awareness via an underlying background of accessible memory and experience of past events. Were this not so, we would enter each dream as a lost soul with total amnesia. This background, I believe, is the same foundation upon which we build our daily conscious mentation, the nature of which we shall explore in a later chapter on `consciousness'. Dreaming, I know that I am precisely the same entity which inhabits my body when awake : it is as if I am locked in a dark cupboard alone to view episodes on a portable TV screen, but there is no sense of panic, because I am comfortably aware that I can escape into the real world any time by awakening.

Yet paradoxically, that reality does not exist for us at all when we are in the cupboard. We have no perception of the world which accommodates our sleeping bodies, or of interval or time lapse in the real world. We have escaped from the communal Present Moment which others, wide awake, still experience. We are out of Time - but where are we ?

We are in another world in which there is movement and duration which we can recognise, but not the real-world Present Moment; whilst we still exist in Space 1, there is no sensory connection with it. For this reason, our dream world cannot be the Fixed Time Field of Space 2 : it is, perhaps, a Halfway House, from which the self can journey outwards into Space 2, or inwards to the conscious reality of Space 1. Just for a while our lifeline to reality has been cut - for reasons we shall try to establish.

Dreams possess an extraordinary quality of realism comparable to our conscious sensory perception of the real world, in full colour and what seems sometimes to be stereophonic sound, and in very fine detail. Yet strangely, even when a dream becomes lucid (the dreamer perceives that he is dreaming) the images still retain an extraordinary semblance of reality. Frequently, we are unable to decide if we are asleep or wake. The dreaming mind disregards the limitations of the real world, recognising no natural laws, and we are able at will to fly like birds, travel instantaneously between one location and another, and perform impossible feats. In the Land of Dreams, nothing is impossible and Magic is King. Perhaps the intrinsic attraction of dreaming is that we are master of our own domain. Heraclitus of Ephesus described it thus :

> *`The waking have one world in common but the sleeping turn aside each into a world of his own.'*

4. The Purpose of Dreams.

Of two possible explanations, I favour the second :

1. All dreams are event-scenarios imbued with clear, obscure, symbolic or implied meaning, intended for the enlightenment of the recipient.

2. They are mentative images, byproducts of some autonomous function intended as a therapeutic panacea for the strains and stresses of everyday life.

Dreams, I suggest, cannot be regarded seriously as ongoing symptomatic reports of the unbalanced mental state of the dreamer, provided for the benefit of analysts and psychiatrists. But since some dream material clearly emanates from the imagination, the dreams of a Broadmoor inmate will be more incoherent than those of a High Court judge (although the activities and sentencing policies of some judges beg the question !). A lunatic may well have bizarre dreams - but we can hardly say that all who have wacky dreams are crazy ! Yet this is the absurd premise on which many psychiatrists work.

Occasionally dreams do contain data which, if acted upon by the dreamer when awake, may be of lasting benefit to him. Such information can exist in its own right as a ready source of reference, or be passed from one sentient being to another by various means. Such a process requires a sender and a receiver, but here we encounter the first dream paradox : a sender must have some motivation for transmitting a message in the first place — but what if we cannot identify the sender ?

We are face to face with the primary dilemma. There are two options : the dream-constructing entity may be just a facet of the dreamer's own personality, or perhaps it may be some external and hitherto unidentified organism. But which entity has access to the unlimited data on future events available in Space 2 duration-extensions, and also to the human memory banks in the associated neuron networks of the brain in Space 1 ? Let us review the evidence : dream data may be :

* Meaningless images created autonomously for therapeutic purposes.

* Meaningful images designed by an observant external entity.

* Meaningful images deliberately created by the self for its own purposes.

All these alternatives require an entity or autonomous system capable of creating the dream images.

5. The Dream Producer.

To theorise the working of the dream mechanism I evolved this rather strange entity, which is not an external observer operating in Space 2. It is rather an autonomous system similar to the sleeping `nightwatchman' which monitors heartbeat, respiration and the other vital basic processes. The task of the Dream Producer is to generate an ongoing series of trivial and meaningless dream scenarios for viewing by the human self in sleep, providing therapeutic benefits. Indeed, dream-deprivation is detrimental to general health. The question of the motivation of the producing entity does not arise.

But what of precognitive dreams containing a specific message aimed at the dreamer himself ? And the dramatic `flashes of intuition' and premonitions many people experience ? There is certainly motivation here, and clear evidence of the DP's ability to access to events existing only in potential in Space 2. The DP seems to inhabit the frontier region between our prosaic Space 1 and the wonders of Space 2, and there are two possibilities : it may observe events itself, passing details to the conscious mind in the instant of awakening. Alternatively it may obtain data from the migratory self, which has full access to Space 2, which seems to be the logical format since the DP appears to be a wholly autonomous self-contained system, whilst being part of the mind and self.

6. Jung and the Id.

Swiss psychologist Carl Gustav Jung[26] (1875-961) was a contemporary of Freud who refuted the latter's obsessive belief in the sexual nature of dreams and founded the school of analytical psychology. There is no space here to describe Jung's theses in detail , but his view of dreams was revolutionary for his time. They were, he said, manifestations not only of mankind's `*id*' or personality but also of the `*Collective Unconscious'* (CU), a species of group gestalt formed by the joining of many `ids' in some unspecified but extra-spatial continuum to which sleeping minds have access.

There are immediate similarities here to Space 2 and the dream domain, and there appears to be no reason why an unlimited number of `self' entities cannot access Space 2. The Dream Producer is not the self itself, but a by-product of it. Self is another name for id.

Jung suggested that many `ids' gather on a non-material level, combining to form a near-omniscient super-intelligent entity, but made no attempt to define the environment in which this occurs, suggesting merely that we do dream constantly, even when awake (when the `white noise' of the conscious mind blanks out the dream images).

Now, this does not tally with what we experience in real life. When we daydream, we experience an instantaneous shift from reality to fantasy, the effect being not so much a fading of `white noise ' as a temporary shift to an altered consciousness state where dreams hold sway. We are in a hypnagogic state in which we are still aware of our surroundings, of the insidious drone of a lecturer's voice or the rumble of distant traffic. In sleep, we sever all contact.

The mind functions in three modes : the hypnagogic; when awake and fully conscious, and when asleep - but not necessarily *unconscious* (which describes the zero mentation state associated with anaesthesia or following a blow on the head. `Unconscious', *per se*, implies a total absence of mentation; the more preferable term `subconscious' refers to mental activity on one or more alternate levels of consciousness beyond the waking state). I believe that the mind functions in both conscious and subconscious modes, but not in the sense of dual minds operating independently in cranial hemispheres. Yet there is still a modicum of support for dualism today, as we shall see.

Whilst Freud was convinced of the therapeutic nature of dreams as instruments of `wish fulfilment', Jung rejected the idea along with Freud's favourite hobbyhorse of symbology in dream construction. Jung believed correctly that we dream constantly, but recent research into rapid eye movements (REM) during dreaming confirms that we *experience* dreams only at irregular intervals throughout a night's sleep, the cycle commencing between 1 and 2 hours after we fall asleep. Remarkably, dreams have neither beginning nor end : we enter them abruptly and apparently as soon as we fall asleep, but this is solely because we are unaware that an hour or so has passed in the waking world. The mind may initially enter some dreamless domain for a period (not found in daydreams). Sitting in a warm stuffy lecture-room trying to concentrate upon the speaker, abruptly we are in the midst of a dream with no delay — yet we may still be listening to the droning voice and be aware of Space 1 time lapse.

This points strongly towards a continuous round-the-clock dream production programme, ready for the arrival of our migratory self. We construct dreams *all the time* but experience them only *part of the time.*

7. The Collective Unconscious.

Whilst it has become traditional to refer to various locii of mentation as `levels of consciousness', it is semantically misleading but convenient. `Levels' may refer to graduations of consciousness; to the physical zones of mentation in the brain, and to domains like Space 2. In trying to locate the Collective Unconscious, Jung described it as a stratum of the mind common to every human being, able to produce a range of images - dreams, visions, advanced religious concepts and the like. In some queer way, he believed, a merging process was possible between many human intelligences. The CU is part of the subconscious mind incorporating patterns of memories, experiences and instincts common to all mankind, usually inherited and expressed in dreams. Jung categorised specific groups of these patterns as `archetypes'.

Whilst I found this hypothesis difficult to accept in terms of a `group mind', it seems logical to use deeply-ingrained and inherited tendencies imprinted on the genes to explain why people, faced with a particular situation, will react in a particular way - a standard reflex. Indeed, it would be strange if they did otherwise. Identical basic reactions are deeply-rooted in societies world-wide : human nature is essentially the same everywhere.

Intriguingly, aboriginal tribes like the Australian Bushmen refer to the *Alcheringa* or Dream Time, a mythical Golden Age when magic was the norm, the world young. I suspect that dreams of prehistoric man were fundamentally different to ours. Who knows - the abilities of levitation and psychokinesis we experience only in our dreams may have been commonplace in early man, as racial memories of the past. This may be why telepathy occurs occasionally in identical twins, and why children are invariably associated with poltergeist activity.

8. Jungian Dreams.

What does Jung make of dreams ? They are tools useful in psychoanalysis of disturbed patients, but I must repeat - dreams are notoriously ephemeral, unreliable, spasmodic, incomplete and almost invariably forgotten completely on waking. Dream stories are distorted, haphazard, illogical and bizarre, concocted from a random selection of remembered and/or imaginary trivial incidents. How can any psychoanalyst be sure he has the full story of a dream ? Or that the patient is not making it up as he goes along, just to please his doctor ?

Such narratives introduced as evidence in any court of law, would be ridiculed and discounted - and claims that dreams are indicative of the state of mind of the dreamer are almost as illogical. If I indulge myself with a chunk of over-ripe Stilton before retiring, I can assure myself of adventures and horrors which would put Stephen Spielberg and Indiana Jones in the shade ! Finally, since we dream several times nightly but may remember only one episode, how can a psychoanalyst be sure that we have recalled the dream he associates with our problem ?

Since the beginning of the century when interest in the mind-process was aroused, dreams provided the only available avenue of research. I am not discounting hypnotism, which is another far from infallible way of getting into the patient's mind. Psychoanalysts were quick to employ the content of remembered dreams as a means of diagnosing mental problems, largely because they had no other viable method. But the Establishment is slowly coming to terms with the fact that the dream analysis may not fully identify the problem and enable the patient to cope with it. And since the problem is already known (why else visit a shrink ?) dreams appear to be irrelevant in this context.

This, I accept, is an extremely simplistic viewpoint. In rare cases, specific fears may be encapsulated in dreams, assisting in identifying the problem, but when the data is buried deep within the patient's mind, the problem devolves into one of memory retrieval. In the treatment of agoraphobia for example, dreams have no relevance, in that sufferers have no such problems in dreams. In my view the average dream is 99% a therapeutic process designed to alleviate the stresses of everyday life - a form of battery-charging. Fortuitously or otherwise, a small proportion of dreams contain details of previewed future events, and the mechanism by which data is transmitted to the conscious waking mind is central to the whole problem.

9. Channels of Communication.

The incoherency and trivial nature of dreams, and the autonomous 'forgetting' syndrome *oneirolysis* ensures that most dreams are forgotten, negating Freudian and Jungian theories that dreams have meaning. It avoids memory-overload, just as we tend to forget yesterday's newspapers today, and the existence of alternative data channels such as intuition, premonition and simple hunches suggests that the main transmission channel of dreams is inherently flawed and unreliable.

When the Dream Producer needs to transmit a warning message in clear unambiguous detail, the secondary channels mentioned above may not function viably in passing on a precognitive dream. People experiencing premonitions know that feeling of indefinable unease, a remote sensation of impending disaster - but a clear picture is lacking. It is like trying to recall a nightmare on waking : vague and amorphous images of terrible events of which hover on the brink of recollection but dissolve into undefinable misgivings and fears.

This transmission-mode is clearly unreliable in bridging the consciousness-interface which exists ephemerally between left and right brain lobes on waking. There is a correlation between the strength of message and nature of emergency ; when imminent danger involves the subject, a friend or close relative, there may be a `verbal' warning, a voice apparently speaking in the subject person's ear. It is implanted directly into the ear-brain neural circuit, since the `voice' is rarely if ever heard by persons nearby. The following cases are from `*Premonitions'* by H.B. Greenhouse, unless otherwise stated.

The Gracie Case.

At the time of the *Titanic* disaster, American passenger Colonel Archibald Gracie was on deck at 2.20 am when the great ship's stern rose for the final plunge. Gracie prayed as never before, that his last thoughts would reach his family in New York. At that precise instant his wife woke up with a start to hear a voice in her mind saying `*On your knees and pray'*. She realised at once that her husband himself was praying for her and she rose hurriedly, opened a prayerbook at random and found the words: `*For those in peril on the sea'*. Colonel Gracie was sucked under as the ship went down, but survived.

The Adrienne Coulter Case.

During the 1960 Presidential campaign when Robert Kennedy was battling Nixon, Adrienne (a well-known psychic) heard a voice say `*Nix on Nixon. Kennedy will win and be assassinated.'* This case was widely publicised at the time.

The Jeanne Gardner Case.

On June 3 1963, a Voice told this West Virginia housewife to write down a message : that Robert Kennedy would be assassinated. He would be in a `galley', which she took to mean a kitchen, in the early hours of June 5. No location was given, but the Voice said `*Tirhan Tirhan'*, which she assumed to be a place name, possibly in Iran. Jeanne showed publisher friend Mrs. Moore her journal entry, and next day told booksellers and salespeople at the convention that Kennedy would be killed in a kitchen early on Wednesday June 5. When asked subsequently if she thought the murder could have been prevented, Jeanne said `*No - if it had been inevitable, the Voice would not have left out a single fact.* This seems to be a self-contradictory statement. The odds against Jeanne identifying a killer by his very unusual name are astronomical.

Joan of Arc.

When a child, `Voices' told Joan there would be war between France and England, that she would lead the French armies. Her first experience was at age 13 in her garden at Domremy, when a `voice' said three times: `Jeanne ! Jeanne ! Jeanne !'. She saw, apparently, a light of extraordinary brilliance and the Voice said : `*Jeanne, go to France where there is a great pity. . .'* It said she had only `*a year and a little more'* to accomplish her mission. She learned in advance her own fate and that of France. . .

The Mrs. Davidson Case.

Quoted frequently, with good reason. One July, an American housewife Mrs. Davidson, mother of baby Lettie, began having premonitions that tragedy involving a burning cradle would soon befall her family. She confided in her husband and a sister in neighbouring Connecticut : the latter did not believe in such things and said so in no uncertain terms. But the feelings persisted, growing stronger. Alone one day, Mrs. Davidson mused that Lettie would have her own bedroom when she was older. At that instant a Voice said : `*She'll never need it'.* As a precaution, the mother decided to destroy all loose matches in the house but somehow never got round to it. Writing one November evening in a diary she kept about Lettie's progress, which the child could read when she was older, the Voice returned. `*She'll never need it'.* Two weeks later Lettie was running around in her old shoes, and her mother said `*We must get you another pair'.* Right on cue, the Voice said : `*She'll never need it'.* Putting the child to bed, she thought again of the need to put away the matches; picking up the box from the bedside table, she decided she needed them to light the gas stove and slipped them under the cot mattress. She would dispose of them later.

As she laid the child in the crib, the Voice returned. `*Turn the mattress'.* But she was in a hurry : she could do that later. Half an hour later she heard Lettie crying and rushed upstairs : the room was full of smoke, the crib on fire. The badly-burned child had found the matches under the mattress, and died three hours later.

Clearly, the warning entity - the mother's subconscious mind, or perhaps the child's surviving self - knew from the outset that these events would end in tragedy, and was in contact with her conscious mind. Undeterred by unheeded previous warnings, it made one last effort by telling the mother to turn the mattress - to no avail. The tragedy seems to have been an inevitable single-version event - but what motivated the entity to issue the warnings ? I believe it may have `seen' other potential versions which could have achieved reality, had the mother heeded warnings which she twice ignored. The Probability Field in Space 2 must have been so strong that its effects were felt in Space 1 in the minds of other people like Mrs. Davidson's sister, exerting pressure to prevent trends towards intervention. But this is only speculation.

10. The Content of Dreams.

Dream settings contain material drawn from past memories, whilst the fragmented and ephemeral dream story is a product of imagination based on the limitless store of minor events we experience in life. The Dream Producer is unrestricted in choice of subject : almost every event, acquaintance and article in everyday use, every TV programme, movie and newspaper headline and book we read is potential dream material. Since 99.9% of all we do, read, see and hear involves inconsequential events and artifacts in our mundane lives, almost all dreams are trivial. They are montages of playbacks, re-runs of past incidents but featuring new characters and locales, fragmentary in nature, unimportant in context. Even a skilled Dream Producer cannot compile a credible full-length dream story with a real beginning, end and cast of speaking characters, around a simple daily occurrence such as knocking over a pair of stepladders. The Producer, doing his best, may create a cameo in which the dreamer is hanging by his fingertips from a roof gutter (probably a scene stolen from some old Harold Lloyd movie shown on TV !).

In-depth search of memory files may dredge-up incidents long forgotten by the subject. In my dreams I have met old friends last encountered 55 years ago during my R.A.F. engineering apprenticeship. Their names and youthful faces are truly presented - a feat I would find impossible when awake.

Some scenarios are exceptionally creative, featuring musical or artistic themes. Ever a humble fumbler at the piano, never having taken lessons, I have dreamed of performing in some huge auditorium, producing music of such beauty and complexity that even when dreaming, I am wishing and hoping that I can recall the themes and harmonies my hands are creating; I find tears on my cheeks when waking up. Admittedly, this is wishful thinking in the extreme - but if dreams are the therapeutic entertainment we believe them to be, my Albert Hall debut lifted up my spirit and left a lasting legacy of pleasure.

Such fulfilment dreams are frequently reported, forming a large proportion of `remembered' cases. Freud named this process `condensation' because the end-product seemed to coalesce a number of conventional images, already known to the subject, into something entirely new. Samuel Coleridge Taylor, Charles Mycroft wrote, called it *`secondary* *imagination which dissolves, diffuses, dissipates in order to create'.* I believe we are talking about the process of inspiration, which provides substantial proof of the existence of the Fixed Time Field in Space 2, as I shall show.

All dreams are personalised. Subconscious minds carry an inherent self-image of our physical bodies : the `I' in my own dream is identical to the `I' in the real world. I know of no example in which a dreamer is a person not himself : whether participant or spectator, he is still `his own self' in every respect. We have no conscious control over dream subject matter or our personal involvement; the act of falling asleep transports us instantly into a theatre auditorium with no finite division between audience and cast. We may begin as a spectator and become a participant; in some respects we become no more than robots but it does not matter, because we do not know we are being manipulated : we have no recollection or perception of the outside world, no sense of Time. We accept without demur the extraordinary situations in which we find ourselves, lacking a data base against which we can compare them and formulate an opinion.

In some queer manner, dreams occasionally become `lucid'; we are able to control the dream story to a degree, and we become aware that we are dreaming, just as I did on that shadowy racecourse many years ago. Further, when dream becomes nightmare and we suffer agonies of fear, we can break the sequence and wake up of our own volition. Alternatively, we can simply assure ourselves that we are having a `bad dream' and go through the motions with a kind of detached sardonic amusement.

This is fundamentally different to classic nightmares from which we are released just before some terrible climax by an autonomous and protective reflex - but how ? I suggest that the human self is migratory, moving from the conscious (left lobe) mode in Space 1 to the subconscious (right lobe) mode in sleep. Still in Space 1, it is in total permanent contact with Space 2; within the right lobe it views dreams constructed by the Dream Producer as a therapeutic process, choosing its role as spectator or participant. But when involved in nightmares, it may abandon its `participant' segment, moving wholly into the scenario which becomes a lucid dream, whilst retaining contact with Space 2. It will intervene if the Dream Producer is going `over the top' using material which might seriously impair the therapeutic benefits of the dream process. This confirms that the Dream Producer is definitely an autonomous self-programming system capable of being over-ridden by the mind and self.

The original hypothesis taking form in my mind involved a physical body manipulated by a single `mind' entity handling constant sensory data input but deferring decisions to the dominant `self'. The mind functions in two modes : waking left-lobe `conscious' state and sleeping right-lobe `subconscious' state. In both modes, bodily processes are maintained by autonomous systems. In sleep and other altered states of consciousness, the conscious mind closes down and the self moves to the right lobe.

There, the subconscious mind (including the Dream Producer with full access to memory banks) provides the self with therapeutic dream material. The mind is an electrochemical mentation-system generated within the neural network of the brain, whilst the self appears to inhabit the electromagnetic field surrounding the human body.

This early thesis seemed reasonable as a starting point, but correlating it with the contents of dreams, I found a number of inconsistencies.

11. The Quality of Imagery.

Francis Galton (a cousin of Charles Darwin) became noted for his work on the concept of correlation. In 1883, his experiments in the psychological field (which was then comparatively new) sign-posted new avenues of research. What, he wondered, was the origin of `visions' and `thought' ? The current world view held that all thinking was based in and generated by images, but Galton conducted lengthy research for an alternative thesis. Astonishingly, there was substantial evidence that ordinary people reported a richness of imagery similar to his own imaginative style, which was lacking in scientists, by their own admission !

> *`I saw at once that the brain was vastly more active than I had previously believed it to be and I was perfectly amazed at the unexpected width of the field of its everyday operations. . . they (the scientists) protested that mental imagery was unknown to them. . . they had no more notion of its true nature than a colour-blind man. . . has of the nature of colour.'*

The explanation, identified almost 100 years later, lies in the interaction between left and right, frontal and occipital brain lobes. We are all familiar with the extraordinary clarity, sheer complexity and vividness of images constructed by the Dream Producer; manifestly it is quite a different process to image-construction by our waking minds. To demonstrate, let us perform an experiment in visualising a red square. Sit down, relax completely and with eyes closed, examine the dark field of non-vision. It looks rather like the sky at night, filled with remote tiny stars or flecks of light, or an inactive monochrome TV screen. Regard it as a window into space, a void ready for creation, and begin to assemble a picture of the square against the opaque backdrop of the void. Presently, it will begin to take shape; you will achieve a square of sorts, wavery and unstable with a pinkish tinge, but if you analyse what your mind is doing, it is experiencing difficulty in maintaining even the outline of the square, let alone reproducing a satisfactory red colour. If you repeat the experiment daily, your imaging ability will slowly improve, but having achieved a reasonable simulacrum of a square, you will find that despite superhuman efforts you cannot keep it in focus more than a few seconds.

Our conscious minds have extremely limited powers of image creation, compared with the Dream Producer. We experience nightly dreams in brilliant colour and stereo-sound inhabited by strangers and also by friends who are recognisable and in turn recognise us. The dream possesses an incredible aura of reality; we accept what we see as real because we cannot conceive in the dream that such scenes can be part of an artificial imaginary sequence. Another experiment : in a familiar waking environment, look around and try to convince yourself that what you see is unreal, part of a dream. The world appears to be so firm and solid that it is impossible to think of it in any other way ! This belief is an integral part of the dream structure, because the foundation of successful fantasy is total acceptance of a new world where Magic is King. This may explain the popularity of books like *`Lost Horizon'* by James Hilton (MacMillan, 1933), and the tales of J.Rider Haggard.

The quality and realism of the imagery convinces the visiting dream-watcher, augmented at times by participation in the scenarios. Presentation may resemble a clipping from a well-produced and directed 3-D film in full colour/sound, featuring characters indistinguishable from living persons. Whilst the dream-story may be puerile and trivial, frivolous and petty, the observing self sees nothing untoward about this. It is not surprised that the dream has no beginning or end, and reacts blandly when pitch-forked into a new world. Every dream gives the impression that it commenced well before we came on the scene, and that it will continue after we have gone on our way. And the dramatic character of many dreams is startling. . .

At one instant we are dozing off in a familiar bed. In the next, we are part of a crowd in some noisome alley-way at dead of night, watching a scene which cries out for explanation. A man with one hand locked in the hair of another pins his victim against a wall under an old-fashioned gas street light with square panes, an intricate construct of black wrought iron which throws an amorphous pattern of light on the scene : we stare at this for a while, transfixed, and the attacker turns his head to glare, obviously aware of our presence. We hear the panting, cursing and heavy breathing of the struggle. We sense in the anonymous crowd a mood of rapt attention and expectancy and the detail is extraordinary. We see the twisted mouth of the victim, the gap of a missing tooth. . .in our dream we speculate briefly : what happened to that tooth ?

Suddenly, the assailant produces a long knife, puts the point under the other's chin. We see the knife driven up through the brain to protrude beyond the skull, and the combatants relax : arm in arm they walk off down the alley, the knife still *in situ*, but we see nothing unusual in that. Slowly the crowd disperses and abruptly, we stand outside a window staring inside. In dim light a woman sits at a table. Before her, an opened letter has been put aside, and a small box lies close to her hand. In our dream, we ponder the meaning of this : what does the box signify ? What was in the letter, to make her weep ? We cannot tell, and abruptly we are swept into yet another episode. Then starkly, without the slightest warning, we are awake and back in our real and familiar world.

At this instant, memories of our dreams begin to slip away : we may forget them completely, or we may recall isolated images of events and images, the way a person spoke but nothing of their conversation. Perversely the harder we try to remember, the less we can recall : reminiscent of the Heisenberg Uncertainty Principle, our own clumsy efforts defeat themselves and everything slips away into oblivion. Finding an explanation for this effect is difficult.

How deep and profound is the imagery of dreams ? Are they mere electrochemical impulses self-generated in the neural networks of the right brain lobe, similar to bodiless `voices' and apparitions visible to just one person ? I believe we shall find no simple answers here. I can recall dreams in fine detail and quality, probably because I have been recording them for many years, yet I have difficulty in believing they are only flickering images on some mental movie screen. There is an enormous disparity of quality between them and the primitive images we can produce consciously. Dreams are a calculated attempt to simulate reality, ensuring the dreamer sees nothing which might break the spell. True, magical and extraordinary things do happen in dreams, but in some queer way we accept them : anything goes in this world of phantasms, for to the dreaming mind, it is the only one which exists. There is no opportunity to relate our ongoing dream to the real world.

Our search for the mind/Space 2 inter-face will be focussed on three target areas :

1. The way the brain/mind combination works in the thinking mode.
2. The mechanism which produces dream images of such clarity.
3. The nature of the entity or entities which have access to Space 2.

In a dream I am walking down a dark road flanked with houses. I look down at my body : I am naked, but this is not unusual in dreams and I feel no embarrassment. I hear my bare feet padding on the road and suddenly I am wearing shoes. The houses stand in gardens behind low hedges, and some windows are lighted : I see human silhouettes within and wonder briefly what they are doing. A shadowy figure approaches : I recognise a familiar but nameless face; he walks past with no sign of recognition and I sense disappointment. Without warning, I am driving a car down the same road, and I accept the sudden transition calmly. Beside me sits a nebulous and anonymous figure whom, I feel, I should know but do not. I hear the engine, the swish of air past the window, feel the gear lever in hand, my foot on the pedal, and the sensations are familiar. My companion gives directions and we accelerate; flashing down a narrow lane the car arcs twenty feet before plunging into a river. We sit placidly watching the water rising until it reaches my mouth and I begin to choke : I know that I am about to die. Then abruptly I am awake with a corner of the sheet in my mouth obstructing my breathing.

The quality of such imagery generates important questions. Did the house occupants have complete bodies, or only the upper half visible in the window ? How far does the Dream Producer go in search of reality ? Were the rooms fully furnished ? Were the houses real constructs with sides, walls and roofs, with perhaps a garden beyond ? Or mere facades like those on movie lots ? If complete replicas, did the entire world incorporate space and time, sky and heavens - created by the Dream Producer ?

Reason suggests otherwise. I believe the images we `see' resemble TV transmissions projected onto the consciousness-background of the mind, precisely as our eyes absorb a vista which the brain decodes into a coherent pattern. The mind scans and identifies part or all of this field of presentation by reference to the neural networks, presenting it to the self which decides what action if any to take. The Dream Producer assesses data obtained via our normal senses for suitable scenario subjects; in the dream I described, it may have picked up a sequence in which I was searching for an address, possibly from my experiences as a salesman. I was naked quite literally because I brought no material objects with me : my mind is non-material, but the Producer - a logical entity - takes care of that ! Images of houses from my memory banks are added to the scenario, and because once I took a walk down a dark road, I become a participant, rather than spectator. The process goes on, the Dream Producer constantly amending or adding to the scenario : when he has exhausted its creative possibilities he switches without warning to another.

What he constructs is a series of electrochemical electromagnetic signal sequences delivered to the same analytical circuits of my mind which handle external sensory data input : the signals are decoded and translated into images imprinted on the thought-background of the mind, rather as a TV picture is transmitted and received - precisely the same process which occurs in the waking mode as my body/brain/mind combination converts visual data input into understandable images.

Yet in dreams I `see' only what the Dream Producer wants me to see, and because Nature abhors complication, he needs nothing more elaborate than a two-dimensional presentation which I accept as real, just as I accept television pictures which are no more real. But some dreams have a terrifying quality of reality : for example, that experienced by a close friend whom I shall call Charles (not his real name). He knew of my interest in the subject.

Normally level-headed (he was an aircraft pilot for 30 years) with an impeccable character, he came to see me in an extremely disturbed frame of mind. In a dream he and two other men had broken into a large private house, bent on burglary. In a vicious fight the two occupants, a married couple were brutally killed. Charles took no part in the butchery, but stood aside casually to watch it done, whilst the others ransacked the house and a safe, taking valuables and a large sum of money, stuffed into two green velvet embroidered cushion covers. The bodies were taken away in a large white van and, driving far out into the countryside, the thieves buried them near a small stream spanned by a level wooden bridge. The loot, excepting the money, was laid on top of the bodies and the grave filled in.

There the dream ended, and Charles's terror began. He believed it was absolutely real, and had happened during a black-out, of which he had had several following a car crash some fifteen years previously. These symptoms had passed and he regained his pilot licence. He was convinced the dream was a replay of the actual crime, and that he could identify the grave location. But how could he go back and uncover the evidence of his crime ? He was a happy and secure husband and father with few cares or worries : why should he deliberately destroy his life and his family ?

I saw him three days after the dream, and eventually I was able to help him rationalise the experience : we made many unproductive journeys into the countryside, but it was many months before he was able to forget the nightmare : he talked about it morbidly, describing its intensity, the cries of the victims, the sight of blood, the callous jubilation on finding the loot, the harsh argument about disposing of the bodies. What appalled him most was his own lack of compassion for the victims; he had stood aside and let it happen.

It is difficult to rationalise this strange dream. The visual images and conversations were of startling clarity, and it has been suggested that Charles, whilst asleep, had somehow picked up the story telepathically from the real murderer, who would always brood obsessively about the killings. But one can only speculate.

12. How Long does a Dream Last ?

For years it had been assumed that dreams occurred in accelerated Time, perhaps only seconds, an idea which may have originated in daydreams in which the subject may doze off in the middle of a conversation , experience a lengthy dream and awaken almost at once. The daydream may be protracted and absorbing, yet the dreamer may awake abruptly to hear the speaker conclude a sentence he had barely commenced when the daydream began. I have been astounded, after total anaesthesia for an operation, to find I have been unconscious for eight hours or more: to my mind, only seconds have elapsed since the man in the green mask jabbed me with a hypodermic the size of a pneumatic road drill and asked me to count to ten.

But current research suggests that we dream several times a night, the first time after a deep sleep lasting an hour or more. During dreams, REM (rapid eye movement) occurs, as the subject follows the action in the dream story.

More than any other example, the Maury Paradox has attracted constant interest for many years. A French writer at the time of the Revolution, L.F. Alfred Maury performed a series of experiments confirming that even in sleep the senses transmit data to the brain, which responds with appropriate imagery. Dreams, Maury maintained, were caused by external stimulation. He applied various stimuli to sleeping volunteers, including tickling, drops of water and fumes from burning feathers. The resultant dreams supported his thesis : a burning match held under his nose caused Maury to dream that he was at sea and the powder magazine of the ship had exploded. He found evidence that dreams incorporated extensive memories of past events, names and places beyond the capability of his waking memory.

But Maury is best-known for his extraordinary dream of the guillotine. In it, he had been arrested and tried, found guilty and condemned by Robespierre and Marat. He was taken to the scaffold, tied to a board by the executioner and beheaded. He felt in his dream the blade of the guillotine slice his head from his shoulders - and in that instant he woke up, only to find that the head-board of his bed had fallen, to land on his neck.

Controversy raged around this dream. If the displaced head-board caused his mind to construct the dream sequence, the dream was compressed into the instant between the board falling and Maury waking up. But another explanation is that his Dream Producer, pre-viewing the head-board incident in future Time, developed a dream story around it. That dream could have begun *before* the board fell, its ending coinciding with the execution sequence and Maury waking up. This seems to me to be the most probable explanation.

But what were the Dream Producer's motives ? Did it have a motive of any kind, or was it routinely using as dream material a future event only seconds away ? The resemblance of the head-board to a guillotine blade is unmistakable, and the Producer knew Maury would come to no great harm : indeed, he was more likely to die from a heart attack after such a dream ! The dream-producing system has no feelings of responsibility for the dreaming subject, manufacturing dreams on any subject it can find - including sex, violence, death, torture, rape, bug-eyed monsters and invisible unnameable horrors in hideous nightmares from which there is no escape save waking up. There is nothing in its terms of reference involving protection of the dreaming mind from side-effects, no British Board of Film Censors or the American Hayes Office to monitor the impact of dreams on the subject.

To the contrary : evidence suggests that hundreds of people may die of fright each year in their sleep. Increasingly I came to believe that the Dream Producer was far from being the creative genius I had first envisaged him to be. He didn't care how much he terrified Alfred Maury with his dream of execution by the guillotine ! It wasn't his job to care. And why a guillotine anyway ? Well, Maury lived in France at the height of the Terror when bad dreams about being executed had a nasty habit of coming true - it was the Revolutionary equivalent of a parking fine. No wonder Maury's idiot dream-merchant saw the analogy of the head-board and Madame Guillotine. . .

13. Dream Programming

The evidence to date supports the concept of a continuous ongoing autonomous process of dream construction, probably located in the right brain lobe, with access to the neural memory network. The self supplies data from Space 2 to the Dream Producer, and thus to the conscious mind on waking, using the inter-lobe link of the *corpus callosum.* Normally the self cannot pass Space 2 data directly to the conscious mind in waking mode, using instead circuitous methods in emergency. It implants the information in the subconscious mind and generates audio or visual warnings as described in the chapter on Precognition.

14. Menzones

I have suggested that the Dream Producer constructs dream scenarios continuously, using material from three sources : imagination, future events in Space 2 and memories. The self in sleep migrates from conscious mind to subconscious, where it has access to the dream theatre. We do not begin dreaming at once : an hour or more may elapse before the first dream commences. The reverse occurs in daydreams - but what is our sleeping mind/self doing in the non-dreaming state ?

In Fig. 15, we see an array of consciousness zones accessible to the migratory self. Rather than `levels', they are domains in which consciousness functions, located within the brain. Some extend beyond our ordinary universe into other co-existent continuums, one of which is Space 2. I call them mentation zones or `menzones' in an abbreviated form.

Fig. 16 is a purely diagrammatical illustration. In sleep the migratory self has direct access to the dreaming subconscious menzone, but normally enters first a non-mentation mode, a battery-charging sanctuary in which the stress of conscious daily burdens and responsibilities is relieved. This is not the `unconscious' state of zero mentation, but a region of pure thought and contemplation; many adepts of Eastern philosophical schools such as Hatha Yoga train themselves to enter this `alpha' state of cerebral activity associated with the meditation zone. An intermediate menzone level familiar to all of us, the half-asleep, half-awake hypnagogic state assumes considerable importance in regard to inspiration, characterised by a queer feeling of dissociation : we are distantly aware of the material world around us, whilst viewing the images our dreaming mind generates : it is almost as if it is another person who is involved : we watch with feelings of remoteness, unconcerned, almost clinically reserved.

When a daydream is imminent we notice a diminution of ambient sound terminating in complete silence. The room takes on a lambent glow as if seen through a prism, and superimposed upon it the flash images and visions of the daydream. In this temporary gestalt we are half-way between worlds, and the experience contains its own measure of elation, pleasure and thinly-disguised guilt, similar to semi-trance states such as the early stages of hypnosis itself. We stand poised upon the threshold of some other domain, in an altered state of consciousness. Elmer and Alyce Green discovered that theta rhythms generated in hypnagogic states produce deeper states of reverie than the alpha waves associated with meditation.

After a suitable interval spent in `battery-charging' in the meditative zone, the self migrates into the nearby dream theatre, where the Dream Producer's creations are being continuously `screened'. The self may enter randomly at any stage of the dream story as a spectator or participant and the scenarios are flexible for that reason.

On the far side of conscious Space 1 we find the co-existent Space 2. The self, embodied in the electromagnetic field of the body, is at home in both domains, for like all moving objects it has a duration-extension in Space 2 where it is omnipresent. The self can migrate directly into the dream zone as in daydreams, bypassing the meditation level. In Fig. 15 we see the zero-mentation level of anaesthesia, and beyond the co-existent zone of Space 2, two higher levels, which we shall examine in detail in a later chapter. One is an intermediate level, possibly that domain seen in `out-of-the-body' experiences, and beyond that the numinous.

To clarify Fig. 16, the reader may imagine himself to be the `self', existing not only in Space 2 outside the diagram (which represents the human brain/mind in Space 1) but also in Space 1 with access to all parts of the diagram. Extending the analogy, the room in which you sit represents the intermediate zone, the rest of the world is the numinous.

15. Dream Production

At this point we must clarify our ideas about the characteristics of the self - the personality. Using again the aeroplane analogy, the human body is the aircraft, with a number of `automatic-pilot' autonomous systems ensuring its safety. Should an emergency occur, the mind (pilot) is alerted, reacting in response to trained reflexes whilst exercising control over the aircraft. But behind the pilot is the `aircraft commander', the `self' which makes vital decisions about destination, route and purpose of the flight.

The judgment of the `mind/pilot' consciousness is restricted to what he can see and hear : should problems or danger lie ahead, he will need more than his five normal senses, and seeks an alternate level of observation by referring the problem to the `commander' (the self). Calling the ground radar controller, the self can advise the mind/pilot that the sky is clear, the weather good for the next five hundred miles. In effect, the `commander/self' has been able to look forward perhaps 2 hours into the future : the probability of a safe landing is extremely high. Conversely, there may be a great storm an hour ahead : the commander advises the mind/pilot to alter course to avoid the storm, and a possible accident is averted. This is an example of a precognitive experience.

Since the brain neural circuits work on electrochemical processes, the mind appears to be a sentient entity generated within the electromagnetic field of the brain itself. It is clearly non-material - whilst most cells in the body are replaced on average every nine or ten years, the mind, with memory data-base and emotional background, still functions precisely as it did in earlier years.

In regard to visual images, the eye does not `see' the picture the mind eventually observes (Fig. 17) : components of the observed frame of reference are transmitted as electric signals via the optical nerves to the brain, where the enormously-complex neural cortical network converts them into a coloured image projected upon the thought-background of the mind. The mind, meanwhile, is assessing each image and by comparing successive frames of reference, perceives motion and change. After analysis and extraction of all associated data, the completed image is presented to the self, as basis for future decision-making. But the image-making part of this process is of paramount importance, for I will show that precisely the same process is used by the Dream Producer in creating his scenarios : since the real-world images our brain produces are presented in full colour and stereo sound, the thought-background is capable of similar image quality when used by the Dream Producer. And herein lies the explanation for the extraordinary quality of dream imagery.

Is there proof of that statement ? I believe so. In waking mode the eyes move constantly to scan each Present Moment frame of reference presented on the thought-background of the mind, in a continuous feedback loop : the eye detects a change, sends signals to the brain to modify the background presentation and instantly resumes scanning *the real world and the thought-background at the same time !* But in sleep, the eyes are closed and the optical nerve-circuits scan only the thought back-

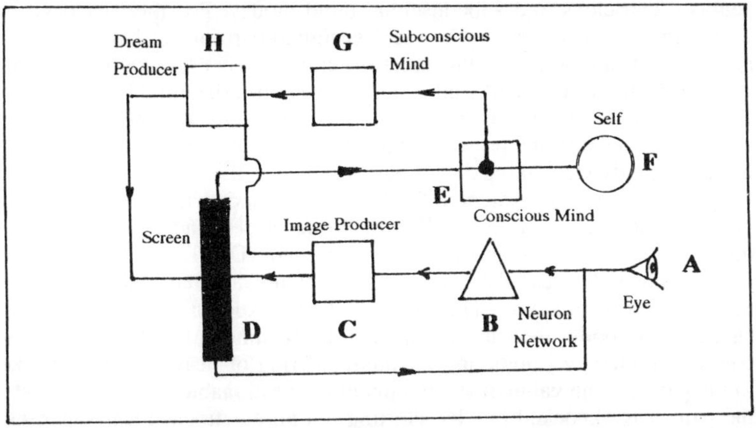

Fig. 17

ground dream images : any motion in the dream is followed by the eyes, in REM (Rapid Eye Movement).

The process of image and dream production is shown diagrammatically in Fig. 17. In waking mode the eye (A) observes movement in Space 1 frame of reference, scanning such motion for continuity. Signals transmitted via the optical nerves are assessed and analysed by the associational neuron network (B) and sent to the image-producing circuit (C). Here, the full colour presentation simulates the viewed external frame of reference, which is superimposed on the thought-background` screen' (D). This image is presented to the conscious mind (E) which reacts appropriately under the guidance of the self. For example, driving a motor vehicle, the mind will react to the constantly-changing situation by issuing control commands to the body, and this process becomes continuous and autonomic until the time arrives when a decision much be made, such as a change in destination : such decisions are made by the `self' entity (F) and passed on down the line. We can imagine the `self' as the entity now looking down at the diagram from outside the 2-dimensional world of the paper.

In sleep, the process undergoes a sea change. The self migrates into the subconscious-mode right brain lobe (G) where the Dream Producer (H) beavering away producing scenarios has access to past memories, future events in Space 2 and powers of imagination. Using the same image-producing system (C) on the thought-background, he projects dreams which are observed by the self, and because the created images are integral with the eye/assessment/image-producer system (B) the eyes react to movement in the thought-background screen, producing REM (Rapid Eye Movement).

Diagrammatically, at least, we can assume that the thought background forms part of the physical linkage between left and right lobes, between conscious and subconscious mind-modes. Possibly, psychiatric symptoms involving hearing `voices', seeing apparitions or hallucinations may arise from faults in the electrochemical synapses controlling the waking mode. That circuit connecting the eye with the mind by producing comprehensible images is necessarily one-way. In waking mode, the created dreams are not projected onto the thought-background, which is presenting only the waking data input.

But suppose the system is faulty : that in waking mode, visual/audio images leak through from the Dream Producer (H) and the data assessment circuit (C) onto the thought-background (D). The subject, whilst fully awake, will `hear' the voices of the dream characters and `see' flashes from the dream action. The cause of the breakdown may be electrical, chemical or both; the current method of treatment is ECT - electroconvulsive therapy - involving the administering of heavy electric shocks to the patient. The value of the treatment is questionable, to say the least : the patient is `knocked-out' by shorting-out all electrochemical synapses, but whilst healthy circuits soon recover, faulty systems takes much longer resulting in loss of memory, lassitude and confusion in the patient.

Since the DP has no prior warning of the arrival of the migratory self when sleep occurs, a constant flow of scenarios is essential. Episode strings, possibly, may last only an hour or so, before the DP must fabricate the next string; this may be why we dream intermittently. During intervals, the self drifts into deeper meditative sleep. There will be, one hopes, no commercials ! But knowing the ingenuity of man. . .

The DP is never short of material. His terms of reference are very wide : dream scenarios need no story line, recognisable beginning or end, no explanations or apologies. A segment lasting only a minute may feature nothing more exciting than addressing an invisible audience on matters important at the time, but forgotten on waking up. These `film clips' involve almost any subject, object, topic, person, animal, action or activity and each can be treated differently. Funny, tragic, frightening, ludicrous — how many adjectives and adverbs are there ? The DP need not rely on real people, but creates total strangers of either sex, with a thousand different descriptions. How many dress patterns are there ? He manipulates his characters, having them walk, run, stroll, shuffle, hurry, drive, fly, ride or swim : how many verbs are there ? A hundred characters, each in a thousand different situations with different locations and end-results. Sixty million British people dreaming three times a night, a thousand a year, 60,000 million different original dreams, each one personalised to the dreamer himself ! There is no limit : each day that passes adds a hundred more trivial or important events to complement past memories.

In an average life a person may experience 50,000 dreams, many of which are standard archetypal scenarios. We have no way of cross-checking, analysing, comparing, but there may be a vast number of coincidences in which two or more people have the same dream. But I found no example in which two or more people shared the same dream and met within their sleeping minds.

16. Sources of Dream Data

We have evolved some fundamental ideas summarised as follows :

(a) Co-existent with our familiar 3-D universe is a second 3-dimensional continuum, Space 2. The duration-dimension is common to both.

(b) There is no motion in Space 2. All moving bodies in Space 1 appear as duration-extensions in Space 2.

(c) The advancing discontinuity of the Present Moment moves along the duration-extension in the form of a Life Wave.

(d) The electromagnetic field of the human body, encapsulating the self, has a Space 2 duration-extension extending from birth to death. Thus the self is omnipresent, existing simultaneously at all points along its duration-extension.

(e) The autonomous Dream Producer, via the self, has access to all data in the duration-extension in Space 2, and also to the mind's memory banks.

(f) During sleep, dream scenarios are projected onto the thought-background of the subconscious mind.

(g) On waking, the tenuous bridge between conscious and subconscious minds collapses. Before dream data can be transferred to the waking mind, the inter-lobe link is broken and the dream forgotten. This process is called `oneirolysis'.

(h) The thought-background functions as a `projection screen' in the sleeping and waking modes. In conscious mode the images reproduce what the eye sees, and in sleep the dream scenarios. Both modes produce `rapid eye movement'.

The concept of an omnipresent self inhabiting both Space 1 and Space 2 may be difficult to grasp. Take this simple analogy : imagine our solar system is a very long corridor train travelling on an endless line. Countryside seen by front coach passengers will not be seen by rear coach passengers until they reach that point. If a passenger in mid-train leaves his seat and walks back along the corridor, he will see again the vistas already seen, which exist in his memory and also in the real world. He is, in fact, travelling back into the past.

Similarly, by walking forward he will observe views normally inaccessible to him until the train reaches that point. But if he runs up and down the train so fast that he is to all intents and purposes in all locations at the same time, he becomes omnipresent, with instant access to *all* data outside the train, including future, present and past. The self can access instantaneously all knowledge and events throughout the journey or duration-extension. It is omniscient.

This analogy does not take into account the indeterminate nature of future events. An external observer flying above the train will see that the rail line is not a single track : on each side at intervals, lines branch off to alternative vistas of countryside and events. To passengers the random `points' setting does not cause concern because they have no information on events on the branch lines. An occasional prescient traveller may foresee disaster ahead on this line : and by changing trains at the next station he successfully evades the catastrophe.

Our flying observer, perhaps a self recently migrated to Space 2, is aware of all potential future events and may decide to alert his own mind/

body to the danger, and this would result in a precognitive dream or warning. But why are such dreams so rare ? I believe that most people go through life unimperilled in any way, except by sheer boredom. Trivial previewed events mean nothing to the waking mind, and the self must resort to stronger methods.

17. Disaster Premonitions

The self-preservation instinct is deeply rooted in all of us, evidenced by instant emergence from sleep if our `night-watchman' detects unusual sounds nearby; another example is the reflexive duck to avoid a flying cricket ball. But I would go further. What makes us start to duck even *before* we see the ball approaching ? What makes us decide, quite without reason, to miss the approaching bus and take the next ? What makes us feel uneasy about taking a proposed trip, making an imminent important decision ? What makes us abandon a trip, get off the train at the next station and hurry back home - to find the kitchen in flames ? They are messages from our innate omnipresent self, which observes the danger and sends a warning - either in a precognitive dream, a hunch or premonition, or in extreme emergency, a seemingly-audible voice breaking into our stream of consciousness.

Given vital information on one or more versions of a future emergency by the self, how does the Dream Producer proceed ?

(a) By selecting the most probable version and incorporating it into a dream scenario.

(b) By ensuring that the sleeper remembers the dream warning after waking up.

(c) By ensuring that the subject wakes up before the next dream scenario begins.

(d) In extremely urgent cases, provide repetitive dreams by rerunning the original scenario.

(e) If necessary, using other individuals as channels of communication - people known as `sensitives' or psychics.

Regardless of such efforts, warnings may end in failure, because the process is neither normal nor natural : the oneirolysis process may function too well and erase the dream details. The dreamer may recall some previous dream and miss the warning completely. On waking, there may be only a residual uneasiness and forboding, an indefinable sensation of imminent but undefinable disaster. Even if the message gets through, it may encounter mankind's universal reaction of disbelief in the face of the unknown. Such rejection can be nullified, as in Dunne's case, but only by skilled investigators. There is the ever-present risk of ridicule : it requires considerable courage to walk out on a job because we `sense' the roof will soon collapse. For example, two GIs leaning against a wall in London during World War II were approached by a white-helmeted Military Policeman. He said :

"Okay, you guys. Move on ! Whaddya doin', holdin' up that wall ?
"Yes, Sarge. . ."
"Move on - now !"
So they moved on - and the wall fell down. . .on the MP.

\+ + +

SUMMATION

I have asked the reader to take a great deal for granted in the absence of evidence supporting the theses of the Fixed Time Field and the nature of precognitive dreams, in the interests of maintaining orderly progression in the narrative. Indeed, the paramount requirement in dealing with so many regimes and domains lies in determining the optimum order of presentation. I have tried not to lose sight of our primary target : demonstrating a link between human consciousness and the fabric of the future. Happily, the next chapter on `Inspiration' will serve to rectify past omissions, and meantime, we can summarise this chapter briefly as follows :

* The average dream is basically therapeutic in purpose to provide a form of `battery-charging' environment for the stress-weary self in the subconscious mode. Dream-deprivation can be inimical to general health.

* Ordinary dreams consist largely of trivia built into meaningless action-scenarios like film clips.

* Whilst dream content can be influenced by external stimuli, rich food or similar sources, the average dream contains no hidden messages, no direct indications of the dreamer's mental state and provides no basis for any treatment except by a process of autosuggestion.

* Channels of transmission between the dreaming and conscious minds are so unreliable, ineffective and frequently blocked by oneirolysis that it is unsafe to regard dreams as viable mental health indicators.

* Nonetheless, experience and recollection of precognitive dreams may occur in cases of extreme urgency. Where this channel fails,

the dreaming self may resort to hunches, premonitions, pseudo-audible warnings and other measures.

* Dream content is drawn from past memories, future events and imagination.

* The 3-dimensional Fixed Time Field containing all future and past events is coexistent with our own 3-dimensional universe, and is accessible to the human self. This information is made available to the conscious mind in PCG dreams.

* An autonomous Dream-Producing system projects continuous scenarios onto the `screen' of the thought-background in sleep to accommodate the arrival at any time of the self `dream-watcher'.

* Menzones, regions of cerebral mentation, are shown in Fig. 16.

+ + +

CHAPTER FOUR

INSPIRATION AND THE TIME SHUNT

`Why, this is not drawing but inspiration !'

Blake, commenting on Constable drawing.

`...it is not by wisdom that the poets create their work, but by a certain natural power and inspiration. . .'

Socrates 470-399 BC

`The description of Apollo in the third book of "Hyperion" . . . came by chance or magic. . .something given to me. It is odd - it strikes me more as the production of another person than myself. . ."

John Keats 1795-1821

`There is a "not-myself" which takes possession of me. . .I feel that my own personality is only the instrument through which this "other personality" is acting. . .'

George Eliot (Mary Ann Evans) 1819-1880

`The wind plays my old harp as it lists. It has its high notes, its low notes, its heavy notes - and its faltering notes. In the end it is all the same to me provided the emotion comes, but I find nothing in myself. It is the "other" who sings as he likes, well or ill. . .'

George Sand (Amandine Aurore Lucie Dupin) 1804-1876

`Whenever I write, the feeling of being a "receiver", an instrument, a mouthpiece. . .'

Dobell, French writer.

`I have been surprised at the observations made by my characters. It seems as if an occult power is moving the pen. . .'

William Makepeace Thackeray 1811-1863

CONTENTS

1. General World View
2. A World of our Own
3. The Legacy of Misdirection
4. The Purpose of Dreams
5. The Dream Producer
6. Jung and the Id.
7. The Collective Unconscious
8. Jungian Dreams
9. Channels of Communication
10. The Content of Dreams
11. The Quality of Imagery
12. How Long does a Dream Last ?
13. Dream Programming
14. Menzones
15. Dream Production
16. Sources of Dream Data
17. Disaster Premonitions

SUMMATION

4

INSPIRATION AND THE TIME SHUNT

1. Inspiration - Nature's Gift

THOMAS Alva Edison is famous, among other reasons, for saying : `*Genius is one per cent inspiration and ninety-nine per cent perspiration*'. In fact, the reverse is true - the history of invention shows that the initial concept is by far the greatest hurdle to jump - thereafter it is a matter of sustained development, refinement and manufacture. Indisputably, almost all the great creations of the human mind bearing the hallmark of enduring greatness and originality have emerged from the subconscious mind. The subsequent development, perfecting or realisation of the primary concept may require considerable physical and mental effort, be it painting, music composition, sculpture or writing : all great artistes require a template, a vision of the completed work before devoting their great personal skills to its creation. Genius in the creation of the original work as visualised is one thing : the gift of inspiration is something else.

But how to describe it, to evaluate it, or trace the origin of that spark of vision that sets the artist's mind aflame ? Many have tried. G.N.M. Tyrrell wrote :

> `*Those creations. . . have come from beyond consciousness, knocking at its door for admittance; they have flowed into it, sometimes slowly as if by seepage, but often with a burst of overwhelming power*`.

Rosamond Harding[36] from whose work all the quotations in this chapter are extracted unless otherwise stated, maintains first, that the source of inspiration is clearly located elsewhere than in the conscious mind, and has thus far not been identified. Second, that the inspirational experience is extremely traumatic, frequently leaving a lasting effect on the recipient.

We must distinguish clearly between classic inspiration and the end-results of dedicated and extraordinary efforts to solve intractable problems. The final breakthrough in many such cases may resemble pure inspiration; in fact, the subconscious works doggedly on the problem when the conscious mind is preoccupied with other matters. For example, we may experience difficulty in recalling a name or telephone number and, irritated, put it out of our minds and get on with life. Yet without warning the elusive data surfaces in our thoughts, rather like a white rabbit from a magician's top hat.

How can the subconscious mind succeeded when the conscious mind has failed ? Is this an example of genuine inspiration, or simply the product of a relentless search of the memory banks by our subconscious mind ? This has puzzled researchers for more than a century, but I hope to provide an answer in the course of this chapter.

2. The Connection with Time

I know of no other investigator of the inspirational process who has made the vital connection between the Time mechanism and inspiration, but there is a simple explanation for that. I perceived the link only after devising the Fixed Time Field theory of two co-existent universes. Lacking that starting point, writers have been restricted to quoting and rehashing all the hackneyed examples of inspirational episodes recorded by great artistes of the past - yet each carries the vital clue.

Frequent attempts have been made to explain inspiration : it has even been attributed to involvement with the minds of long-dead geniuses - poets, painters, sculptors and musicians who occupy, justifiably, their niches in the Hall of Fame. Yet looking back on this chapter, I marvel that the link with Time, so blindingly obvious now, has remained unrecognised and undetected for so long.

My thesis is not difficult, and mathematics are unnecessary for full understanding. Any reader still not entirely `sold' on the idea of the human self, with its own duration-extension, having total and permanent access to the co-existent Fixed Time Field, should first read Chapter 5.

3. The Characteristics of Inspiration

All great ideas appear to fall into one of two categories :

(a) Major : the involuntary and unexpected appearance of the entire concept in the mind of the subject.

(b) Secondary : the sudden perception of the final solution to a problem upon which the subject may have worked for a long time.

In category (a) a writer may `receive' the full outline of a story or play in a single furious injection of data in great volume; an artist may see an inner vision of a completed painting, or a musician may `hear' a new and original score, often in fully-orchestrated form. The material may appear in a dream or a hypnagogic state, or via a brief flash of intuition whilst fully conscious : sometimes it is `heard' (but only by the subject) as a voice or a solo instrument, and at other times as speech dictated too fast even for a skilled stenographer. The hapless recipient can only strive to recall all that he heard in a few moments of time. The thing happens without warning, and in adherence to Murphy's Law, invariably at times when there is no pencil or notepad at hand, or the recipient is surrounded by distractions. There is no better example than Samuel Taylor Coleridge's experience when writing the legend of Kubla Khan, quoted by hundreds of authors. He was an opium addict; in the summer of 1797 during a period of illhealth, living in a remote farmhouse between Porlock and Linton on Exmoor, he fell into a deep sleep whilst reading how Kubla Khan commanded the building of a palace surrounded by extensive grounds and gardens, enclosing some ten square miles of landscape. In his dream Coleridge constructed a masterpiece of poetry of which, he felt, he could write two or three hundred lines, and this without minimal effort, enhanced by the wondrous images his mind observed.

On waking with an intuitive grasp of the whole work, Coleridge began writing furiously line after line of the poem which would bring him immortal fame. But, according to Lord Byron, he was interrupted by a `person on business from Porlock' who stayed for an hour. After he departed Coleridge, to his mortification and fury, found that despite retaining vague memories of the vision he had seen, he had forgotten the remainder of the poem.

Secondary inspiration is more difficult to define. A subject may be engaged on a deliberate self-initiated programme to reach a particular goal or solve a specific problem; the final barrier may be surmounted, the solution identified by a single blinding flash of intuition, but I suggest two possible explanations.

First, the involvement of the subconscious mind in long-term examination of the problem, based on the whole of the accumulated data : the ultimate solution is found by deduction, rather than inspiration. Second, an explosion of genuine inspiration, unrelated to a specific problem. Sometimes the revelation occurs *before* the problem itself is identified !

We are specifically interested in the true phenomenon of inspiration, i.e. the involuntary reception of new data totally unrelated to any current work or thinking by the recipient. Its main characteristics are :

(a) A feeling, literally, of `possession by some other intelligence'.

(b) A deep-rooted compulsion to record the data input, before forgetting it.

(c) The data input may occur whilst the subject is awake, asleep, in a daydream, trance or similar altered state of consciousness.

(d) The process often features extraordinary feats of calculation etc.

(e) It is involuntary, uncontrolled, spasmodic and impossible to reactivate once the flow of data has ceased.

(f) The phenomenon is often accompanied by moments of great lucidity and clarity of comprehension comparable to religious revelations.

(g) It is invariably of brief duration and highly concentrated form.

(h) Significant loss of data, as in the Coleridge example, may result if the recipient lacks skills and/or equipment for recording or recalling the data.

(i) The experience is often holistic in nature, the recipient `seeing' or `hearing' the whole of the revelation, be it a painting, music, writing or invention. The `sender' fails to appreciate the problems of recording or reproduction precipitated by the large-volume transmissions without warning - yet this characteristic provides in itself very strong corroboratory evidence of the Time connection, as we shall see.

(j) A marked feeling that the data is being `given' to the subject by some exterior agency.

(k) A range of sensory input channels is employed - sight, hearing and smell but not (significantly) via senses involving direct physical contact with the data source.

(l) A feeling of `duality' : of being not only in two places at the same time, but of being two distinct personalities. The inspiration mechanism I postulate explains this and similar effects.

(m) It is an intuitive process which apparently `opens the mind' to receive a flow of data, after the initial penetration or contact. The result is a strong mental compulsion to keep the contact open, and there is a real sense of deprivation when the link is broken. It is noteworthy that many cases of inspiration occur in the hypnagogic state when the mind is relaxed, open and receptive.

4. Capitalising on Inspiration

What happens after an inspirational experience ? Rosemary Harding describes the more common reactions :

(a) The idea is briefly noted and checked.

(b) Immediate and dedicated recording is initiated.

(c) Alternatively, the idea may be temporarily shelved, to `gel' over a period.

(d) A rough initial draft of the data is prepared. This may be a pencil sketch in the case of a painting, a few bars of music recording a theme, a few lines of prose or poetry.

(e) Other work may proceed during the `gelling' period.

(f) The basic idea is improved and refined by using the imagination to reproduce the quality of input first received.

(g) Most recipients place complete trust in the intuitive process, allowing their subconscious minds to work on the data input whilst other work is in progress. (See previous page).

5. The Time Shunt

My first substantive proof of the connection between Time and inspiration came in 1979, in the form of my best-seller novel *DOWN TO A SUNLESS SEA* (Hale, London). It was my third book; the previous two were published 18 years earlier with indifferent success. Employed at the time as a technical author on hovercraft, I had not the slightest intention of starting a new novel. But I woke up one morning in Southampton *with the whole of the last chapter of a book crystal-clear in my mind !* For the benefit of readers unfamiliar with *DOWN TO A SUNLESS SEA*, a few survivors of the nuclear holocaust fly south to the Antarctic to escape the lethal fall-out. Jotting down all I could recall of the dream, it was obvious that I had been reading a full printed version of this book; I recalled the names of at least five main characters, as well as the locale of the story. There was some subconscious association with the ill-fated Scott expedition to the Antarctic, because the hero was a pilot named Jonah Scott.

I fought to recall the rest of the dream, five months of agonising concentration and frustration, working *backwards* to the beginning of the book to learn how the tale began ! It became easier with time as the story unfolded, and happily I left the survivors rebuilding a life of sorts, leaving the way open for a sequel.

A strange experience, to say the least - but there was more, a twist in the tale. In the Epilogue of the British version published by Robert Hale, the last few survivors perish when the fall-out reaches the Antarctic ice-cap. But when US publishers Simon and Schuster produced their own version, they wanted a happy ending and deleted the Epilogue ! Incredibly, I had dreamed about the US version of the book, which would not be published for two more years !

In some precognitive dreams the subject previews not an actual occurrence but a newspaper or television report of that occurrence. Dunne quotes several examples in `*Experiment with Time*'; we find others in the *Titanic* disaster cases, but in this unique experience I had read an entire novel whilst asleep - two years before it was written or published. Incredible ! Even a skilled high-speed reader would require several hours to absorb the book in its entirety. This was totally at variance with the usual precognitive dream in which the subject awakes recalling vague memories of some impending disaster. True, I could recall only the last chapter encapsulating the story line, from which I reconstructed the rest - i.e. my Dream Producer knew that transmitting the whole text at once was impossible.

This was a classic example of inspiration. I experienced text-book symptoms of awe and incredulity, a feverish urge to write down as much as possible, for as a writer, the book's potential was immediately obvious. At that time (1979) I had been researching Time for many years, evolving a hazy concept of the way it might work from the precognitive death-dream of my friend Doug Worley in Germany. All future events, I was sure, existed in potential outside this universe - in some queer way we can preview such events, transmitting data to the Present Moment. From this emerged the concept of the Time Shunt : Fig. 18 illustrates my own experience, and it will be advantageous to follow the explanation through on the diagram.

At Present Moment A in 1979, I wake from sleep with the inspiration - the theme of the book. It is completed early in 1980, published by Hale in London and later in 1982 by Simon and Schuster in New York, (Time Location C) after a Time Lapse B in ordinary time. At that time my conscious self reads a complimentary copy of the U.S. version, but since my `self' is omnipresent at all points along my life duration-extension the material is also accessible to that entity back in 1979 in the Fixed Time Field D, and at all other points too. My Dream producer in Present Moment A in 1979 receives the material, and unable to inject all of it into a dream, settles for the last chapter.

The discerning reader will realise that this is, in effect, a closed loop Time system, similar to that used in many a science-fiction story. But this time it is for real, and a little thought reveals that it does not in any way

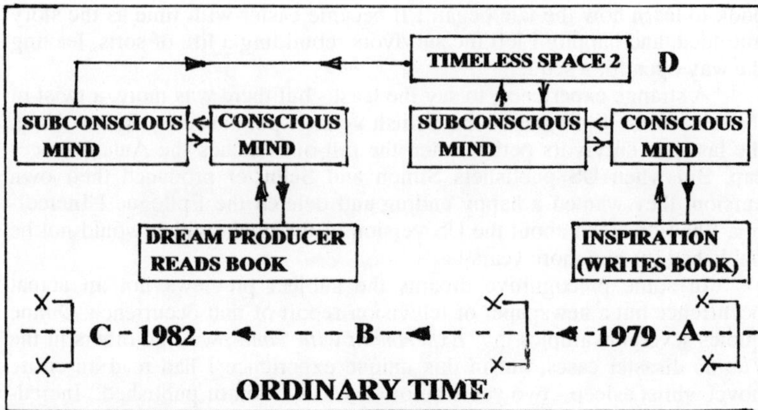

Fig. 18

The Time Shunt

contravene the Law of Causality. All these events occurred along a line of duration in universal time extending from 1979 to 1982 - and it is no use debating which came first : the book or the inspiration. In fact, the whole closed-loop system exists in the Fixed Time Field as a single autonomous potential event in its own right. There is no question of cause or effect, when both exist simultaneously in the FTF continuum. The whole event was activated when the solid material of Earth and the moving discontinuity of the Present Moment reached the spatio-temporal location of my dream - Point A.

The dream was a potential Time event, waiting to be activated into reality when the Earth reached the Space-Time location encapsulating it. In other words, the dream was all set to occur, and did so when the `time' was right. And the loop-system total-event is completed when the moving Present Moment reaches that time in 1982 when I read the last page of the book. (Point C).

Because it is omnipresent, the observing self does not `travel back in time' after reading the book. In the Fixed Time Field, `Time' as such does not exist and temporal locations A and C coincide.

6. The Analysis of Inspiration

To prove that Time Shunts do occur, I propose to review a number of well-documented cases of creative inspiration as quoted by Rosemary Harding. Remember that Shunts invariably occur in altered states of consciousness such as the hypnagogic state, sleep, trance or hypnotism. I will let the examples speak for themselves.

7. The Involuntary Experience

Tchaikovsky : *`Generally speaking, the germ of a future composition comes and unexpectedly - I sketched the whole of the "Tempest" overture, as if possessed by some supernatural force -'*

J.Marchant : *`An explanation, a theory, a discovery, the plan of a new book to him like a flash of light. . .and with it not only the plan but the material, the arguments, the illustrations.'*

Th.Hardy : *`Wandering about the countryside. . . ideas often came into his head suddenly without warning.'*

Wm.James : *`Fevered states, when ideas are shooting together. . .'*

Daudet : *`As I listened to two women calling to each other across a valley, the plot of "L'Arlesienne" came to me, as if in a sudden hallucination. . .'*

Shelley : *`...the mind in creation is as a fading coal which. . . some invisible influence wakes to transitory brilliance. This power rises from within -'*

A.E.Wallace : *`Ideas and beliefs are certainly not voluntary acts. They come to us - we hardly know how or whence. . .'*

8. Dreams and Inspiration

Van Gogh : *`A terrible lucidity at moments when nature is so glorious - the picture comes to me like in a dream. . .'*

Victor Hugo : *`Let poets dream. . . let artists dream. . . let philosophers dream. . . Let all thinkers be dreamers. . .'*

A.E.Wallace : *`In one of my daydreams. . .'*

H.R.Haggard : *He embodied one of his dreams in "The Mahatma and the Hare".*

Sir W.Scott : *`My life. . .has been a sort of dream.'*

Burn-Jones : *`Daydreams so vivid that they seemed almost to be recollections.'*

W.B.Yeats : *`Being both asleep and awake. . .'*

W.H.Rivers : *`Ideas and the language in which they were expressed came to me in the half-waking, half-sleeping state directly continuous with definite sleep.'*

Wordsworth : *Said that the beginning of his Ode ("Fallings from us, vanishings,") referred to the trance-like states to which he was subject.*

Tartini : *He dreamed that the Devil played him a violin solo of surpassing beauty and brilliance. Waking, he used the theme for his violin sonata* "Trillo del Diavolo".

Shelley : *`I made a fair practice of noting down my dreams'* (perhaps an early Dunne experiment ? Auth.)

Swinburne : *After failing to write a poem on which he had been deliberating, he went to bed. But early next morning he wrote the "Ballade of Dreamland" in one continuous session without pause. Also, the three opening stanzas of "A Vision in Winter" came to him in sleep - remembered on awaking.*

C.Bronte : *`After weeks in which inspiration had "dried up", some morning I would wake up and the progress of my tale lay bright and clear before me.'*

Poincarre : *The solution to a problem came to him as he lay dozing in bed.*

Descartes : *Lay half-awake until a late hour until although still awake his brain "began to work"'.*

Mark Twain : *Found that lying in bed. . . produced a more scintillating action of the mind.*

Brindley : *An engineer, faced with difficulty, he would retire to bed for two or three days, emerging with a solution to his problem.*

Robert L. Stevenson: *In a chapter on "Dreams" he tells how his "Brownies acted out his stories for him -"* (perhaps a rationale to account for the seemingly impossible, i.e. inspiration.)

Mozart : *`. . .what a delight I cannot tell ! All this inventing, this producing, takes place in a pleasing lively dream. . .'*

Wagner : *Discovered the opening of "Rheingold" when half-asleep on a Sofia hotel sofa.*

Sir H.Parry: *`. . . a new version of Symphony Number Three came suddenly as I lay trying to sleep in the afternoon'.*

Dobell : *`curious experiences which came to me spontaneously - I called them "involuntary efforts to recall dreams."'*

Elgar : *`The all-but unconscious medium by which works come into being. . .'*

9. Unknown Sources of Material

Mme Guyon : *`Before writing, I did not know what I was going to write. Whilst writing. . .I saw that I was writing things that I had never known.'*

Blake : *His poem `Milton' was written as from immediate dictation, sometimes 20 or 30 lines at a time, without premeditation and at times `even against my will - '*

Keats : *`The description of Apollo (in the third book of Hyperion) came by chance or magic. . .something given to me. It is odd - it strikes me more as the production of another person than myself'.*

Dobell : *`Whenever I write. . . the feeling of being a "receiver, an instrument, a mouthpiece" -'*

George Eliot : *`- there is a "not-myself" which takes possession of me - I feel that my own personality is merely the instrument through which this "other personality" is acting'.*

Dickens : *`. . .writing, some beneficient Power showed it to me. . .'*

Thackeray : *`. . .I have been surprised at the observations made by my characters. It seems as if an occult power is moving the pen -'*

Enid Blyton: *`I shut my eyes for a few moments. I make my mind blank and wait. . . and as clearly as I would see real children my characters stand before me in my mind's eye. . . I see them in detail. . . I don't know what anyone is going to do or say. . . I am in the happy position of being able to write a story and read it for the first time at one and the same* *moment. Sometimes a character makes a joke. . .that makes me laugh as I type it - and then I think - "Well - I couldn't have thought of that myself in a hundred years !" And then I think - "Well, who did think of it, then ?"'.*

And a further example from Tyrrell in `*Personality of Man'* :

`George Sand, after describing Chopin's creation as miraculous and coming on his piano suddenly complete or singing in his head during a walk, says that afterwards "Began the most heart-rending labour I ever saw : a series of efforts, of irresolutions, and of frettings to seize again certain details of the theme he had heard. *Chopin would shut himself up in his room for whole days, weeping, walking, breaking pens, repeating and altering a single bar a hundred times. . . spending six weeks over a single page, only to write it at last as he had noted it down at the very first."'*

This is an absorbing example. Chopin, quite clearly, had `heard' the entire composition in his mind, fully orchestrated. His subsequent efforts were not devoted to composing, as such, but recording in musical notation the theme he had already heard in his mind. The actual composing had already been done - but by whom ? Or what. . .? The only viable explanation is that his subconscious mind had listened to a performance of the complete orchestrated work - at some time in the future.

10. Presentation of Material

Gowan suggests that the right hemisphere of the brain is the abode of the subconscious Dream Producer (which he calls the `scanning entity') and discusses the `mechanics of inspiration' (P.290). He takes examples of classic composers, in which they were obviously functioning in some altered state of consciousness when composing.

Brahms : *`In this exalted state. . .the ideas flow in upon me. I have to be in a "semi-trance" condition to get such results. . . when the conscious mind is in temporary abeyance and the subconscious is in control. . . for it is through the subconscious mind. . . that the inspiration comes.'*

Strauss : *Talking about two operas (Elektra and Rosenkavalier) : `when the ideas were flowing in upon me - the entire musical, measure by measure. . .it seemed to me that I was dictated to by two wholly different Omnipotent Entities. . .'*

Pucchini : `. . .*faith opens the way for vibration to pass from the dynamo which is the soul-centre. . . into my consciousness.'*

Humperdinck: . . .`*I have very definite impressions while in the trance-state, which is the prerequisite of all true creative effort. . .'*

And Rosamund Harding again :

Daudet : *He `saw' what he was creating and `heard' what he was writing.* This is noteworthy because, whilst data transfer occurs in the brain's neural network between Space 1 and Space 2, it cannot be via direct or physical links : it may be analagous to telepathy. Daudet's `hearing' words seems to confirm that telepathic communication involves the use of words as well as images, and that the `scanning entity' postulated by Gowan may find it easier to transmit words across the barrier to the conscious mind than images. Sir Francis Galton thought without the use of words, but I cannot imagine how that could be possible.

Shelley : *Was able to `throw a veil over his eyes' - and see the features of a scene reproduced in a form more perfect and pure than that presented by external sources.*

This example is particularly interesting :

Elgar : `*Asked by William Reed how he produced the terrifying sound in* "The Apostles" *when Judas goes out and hangs himself, he replies : I "saw" Judas at the extremity of his remorse and "heard" the noise on a muted horn.'* Elgar clearly received both `sound' and `vision' within the inspirational message - a fairly common occurrence with many composers who `hear' fully orchestrated versions of the music they are about to compose. Gerschwin, for example, wrote the whole score of "Rhapsody in Blue" on a train, without a piano or keyboard at hand, after `hearing' an orchestrated version in his mind.

11. Holistic Reception of Material

Continuous input of information over a very brief period is a common feature of the inspirational process, but in view of the brevity and intermittent nature of many PC dreams and similar paranormal experiences, added to the impossibility of re-establishing contact once broken, holistic inputs at high speed would appear to be logical and predictable. The Dream Producer will be aware of the situation when constructing a precognitive dream or inducing a premonition or warning to the conscious mind. In an effort to transmit the maximum volume of information before the contact channel breaks down, the input would necessarily be holistic and rapidly-transmitted. For example :

Tchaikovsky: *`All this fires my soul and provided I am not disturbed, my subject enlarges itself, becomes methodised and defined, and the whole, though it be long, stands almost complete and finished in my mind.'* In fact, he sketched out the whole of the *`Tempest'* overture from start to finish nonstop as if possessed by some supernatural force.

George Sand: *Wrote for hours without pause or erasure and sent her MSS to the printers without even reading it through.* (I see this as a copying process in which Sand is receiving in full from her scanning entity the MSS exactly as it would be duly printed, up there in the future. Sand obviously senses this and needs to make no changes.)

Coleridge : *`Writing the poem* "Christabel", *I had the whole present in my mind, with the wholeness no less than the liveliness of vision. . .'*

There is an important clue here in regard to poetic inspiration. As a writer of modern poetry myself, albeit one comfortably addicted to old-fashioned ideas about rhyme and metre, I know that rhymes do not flow spontaneously from the imagination : there may be a choice of half a dozen rhyme options, all different-length words which affect the correct metering of each line. It is necessary to try each on for size, and often I resort to a thesaurus to find an appropriate word which both rhymes and `fits' the metre. It can never be a mechanical process, and the transmission of long rhyming poems during a period of inspiration can only mean that the `scanning entity' is reading from a prepared and printed script. But if the reader feels this contravenes the Law of Causality, I refer him back to the Time Shunt fixed loop system : it is unproductive to ponder which came first - the poem or the inspiration which gave it birth. Both are integral parts of the single Time event.

12. Chronological Order of Transmission

All the examples I have quoted thus far support the concept of Time-generated inspiration. We find additional corroboration in many haphazard selections of extensive material transmitted in non-chronological sequence, as in my own novel DOWN TO A SUNLESS SEA. Instances also occur of material being received over an extended period by means of multiple transmissions :

Berlioz : *When composing his Trio "Ange Adore" he was surprised at times by the unexpected order in which ideas came to him.*

Mark Twain: Writing to his mother:`*I am trying to think out a short story - I've got the closing sentence of it all arranged. . .'*

Daudet : *One evening in front of the Tuilleries Gardens he had a vision of his book entitled* "Rois en Exil", *together with the sentence with which it ends - "A mighty thing lies dead".*

Compare the example above with my own experience of dreaming about the final chapter of an as-yet unwritten novel. . .

Lewis Carroll: `*I was walking on the hillside, when suddenly there came into my mind one line of verse - one solitary line.* "For the Snark was a Boojum, you see." *I knew not what it meant then, and I know not what it means now. But I wrote it down and some time afterwards, the rest of the stanza occurred to me.*

R.Korsakov: `*When writing "Christmas Eve" there came into my mind mind some new ideas for "Sadko-"*

Thackeray : *Whilst still writing "Esmond" he mentioned to Anna, his daughter, that he had thought of a new novel - "The New-combes".*

13. Flashes of Inspiration

I can identify no relationship between the brevity of contact and the volume of data passed in a given period. The relevant factor appears to be the physical ability of the recipient to absorb and/or record the material. The `flash of intuition' varies in intensity from subject to subject, ranging from an indefinable `hunch' to brilliant aural/visual manifestations which are neither seen nor heard by other persons present at the time. These experiences resemble religious manifestations such as those allegedly `seen' by Bernadette at Lourdes. Some cases involve others present reporting `seeing' the same vision, but one cannot discount the possibility of infectious religious hysteria. Light of an extraordinary quality of brilliance and amazing clarity of colour is frequently cited. Such images are characteristically ephemeral and usually persist only for a brief period of time before they fade or vanish abruptly.

Observers describe a pervasive feeling of ecstasy or exhilaration, often attributed to Divine intervention. However, precisely similar effects are widely reported in drug-induced trances, usually by people whose motivations are far from religious. . .

Gowan in `*Operations of Increasing Order'* wrote :

> *`The unconscious thought processes in mathematics are unidirectional, not only in Time but in logic. Again and again mathematicians have recorded their experience of the sudden flash of insight. This communication comes quite unexpectedly, after a long process of conscious thought has failed to produce a solution. The flash of insight then presents the whole solution in a way quite unconnected with the previous conscious thought processes, and all at once, rather than over a time interval in logical order. The experience is not confined to mathematics but forms a crucial part of the art of creation in any scientific activity and in many non-scientific activities. Its most important characteristic is the simultaneity with which the complex solution arrives in the conscious mind, which is an indication of the timeless nature of the unconscious. . .'*

14. The Universal Unconscious - the Source of Inspiration ?

The `coexistent continuum' is accessible by the self, including all past and future events. The FTF, however, is certainly not the domain named the `numinous' (See Figs. 15/16) but I believe the latter occupies the same spatial volume as the Fixed Time Field *and* our material universe, for whilst there is no Time as such in the FTF (a domain inhabited solely by the `self' entities of sentient beings) the numinous concept can be derived in the same way as the Fixed Time Field. If movement was possible in Space 2 in the FTF, it would produce a secondary duration-dimension forming the first of three dimensions in what we can now call Space 3 - the numinous !

The numinous domain is the third in our series of dimensional continuua and we have certain clues as to its characteristics. Almost all races believe in some realm of universal peace and happiness to which the souls of the dead migrate to enjoy the fruits of immortality. It is known by many names : Nirvana, which to Buddhists and Hindus represents final release from the eternal cycle of birth, physical existence, death and rebirth. The Scandinavian races have their Valhalla - in Norse mythology the Great Hall of Odin where all warriors killed heroically in battle live on. Some call it Paradise, others the Garden of Eden, whilst Christians call it Heaven - but it always embodies the concept of the ultimate abode of the righteous, and as such is a very exclusive kind of club.

A fourth domain, apparently a yet another vibrational level to the three we have described, is that strange place we enter at the moment of death. It has been widely described and recorded by people who have come very close to physical death. If it exists (and there is considerable corroboratory evidence to that effect) it is certainly not the Fixed Time Field, in which no movement occurs, nor yet the numinous. Rather it seems closely related to our homely physical universe, as described by many people who `died' but returned to life, with a remarkable degree of coincidence and corroboration. It is a place of pleasant warmth illuminated by a light of extraordinary brilliance with no identifiable source, but lacking seasons as we know them, and it is always glorious summer. In it, `dying' persons meets friends and relatives who have passed on, and were it not for the remarkable global similarity in such accounts, one might suspect that they were hallucinations induced by illness or drugs.

15. Collating the Evidence

G.N.M. Tyrrell asks :

`Where does the material which forms the content of an inspiration come from ? Has it entered the mind at some time through the bodily senses ? Or does it come from sources unknown to us ?

We have made considerable progress since he wrote *`The Personality of Man'* in 1946 but Tyrrell, as with many others, failed to note the connection between inspiration and Time. If my own postulate is correct, we can define it as follows :

`Involuntary inspiration springs from the observation in future Time of the end-product of that same inspiration, by the subject's `self'. The material is transmitted to the subject's conscious mind paranormally via communication channels including premonitions, visions, day-dreams and precognitive dreams. The process constitutes a Time Shunt which does not contravene the Law of Causality because the entire time-loop system is a potential Future event in its own right awaiting the transit of Earth through the Space-Time location of the inspiration-event itself.

Further, we may postulate interchange of data between other `self' entities in the Fixed Time Field, and between those entities and human conscious minds,via the inter-lobe link of the *corpus callosum* - a logical basis for telepathy. The reader will already have noted a possible connection here with the `mediums' and `spirit guides' involved in Spiritualism.

15. The Puzzle of *Déja Vu*

If there is one single phemonemon which demonstrates the viability of the Fixed Time Field and the Time Shunt thesis, it is that of *déja vu* - that sensation of having seen or experiênced an event for the second time. It has occurred to almost every living human being, and we can take a hypothetical example : I awake one morning with a fading memory of a dream in which I am standing in the street staring up at a twelve-feet tall man dressed in yellow trousers, a red jacket and blue top hat. He is huge, and smiles down benevolently at me as he passes by, raising his hat in salutation. Predictably, I laugh at the strange memory, which fades quickly and is lost for ever. *Or is it* ?

A few months later the circus comes to town. I watch the parade go by, the elephants, clowns and horses and acrobats in gleaming tights. And there in the parade is a man on high stilts, wearing long yellow trousers, a red jacket ! He catches my eye as he strides past, doffing his blue top hat in salute. In that moment I am totally convinced that I have been here before, that I have already seen in some other time this extraordinary spectacle - but where and when ? I am beset with unease, a sense of personal dissociation, as if the very framework of reality trembled and shivered for a moment before resuming normality. It is all nonsense, I tell myself - and of course I cannot consciously recall the dream episode. But my subconscious mind does so, and instantly notes the similarity between the Present Moment and the stored dream memory.

The feeling of unreality is very striking. I know this experience is nonsensical, impossible - yet it has happened, and my greatest difficulty lies in accounting for it, lacking a logical explanation such as the Fixed Time Field concept. The brain functions largely upon a basis of comparison, working constantly on comparing external data input with that stored in the memory banks, updating them with added experience. For example, walking on a smooth wet concrete floor, experience tells me there is a danger of slipping. My memory pinpoints an earlier incident and I remember I slipped on that occasion because I was wearing smooth leather-soled shoes. My subconscious checks instantly on what I am wearing today - corrugated rubber-soled walking shoes. End product verdict : it is safe to walk.

In the case of the clown on stilts, my conscious mind tells me I am apparently seeing him for the second time - but it is, in fact, the first time : at that very instant, my observing self (omnipresent in both past and present) is incorporating the incident into the dream I had months previously. Thus I see the clown in a dream *before* I see him in reality. There is no other possible explanation - and it vindicates totally the Fixed Time Field theory.

SUMMATION

1. There are two basic categories of inspiration : the involuntary input usually encountered in altered states of consciousness, and voluntary

inspiration appearing as a flash of intuition leading to the solution of a problem with which the conscious mind has been grappling fruitlessly.

2. All available evidence suggests that true inspiration emanates from a source outside the physical body in our 3-D universe.

3. That source is the migratory omnipresent element of the human personality which has its own duration-extension in Space 2.

4. In the Fixed Time Field the observing entity has access to all past events in the duration-extension. It can also perceive in one or more versions the potential future events which lie ahead of the travelling Present Moment discontinuity.

5. The information obtained is passed to the conscious mind in various ways using the ephemeral `waking-up' link between right and left brain hemispheres. It may take many forms : daydreams, premonitions, hunches, visual or aural messages, visions and precognitive dreams, and either as images of events or printed or written scripts.

6. In most cases there is an impression of information being supplied or `dictated' into the mind of the recipient, sometimes as a voice, and at other times as printed material.

7. On waking, only the memory of the work remains, which begins to fade at once.

8. Involuntary inspiration takes the form of a `Time Shunt' in which the material of the creative work is previewed by the subject before actual creation occurs.

9. The Time Shunt is a loop-system existing as a future space-time singularity, which is activated the moment the dreaming subject's travelling Present Moment discontinuity reaches the beginning of the loop, i.e. the precognitive dream sequence.

10. The Time Shunt thesis provides a reasonable explanation of the *déja vu* phenomenon. The migratory entity observes a future event, incorporates it into a dream scenario which is remembered on waking. Months or years later the actual event occurs, watched by both the waking conscious mind and the observing entity in the past (which is coincident with the future in Space 2). The conscious mind forgets the dream, observes the actual event and assumes it has already happened before !

11. Reading the personal case-history files of involuntary inspiration, the connection between inspiration and Time becomes obvious.

12. If one migratory entity can enter the Fixed Time Field dimension, so too can countless others. Exchange of data between such entities may result in the transfer of material from one conscious mind to another - telepathy.

13. Time Shunt inspiration is a by-product of precognitive dreams using material of future events obtained from the Fixed Time Field in Space 2. As such, each provides conclusive evidence of the other, and that proof is reinforced by the case of identical twins who have individual but identical duration-extensions in Space 2.

To evaluate the Fixed Time Field thesis in its entirety, it is necessary to explain how the postulate fits in with what we know of our material universe - or conversely, what kind of universe can accommodate the coexistent Fixed Time Field.

\+ + +

CHAPTER FIVE

WHAT KIND OF UNIVERSE ?

`Worlds on worlds are rolling over
From creation to decay
Like the bubbles on a river
Sparkling, bursting, borne away. . .'

Percy Bysshe Shelley 1792-1822

`The resistance to new ideas increases by the square of their importance. . .'

Russell's Law

`The universe is not hostile, nor yet is it friendly. It is simply indifferent. . .'

Rev. John H. Holmes 1879-1964

`The wise man looks into space and does not regard the small as too little, nor the great as too big, for he knows there is no limit on dimensions.'

Lao Tzu Chinese philosopher

A dark
Illimitable ocean without bound,
Without dimension, where length, breadth and highth
And time and place are lost.

John Milton 1608-1674 Paradise Lost

CONTENTS

1. Einstein and Beyond
2. The Expanding Universe
3. Space and Time
4. Particle Consciousness Demonstrated
5. The Implications
6. The Shape of the Static Universe
7. Before the Big Bang
8. The Fixed Time Field Universe
9. The Big Bang Universe
10. A Question of Size
11. Black Holes and Other Possibilities
12. A Question of Gravity
13. Theosophical Aspects

SUMMATION

5

WHAT KIND OF UNIVERSE ?

1. Einstein and Beyond

THE cosmos extends from the infinitely small to the infinitely large. Not many years ago, the smallest body was thought to be a molecule, whilst the largest, Earth, was the centre of the universe. Man's knowledge of the universe has increased exponentially since the Middle Ages and in recent years it was suggested that all Nature's secrets had been discovered and further research was unproductive. But we have barely scratched the surface, using little more than a process of `guesstimation' and `trying on for size' theory after faulty theory in too few organised research programmes. Worse, inexplicable paranormal phenomena appeared to contravene the laws of nature, but undeterred, we sought explanations, not so much for the awesome immensity of the universe but for our own existence in it. Answers were slow in coming; to compensate we did not attempt to fit our own existence into the universe, but assumed that the universe had been created especially for mankind.

This is not only unduly optimistic but impertinent, in view of our precarious presence on the third planet of a G-type sun on a minor spiral limb of the galaxy. Current calculations point to some 100 million stars capable of owning families of planets in this galaxy; our Sun was a late arrival in galactic history and many races out there, humanoid and other wise, were probably civilised and well-advanced millions of years ago. Yet in our vanity and arrogance we firmly believe we are the dominant and perhaps the only civilised race in the galaxy, and to justify that statement we assume we were created and protected by a God who cares only for mankind, to the total exclusion of all other living species. Incredible !

`Seeing is believing' : for two millennia we believed the Sun rotated round the Earth, until Polish astronomer Nicolas Copernicus (1473-1543) proved that the Earth orbits around the Sun. The Inquisition forced Galileo Galilei to recant the Copernican theory (which he had verified himself, using the refracting telescope he invented).

Accurate observation of motion is no simple matter. Any passenger in a halted train at a station will confirm that, when a train on the next line begins to move, it seems that his own train is moving - an optical illusion dissolved only by reference to the platform or some other stationary object. I quote Aristotle :

`We apprehend Time only when we have marked motion.'

Because humans tend to believe what they see, he concluded (watching a tossed ball) that moving bodies tend invariably to come to rest. Nothing moves of itself. Yet how did Aristotle reconcile this statement with constant motion of the heavenly bodies he saw each night ? He could not; in considering Time he was obliged to link together Time and motion.

Galileo exploded Aristotle's ideas on moving bodies and went even further. Timing and watching a ball rolling down a tilted plane, he deduced correctly that velocity alone was insufficient to define *motion involving a change of rate of motion.* Today every student knows the meaning of acceleration, but in Galileo's time the concept was both revolutionary and of supreme importance in understanding the rotational pattern of the Solar System.

And so to Isaac Newton. Grappling with the problem of the `natural' deceleration of moving bodies, he rejected Aristotle's basic assumption, and there is no need here to relate the way in which he made his famous discovery. He saw that, where no external forces affected a moving body, it would continue to move *in the same direction at the same velocity.* In addition he identified the two unseen forces which brought bodies such as balls and carts eventually to a halt - friction and gravity.

Taking Galileo's work a stage further, Newton established that velocity, being logical and self-explanatory, was largely irrelevant : the vital element was `acceleration' - *the rate of change of velocity,* produced by applying a force to an object, the rate of acceleration being proportional to the force applied and duration of application. He demonstrated that uniform constant motion was not absolute but relative (e.g. the apparent motion of our stationary train is relative only to the passengers— a person on the station platform would see nothing untoward). Another example : we can walk up and down a train travelling at a steady 60 mph as if it were standing still - until the train brakes or accelerates suddenly. And magically, we are once more part of the outside world.

Newton outlined in his `*Principia*' a material universe governed by simple laws, existing in `absolute' Time and Space, where terms like `absolute motion' and `absolute rest' made sense. Johann Kepler, who died some 12 years before Newton was born, had discovered (strangely, in a precognitive dream) that the planets travelled around the Sun in elliptical orbits at various speeds.

Progress from theoretical calculations to physical experimental confirmation was slow, because the technology simply did not exist. Observations of movements and characteristics of celestial bodies (which might have confirmed scientific theories) were impossible because of an inability to cast and grind telescopic lenses. The way was - and is - paved with the ruins of scientific theories, but I do not see that as a negative process : in dealing with problems involving multiple possible solutions, sheer dogged persistence, calculation, and a simple process of elimination may prevail. True, we can wait patiently for inspiration, for the thunderbolt to strike - but not for long. It can hardly be considered a viable research technique !

2. The Expanding Universe

Steps along the way. . . Slither discovered the `red shift' in starlight revealing that the whole universe is expanding outwards from the hub. Hubble discovered in 1920 that the magnitude of the red shift was proportional to the brightness of a star. The extraordinary age of the universe is seen in the stars : their light began its journey to earth countless millions of years ago. With more powerful telescopes the age of the universe is estimated at somewhere between 13 and 20 billion years, and it will probably continue to exist three times as long as that. Much was expected of the Shuttle telescope recently placed in orbit, but a slight manufacturing error reduced its effective range by at least a half. As a result we are still unable to observe what happens when the hurtling galaxies approach the speed of light on the outer limits of the universe. An imminent Shuttle mission will attempt to rectify the defect.

The universe features total disequilibrium of conditions : a dark, cold and virtually empty void filled with super-hot super-bright objects. With the amount of background light in the universe, we should experience illumination some 40,000 times greater than daylight ! But the nearer stars and galaxies obscure the more distant constellations. This effect, known as Olber's Paradox, confirms our ideas of a constantly-changing expanding universe : the huge Catherine wheel of gas and stars which is our galaxy rotates around its centre once every 200 million years.

The Earth, with other planets and asteroids, rotates around the Sun in the plane of the ecliptic, a solar system rotating round the hub of a spiral galaxy which itself rotates around its own centre whilst travelling at ever-increasing speed towards the periphery of the known universe. That speed will approach eventually the velocity of light C (300,000 kilometres per second) at which extraordinary changes occur to moving bodies - their mass increases to infinity and they expand at right angles to the direction of motion. Einstein shows us that no moving body can exceed the speed of light in this universe, and long before reaching that velocity the body's enormous mass will distort and rupture the Space-Time fabric and it will pass into another continuum.

Other strange bodies exist : dark stars undetectable by light telescopes, revealing their presence by emitting radio waves. The further out we go, the more radio stars we find - but only up to a point. Beyond that, a sudden change - a sharp reduction in the number of radio sources, indicating that recently (astronomically speaking) the nature of the universe changed fundamentally. But to what ? Why ? And how ? So many mysteries, paradoxes, strange bodies with even stranger-sounding names such as quasars, pulsars, novas, black holes . . . I do not intend to delve deeply into such matters. Physicists searching for the Great Secrets approach the subject on a wide front :

A. The nature of Space and Time.

B. The nature and velocity of light.

C. The origin and age of the universe.

D. The cause and progress of the galactic expansion process.

E. The nature of matter itself.

F. The quantum discontinuity beyond which matter loses solidity.

G. Mankind's existence in, and relationship to, the universe.

3. Space and Time

I have suggested that the Fixed Time Field (Space 2) is a three-dimensional continuum coexisting with our own Space-Time universe (Space 1) within which the duration-extensions of bodies moving in Space 1 contain potential future events in multiple versions. Earth events involve the animate as well the inanimate; each event is activated and assumes singular reality at the instant Earth and its inhabitants reach the Space-Time location of the event-start in Space 1. Viewed in Space 2, it occurs when the moving discontinuity of the Present Moment reaches the equivalent event-point along the duration-extension.

Behind the Life Wave of the advancing Present Moment, that event-reality is now irrevocably embedded in the ever-lengthening `past'. When the last galaxy finally reaches light velocity on the edge of the universe, it will (as Einstein postulated) assume infinite mass, distorting the Space-Time continuum and vanishing into another continuum. But in the Void remaining, the gravitational matrix of the Fixed Time Field in Space 2 still contains the moulds of potential events, duplicating the conditions before the preceding Big Bang.

At this point I would ask the reader to consider the following :

'If a second Big Bang occurred, injecting vast volumes of expanding matter into the Space-Time Void, would the same events be repeated faithfully within the limitations of the Probability Field governing which event-version achieves reality ? Will the same things happen again to the same people ? This question has fundamentally important implications for every human being.'

For an answer we must go back to the moment of creation - the Big Bang - and trace the development of the universe and its contents. In this explosive and controversial issue, we can make an educated guess at the probable state of the universe in its early stages, soon after the Big Bang. This term is attributable, I believe, to the British astronomer Fred Hoyle in a paper he published in 1950. It is somewhat misleading because it conveys the impression of a huge explosion occurring in empty space : it is more accurate to say that space itself was expanded by the force of the detonation, and carried along with it the vast cloud of material which now fills the cosmos. From Einstein's Special Theory it is possible to create a model of the universe and trace it back to its beginning : it originated in a mathematical singularity, an extremely small body with enormous density. We can imagine all the matter in the universe compacted into a volume smaller than an electron - not a difficult concept to grasp, since spaces between nucleii and particles are similar (given their extreme smallness) to the distances between the Sun and its outer planets.

John Gribbin[38] shows that the curvature of space discovered by Einstein is found regardless of the universe model postulated : taking a two-dimensional universe, the curvature may be positive, e.g the surface of a sphere where two parallel lines must eventually cross and the angles of a triangle add up to 180°+. A negative curvature produces an open construct - for example, a sheet of paper partially folded so that the ends do not meet. Here, parallel lines diverge from one another and the angles of a triangle add up to less than 180°. Flat Euclidean space, as we encountered in 'Flatland' in a previous chapter, is the exception, forming the halfway house between the positive and negatively-curved models, and where parallel lines remain equidistant and the angles of a triangle add up to exactly 180°. Gribbin points out that our own universe is, in fact, almost flat. There is, however, a fourth model - a universe curved like a Mobius strip (Fig. 11. P.83).

This curvature of Space-Time necessarily modifies our concept of the three dimensions in Space 2 (the Fixed Time Field) which were shown in Fig. 5, for the same of simplicity, as straight lines. In fact, the duration dimension is very slightly curved, proportional to the strength of any local high-mass body which distorts the Space-Time fabric. Indeed the distortion may be almost unmeasurable - but it will not affect the disposition of the Extension and Form dimensions, set at right angles to the duration-dimension, as shown in Fig. 19 :

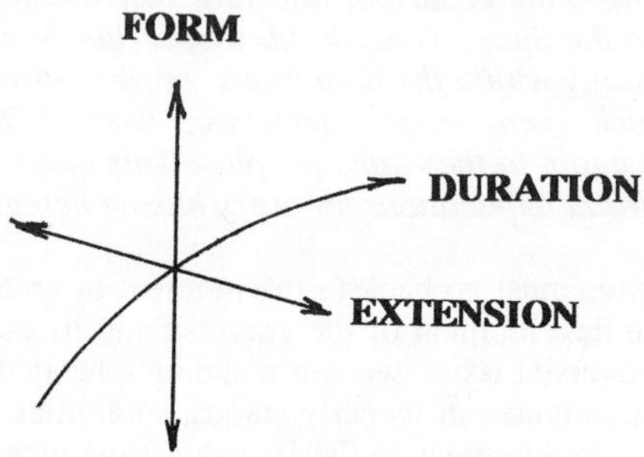

Fig. 19

A map of the radio stars shows an ever-expanding universe evolving over immense periods of time into a great irregular sphere of matter - solid and gaseous - filling the void which existed before the primeval explosion itself. It originated from an extremely-hot high-density singularity, spreading out in all directions over millions of years until an abrupt fundamental change occurred at approximately one-tenth of the estimated age of the cosmos. Astronomers detected a weak but universal background radiation on the 1 centimetre wavelength - the type one might expect to be emitted during the first few hours of expansion.

Thus far we have not paused to identify the great imponderables : What existed before the Big Bang ? Is Time infinite ? Was the universe created solely by chance ? If not, who and what was the Creator ? And if such an entity exists, who or what created *it* ? And so on, *ad infinitum*. . .

We have encountered a basic dichotomy. From a theosophical viewpoint the Creator is the Supreme Being by whose hand the universe, mankind and all living creatures came into being out of nothingness. Against that, we have the wholly scientific and material view that the universe evolved naturally from a set of natural conditions which made its debut inevitable. Scientists point to the development of life when a particular set of conditions occurs - a primeval soup containing all the necessary ingredients for living cells plus the primary spark - probably from electric storms - which sets the process in train. Asked from whence came all the matter which makes up the universe, the scientists will reply simply : from another set of natural conditions including an empty but limitless void and the sudden injection of matter under great heat and pressure from a single tiny and immensely dense core.

It is not for us, they say, *to debate who or what designed and built the universe, if it is indeed a creation and not a simple natural development. And if there are divine or religious connotations, we do not wish to know.* Yet there is no mutual exclusion here : many scientists believe in the existence of an omniscient Creator and the natural laws which govern the universe. Many theologians accept the mechanical principles on which the universe functions, whilst insisting on the necessity for a Supreme Creator.

Let me restate, at this point, my motivations in writing this book. I am not interested, *per se*, in proving or disproving any theological theories. I may discuss later in this chapter the religious implications of the Fixed Time Field theory that survival after physical death may be a natural function of the universe, with no religious connotations of any kind. Meanwhile, my immediate aim is a paradigm of a universe which will firstly accommodate the Fixed Time Field theory and secondly, explain some or all of the major paradoxes and paranormal phenomena.

This postulate will be sketchy and abbreviated, quoting (without specific proofs) universal laws the reader may confirm elsewhere. I would not be so presumptuous as to try to write a basic cosmology primer.

The last century has seen the development of several Time theories based on recent discoveries, but all have been gradually superseded in the light of later research. Ouspensky and Dunne went some way to identifying the Fixed Time Field, only to be diverted down some arid cul-de-sac. In my case, the Doug Worley experience provided irrefutable proof that future events do exist in potential multiple versions, leading me to study duration and dimensions and the means by which information on future events could be transmitted to the conscious mind. This necessitated a study of brain physiology and thought processes, altered states of consciousness and dream imagery. The last demanded some knowledge of particle characteristics, quantum physics and electromagnetic phenomena in the brain. Let us begin with particles.

In 1900 physicist Max Planck was studying black-body radiation - the emissions produced by colourless black bodies when heated, by virtue of added energy. Hitherto it had been assumed that electrons emitted energy until they were exhausted, but Planck discovered that such oscillating radiating bodies emit and absorb energy only in specific amounts ! This is tantamount to saying that the temperature of heated water rises only in 10° stages ! It was a radical discovery.

Planck found that electrons radiate energy in `spurts', their remaining energy falling to successive finite levels until exhausted. Energy loss or gain took the form of little `chunks', the size of which could be calculated by using a constant - a specified number which never changes, introduced into calculations. He found that low energy `chunks' (e.g. from red light) are smaller than high energy examples (e.g. white light).*

In 1905 Einstein recognised certain connections between energy and mass which would give us a much deeper insight into the nature of the universe. One major link involved the nature and behaviour of light, and at age 26 Einstein produced five significant papers. Three were fundamental to the development of physics; the first (which earned him the 1921 Nobel Prize for physics) described the quantum (particle) nature of light. The second described molecular motion, and the third set out the Special Theory of Relativity.

He conceived light as a particle phenomenon - numbers of photons (light particles) forming a beam, but there was a serious problem : some 102 years previously an Englishman named Thomas Young had proved that light was a wave phenomenon ! Now, Newton's physics had always implied that light was a particle phenomenon and he set his laws in Absolute Space and Time. But they are unviable in the real universe, and as long ago as 1818, Young and a friend named Fresnel set out to disprove the particle theory. Gary Zukav[30] describes their experiment with great clarity.

The issue is this : a particle is a self-contained `something' located in one particular place (in motion or otherwise) whilst a `wave' is something that is spread out. Here is a simple wave :

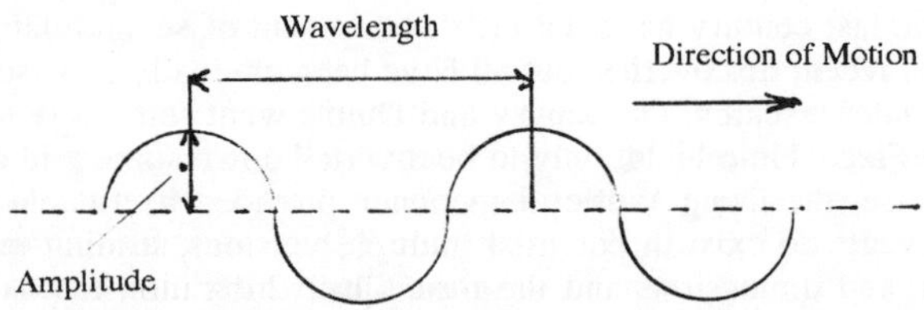

`Wavelength' is the distance between wave peaks : some radio waves exceed six miles in spacing, whilst X-rays are about 100 millionths of a centimetre long. `Amplitude' is the height of the peak from centre-line, and the number of peaks passing a given point per second is the `frequency'.

Now : Wave Velocity = Wavelength x Frequency

The velocity of light and most types of electromagnetic radiation is approximately 300,000 km per second. Light velocity C is a constant - but Einstein's unique contribution was that C is constant in *all* circumstances, regardless of its characteristics (wave or particle) and whether its source is approaching or receding from the observer.

* Could such energy levels correspond to event-versions in Space 2 ? An interesting speculation.

Light can be a wave or particle phenomenon, depending on the circumstances - but in Young's time the major puzzle was this :

> *`How can light, which is composed of particles or waves, travel through Space which is devoid of any means of supporting it, as air supports sound waves ?'*

Prior to 1887 scientists postulated the `ether' - a very odd invisible and undetectable substance which `supported' light in space. But in that year, Americans Michelson and Morley reasoned that the movement of the Earth through the `ether' would necessarily affect the speed of light - that a light ray shining in the directions of the Earth's motion would be travelling `against the stream' as it were, and be slower than a light ray directed back `down-stream'.

But their experiment showed no difference at all and the existence of the ether remained in doubt until Fitzgerald and later Lorentz suggested that objects contract in the direction of motion through the ether - the contraction being precisely the value needed to account for the non-appearance of the anticipated light-velocity differential ! This is a classic example of tailoring the question to fit the answer, and there is no `ether', of course, but like many such failures it pointed the way.

Planck calculated the energy increase in a light quanta (photon particle) with increased frequency : the higher the frequency, the higher the energy. Because of the higher frequency, violet light photons release higher-energy electrons than those of red light.

The reader is no doubt complaining : "Hold on ! Here we are talking about particles with - apparently - wave characteristics !" Can light be both particle and wave at the same time ? It is essential to understand the difference between these states : in the Space 2 duration-extension of any object moving through Space 1, all matter behind the advancing Present Moment is in solid particle form, whilst the matter ahead of the moving discontinuity is in indeterminate wave function. The PM is constantly collapsing the matter of the wave-function Probability Field into particles, forming molecules and solid moving matter which produces events.

Thus the wave is very different from the particle, although both are associated with motion - all particles move in our universe, and waves are fundamentally a product of motion. The frequency and wavelength of a wave depends upon the spatial and temporal extent of the wave : the greater the extent, the better the definition. The wave, *per se*, is spread out over space while the particle is strictly localised - and where electromagnetic radiation is in a mode combining both, the result is a wave packet - a moving vibratory disturbance of limited spatial extent which behaves in many respects like a particle, but is generated by the interactions between atoms - a collective motion of all the atoms in a material (which may equally be a liquid or a field of electromagnetic radiation). Here is a diagram of a wave packet :

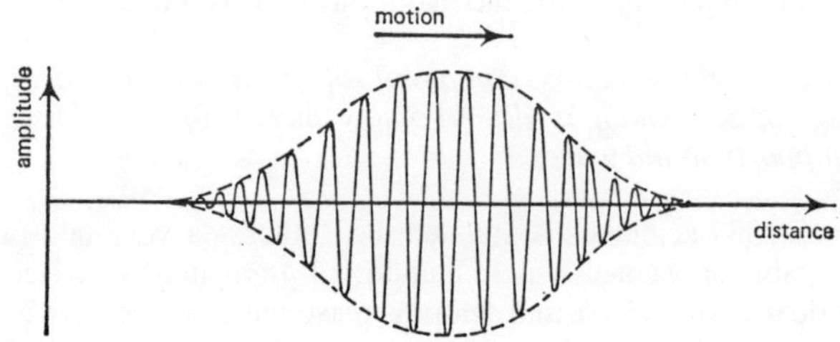

(From Time,Space and Things - B.K.Ridley, Penguin 1976)

Both particle and wave packet carry their charge of energy and momentum; each occupies a finite volume of space- but their behaviour is very different. If two particles collide they bounce apart - but if two wave packets meet, they merge into each other and the amplitude of vibration fluctuates up and/or down. In other words, interference occurs - and if a particle is directed towards a slit in a partition, it either goes through or stops. A wave, on the other hand, will always get through (in part, at least) but its direction of motion is changed to some degree because of diffraction. Further, it can be reduced in amplitude progressively, and may be collapsed by external influences into `solid' particle mode : the particle's resultant mass, momentum and direction of motion are subject to probability effects as predicted by Schrödinger, producing a range of event versions - and the two major external influences are the arrival of the Present Moment discontinuity and the imposition of the human will upon a wave packet Probability Field. We may have here a logical explanation of paranormal phenomena such as psychokinesis : the fall of thrown dice is a good example. Before they come to rest, their final presentation is a function of a wave packet Probability Field : ahead of each Present Moment (of the dice) their Space 1 location is only an indeterminate wave function. But the psychokinetic dice thrower, visualising the winning display of 3 and 4, wills the final movement of the dice to the desired effect by collapsing the wave function and distorting the Probability Field.

Precisely how does he do so ? His self is a wave function EMF existing in both Space 1 and Space 2, by virtue of its own duration-extension. Further, it is omnipresent at all points along that extension and by interacting with the wave packet Probability Field ahead of the dice's Present Moment, interference and diffraction occur, producing a new matter structure and a new sequence of events - i.e. the dice will show 3 and 4.

This particle/wave packet duality is yet another discontinuity, similar to that of the Present Moment and also of matter solidity, which remains reassuringly visible down to molecular level, but at subatomic level becomes empty space containing atoms - electric nucleii with orbiting electrons and other particles which are also positively or negatively-charged ! And light photons can be particles or waves, or both at the same time, in given circumstances. This is the frontier of magic itself : at quantum level subatomic particles - rotating wave packets with characteristics of spin, charge and mass - exist only in potential, such that efforts to examine them closely will alter their characteristics - the Heisenberg Principle of Uncertainty.

Electrons cannot be `split' in any experiment involving firing a particle through a slit. But we can arrange to divide a wave packet in two, using a `shutter' which operates fast enough to close after half the wave packet has passed through. Yet strangely, the electron displays a diffraction pattern exactly like a wave, whose wavelength is Plank's constant divided by its momentum. So the electron, in fact, is neither a particle nor a wave, but something quite different.

How can this be ? How should we regard these wave patterns ? We can assume they are created by waves following the possible paths an electron may use - and here probability enters the equation. The energy in real waves (which determine whether or not they can be detected) is a function of the square of the amplitude : with electron waves, we can associate the square of the amplitude with the probability that an electron may be found. The more intense the wave, the higher the chance of finding an electron, and the astonishing fact is that these are probability waves which reach out along the direction of travel and define statistically the chances of an electron being at a given locality. And the essence of probability is the *action quantum* - literally a measurement of the intrinsic freedom of motion of fundamental particles. In a later chapter we shall meet this action quantum in the form of a Restraining Field which forces events to remain on or close to the Probability Geodesic - the most probable version of events to come. The photon is a good example of a Probability Wave.

A side effect of this development was the degradation of the Bohr model of the atom : in the new model we still have the nucleus, but the orbiting electrons are replaced by patterns of standing electron waves. Further, Pauli's Exclusion Principle states that no two electrons can have identical properties in the same region of space - that no two objects can occupy the same space at the same time. Protons and neutrons also obey the Principle, and in large numbers they are described by a scheme of statistics developed by Fermi and Dirac. As such, they are called *fermions.*

Photons, however, do not conform. Any number can have identical properties in the same region, and tend to accumulate in large numbers : they obey statistics developed by Bose and Albert Einstein, and are called *bosons.* Photon bosons form electromagnetic fields, whilst the postulated *graviton* boson forms gravitation fields.

Incredibly, the Bell Experiment indicates that particles (electron waves) may even possess consciousness or awareness, with important implications when studying thought processes. `Consciousness' does not automatically imply intelligence : plants are conscious of activities around them and may show improved growth and health when music is played nearby, but no one would credit them with any degree of intelligence. Particle consciousness is more an awareness of general sets of conditions and an ability to form associations with other conscious particles, with no limitation on distance. The experiment also confirms instantaneous superliminal communication between separated twin particles, whilst the Young experiment (a photon gun firing particles through twin slits in a partition) shows that photons in some queer way become aware (before firing) that one or the other of the two slits may be closed !

4. Particle Consciousness Demonstrated

Can we prove particle consciousness exists ? What do we mean by consciousness ? A definition springs to mind : self-awareness. Species below certain levels of evolution do not realise they exist, cannot differentiate between existence and non-existence. Only man, of the higher mammals, is aware not only of his own existence but that of the universe and the conditions necessary for survival in it.

The idea of awareness in a particle may seem strange, but the experiments I shall describe appear to confirm the fact. At quantum level (the term is derived from Max Planck's small finite bundles called `quants') some particles do not comply with natural laws. The tachyon ignores the limiting velocity of light in this universe - it may function partially at least in some other continuum. What better domain than the Fixed Time Field, where all movement is instantaneous, as is the speed of thought ? A `conscious' tachyon may well be aware of its own existence and environment, whilst in the Bell Experiment involving reversal of spin in one segment of a divided twin particle, the second instantly followed suit *with no detectable time lapse !* This suggests that each segment was aware of the existence, location and state of its partner, regardless of distance - instant perception possible only in the Fixed Time Field.

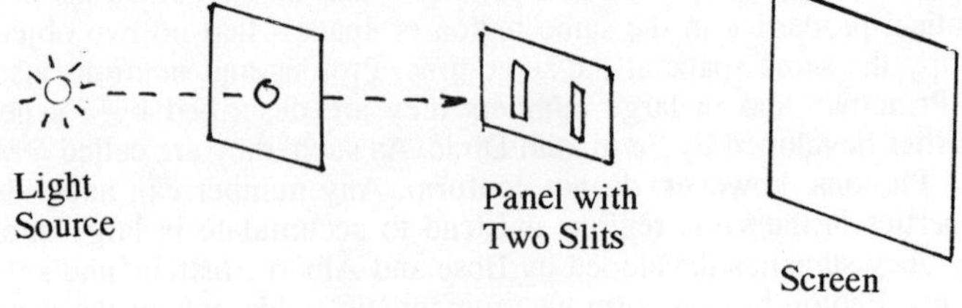

Fig. 20

The Young Experiment

In 1803 Thomas Young experimented with a screen with two vertical slits located next to a light source (see Fig.20). Each slit could be covered with material, such that light passing through the slits would form patterns on a wall or screen beyond. But when Young covered one of the two slits, the resulting pattern was as shown in Fig. 21.

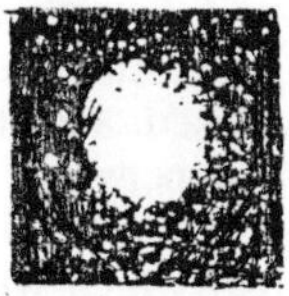

Fig. 21

Diffusion Pattern - 1 slit closed

With two slits open the pattern should have shown the result in Fig. 22 - two patterns similar to the 1-slit open display, as shown.

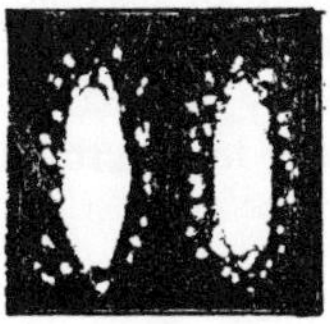

Fig.22

Anticipated Diffusion Pattern - Both Slits Open

But Thomas Young was amazed to find the actual pattern shown in Fig. 23, with four light areas !

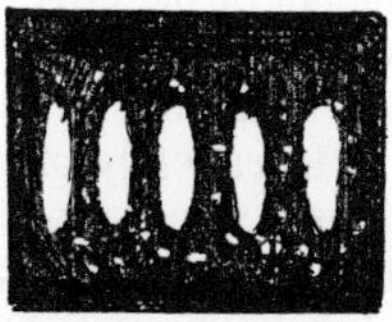

Fig. 23

Actual Diffusion Pattern - Both Slits Open

How could this be explained ? Young recognised the last pattern as `interference', a typical wave mechanics phenomenon when light waves interact when emerging from the slits. Sometimes they overlap and reinforce each other : at other times they cancel out.

Now, Young's experiment showed that light was a *wave* phenomenon, whilst Einstein's own photoelectric experiment a century later proved equally conclusively that it was a *particle* phenomenon ! Later researchers have duplicated Young's experiment using a light-gun firing photons (light particles) with one slit closed, and the results have been bizarre in the extreme ! But why ? What happens ?

We fire a photon through one open slit to impact upon a photographic plate. It lands in a light area (which would be dark if both slits were open, i.e. one of the dark separation areas in Fig. 23). Now we repeat the experiment with both slits open - and no hits are observed in the first experiment's impact area ! In effect, with both slits open, there are always light and dark alternating bands - yet regardless of whether one or both slits are open, the photon always avoids dark areas !

The conclusion is unavoidable - and startling. In some queer way the photon `knows' if the second slit is open or closed ! Even more incredible, it seems to be aware that two slits exist. . .

This is a second example of particle consciousness, the first being the Bell Experiment in which one particle of a separated twin system not only reproduces instantaneously the characteristics of its twin - but knows precisely where it is, in order to determine the changes which have occurred !

5. The Implications

Obviously we are dealing with a quantum discontinuity. Down to a certain level matter obeys natural laws, but beyond that, subatomic particles contravene these laws. Presumably they function partially, at least, in another but necessarily co-existent continuum. Such examples of superliminal communication - e.g tachyon and twin particle systems - offer a feasible explanation of data transmission on future events to a present-time conscious mind.

We can construct a model of the effect : assume that all particles in the human brain/mind EMF and the `self's EMF surrounding the whole body have a degree of self-awareness. The self, dissociated from both mind and body, functions independently of both and is immune to aging. The mind deteriorates with age, since some brain cells are not replicated, and succumbs with the physical body. The self EMF, functioning both in Space 1 (governing mind functions) and Space 2, has a duration-extension independent of the body and generated in the foetus EMF at the moment of conception, growing in volume and experience to adulthood. But from where does the self originate ?

There are three possible solutions. First, it may self-evolve within the body, incorporating inherited characteristics embedded in the genes and DNA. Second, it may be a migratory entity from the FTF continuum which inserts itself into the fertilised cell at conception. Third, it may be a combination of both these options.

The implications are of overwhelming importance to mankind. If the self is self-generated within the foetus in conjunction with the mind/brain combination, there can be no life after death. However, if it is a free and migratory Space 2 entity, it will return to Space 2 on physical death of the body, ready and waiting to embark yet again on life's stormy seas at the right time. The waiting will not be onerous - for Time does not exist in the Fixed Time Field, and a billion Space 1 years pass as if they do not exist.

In other words, reincarnation : an unending cyclic rebirth which continues until the pattern is broken. Buddhist, Hindu and other religions believe this to be the divine shape of the cosmos.

\+ + +

Another spin-off from the Fixed Time Field universe appears to explain telepathy and other paranormal phenomena. An observing `self' in Space 2, whilst concerned mainly with events along its own duration-extension, can also communicate with other `self' entities - and not solely those in close physical proximity in Space 1. In the FTF distance and Time are meaningless; in telepathic communication, a Space 2 scanning entity A in contact with its own physical mind/body in Space 1 Present Moment is aware of certain information. It passes the data to a second Space 2 scanning entity B, which in turn transmits the information to its own mind/body in Space 1 Present Moment - with no apparent time lapse. Predictably, telepathy between twins and close relatives occurs more easily since their duration-extensions are interlinked in Space-Time. In hypnosis, communication between the hypnotist and the subject in a hypnagogic state may involve contact between their selves in Space 2. The hypnotist's conscious mind may gain access to the subject's by way of Space 2 and the physical bridge between right and left brain hemispheres.

6. Shape of the Static Universe

`Static universe' is another term for the Fixed Time Field (Space 2). In Space 1, motion generates duration which we experience both subjectively and objectively. A Space 2 observer will observe no motion at all. Physical space exists between the heavenly bodies, but the Sun is an incandescent virtually-endless cylinder, slightly curved to follow its orbit around the Galactic hub. Light photons and other radiation with their own duration-extensions fill Space 2 with a brilliant light of indescribable density, an all-pervading luminosity, of which many descriptions are on record.

The Space 1 plane of the ecliptic - the Catherine wheel of the solar system - is tilted to its direction of motion at an angle of 67° . In Space 2 the Earth will be a delicate blue-green spiral around the Sun cylinder. It is impossible to describe fully what the human eye might see in that fabulous domain, and I believe that no human mind could survive the shattering impact of such a revelation and remain wholly sane.

This co-existent double-universe is located in a Void of unknown dimensions, featuring a number of anomalies. First, Space and/or Time cannot be considered separately. If all the material in the universe vanished, the remaining void does not have three dimensions, but six - three in Space 1, three in Space 2. Einstein in 1915/1916 envisaged Space-Time as a continuum which can be bent and distorted by the gravity fields of material objects. John Gribbin illustrates this distorting effect in Fig. 24.

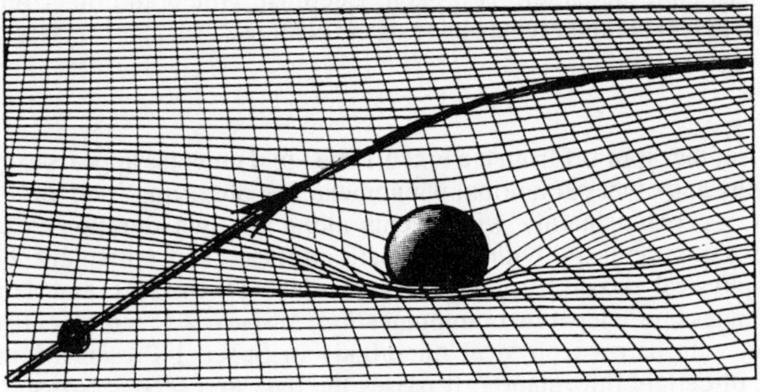

Fig. 24

Space-Time Distortion

Imagine a flexible rubber sheet marked with a grid of lines stretched over a flat frame, over which one rolls a small light marble. Resultant distortion of the sheet is very small, the marble following almost a straight line. Using a heavy ball, grid distortion will be proportional to the mass, as shown. If a marble is now rolled across the sheet, it will be deflected by the mass of the heavy ball as shown, proportional to the separation distance. Too close an approach entraps the marble in the ball's gravitational well and they will eventually impact. Similarly, celestial objects of large mass distort the fabric of Space-Time.

All Space 1 moving bodies follow paths formed by the template of gravity, a vast honeycomb network of channels along which the material of the expanding universe must pass, like a metal mould which cools and solidifies material as it flows. Future positions of celestial bodies, therefore, can be predicted with great accuracy, but movements of living inhabitants are restricted by the Probability Field in Space 2.

Einstein pointed out that there is no detectable force of gravity as such : moving objects simply follow a path of least resistance, much as

Newton's apple fell directly towards the centre of Earth rather than at an oblique angle. The effect deflects light beams passing close to large-mass bodies : photon streams would need to expend much energy in resisting the gravity field against the line of least resistance. The General Theory of Relativity predicts accurately the deflection found in a light beam passing close to the Sun. The Special Theory links Space with Time in a definition which involves geometrically flat Space; since all Space is curved by gravitational effects to a greater or larger extent, this was a `special' case : Space-Time itself is curved. Galactic expansion, Einstein said, is not the result of the original primeval explosion, but of the expansion of Space-Time, which draws the material along with it. But Newton's Laws tell me that if a force is applied to a body unaffected by other external forces it will continue to move in the same direction. If two or more particles are expelled from a common source (Fig. 25) the distance between them increases with time and distance, producing the phenomenon of expansion.

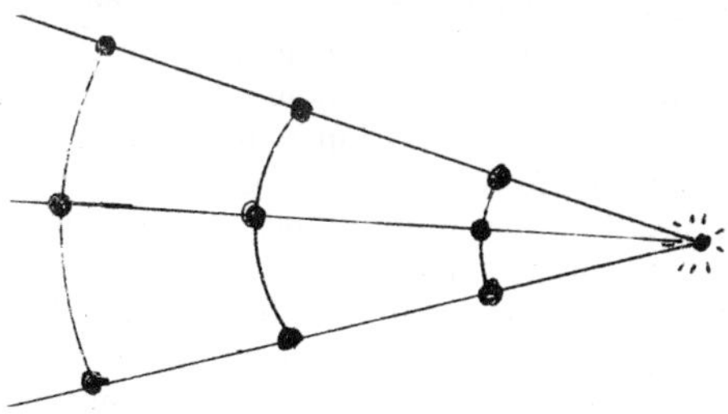

Fig. 25

Radial Expansion from a Single Discontinuity

The Big Bang occurred approximately 14 to 20 billion years ago, and we believe the original material is still in motion on the distant edges of the universe - but can we be sure ? How far away is the end of the universe - if indeed it does end ? The recession velocity of the galaxies increases according to Hubble's constant : some of the more distant constellations are already travelling at a high fraction of light velocity. So what happens when they reach C ?

Light travels at a fixed speed of 300,000 km per second. The most convenient way to describe huge interstellar distances uses light-years - the distance light travels in a year. Observing light emissions from a star five light-years distant, we are in effect looking back the same period into the past. Meanwhile, the star may have gone nova and exploded, but we will not know until the light of the nova reaches us - years after the event.

7. Before the Big Bang

Going back to the last few seconds before the Big Bang occurred, we encounter the first paradox. Did Time begin with the Big Bang - or was the Space-Time Void always there ? No matter how far back in Time we go, there is always a `before-Time' : conversely, Time must have no end because there is always something `after' that supposed end. But matters are complicated by the second paradox : where did the Space-Time Void come from ? Was it created at the instant of the Big Bang ? If so, what existed *before* that moment ? It is difficult to imagine `nothingness' - we must ask what surrounds that `nothingness' - if it has no limits. I see two alternatives : one, the Void may not have existed at all, in which there would be no one around to speculate. Two, since it does exist, we must try to determine its origin. Again, two options: first, that it appeared autonomously with no outside interference, or second, that it was created.

The problem diversifies : the existence or otherwise of a Creator introduces theological arguments outside the scope of this book. We have enough problems trying to isolate the Time Mechanism, without becoming involved in interminable religious arguments. The primary factor is limitations, natural or imposed. Nature is logical and abhors closed systems : no matter how many times we magnify a particle, the only limit to the process is mechanical expertise. No matter how often a unit is divided, the parts may be sub-divided again and again. . . if not physically, then mathematically. Conversely, we can multiply anything indefinitely - including the estimated size of the universe.

Similarly, we may assume that Time is infinite. Whether or not a universe exists at each end of the vista of unlimited Time (assuming a Void incorporating Space-Time) Time must have begun with the formation or creation of the Void. The estimated age of the universe reveals a mighty ocean of time on which we are embarked, and we can detect no nearby or distant shore. Our best assumption is that both Void and the underlying Space-Time matrix are infinite, eternal and limitless.

8. The Fixed Time Field Universe

At the instant of the Big Bang, the empty Void was a Space-Time continuum embodying the curvature associated with the gravity fields of duration-extensions of moving bodies to come, a gigantic lattice of predetermined forces comprising the Fixed Time Field. Within it, every particle of expanding non-sentient material follows the line of least resistance. With living matter, a Probability Field ensures that potential future events fall within the limitations of probability and possibility.

Employing the analogy of a vast tract of dry desert and mountains, a cloudburst erupts - the first rain ever known. Torrents of water cascade down mountain-sides onto the plain, and the resultant streams and rivers do not wander over the landscape indiscriminately. They follow the ground contours along lines of least resistance, using the valleys as ready-made moulds. Eventually all the water disappears, leaving the dry empty desert. But if a second rainstorm occurs, the water will follow precisely the same courses. Each dry valley is a space template for a potential future event - the arrival of flood waters to form a stream.

Moving Space 1 bodies follow predetermined paths through Space-Time along the duration-extensions in Space 2. As the material of the universe reaches velocity C and enters a different continuum, it leaves behind an empty Void containing the same Space-Time lattice, ready for a new injection of matter. In other words, identical pre-Bang conditions are ready for another cycle - and a new universe is born.

This repetitive endless process is encapsulated in the Cyclic Universe theory embraced by many Earthly religions. They believe that the human self, surviving physical death of mind and body, dwells in the co-existent universe until it enters once more a newly-conceived human foetus; each time, the process improves and refines the personality until it achieves eternal existence in the ultimate non-physical domain - nirvana, Paradise, call it what you will.

Many alternative scientific theories of creation have been evolved. It has been suggested that prior to the Big Bang there was nothing - not even a Void. `Bubbles' of Space-Time appeared and a form of `negative pressure' initiated the galactic expansion process, resembling in some ways Hoyle's own theory of continuous creation of material. But no viable Time Mechanism ! I found that odd. But Hoyle himself said :

> *`The whole idea of creation is queer. . .all the material of the universe is supposed to have appeared in one instant of time, the whole creation taking the form of one Big Bang. For myself, I find this idea much queerer than continuous creation'.*

9. The Big Bang Universe

More accurately, the Friedmann-Gamov general astrophysical model, beginning with the concentration of all matter into one hot dense ball - but at once we see problems. What could produce such a ball ? What existed before it ? How much time was required to construct it ? A considerable time-consuming process of compression would be involved. Professor Allan Sandage (Mount Wilson Observatory) believes that the universe at some point will cease to expand when the expansion force is equalled and finally exceeded by the gravitational force, collapsing within itself and beginning a period of contraction ending in a microscopic singularity which again explodes - another variation of the Cyclic Universe. Others suggest that the Void and its Space-Time curvature existed before the Bang ruptured the fabric of Space-Time, linking the universe to another continuum containing matter subjected to enormous pressure and heat.

If the `rupture' theory has any substance, it would occur at some weak point in the fabric of Space-Time - but why there was there only one such point ? Further, a process of pressure equalisation would occur, in which influx of material would slow down and cease, lacking pressure differential. As for the ball itself, we know that some neutron stars not much larger than footballs contain more material than the Solar System.

10. A Question of Size

We do not know the distance to the edge of the universe, i.e. to the frontal wave of expanding galaxies. But reason suggests that the Void itself is infinitely larger than the material universe - yet we have observed galaxies more than 10 billion light years away travelling at .9 C. We hope to locate still more distant constellations through the Hubble telescope now in Earth orbit. Clearly, the outermost galaxies are close to attaining the velocity of light, which according to Einstein cannot be exceeded by moving objects in this universe. They will reach C before arriving at the far edge of the Void - if there is such a boundary. The logical solution lies in an endless Void, within which our universe and countless others are accelerating to the location where they achieve light speed.

What happens at that point ? The problem is one of size. In a science-fiction story about a ship full of friendly aliens approaching the Earth on initial contact, scientists guide the ship in for a landing at a vast airfield using radar for detection, radio for communication. But something goes wrong : the alien ship disappears from the radar screen, whilst radio contact is maintained up to the moment of landing. The aliens, disembarking, find themselves in an impenetrable jungle with zero visibility and the search for them begins. In fact, the 500-strong crew have landed right on target - but their ship is barely a millimetre long, the jungle is uncut grass - and the boot of a passing searcher crushes the tiny ship out of existence.

Are there gravity-free areas in this universe ? General Relativity shows that the inertial mass (of a moving object) is equal to gravitational mass - explaining why a 200-pound astronaut and a feather fall at the same rate. In fact both have equal inertial mass, i.e. a disinclination to move. Einstein named this the Principle of Equivalence, applicable to accelerating (free-falling) objects. Special Relativity, conversely, describes uniform zero-acceleration motion of objects in a co-ordinated system, assuming the system itself is in uniform zero-acceleration motion. For example, inside a descending elevator. Gravitic effects can be ignored in two areas :

(a) Remote areas of space far from large matter concentrations, and
(b) In very small areas of space.

In the analogy of a three-dimensional network of strings forming 6" cubes, each knot is a magnet attracting nearby ferrous objects, including a steel ball travelling through the network. It is deflected at various points by the magnets and its position can only be determined in relation to the grid and not to the surrounding space. Repeating the experiment results in an identical trajectory : the network is forming a gravitic matrix similar to that in the Fixed Time Field. An object passing midway between two magnets will be unaffected, whilst other objects will be deflected by an amount equivalent to the gravitic force and the period under its influence. If the magnets were 6 feet apart, the deflection would be much smaller : conversely, if the transit time was brief, deflection would be negligible. Gravity, therefore, manifests itself as :

(a) The equivalence of inertial mass.
(b) Gravitation effects proportional to the body's mass.
(c) An overall resultant gravitational field forcing bodies to follow pre-determined tracks through the FTF and the physical universe.

Zukav in `*The Nature of the Space-Time Continuum*' quotes the famous analogy of Lord Russell, which likens the continuum (STC) to a hilly countryside. The hills are caused by pieces of matter (objects). The larger the object, the more its gravity field distorts the STC, which in remote spatial areas resembles a flat plain : an Earth-sized object causes quite a bump and a Sun-sized object a relative mountain. Zukav writes :

> `*As an object travels through the STC it takes the easiest path between the two points : this is called a* "geodesic" *and is not always a straight line. Now, suppose we observe vertically from our balloon a mountain which has a bright beacon on the summit. Rising gradually from the plain it steepens with increasing elevation almost to the vertical at the top. Many villages surround the mountain, interconnected with footpaths, all of which curve away as they approach the steep mountainside. Suppose it is night-time and from the balloon we can see neither mountains nor paths - only the beacon and the torches of travellers. As we watch we note that the torches approaching the beacon are deflected from it gently, when at a distance but sharply when close to the beacon. From this we would probably deduce that some odd force emanating from the beacon was repelling all attempts to approach it - for example, we might speculate that the beacon was extremely hot and painful to approach. With the return of daylight, of course, the truth would become clear - that the torch-bearers simply followed the easiest paths.*'

This analogy illustrates the `channelling' effect of the gravitic fields in Space 2 controlling the movement of matter within the bounds of probability and possibility. We may label the most likely path, incorporating the most probable event versions, as the *Probability Geodesic*.

Does our universe fill the whole of the cosmos, the Void ? Or does it contain billions of similar universes ? Einstein tells us that bodies travelling at near-light velocity increase in mass and decrease in length, spreading out laterally on a broad front at 90 degrees to the direction of motion

(Fig. 26), eventually coalescing into a ball of matter of enormous size which contracts upon itself to become a neutron star about as large as a football, of incredible density. At the speed of light the tiny body containing all the material of a single universe ruptures the Space-Time fabric, erupting into some adjoining continuum at high velocity and temperature.

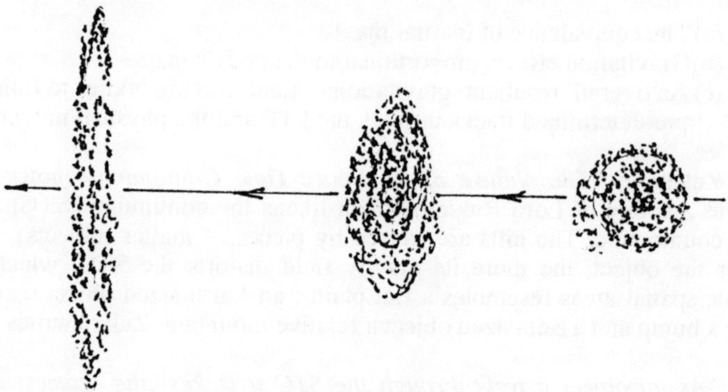

Fig. 26

Galactic Distortion at High Velocities

Suppose that in this infinitely-larger cosmos there is a further Void, a curved Space-Time continuum containing the gravitic matrix of a greater Fixed Time Field, channelling newly-arrived material to convert embedded potential future events into reality. The cycle begins again and continues until all the material reaches C and passes into a third and still larger Void. . . Logically, there may be an infinite succession of Voids and universes stretching from the unimaginably-large to the incredibly-small - and beyond even those limits. Further, as each Void empties of matter, a fresh singularity from some microscopic continuum emerges to create a new cycle.

The sequence from small to large is open-ended and infinite, for nature abhors closed systems. In each domain, whilst the speed of light is a limitation, it will probably vary : C in microscopic universes will be much higher than in macroscopic universes.

There is one interesting link between size and Time. In many puppet movie cartoons, we see miniature oil refineries, factories and ships explode into thousands of pieces which fall much too quickly compared with a real explosion. But by slowing down the film appropriately, the debris would fall at a natural rate, providing an eerie effect of realism. I cannot understand why film producers have failed to grasp this simple fact - but perhaps they have : children accept what they see unquestioningly.

11. Black Holes and Other Possibilities

John Gribbin[40] describes black holes as spatial discontinuities in which matter is so concentrated that gravity will become the ultimate irresistible force, crushing all available matter down to a single point - a mathematical singularity such as we have described. In the development of a black hole, the fabric of Space-Time collapses : to quote our previous example, the ball breaks through the rubber sheet (P.167). Before that point is reached, gravity around the singularity becomes so strong that even light cannot escape - hence the term `black hole'. It is surrounded by a region from which escape becomes impossible, bounded by an `event-horizon'. Beyond that limit, any matter drawn into the hole will pass into some other universe.

Now, this appears to provide a source for the immensely-dense singularity which breaks through the Space-Time fabric into a new continuum as a Big Bang. Gribbin supports this thesis, suggesting that the effect will create a `white hole' in the new cosmos, the hole emitting `anti-matter', but the release of enormous amounts of energy will not cause a deep gravity field and a new mathematical singularity. Instead, matter will disperse in all directions; there will even be a slight decrease in gravity, which will disappear when all matter has vacated the area. I would carry this a stage further : the matter is drawn into the channels and pathways of the Space 2 gravity fields.

Have we any supporting evidence for Gribbin's theory ? No `white holes' have been located in our universe, and if my own thesis of a cyclic universe is correct, the Big Bang must occur at precisely the same point if the same chains of events are to be activated. Pre-Bang material, therefore, may emanate from a microcosmos in which similar chains of events have occurred, and the process may continue into the infinitely small and infinitely large *ad infinitum.*

Whilst supporting the Big Bang thesis, Itzhak Bentov fails to provide an adequate explanation or explain how the superdense `ball' of the singularity originated, what it was before it emerged and the involvement of Time in the puzzle. He visualises the ball as emitting a jet of matter into Space 1 at a velocity less than that of the material's escape velocity from the ball's own gravitational field. It falls back forming an object like a cored apple, a torus which resembles a flattened smoke ring with a small central hole from which galaxies from the sub-universe emerge, travel round the torus and re-enter the central hole. At the `re-entrant' funnel a remarkable effect will occur, since the density of the galaxies will be very high. They will collapse, fall in towards the nucleus and form a black hole. This again coincides with a white hole in the adjacent universe.

This conflicts substantially with the Fixed Time Field idea. Bentov dispenses with the `Time flow' concept, suggesting that it is matter that flows, not Time - but moving matter creates Time in the form of duration. He suggests we move through Space along the `axis of Time' (duration) -

if we could stop our motion dead in space, we would experience no Time at all ! But reason suggests otherwise : even if we could be stationary in space, we would still perceive time by the movements of the celestial bodies. Einstein shows that it is impossible to come to an absolute stop in space, without reference to some other totally stationary object. In an all-moving universe there is no such reference point.

Bentov goes on : `*In an empty universe before the jet erupts from some other Universe into our own, there is no Time'*. This is true - there is no motion, nor an observer to confirm it.

12. A Question of Gravity

The Fixed Time Field with its Space 2 gravitational lattice containing future/present/past duration-extensions of moving bodies will now be familiar to the reader - a domain containing future events in potential mode. The Earth's duration-extension resembles a tunnel and the portion expanding constantly behind the advancing Present Moment consists of solid fixed past-time events. I have shown that the Life Wave of the Present Moment discontinuity converts the wave-function indeterminacy of the future into solid-particle reality. Whilst the `future' sections of celestial body duration-extensions contain fixed events which are generated inevitably by the body's passage through given spatial locations, human beings may influence the characteristics of future events affecting themselves.

We will discuss this further in a later chapter, but by way of clarification, consider a single human duration-extension as shown in Fig. 27.

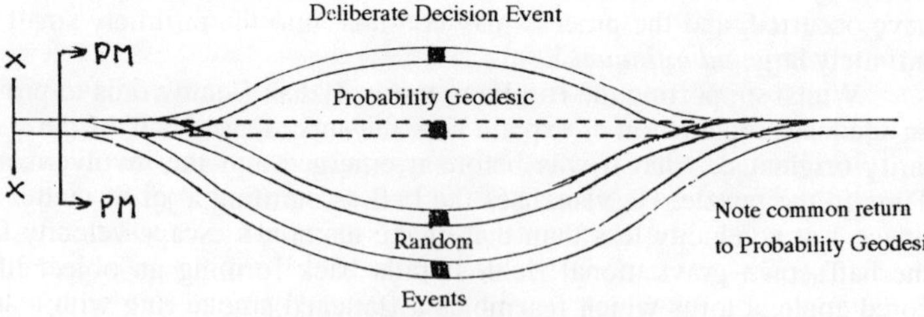

Fig. 27

Human Duration-Extension

Up to Decision Point X the subject makes no conscious decision to sway a future event. The version achieving random reality will incorporate the most probable sequence of events, i.e. following the Probability Geodesic. At X there is a choice of decisions : unable to identify which will be most beneficial, the subject makes a random choice which may divert his Time track into either event version. Alternatively, the subject may have a strong conviction or premonition that a particular decision will be beneficial, and succeeds in collapsing the wave-function by an act of will. But how does he achieve his aim ? I believe it to be a four-fold process including :

1. Thought background processes in the brain.

2. `Particle-consciousness' in the self's duration-extension.

3. The wave-function mode of potential future events.

4. The strength of the Space 2 Probability Field which influences the most probable version in achieving reality. The self-entity in Space 2 over-rides the Probability Field sufficiently to allow the desired version to occur.

This is akin to psychokinesis. If the mind/self can move relatively heavy artifacts, it can apply the necessary bias to collapse the wave-function indeterminacy of future events and produe the event-version required. We will return to this point when discussing the *I Ching*.

13. Theosophical Aspects

The outline of the co-existent Fixed Time Field theory was taking shape in my mind as a logical Time Mechanism, and despite rigorous examination, it seems to provide satisfactory answers to certain paranormal occurrences including precognition, *déja vu*, telepathy, inspiration and similar phenomena. In so doing, it contravenes no natural laws of this universe, but points to possible modifications of those laws, enabling them to apply to any adjoining universe. Significantly, it suggests a cyclic universe embodying survival after death as a natural function of the universe without religious connotations. It demonstrates the eternal relationship between man and universe, and for the first time we have some intimation of man's place and purpose in the universe.

Inevitably, the theory conflicts with established theosophical beliefs, since no attempt has been made to address the ultimate puzzle of the creation of the co-existent universes. My own feelings are clear : whilst being totally agnostic, I agree unreservedly with David Foster[32] that the cosmos could not have come into being by accident. Statistical odds against that are extremely high - billions to one, and I am forced to believe in the existence of a supreme Creator - who can deny it ? Yet I cannot and will not accept that we are the sole intelligent race in the universe, that we were placed here on Earth by the Creator as a special project requiring His personal attention. Against the vastness of a cosmos containing millions of inhabited planets at a far higher state of evolution than ours, such a proposition is unworthy of mankind but typifies his vanity.

In my view, Creation and the nature of the Creator are so far beyond human understanding that it is a waste of time to try. Notwithstanding, I accept that religion contributes something towards the alleviation of human suffering - but totally unbalanced in comparison with the harm done by religion during the last 2000 years (evangelistic religion has killed more than 1000 victims for every person killed in the history of war, and as I write several million Iraqi Kurds are dying of exposure, starvation and injuries inflicted by a self-styled religious Ba'ath Party.) Religion is the greatest killer, oppressor and persecutor of the innocent in known history. Ask any Jew.

I blame unbridled religious fanaticism, seen as an obligation to recruit more believers by whatever means available including torture, rape, murder, assassination and blackmail. The slogan of the Spanish Inquisition was "Recant or die !", whilst the ban on contraceptive appliances by the Roman Catholic Church ensures that an unending supply of little Catholics is born, ignoring the looming world-wide over-population crisis. The Church recommends the `rhythm' method - but few couples have any musical talent. . . Further, the whole basis of the Islamic faith is to recruit anyone prepared to believe in the Koran and kill all those who don't. *`Death to the Unbelievers !'*

I deny no one the right to believe anything he likes, whether Christian, Mormon, Catholic or Moslem, Buddhist or Hindu. I do deny him, in the strongest terms, the right to foist his beliefs on me, or even onto his own children before they are old enough to make up their own minds. Next to terrorism, raw religious fanaticism is the greatest threat we face in this precariously-balanced world. All too often, they go by the same name.

14. The Meaning of the Universe

In the foreword to David Foster's book[41], Colin Wilson identifies our efforts to find some kind of meaning in our presence in this universe as an inevitable extension of the `family syndrome' : we become used to thinking of a father figure, a director creating for us a meaningful world out of the seeming chaos of reality. We make the same error in thinking that the universe must have the same pattern, and seek constantly a parental figure in which to place our trust - in precisely the way the young of wild animals adopt wooden models of the adults of their species as surrogate mothers. But in attributing some meaning or purpose to this universe, our instincts only partially obscure the harshness of reality : soon we perceive the futility of appealing to some imagined and omnipotent Being. This is the essence of Existentialism, which was favoured by writers like Andreyev, Schopenhauer and Beckett.

Has the universe any meaning ? Does it embody some form of awareness ? David Foster regards it as an intelligent entity functioning like a giant computer, identifying the coding systems used in genes, DNA and RNA molecules which are so complicated that such systems could not have evolved by sheer chance. Further, he argues, a primary law of physics is that a highly-complex process requires even more complex energies to set it up - and no energies of Earthly origin are sufficiently powerful to generate, for example, the DNA molecule. In fact, the universe according to Foster may well be a gigantic electronic construct which *demands*, rather than requires the presence of sentient species like *homo sapiens*.

SUMMATION

1. The ancient philosophers including Aristotle, Isaac Newton and Galileo Galilei failed to solve the secret of Time.

2. Light is both a particle and wave phenomenon.

3. The universe may be an intelligent computing device.

4. The Young and Bell experiments suggest that particles may possess consciousness or awareness.

5. Electromagnetic fields exist not only in Space but in Time.

6. The human self inhabits a body electromagnetic field which extends the full length of the subject's duration-extension in Space 2.

7. The Fixed Time Field (Space 2) is a three-dimensional continuum coexisting with our own universe (Space 1) consisting of a gravitational lattice forming a template of all future events.

8. The human self has full access to all future and past events within its duration-extension - a possible clue to the memory process.

9. Being wholly non-material in nature, and taking advantage of the ability of all electromagnetic fields to exist freely in space with no physical connection, the self will survive physical death of the subject, remaining in Space 2 until re-entering a foetus at conception.

10. Before the Big Bang, the Space-Time Void included an empty Space 1 and a coexistent Space 2 incorporating the gravitic fields containing all future events in potential.

11. Time and the Void are infinite, without beginning or end. Within it occurs an endless cycle of Big Bangs, expansion, the attainment of light speed, transition to another continuum and a return to an empty Space-Time Void.

12. Given the Fixed Time Field matrix, repeated cycles will result in similar mainstream events following a `Probability Geodesic' including variable human-intervention events.

13. No cosmic paradigm succeeds as well as the FTF thesis in accounting for paranormal phenomena such as *déja vu*, inspiration, precognition, telepathy, psychokinesis and reincarnation.

14. Black holes may be a source of tiny but indescribably-dense matter `seed balls' which enter our universe to start another Big Bang cycle.

I have now put forward two proofs of the Fixed Time Field Theory : precognition and inspiration. Our third proof is found in the case of identical twins.

+ + +

CHAPTER SIX

THE ENIGMA OF IDENTICAL TWINS

`O'er the rugged mountain's brow
Clare threw the twins she nursed.
And remarked : "I wonder now
Which will hit the bottom first ?"'

Harry Graham 1874-1936 Ruthless Rhymes for Heartless Homes Compensation.

`GIVE US A BREAK' says Mum of twins. . .

Amil Kishal (9) of Totton, Southampton, broke his left wrist playing football. Ten days later his twin brother Nevin fractured his left wrist - playing football. . .

With acknowledgements to Mrs. Koshal and the Southampton Evening Echo

CONTENTS

1. An Old Familiar Question
2. The Egg and I.
3. Twins and Time

SUMMATION

6

THE ENIGMA OF IDENTICAL TWINS

1. An Old Familiar Question

A CLEAR connection can be demonstrated between the phenomenon of precognition and cases of identical twins who are separated in their early years. Despite this deprivation, the subjects often lead near-identical lives. They marry similar partners, have the same number of children and enjoy identical tastes in clothes, books and amusements. All this, to a degree far beyond that which might be expected from chance alone. Yet remarkably, researchers in general became bogged down in the minutiæ of individual cases and made no attempt to identify an operating mechanism to account for these remarkable coincidences.

Colin Wilson[40] quotes many cases, some of which I reproduce here with my grateful acknowledgements, and cites certain evidence of right-lobe activity on the part of some twins. But I can identify no other efforts to explain the coincidences encountered.

2. The Egg and I

There are two categories of twins : those born at the same time from two separate eggs (dizygotic or DZ twins) and those born from a single but divided egg (monozygotic or MZ twins). The great majority of coincidental cases are found in MZ twins who have identical genes producing matching physical and mental characteristics. Some, in fact, have almost-identical fingerprints. It is convenient to use the number of matching characteristics in each case to assess the degree of comparability : from that figure we may calculate the odds against such matching occurring by chance.

3. Twins and Time

In earlier chapters I submitted two sources of proof of the Fixed Time Field thesis (precognition and inspiration) and suggested that further proof may be found in the investigation of identical twins. Recapping briefly, I have suggested that each human being living in Space 1 (our 3-D universe) has a duration-extension in Space 2 (the Fixed Time Field) which extends from conception to death. A cross-section at any point along the duration-extension will identify a specific date in history, a three-dimensional frame of reference in real time - perhaps a single second, hour or minute of a person's life. Where that cross-section coincides with the travelling Present Moment life-wave, previous events existing in particle-mode reality are fixed in the immutable past. Ahead of the PM all particles are in indeterminate wave-function mode, coalescing into the version closest to the Probability Geodesic as the wave-function mode collapses. Human beings have the ability to influence which potential future event achieves reality, by collapsing the adjacent wave-function indeterminacy without disturbing the mainstream flow of events.

Whilst every duration-extension is individual in nature, it may make contact and intermingle with others in Space 2. A human couple may first meet after years of independent existence, marry and spend the rest of their lives together. In effect, their duration-extensions, which meet and remain together in Space 2 and include all their life-events, were *in situ* in the Space-Time matrix long before they were born. That close association will be duplicated in the case of identical twins who, but for a freak of nature, should have been a single individual. Their life-events in both cases will correspond to their Probability Geodesics - *and these will be almost identical.*

Taking a somewhat crude analogy of a dish of spaghetti, each strand has individual existence, but two identical strands emerging from the machine side by side become separated during cooking. Each may become permanently attached to a nearby strand, never contacting its twin again. Yet each will follow an identical existence, first in the can and then in the cooking pot, subjected to the same temperature increase and finally terminated in the process of digestion, all at identical times.

Nature, Fate, call it what you will, has prepared a sequence of events for the human entity which will emerge from the fertilisation of a single egg. The emergence of two identical individuals from that egg will not change their predetermined future life-events. There will be minor deviations as each exercises his option to pre-select trivial event versions which do not affect the main-line sequence of events.

But life contains more than simple event sequences : each twin's duration-extension contains every aspect of his character, preferences and opinions, likes and dislikes, beliefs and disbeliefs - everything that contributes to a single unique personality. All are locked solidly into his life-track, together with important mainline events such as first job, marriage, birth of children, death of parents, serious illnesses and the like. Take the example of a single female fertilised egg. Her whole life is encapsulated within her duration-extension in Space 2 along a Probability Geodesic - the most probable sequence of events. Each event exists in potential ahead of the Present Moment in multiple versions, and whilst important mainline events are controlled by the Probability Field, minor events exist in multiple versions, unformed and undeveloped in the swirling clouds of wave-function particles ahead of the Present Moment. And whilst we can influence which version achieves reality, we must be aware in some way of the nature of events on the Probability Geodesic. We will return to this point presently : meanwhile, we can outline a hypothetical life history of the child :

1961	Conceived		
1962	Born		
1963	Age	1	Takes first steps.
1964		2	Speaks first words.
1965		3	Falls, breaks forearm.
1966		4	Starts nursery school.
1967		5	Contracts mumps and measles.
1968		6	Prefers boy's toys to dolls.
1969		7	Develops liking for butter beans.
1970		8	Starts piano lessons.
1971		9	Learns to swim.
1972		10	Has night terrors.
1973		11	Contracts chickenpox.
1974		12	Prefers blue for clothes.
1975		13	First boyfriend named Peter.
1976		14	Studies biology, computers, French.
1977		15	Cycle accident, breaks left leg.
1978		16	Becomes pregnant, has abortion.
1979		17	Becomes engaged to boy named Bryan.
1980		18	Marries in St. Margaret's Church.
1981		19	First child named Stephanie.
1982		20	Mother dies, followed soon by father.
1983		21	Second child named Robert.

A typical life story - but on closer examination we find that several events involve active choices : her toy preference, liking for butter beans, her liking for blue clothes, learning to swim, choice of studies, electing to learn piano, pregnancy and abortion, and choice of children's names. All these, of course, result from her adherence to her Probability Geodesic, and occur without conscious effort on the child's part. Other events on the list have an element of chance : which forearm would be fractured at age 3, contracting diseases (although mumps and measles are very probable in all children who have not been immunised). Similarly, which leg would be fractured at age 15, meeting and marrying a boy (whose name happens to be Bryan) and her resultant pregnancies. Only a few events are the result of external influences : starting school, and the deaths of her parents.

Of those events triggered by her own decisions, most are unpremeditated or trivial and we can identify only two important mainline decisions she is forced to make : firstly, her abortion following accidental pregnancy and secondly, her marriage to Bryan (her children are consequences of that decision). Out of the 21 listed events, only three appear to be variable - her two accidents and her pregnancy; the remainder of her life conforms with the Probability Geodesic. For example, her first accident could have taken several forms :

(a) She could have been knocked down, instead of falling.
(b) Either arm could have been broken, or other injuries sustained.
(c) She could have been struck by a passing vehicle and been killed.
(d) She could have survived the fall without injury of any kind.

Now, let us suppose that this is a single MZ egg which splits into twin embryos. Both children will have near-identical Probability Geodesics ahead of them, and they will encounter similar events at comparable times, regardless of whether they are together or separated. In cosmic terms separation distance is irrelevant; further, each will make individual decisions resulting in slightly-different versions of the same event, decisions largely influenced by common tastes and preferences locked into their identical genes. In fact, they cannot avoid leading near-identical lives as their exactly-coincident Present Moment moves along the same Probability Geodesic. The Fixed Time Field is the only possible explanation of the phenomenon.

Predictably, some will dispute the facts, but the evidence cannot be ignored when we examine examples of MZ twins. Unless otherwise stated, the following are quoted from Colin Wilson with his kind permission and annotated `CW'.

The Lewis Twins (CW)

The boys, born in August 1939, were put up for adoption. Jim was adopted by the Lewis family in Lima, Ohio. The second, as yet unnamed, went to the Springer family in Dayton, Ohio, and they too named their boy Jim (unaware that his twin bore the same name). Jim Lewis traced his twin brother in 1979 and a staggering series of coincidences came to light.

1. Both were habitual nail-biters.
2. Both suffered from insomnia.
3. Both experienced migraine from the age of 18.
4. The migraine disappeared at the same time in each case.
5. Both had cardiac problems.
6. Both had developed haemorrhoids.
7. They were exactly the same weight.
8. Both had gained some 10 pounds - and lost it - at identical times.
9. Both married girls named Linda.
10. Both divorced their first wives - and then married girls named Betty.
11. Both named their son James Allan.
12. Both owned a dog which they named Toy.
13. Both had worked as a Deputy Sheriff.
14. Both had worked in gas stations.
15. Both had worked in McDonalds restaurants.
16. Both spent their holidays on the same Florida beach.
17. Both chain-smoked the same brand of cigarette.
18. Both had basement workshops in which they made furniture.

The Shirley Johnson Case

The twin Johnson sisters born in April 1943 were parted when babies and lived apart for 42 years, until Shirley learned in 1981 that she had a twin sister Sheila. All efforts to trace her were unsuccessful but in 1967 Shirley collapsed with pseudo-labour pains. She is certain that Sheila was giving birth to a child at that time. She is still searching for her sister.

The John Watts Case

When John met his twin brother Peter after 48 years of separation since babyhood, he found some amazing similarities :

1. They were physically identical.
2. Both wore the same hairstyle, spectacles and clothes.
3. Both had similar jobs.
4. Both had married teachers.

The Barbara Herbert Case

After being parted as babies, Barbara Herbert met her twin sister Daphne by arrangement at Kings Cross railway station in London 39 years later. They found little difficulty in recognising each other, for both women :

1. Arrived at the meeting wearing identical brown velvet jackets, beige dresses and white petticoats.
2. Miscarried a first child and went on to have two boys and a girl.
3. Fell downstairs at age 15, leaving them with weak ankles.
4. Met their husbands at age 15.
5. Had identically-distorted little fingers.
6. Had homes furnished identically.
7. Their adoptive mothers died when the girls were children.
8. Had heart murmurs and slightly-enlarged thyroid glands.
9. Read the same popular novelists and took the same magazines.
10. Had used the same aubourn hair tint when they met.

The Margaret Richardson Case

British identical twins Margaret Richardson and Terry Connolly, who were separated as babies, married on the same day within an hour of each other.

The Killian Twins

Gail and Carol Killian were not separated as babies, but their record of births of their own children is extraordinary : twice in succession they gave birth on the same day, in the same hospital, and the same doctor attended both mothers.

The Edith Heys Story

Edith and her identical sister died in April 1990 under amazing circumstances. They were 82 years old; both collapsed and died at the same moment in the same rooms in their identically-painted houses in the same Barnoldswick street - both from heart failure. Invariably dressed alike, they were buried together.

The Dorothy Low Case (CW)

Dorothy and twin sister Bridget (who lived apart) decided to keep a diary for just one year - 1962. They filled in precisely the same days, left others blank ; the diaries were of identical colour and size. Both had learned piano as a child, giving up at the same time. Both liked eye-catching jewellry.

The Jeanette Hamilton Case (CW)

In 1979, Jeanette and her twin sister Irene were reunited after many years. Comparing notes, they found that both :

1. Suffered from claustrophobia.
2. Disliked water.
3. Sat with their backs to the sea on beaches.
4. Hated heights.
5. Experienced pain in the same spot in the right leg in wet weather.
6. Were compulsive calculators.
7. Had led scout packs as children.
8. Worked at one time for the same cosmetics company.

The Oscar Stohr Story (CW)

After Oscar and his brother Jack were born in Trinidad in 1933, their parents separated, taking a child each. Oscar went to Germany and joined the Hitler Youth. They met for the first time at an airport in 1979, and found that both men :

1. Wore square wire-rimmed glasses.
2. Wore blue shirts with epaulettes.
3. Had identical moustaches.
4. Flushed the lavatory both before and after use.
5. Stored rubber bands on their wrists.
6. Liked to eat alone in restaurants, so they could read.
7. Had identical speech rhythms, despite one speaking English and the other German.
8. Had identical walking gaits.
9. Sat in chairs the same way.
10. Had the same odd sense of humour : both used to sneeze loudly and deliberately in elevators to startle other passengers.

The Chaplin Twins (CW)

Freda and Greta were in a York court, having both fallen for a Mr. Iveson. They attracted considerable attention, making identical gestures at the same time, apparently without thought or discussion. Subsequent investigation revealed many fascinating details :

1. Both were described at school as slow, neat, clean and quiet.
2. Their mother dressed them identically and they had no friends.
3. They demonstrated `mirror-imaging' commonly found in MZ twins - where one was right-handed, the other would be left-handed. One sister exhibited clock-wise hair-whorls, the other anti-clockwise.
4. Aged 37 and unmarried, they lived together. Both would hold the frying pan whilst cooking and they wore identical clothes. Where their coats may have had different buttons, they would transfer half the buttons to the other coat. Given different pairs of gloves, they made up `odd' but identical pairs.

Colin Wilson suggests that in the Chaplin case, there was clear evidence of telepathy in their behaviour and communication : they told one journalist that they had one brain and were really just one person. Undoubtedly many similar case histories exist, as yet unreported or recorded, and I would be pleased to hear from any readers with such experiences. But I submit that this brief selection provides definitive proof of the Fixed Time Field thesis, even after eliminating coincidences attributed to gene-based characteristics and environmental effects. What remains are specific real-time events of extraordinary similarity, which cannot be explained by coincidence or chance. The odds against 14 of the 18 examples in the Lewis case coinciding by chance are more than 480,000,000 to 1.

+ + +

Whilst this `twins' enigma has puzzled researchers for centuries, no one to my knowledge has advanced a satisfactory explanation, or identified a connection between the correlations and a working Time mechanism. Precisely the same situation occurred with inspiration. Remarkably, but for an accident of birth which bisects their common ovum, MZ twins would live as a single individual destined to encounter most of the events in a single Probability Geodesic. This evidence goes far towards proving the Fixed Time Field thesis, and it is remarkable that the connection became evident only in an investigation of the Time Mechanism itself.

One final point. Some may attempt to disprove the thesis by citing coincidence and identical gene-based behaviour/characteristics, but the weight of evidence is against them. As Oscar Wilde wrote in `Lady Windermere's Fan' : *"To lose one parent, Mr.Worthing, may be regarded as misfortune : to lose both looks like carelessness"*. And it is all very well quoting Mark Twain (as did Disraeli) : *"There are three kinds of lies : lies, damned lies and statistics"*. There may yet be a fourth - coincidence.

+ + +

SUMMATION

1. Case histories demonstrate a remarkable degree of correlation between monozygotic identical twins, not only in regard to personal characteristics but the events each encounters during their lifetimes.

2. No viable explanation other than coincidence has been put forward.

3. The degree of correspondence is far beyond that which can be accounted for by coincidence or genetic similarities. The latter cannot account for twins experiencing identical events at the same periods in their lives.

4. The Fixed Time Field thesis accommodates all the correspondences found in each case of MZ twins.

Thus far we have mentioned only in passing the relevance of probability theory in discussing the Fixed Time Field, whilst describing the limited ability we possess to influence future events. Our next target is to evolve an explanation of this phenomenon.

\+ + +

CHAPTER SEVEN

PROBABILITY, SYNCHRONICITY, DESTINY

`Just as doctors' orders mean such and such treatment as specific for such and such complaint, so every individual has circumstances ordered for him specifically in the way of destiny. Nothing happens to a man that nature has not made for him.

Marcus Aurelius Antoninus 121-180 AD

`It matters not how strait the gate,
How charged with punishments the scroll
I am the master of my fate
I am the captain of my soul. . .'

W.E.Henley 1849-1903

`Necessity and chance approach me not
And what I will is fate. . .'

John Milton 1608-1674 *Paradise Regained*

`The probability of life originating from accident is comparable to the probability of the Unabridged Dictionary resulting from an explosion in a printing factory. . .'

Professor Edward Conklin Princeton University

Chaos umpire sits
And by decision more embroils the fray
By which he reigns : next him high arbiter
Chance governs all.

John Milton 160--1674 Paradise Lost

CONTENTS

1. Man's Place in the Universe
2. The Moving Finger. . .
3. The Bounds of Possibility
4. Synchronicity and Coincidence
5. The Effects of Entropy
6. Pressure in the Probability Field
7. A Paradigm of Probability
8. The *I Ching*

SUMMATION

7

PROBABILITY, SYNCHRONICITY AND DESTINY

1. Man's Place in the Universe

IN a previous chapter we discussed the implications for mankind of an absolute deterministic physical universe - that is, movement of matter through Space pre-set by the gravitic effects of the Fixed Time Field in Space 2. We saw that the precise location of the Earth 100 years from now can be determined, as a location on the world's duration-extension. Whilst any future location of human beings conforms with the general context of the Earth's location, precise location is impossible because of our ability to move at will within certain limits imposed by the Probability Field.

The actions and existence of all Earthly living creatures, therefore, are virtually irrelevant and will not deflect the Earth from its course in the slightest degree. (I use the term `virtually' advisedly, since it not altogether impossible that simultaneous detonation of even a small proportion of the world's nuclear devices could deflect the Earth from its orbit, banishing it into the icy wastes of interstellar space or plunging it into the Sun).

Thus, the destruction of one little planet in a minor solar system, one of a hundred million in our galaxy, would have less effect on the universe as a whole than dropping a grain of sand in the Pacific Ocean.

The presence of mankind, *ipso facto*, is not essential to the survival of the Earth, Solar System, galaxy and universe, and this is a very bitter pill to swallow. Humanity has been historically motivated to assume that we occupy a unique and essential place as the only intelligent race occupying the sole inhabited planet in the entire universe - a self-centred view hardly dented by the discovery of at least 100 million stars with planets capable of supporting life of some kind.

That life may take unimaginable forms. Further, most potential life-supporting solar systems are much closer to the galactic hub (we are far out on a spiral arm). As many as 100,000 advanced civilisations may exist within 20 light-years of us. Currently we are exploring our own back yard at snail's pace, and perhaps a hundred years will pass before the first man steps uncertainly on the moons of Jupiter and the sands of Mars. It will take an estimated 500 years to develop faster-than-light ships craft with the instantaneous-communication devices FTL craft will require.

What are our chances of discovery by some space-travelling race ? Logically, an old Galactic civilisation would explore initially the closer systems, and might consider it unproductive to visit outlying systems with no guarantee of finding life.In the final analysis, the ultimate trade goods bought and sold will be information and technology, in which ancient Hub civilisations will be vastly more wealthy than us.

Until the first gigantic discs arrive simultaneously over every capital city in the world in answer to a movie-maker's dream, we will remain doggedly convinced that we are a unique species placed in this universe for some special but unfathomable purpose by a Supreme Being of whom we know nothing. That purpose, and the motivations behind it, is a matter for conjecture : consistent with the vanity and braggadocio of mankind, we will continue to insist that we are - and always shall be, the controllers of our own Destiny.

2. The Moving Finger Writes...

In life, we seek a compromise between what we would *like* to see happen, and what in all likelihood *will* happen, despite our hopes and preferences. Individually, we base our actions on our passivity or aggression, humility or extroversion, taking day to day decisions in a state of groundless optimism in the hope that end results will be beneficial and long-lasting.

Predictably, most of us are disappointed, but shrug shoulders philosophically and get on with the business of living. Our actions and decisions are influenced by present circumstances : at times, decisions are forced upon us with limited choice of action, and at others, we have time to consider at length the probable consequences. The effect generates a need to probe the future, to make predictions on the basis of current knowledge.

Yet few people make good use of the available time to consider fully the implications of a decision. Those who do so are regarded as `wise' and are very much in the minority : the majority take a blind jump headlong into decisions later regretted. Typically, we seldom acknowledge the good judgement of those wiser than ourselves, attributing their success to chance and calling them `lucky'. We blame our own lack of foresight and caution on the laws of chance, adhering to a steadfast belief in the law of causality - that all events are caused by, or are affected by, some previous decision or event. Ludicrously we abandon our inherent right to consider carefully the implications of a current-time decision, saying *`what will be, will be '* in the words of a popular song.

3. The Bounds of Possibility

All events involving human beings lie within a spectrum of *possibility* from `total possibility' on the one hand to `sheer impossibility' on the other. Within this spectrum lies a further range of *probability* options from the `highly-improbable' to the `extremely probable' (the Probability Geodesic). The first range of parameters defines the limitations of reality imposed by natural laws, whilst the second offers a framework of statistical calculation to determine the chances of a given event occurring. `Possibility' quoting Collins English Dictionary, is *`the capability of existing, taking place or proving true without contravention of natural laws.'*

In my view that definition is incomplete, in regard to `natural laws'. For example, something we now believe impossible (because it appears to contravene a natural law) may be quite possible in the light of other laws yet to be discovered - as good a definition of the `paranormal' as we may find. The Collins definition might reasonably be amended to : `contravening no *known* natural law'.

There exist laws which govern the behaviour of large numbers - the laws of probability. Applied to an event, probability statistically is a measure of the relative frequency or likelihood of an event occurring, and it ranks equally with such other basic concepts of physics as momentum, energy, Space and Time. Statistics is the tool we use : the collection, classification and interpretation of quantitive data allied to the use of probability theory. A simple example : a tossed coin may show a head or a tail - half a chance of each, equalling unity, which is the absolute certainty that one or the other will turn up (disregarding the freak `stand-on-edge' case !). If the coin is weighted to fall more frequently head up, there will for example be three chances out of four for a head, one chance in four of a tail. Again, the sum is unity, i.e. 3/4 + 1/4 = 1.

This is only the barest bones of a very complicated subject, closely allied to the Heisenberg Principle of Uncertainty we have already encountered. As a result the laws of physics are essentially statistical in character; quantum theory relates more to the level of expectation than determined quantities, probabilities rather than certainties, and this principle is enshrined in the great Time Mechanism of the universe. In simplest terms the future is always uncertain, but the Laws of Probability govern which of two or more versions of an event is most likely to happen, and each human duration-extension follows the Probability Geodesic - the line linking the most probable events to achieve reality.

Quantum-wise, the classical orbit of an electron in an atom does not exist - instead, a pattern of probability of an electron being in a given location of space. We find no determinism in this universe - rather, there are detailed models describing the interactions between quantum particles and wave packets (always subject to laws of probability) developed by Pauli, Dirac, Heisenberg and Schrödinger. They are astoundingly precise and accurate, showing why we can never know precisely the momentum, energy and position of any particle at any instant in time, because all particles are free-moving entities. Indeed, the source of all electromagnetic radiation is the acceleration and deceleration of particles, almost invariably electrons, which emit wave packets called photons to produce light. They sacrifice, at the same time, some of their precious energy, recoiling like newly-fired guns until halted by pushing against the nucleus.

This is called a *virtual* process, and the light wave packets *virtual protons*; it is seen when an electron changes orbit. Each electron gathers around it a cloud of photons, and changes the characteristics of the atom somewhat unpredictably. The important point is that the electron wave exists only as a probability, a wave function which will change significantly when it interacts with another wave packet.

But how does this quantum indeterminacy affect us in our universe ? Does probability theory govern our very lives ? Take as an example a circus tight-rope walker preparing for a performance (Fig. 28). The probability that he will perform as scheduled is a function of the pressure of certain positive external factors to follow the Probability Geodesic. He needs the money, is under contract, is perfectly capable of doing the job and in good health. There are further connotations of responsibility to his employer, his fellow artistes and the public. Certain negative factors may influence the degree of adherence to the Probability Geodesic : he may be unhappy about the state of the equipment, the condition or lack of a safety net, and worries triggered by some previous accident involving a colleague.

A balancing process follows, in which the degree of first probability (that he will perform at all) is established. The greater the preponderance of positive factors, the greater the probability that he will perform. Assuming that outcome, we can move on to the performance itself (Fig. 28).

The performer stands high above the tense crowd on his small platform, staring at the slender vibrating wire stretching 30 metres to a similar perch and watched breathlessly by the circus crowd. At this juncture we may assess the various possible fates ahead of the performer as follows. This is a spectrum of possibility and probability, and it is important to understand that whichever version occurs, there will be an immediate tendency to return to the Probability Geodesic afterwards. Numbers 1 to 7 are possible outcomes; numbers 8 and 9 represent `extreme impossibility', whilst 1 to 7 display decreasing degrees of probability down to 7. But 8 and 9, we can say, are beyond the bounds of possibility, at least under our known natural laws. Does that apply in all circumstances ?

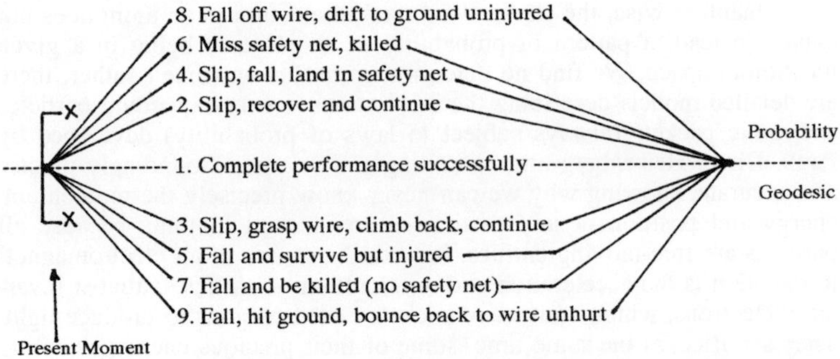

Fig. 28

Probabilities and Possibilities

The startling answer is `no' ! If our wire-walker is performing on the Moon (albeit in a space-suit) it is possible for Numbers 8 and 9 to occur, because of the one-sixth gravity. Similarly, it is improbable that a man would be walking on the Moon (and indulging in wire-walking) *at the present time.* And that is the over-riding factor : Time. A hundred or so years from now, men may feasibly enjoy amusements such as wire-walking on the Moon, probably in specially-created underground Earth environment units.

Neither example contravenes natural laws. However, some laws may work on Earth but not elsewhere. Similarly, whilst they may impose certain limitations now, future developments may eliminate that problem. Notably, the two factors undermining the inviolability of some natural laws are gravity and Time. But laws are not sacrosanct, and we can re-examine our day to day decisions with that in mind.

All human decision-making basically is a straightforward two-way choice. Given two clearly-defined options, we try to assess which will be most beneficial in terms of future events - whether or not to accept a new job, which of two ladies to wed, catching an early train or a late one and the more trivial decisions such as which drinking glass to use, of the two on the shelf. In such matters, we tend to make instant decisions in the certain knowledge that they are of no long-term consequence. However, this random method may become habitual, despite the gravity of a current situation of which we are well aware. Old proverbs tell us to `Look before we leap' and that is good advice.

The spectrum of possibility applied to future events influences the decision process, ranging from `extremely beneficial' to `extremely deleterious'. We have no way of assessing the result without accurate knowledge of the future; because the decisions may involve health, financial status and ultimate survival, acquisition of foreknowledge of the outcome assumes paramount importance and value. This simple fact has generated the universal belief in prophecy, clairvoyance and fortune telling.

If one contemplates making money from gullible people, their absolute belief in the efficacy of both second sight and seer is essential. Here, statistics and probability enter the equation. Making sufficient guesses in a given period, by the laws of chance some will be correct. In the Rhine experiments of the Sixties, a set of 5 different symbol cards were used, 5 of each comprising a pack. A subject attempting to guess the identity of each card would be expected by laws of chance to make 5 `hits' - the measure of `maximum probability'. Guessing all 25 (right or wrong) would be examples of `extreme improbability' - and repeating that feat 25 times in a row takes us outside `probability' into `impossibility' - subject to one proviso : *at the present time.* Outlandish as it may seem, a machine may be built eventually which would augment even the slightest trace of paranormal ability into 100% guaranteed precognition. Again, it is simply a matter of time. T.H. Huxley, in a letter to Herbert Spencer in 1886, wrote : *`I am too much of a sceptic to deny the possibility of anything'.* And Aristotle said : *`Probable impossibilities are preferable to improbable possibilities'.*

Precognition in the Rhine card test may be an example of a Time Shunt. *After* each test, the subject may be shown the actual sequence of cards - but unknown to him, his scanning entity from the previous night is also watching, and transmits the sequence to the subject's memory in a dream. During the test, his conscious mind searches memory banks for any information which may be of help - and up comes the full correct 25-card sequence as a memory ! Again, we must rephrase the law of possibility to read : `Guessing correctly 25 times in a row is impossible - *until it happens'.*

This obviously makes nonsense of statistics - but perhaps I am not alone in believing that one can prove anything statistically : one American researcher showed conclusively that, given a bee's weight and wing area, it is statistically and mathematically impossible for it to fly. However, most natural laws function perfectly well in our universe *as long as normal conditions prevail.* Severe problems arise when abnormality creeps in, for example on occasions when we experience altered states of consciousness. We may use artifacts such as tarot cards and crystal balls, which are devices to precipitate a change in one's state of consciousness. They are not always essential : some people slide effortlessly into such states by means of self-hypnotism and self-induced trances. Perversely, many fringe operators in the sleazy world of phoney mind-readers, phrenologists and con men take great exception to the suggestion that they have genuine paranormal powers ! That would be an insult to their profession. . .

4. Synchronicity and Coincidence

The law of causality indicates a one-way relationship between two time-separated events. Where two unrelated events occur simultaneously, we term this `coincidence' and the likelihood of the occurrence becomes a function of statistics. Taking the simple analogy of a two-horse race, one is the winner because, in passing the post first he established a chronological and acausal sequence of events. If the winner deliberately fouls the second rider, the result is a causal one. If, however, both horses pass the post simultaneously, the result is not only a dead-heat but coincidence : conversely, if the dead-heat is a result of one rider `pulling' his mount, the result again becomes a causal one.

But what of the simultaneous occurrence of two absolutely unrelated events ? Simple coincidence ? Or is there some deeper hidden meaning in the event ? The idea that all events are somehow connected by meaning (which, in requiring the presence of a human being to assess such a meaning, is anthropomorphic in context) has surfaced historically in all parts of the world. Specifically, in the writings of Hippocrates, Theophrastus, Philo and Heraclitus. The idea persisted through the Middle Ages in the writings of Paracelcus and Robert Fludd, almost always with a deeply-religious connotation. `Sympathy' between simultaneous but unrelated events, unexplained by causality, was attributable to Divine intervention.

The advent of astrology as a means of establishing interconnection of such events marked a departure from theosophical explanations which persists even today, in a somewhat discredited and semi-humorous form. Devotees essay to demonstrate some fundamental relationship between a human subject and the relative positions of the planets and constellations at the times of birth and subsequent consultation. But the very generalised nature of the so-called `predictions' suggests that, by the law of averages, one or two people per thousand will find the prediction particularly relevant. For amusement I have compiled genuine-looking horoscopes using only a pencil and piece of paper - generalised predictions which will apply to 99.9% of the general population.

Any predictive exercise involving transfer of money must necessarily be suspect; astrology must fall within this category, but I would suggest that genuine astrologists examine the possibility that they may possess some paranormal faculties. Manipulation of charts and construction of horoscopes, like crystal balls, may induce precognition in some degree.

How are we to regard astrology in the light of the Fixed Time Field thesis ? There is, surprisingly, a remote connection : if the progress of all matter through space is channelled into predetermined evènts, the relative positions of heavenly bodies at the time of one's birth must have some significance - *but only in the context of the universe and its contents taken as a whole.* Any single entity or event has equal importance to any other because all form essential parts (no matter how small) of the whole construct, providing a relationship between simultaneous and otherwise unrelated events which we call coincidence. The dictionary calls this a `chance' phenomenon.

Schopenhauer attempts to account for synchronicity using the analogy of a double pattern of events resembling lines of latitude and longitude on a globe. The latter represents the causal connections of related events, the former cross-sections of acausal `meaningful' relationships. The problem lies in accepting that two events, remarkable only for the fact that they occurred simultaneously, may have some mysterious and hidden relationship. In our world at any one time, millions of separate and apparently-unconnected events occur. At the time of writing, the Gulf War has created more problems than it solved; the country no longer wonders what Tony Benn will think of next; main drains are being laid along our road, the milkman has just delivered his silver-tops and my wife is reading the morning mail. Outside my window a juvenile delinquent of a robin is eyeing me speculatively, my computer has gone on the blink and a car has just back-fired nearby. How in the name of sanity can anyone demonstrate a relationship of any kind between all these events ?

Part of the solution is that at any given instant of time, every subatomic particle in the universe occupies a unique and predetermined spatial relationship to all others - one which will not be repeated in the lifetime of this universe. Because of the rigidity of the Fixed Time Field matrix, each particle must occupy that location and no other : it will do so because it has already done so, and the same principle applies to events, past and future. Further, the Bell Experiment confirms that particles possess consciousness or a degree of self-awareness of their own location in the universe, without regard to spatial separation or direction.

Coincidence cannot be a wholly random process involving chance, given the possibility of communication between the particles of matter involved in the two seemingly-unrelated events. Arthur Koestler[41] wrote :

> *`Whether one believes that some highly-improbable coincidences are manifestations of some unknown principle operating beyond physical causality, or are produced by that immortal monkey at the typewriter, is ultimately a matter of inclination and temperament; the point I shall try to make is that no amount of scientific knowledge can help a person decide which of these alternative beliefs is more reasonable or nearer to the truth. I have found to my surprise that the majority of my acquaintances - amongst whom scientists predominate - are inclined towards the first alternative, although some are reluctant to admit it, for fear of ridicule, even to themselves.'*

Koestler suggested that there are certain classifications (forms of `clustering' of events) which are meaningfully related but causally unrelated, but the difficulty as always is to explain this clustering process. My personal concern is this : how far does one take coincidence ? Where does coincidence end, and magic or the uncanny begin ? How can we exclude the presence of other paranormal phenomena ?

Andrew MacKenzie gives a good example : immediately before D-

Day, June 6 1944, at a time of almost obsessive secrecy about the projected landing areas in France, the Daily Telegraph crosswords from June 3 incorporated a number of military codewords : *OVERLORD* for the invasion plan itself, *NEPTUNE* for the Naval Operations plan. *UTAH* and *OMAHA* were two of the American Task Force bridgeheads on the coast and *MULBERRY* was the code-name for the pre-fabricated concrete port to supply the Allied forces on the landing beaches. Such was the immediate concern that MI5 were called in to investigate, but the compilers were quite innocent of deception : Koestler himself believed that such cases could involve telepathy or precognition, or a combination of both.

The *I Ching* - The Book of Changes - is a 4000-year old book which appears to act as a binary computer to indicate which of two current-time decisions will produce the most beneficial future results. Jung, in his introduction to the Bollingen Version, comments :

> *`The Chinese mind as I see it at work in the I Ching seems to be exclusively preoccupied with the chance aspect of events, and what we worship as causality passes almost unnoticed. Whilst the Western mind carefully sifts, weighs, classifies and isolates, the Chinese picture of the moment encompasses everything down to the minutest nonsensical detail, because all of the ingredients make up the observed moment'.*

This appears to confirmation a vital principle of the Fixed Time Field : that at any given instant, every particle and detail of the universe is in exact and immutable relationship spatially and temporally to everything else. Jung continues :

> *`This assumption involves a certain curious principle that I have termed synchronicity, a concept that formulates a point of view directly opposed to that of causality. It is a curious fact that such a gifted and intelligent people as the Chinese has never developed what we call science. Our science, however, is based upon the principle of causality, and causality is considered to be an axiomatic truth. Causal connection is statistically necessary and can therefore be subjected to experiment. Inasmuch as situations are unique and cannot be repeated, experimenting with synchronicity seems to be impossible under ordinary conditions'.*

Synchronicity, as I saw it, was an attempt to read meaning into a book of blank pages, and the motivations behind it are difficult to establish. Whilst Koestler himself seemed powerless to produce a clear definition, both he and Jung clearly envisaged an alternative to causality - that there was some great intrinsic `one-ness' in the universe. The Fixed Time Field thesis may provide a viable basis for synchronicity, in regard to the Time Shunt which does not violate causality. Future self-contained events (which may extend over a considerable length of the duration extension and include both causal action and subsequent event) may together form a single event within a Time loop. But this is possible only in the Fixed Time Field, Space 2, which contains all past and future events, frozen into a static singularity. And if, as David Foster[39] believes, particles have consciousness, Space 2 could be a single intelligent entity - the `one-ness' which Jung and Koestler sensed but could not identify, in the lack of a working Time mechanism.

A number of people in altered states of consciousness may have sensed this singular `one-ness', in every case being overwhelmed by feelings of awe. Others have experienced the brilliant ineffable white light which permeates Space 2, and my personal view is that of a single gestalt entity in Space 2 formed by the merging of many human `self' entities.

The urge to discover the secret of this universal consciousness or gestalt stems from our need for reassurance that our presence in the universe is neither fortuitous nor accidental, but part of some vast Cosmic Plan - our devotion to a father figure who will love and protect us from all evils when the going gets too tough. Those lacking such reassurance may turn to religion as a substitute, relying on faith rather than knowledge of the existence of the ineffable.

Which brings us full circle to the opening of this chapter : the indispensable presence of man in any attempt to read meaning into the universe, coincidence and the viability of the law of causality. Schopenhauer, commenting on his `network' of connections linking causality and coincidence, wrote :

> `- *both kinds of connection exist simultaneously, and the self-same event, although a link in two totally different chains, nevertheless falls into place in both, so that the fate of one individual invariably fits the fate of the other, and each is the hero of his own drama while simultaneously figuring in a drama foreign to him. This is something that surpasses our powers of comprehension* -"

It is all too easy to fall into the trap of developing a theory or postulate from a diagram (such as Schopenhauer's lattice, P. 203) of the basic structure of a concept, which bears little relationship to reality, and thence to develop a line of thought which will take one down some dry and unproductive cul de sac. One must adhere to basics, as did Jung, who found no proof of a fundamental `cause' producing the infinite variety and number of events in the physical universe. Yet Jung ignores the root of all causality - the Big Bang. Why so ? I believe he sensed that the Bang itself was not a singular event but rather one link in a chain of similar events permanently programmed into the Space-Time Void containing the Fixed Time Field. But they are neither the cause of subsequent events nor products of previous causes. The best analogy I can suggest is that of a circular and endless chain of fireworks, each of which detonates the next in line whilst being instantly reprimed for the next cycle. The chain has always been present, and always will be : each explosion is a finite event which will be repeated in the next cycle.

I believe that Schopenhauer and Jung, whilst on the right track, failed to perceive the all-important essential link between Time and the predetermined universe, in which there is no such thing as coincidence and causality has no place or meaning. But many researchers were performing mental gymnastics postulating some interconnecting manifold encompassing unrelated events. Liebnitz, distinguishing between inner and outer bodily events, thought of body and soul as two synchronised clocks. His souls (monads) had no causal connections but were synchronised in a `pre-established harmony' resembling the universal `one-ness' of the Fixed Time Field. Jung protested that this synchronicity must become the absolute rule, for the number of synchronistic events is so small that far from constituting a rule, they must be the exception. So much so that most people would doubt they existed. In self-defence, Jung resorts to statistics : *`We still do not know whether they (synchronistic events) occur so frequently and regularly. . .that we could speak of them as conforming to a law'.*

I have my own ideas. The underlying causes of the paucity of *observed* synchronistic events in the universe (which Jung believed to be a fraction of all possible events so small as to be undefinable) are first, lack of qualified observers; second, the vast number of synchronous events which go unrecognised, and third, the absence of recognition because of our ignorance of the primary postulate of the Fixed Time Field - that *all* Space 1 events are synchronistic, being fixed spatially and temporally, and related to each other in the eternal motionless singularity of Space 2.

Jung, typically, rejected the idea of simple coincidence and tried to explain synchronistic events by an `equivalence of meaning' involving both physical and psychical states - surely an oblique reference to Space 2. Many early philosophers, I am sure, sensed its existence in some queer way. To raise simultaneous events from the category of coincidence into that of acausal inter-relatedness, Jung considered two areas, as described by M.-L von Franz[44]. These were first, the discontinuities of physics and second, the individual mathematical properties of numbers. It is no coincidence that the first involves the eventual recognition of subatomic particle consciousness below the quantum discontinuity (loss of solidity) whilst the second is related to the numerical coding of what may be an Intelligent Universe.

Much research since that time - 1952 - resulted in the emergence of the concept of `orderedness', which assumes prime importance in our coming discussion of the thought processes involved in human intervention in future events. It resulted in the relegation of `causality' to a principle involving `statistical laws with primal probabilities'. The meaning of this becomes clearer when we refer to John Gowan's work in which he discusses the impact of the gradual dissolution of the old physics, which worked on a simplistic model of reality in which individual objects in space could be visualised, even observed. It assumed the existence of an objective reality which existed without the need for a confirming observer.

As always, people began throwing spanners into the works - the Bell Theorem demonstrated superliminal communication between aware particles; others identified the quantum discontinuity below which matter loses its solidity, and the Young twin-slot experiment confirmed subatomic particle consciousness. Gowan points out that reality is perceivable only in normal states of consciousness : no matter how revolutionary the ideas put forward, there must be changes in scientific thought : we must accept that two kinds of physics exist in the universe. The first - old style - obeys the natural laws to which we have become accustomed. The second does not.

Gowan provides a classic example : the particle called a boson obeys Bose Einstein statistics and has a net spin, i.e. a magnetic field and an electric charge. (See P.166 *et seq*). The fermion, on the other hand, obeys Fermi statistics but has no spin. If the sole difference - the spin - is removed from the boson, the particles should be identical - but *with* spin, the boson can occupy two locations at the same time, whilst fermions cannot ! This concept borders on the fantastic, but remember - natural laws do not necessarily apply at quantum level. A wave packet can pass simultaneously through both slits in a Young experiment : the line between reality and magic is very finely drawn.

5. The Effects of Entropy

Our universe features a state of disorder and asymmetry, with an underlying trend towards eventual dissolution. This is called entropy - a state in which the laws of average are in operation. Gowan considers a state of complete order where the law of averages and most other natural laws cease to rule. In physics, under conditions of high order and low entropy (e.g. at quantum level) we encounter the discontinuity beyond which matter is no longer solid but composed of subatomic particles which are rotating electromagnetic fields with tendencies towards probability. We can never be sure of their characteristics. We may be able to identify either mass or spin, but not both, according to Heisenberg's Principle of Uncertainty.

Gowan[22] suggests that discontinuities at which new orders of reality occur, such as the quantum level, involve environments of increasing order and decreasing entropy - for example, in altered states of consciousness. Those who have experienced such a state retain a lasting impression of a strange clarity of vision, purity of sensation, enlargement of senses - in effect, the characteristic disorganised state of mind gives way to a different level of orderliness.

Another example of a state of increasing order involves the behaviour of Helium-3 and Helium-4 at extremely low temperatures approaching absolute zero. Gowan paraphrases the following account from an experiment by Cohen in 1977 :

> `*Whereas most substances cooled to such a degree become solid, Helium 4 shows a lambda-type phase transition to another liquid state which has super-fluid qualities.'* (Liquid helium is the only known substance which has this quality, defined as retaining very low viscosity , high thermal conductivity and high capilliary etc, at extremely low temperatures). `*If the Helium 3 isotope is present, the homogenous mixture becomes unstable and separates into two parts with a meniscus* (a surface interface, a discontinuity caused by surface tension). *This peculiar behaviour indicates that at critical low temperature levels there is an abrupt change to a different set of laws, the quantum macroscopic. What is happening here is a quantum discontinuity of the type normally found in subatomic particles, but applied to the full-size (macroscopic) level.*

Now, in a system almost wholly entropic and lacking order, the introduction of a small degree of order may be insufficient to go round the whole system satisfactorily, to reduce the entropy level. As a result, the system divides into two domains; one contains all the order in the system (topped up by residual entropy) whilst the other half of the system is in total disorder. Conversely, in a near-perfect order system in which the level of entropy drops to a very low state, the separation occurs at the same discontinuity level. Gowan finds considerable equivalence with the changes that take place in the human brain in altered states of consciousness. He writes :

> `*The process I believe we are seeing is one of slow but inexorable dissolution of the barriers erected by the old science : throughout my research I have been amazed to find that there is an underlying stratum of comparability between so many of the recent discoveries, and there has been a great deal of surprising confirmation of assumptions that, not too many years ago, were considered as fantastic and presumptous. It is true that it requires a vast amount of evidence to sway the beliefs of the more conservative scientists and physicists, particularly in relation to statistics.'*

Translated, this means that new discoveries in the paranormal are making scientists think again. As Gooch[42] suggests, it may be a mistake to use statistics as a basis of argument because synchronicity (and the Fixed Time Field - Auth.) makes nonsense of statistics. How can one calculate the odds against a particular event happening when, in fact, every event of cosmic significance is predetermined ? The patterns of chance are variable only by human intervention, and Gooch concurs to a degree when he says that it is likely that the statistical approach is wholly irrelevant, in terms of the totally different characteristics of the conscious and subconscious minds. As Gowan rightly suggests, in areas beyond the discontinuities (and we have identified quite a few) known natural laws do not obtain, impossibility becomes a redundant term. Magic becomes not only possible but essential in the worlds beyond the discontinuities. In such a context, statistics are meaningless.

Jung appeared to be aware of this. His approach to synchronicity was, in essence, a suggestion that the odds against a particular event happening by chance are so astronomically high that one might be obliged to concede that something other than chance is at work ! Gooch says rightly that this is the approach used by Rhine and others, and is standard practice in most psychological research.

It seems possible, even probable, that we have regarded the universe from a distorted viewpoint : our acceptance of all we see as total reality has become habitual and misleading because our physical senses are as imperfect and useless beyond the discontinuity threshold, as they are limited in the material world. We see only a minute proportion of the vast spectra of radiations which permeate space; our limited world view has prevented recognition of the relationships, eternally locked into Space-Time by the Fixed Time Field, between all material objects and events.

There are some sighted men in the land of the blind. Kant[43] asserted that the outer world comprises the matter of which we are sensorily aware, but our minds assess that input in terms of Space and Time, constructing the concepts by which we understand them.

Throughout history, mankind has sensed the eternal one-ness, the integral relationships between all sensate and non-sensate objects in the universe - all fundamental aspects of the Fixed Time Field. It is impossible to exaggerate the effect on a human mind of even a hint of the Grand Design, and we arrive finally at the inevitable conclusion that this vast construct could not possibly have come into existence by chance alone.

6. Pressure in the Probability Field

I come now to the Probability Field embodied in the Fixed Time Field, which ensures that events follow as closely as possible the Probability Geodesic, the course of maximum probability - including even trivial events resulting from the day-to-day routine decisions we make (Fig. 27). In certain cases the specific event-version is selected by a deliberate decision of the subject himself, over-riding the Probability Geodesic, but this infers that the Probability Field must incorporate a `Possibility Limitation' on the form an event may take. In Fig. 28, for example, some event versions are limited by probability, others by possibility, given our set of natural laws.

In Chapter 4, describing the Time Shunt as a cause of inspiration, we encountered authors who refused categorically to alter their MS in any major respect - for no better reason, they say, than *`It has to be that way'.*

They seem to be under some pressure to ensure that their published work adheres strictly to the original format they envisaged : in some cases, it seems as if the characters in the book are actively dictating the course of events in the book. They take on a life of their own. Here is an example :

Thackeray: *When writing `The Newcombes' he was asked by friends to allow two of the characters, Clive and Ethel, to marry. He replied that the characters, once created, "led" him and that he could not tell the events that waited on Clive and Ethel. Next day, asked if he had slept well, Thackeray replied irritably : "With Colonel Newcombe making a fool of himself as he has done. . . ?" "But why did you let him ?" "Oh," the writer replied, "it was in him to do it. He must. . ."*

I can advance two viable explanations. First, it is a classic example of a Time Shunt : Thackeray knew (or at least sensed) that the story would develop this way - because he had already `seen' it, up there in Future Time. It was not so much that Colonel Newcombe `must do it' - he *had* done it ! Of other characters, Thackeray says "I don't control my characters - I am in their hands and they take me where they please." And if we place ourselves in his position, when asked to modify a story significantly, we perceive the traumatic effect the request may have. A writer is always confident in his own mind that a book will be published in the format he has conceived, by whatever means, but fears that any drastic changes may jeopardise its potential success. It is a feeling every author experiences.

Second, this is a typical result of the Probability Field in action, ensuring that events correspond to the Probability Geodesic. It exerts pressure on the originator to adhere to the original format, even if no logical reason can be put forward, whilst preventing impossible things from happening. Oddly, the pressure is experienced by ordinary people, as well as creative thinkers, in the form of a strange and compulsive urge. It occurs even during trivial day-to-day activities - the need to ensure somehow that everything is `just right'. Papers being sorted must be in the correct order of selection, even if unnumbered : walking feet are directed to miss all cracks in pavements. Where an ornament is disturbed, we feel a compulsion to ensure that it is replaced in precisely the same position.

Why do we do this ? The immediate answer is that we don't : most well-adjusted people shrug off the feeling and tell themselves not to be so foolish. People may take strenuous care not to walk beneath ladders or say `rabbits' in a theatre, and whilst we call this `superstition', an irrational belief with regard to the unknown, I believe we are sensing pressure from the Probability Field - that to adhere to the Probability Geodesic, we must take action to preserve the *status quo*, to ensure that the even tenor of events is undisturbed. Our innate fear of the unknown is an inner conviction that random changes in the sequence of events will divert us into life-paths containing nameless dangers or misfortunes.

If we ask whence such feelings originate, there is only one answer : in the subconscious mind - and since they are associated with future events, the source must be our `self', the scanning entity in Space 2. Unfortunately, individuals unable to rationalise the sensation may develop serious obsessions : they spend endless hours polishing already shining furniture *to get it into the state they think it should be*, moving ornaments again and again to find the precise position their mind tells them is essential if the sky is not to fall on their heads. There are people so sensitive that they know instantly, on re-entering a room, that some artifact has been moved even a millimetre out of position. Others of my personal acquaintance spend their first half-hour every day ceaselessly arranging the items on their desks to the precise position their obsession demands, whilst others are absorbed in ensuring that they don the right sock before the left, that they leave for work at exactly the same time each morning, find the same seat in the train and read the newspapers in the same order every day.

I suspected that they may be equipped (or cursed) with an ability to sense the slightest variation in the Probability Field, the most minute diversion from the Probability Geodesic without understanding it - and we fear the unknown instinctively. This ability is almost certainly an example of the intervention process described on P. 176, but at significantly higher intensity.

7. A Paradigm of Probability

I believe I have succeeded in making a *prima facæ* case for the existence of the Probability Field and Geodesic (possibly different aspects of the same phenomenon) within the Fixed Time Field - fields which ensure that the most probable random version of an event will occur, but strictly within the bounds of possibility laid down by our known natural laws at this time. Yet some apparently impossible events do slip through. The British Ambassador to Austria, Benjamin Bathurst, stopped his coach at a quiet Bavarian country inn for refreshments, disembarked and walked round the front of the team of horses to reach the inn. This in broad daylight, before many witnesses : yet Bathurst never reappeared on the other side of the leading horses, and was never seen again. The *Marie Celeste* is another famous case, and there have been human disappearances which cannot be explained, as Michael Harrison[44] relates.

In September 1880 American farmer David Lang walked out into his 40-acre field in broad daylight, watched by four or five other people. Halfway across the section, he vanished without trace before their eyes. Conversely, men sometimes `emerge' from nowhere - on January 6 1914 a naked man appeared suddenly in the High Street at Chatham in Kent, as if out of thin air and in full view of people standing nearby. He was confused, afraid and spoke some unknown language. Colin Wilson in his

`*Encyclopædia of Unsolved Mysteries*' relates the story of Kaspar Hauser, a youth who appeared from nowhere in the Unschlitt Square in Nüremberg, Germany, on May 20 1828.

Some examples have undoubtedly been exaggerated, but there is an underlying trend : `*The impossible is possible - in certain circumstances*'. A man named Ted Serios can `will' pictures to appear on Polaroid-type film without exposure. Australian aborigines describe events happening hundreds of miles away. There are people who can control by force of will alone their heart rate, blood pressure and alpha brain rhythms. Others have produced stigmata, simulacrums of the wounds of the Crucifixion, whilst at religious celebrations in the remote mountains of Sri Lanka at Kataragama, men and women walk unharmed across beds of glowing coals. And in quiet English country villages, unobstrusive men in tweed clothes locate water a hundred feet underground with no other aid than a forked hazel branch.

I believe we see here a hitherto unsuspected power of the human mind to `bend' the Probability Field a little, allowing magic to work its will. In our case of the wire-walker who may have fallen from the rope, landed unhurt and drifted back up onto the wire, he would be doing no more than St. Thomas of Agostino, who levitated himself and a huge timber cross too heavy for three other monks to lift, depositing it upright in the hole provided. Lastly, we may have a logical explanation for the remarkable phenomenon of the Chinese Book of Changes.

10. The *I Ching*

This ancient book, compiled some 4000 years ago, contains 64 sections, each dealing with common human situations in codified texts. Each section is indexed, named and numbered to represent one of 64 hexagrams - symbols consisting of six short parallel horizontal lines in a stack : here are some examples :

3. *Chun*	16. *Yü*	37. *Chia Jên*
䷂	䷏	䷤

Some lines are broken, others unbroken, forming 64 unique symbols, each associated with a text offering advice to the `operator' (person consulting the *I Ching*). Astonishingly, in some queer way it makes a direct connection between the problem facing the operator and the hexagram containing the advice he seeks. The process begins with the operator, who is usually faced with a two-way choice which will affect later life significantly. Any present-time decision is bound to have repercussions in later events - that is the way we think of causality, and the magnitude of these secondary effects depends upon the importance or triviality of the problem. For example, a Chinese businessman may debate taking an earlier or later train into Beijing. In one variation, if he takes the later train he will merely be late for an appointment, but in another, the earlier train may be involved in an accident. The *I Ching* in some strange way perceives the danger and recommends the operator to take the later train. But most consultations involve minor choices : which of two jobs to accept, which house to buy, which investment to make - all these are decisions with either beneficial or inimical results to the operator in future time.

There has been intense controversy over the way the *I Ching* functions, but the general aspects are widely recognised. First, it seems to sense the mental state of the operator, and incredibly, it will flatly refuse to cooperate with a flippant insincere operator - who will be referred to some totally irrelevant hexagram. Second, there is at the time of consultation an instantaneous but extremely close relationship between the Book, the operator's mind and the nature of the problem, which combine in a momentary gestalt with the whole universe - the `one-ness' we have described at some length. Many attempts have been made to explain this remarkable phenomenon, but in my personal view the operator (who is totally convinced of the Book's magical powers) is subjected to an altered state of consciousness in which he himself guides the course of the consultation. But more of that in a moment.

Millennia ago, an operator `made contact' with the *I Ching* by throwing a handful of yarrow-plant stalks on the ground. By studying the pattern they made, he was able to identify one of the 64 hexagrams and find in the text the answer to his problem. Now we use a simpler method : three coins are thrown at random, each marked with a figure `2' on one side and a `3' on the obverse. A little thought will show that only a limited number of numerical totals are possible :

$$2+2+2=6$$
$$2+2+3=7$$
$$2+3+3=8$$
$$3+3+3=9$$

Each numerical total identifies a variety of horizontal line : for example, 7 produces a positive and stationary (unbroken) line and 8 is a negative moving (broken) line. By throwing the coins six times the operator obtains the horizontal lines of the hexagram, identifies it from the chart in the *I Ching* and turns to the appropriate page of text. There he will find the advice he seeks in making his decision. The attitude in which the procedure is approached is of crucial importance, as I said earlier. The *I Ching* is still in use in China and many Eastern lands, and it is not unusual to find an operator sitting on his stool in the market or main street with his bowl of yarrow stalks, waiting for customers. But a confirmed enthusiast with his own copy begins by finding a quiet secluded spot where he can sit and reflect on the problem facing him. Before him is the *I Ching* and three coins. Presently, he throws the coins six times, reads each numerical total and constructs his hexagram.

At the moment of consultation he is part of a unique gestalt, a perceptual pattern or structure possessing qualities as a whole that cannot be described merely as a sum of its parts. It occurs (in a singular moment of time that cannot be repeated) within his subconscious mind and self, which has access to the infinite one-ness of Space 2, containing all past and future events. He is in an altered state of consciousness in which he is at one with the universe, omnisciently aware of the future events in which he is interested.

From this point the reader may find the process incredible, but if after seeing the evidence he accepts the existence of the Fixed Time Field, he may be obliged to believe in the *I Ching*, however reluctantly. The operator's self, having identified the most beneficial result in Time 2 future, based upon some specific decision he will make at this time, must now identify the *I Ching* text which will point to that decision. This in turn requires the self to identify in the near future the specific hexagram indicating the appropriate text. All that remains is to *ensure that the operator will throw the coins to produce the required numerical totals*, and this is the most difficult part for the reader - not the physical act itself, but believing this entire process really happens.

The mind/self entity uses the power of psychokinesis to manipulate the fall of the coins to produce the desired result.

\+ + +

The point I make here is that the operator himself, albeit quite unwittingly, provides the operating mechanism, but his conscious mind knows nothing of this. He is aware only that whilst thinking very hard about his problem, he is throwing the coins six times and constructing his hexagram. The role of the *I Ching* is that of a supporting artifact precipitating the altered state of consciousness in his subconscious mind, allowing his self to embark on its quest in Space 2 for the information he desires.

There remains only the vexed question of psychokinetic force employed to influence the fall of the coins. The case history for the phenomenon is very strong and supported by much documentary, photographic, film and video evidence which the reader will find in various sources. That the *I Ching* works, there can be no doubt, but we in the west find it extremely difficult to accept. Moreover, the operator's proficiency increases with frequent use, and some of the old men sitting on the street corners of Shanghai and Beijing have highly-developed paranormal abilities. They dip into the future to obtain invaluable information, simply to earn a living. The results can be startling at times : when my best-selling novel *DOWN TO A SUNLESS SEA* was published in 1981, I was interviewed at home by a BBC TV reporter who brought his wife with him. The conversation got round to the *I Ching* and the reporter was openly sceptical; I offered to demonstrate, using them as the subject, and the question I asked the *I Ching* was simple. *Was it going to be a happy year for the couple ?* I threw the coins, found the hexagram and read the text. "This *is* going to be a good year," I told them. "Beginning with the birth of your first child— "

The reporter laughed outright. "That's impossible. Isn't it, darling ?" he asked his wife. She had gone quite pale and looked at me very hard. "But it's true," she said. "I only got the test results myself yesterday. I was going to tell you at dinner this evening. . ."

\+ + +

We have come a long way since my first faltering steps in identifying duration as the first of the three Space 2 dimensions. From that emerged the concept of the Fixed Time Field gravitic lattice locking all duration-extensions into predetermined courses, each containing the solid realised events in the past which follow the travelling Present Moment discontinuity, and the amorphous variable future events in wave-function mode ahead of the PM. We have shown how the Probability Field ensures that events, whenever possible, follow the Probability Geodesic, and remain within the bounds of possibility in accordance with natural laws. Those laws may be modified by the influence of Time, gravity and the human mind. I have shown how the Fixed Time Field accommodates the functions of probability, possibility and destiny, introducing to mankind the proposition that he is in control of his own destiny - but not to the extent we would like. Whilst trivial decisions have little or no effect on subsequent events, mankind has the power not only to observe such future events but to influence, by power of will, the event version which will achieve reality.

Most important, we perceive with justifiable pride and satisfaction that *homo sapiens* does have a meaningful place in the universe. However it came into existence in its awesome complexity, splendour and magnificence, it would have no meaning or purpose in existing, if there was no sentient entity with the intelligence to observe and appreciate it. In his own way, mankind occupies a place in the celestial mechanism equally important as the greatest flaming star or the deepest black hole in the universe. The cosmos exists because we see that it exists : if a tree falls in a remote isolated forest with no life forms within twenty miles, is there a sound of impact ?

The truth is that no event is complete without all three of its elements : cause, result and observation of that result, and the universe would be incomplete without sentient races such as humanity. We do have our place in the cosmos - earned through a million years of evolution. That place may resemble nothing so much as a kindergarten, but eventually we shall make second and higher grades, and in the fullness of Time graduate with honours to take our place in Galactic society.

If, that is, we come to our senses in time. . .

\+ + +

SUMMATION

1. We take minor decisions randomly, habitually, without deliberation, and persist in doing so, even in important decisions.

2. Future events, as a result, follow a random path which is consistent with the Probability Geodesic - the track of the most-probable event versions. Events, therefore, may be beneficficial or inimical, which we ascribe to good or bad luck, and not to our lack of foresight.

3. Those who consider all decisions carefully are called wise - but are simply being careful.

4. Future events coalesce into reality when the wave-function indeterminacy ahead of the Present Moment collapses either at random (see 2 above) when the PM discontinuity arrives, or in a specific selection process of the human will.

5. The Probability Field ahead of the PM influences events to occur in line with the Probability Geodesic whilst restraining them within the bounds of possibility.

6. This process is manifest in many areas, including first, the reluctance of creative writers to alter their work in any way and second, an obsessive impulse to maintain the status quo and adhere to the Probability Geodesic experienced by people abnormally sensitive to the Restraining Field.

7. Human intervention in future events takes the form of a Time Shunt. The self previews the result versions of a Present Moment choice, informs the conscious mind of the need for action. In an altered state of consciousness, the self collapses the wave-function Probability Field to achieve the future-time result required.

8. There is no such thing as coincidence. Since all events - past and future - exist simultaneously and eternally within the Fixed Time Field, there is a permanent and meaningful relationship between all events.

9. Synchronicity is another way of describing this universal `one-ness'.

10. The *I Ching* works on a Time Shunt basis in which the operator in an altered state of consciousness throws coins to determine which two-

way choice will prove to be the most beneficial. The appropriate action is indicated by psychokinetic manipulation of the coins.

11. An altered state of consciousness creates a state of total order and zero entropy in which natural laws no longer rule.

12. There can be no doubt that mankind occupies an important place in this universe as part of the Great Gestalt and the `one-ness' created by the FTF, the co-existent universe of Space 2.

The final part of the jigsaw puzzle of destiny will be found in the swirling depths of the electromagnetic fields and electrochemical processes by means of which we think. The final revelations will, I believe, substantiate for all time the viability of the Fixed Time Field theory.

\+ + +

CHAPTER EIGHT

MIND AND CONSCIOUSNESS

`Today there is a wide measure of agreement. . .that the stream of knowledge is heading towards a non-mechanical reality; the universe begins to look more like a great thought than a great machine. Mind no longer appears as an accidental intruder into the realm of matter : we are beginning to suspect that we ought rather to hail it as creator and governor of the realm of matter. . .'

Sir James Hopwood Jeans 1877-1946

`Remembrance and reflections, how allied
What thin partitions sense from thought divide. . .'

Alexander Pope 1688-1744

`Our normal waking consciousness. . . is but one special sort of consciousness, while all about it, parted from it by the flimsiest of screens, there lies potential forms of consciousness entirely different.'

William James 1842-1910

`Every soul comes into this world strengthened by the victories or weakened by the defeats of its previous life. Its place of honour in this world as a vessel appointed to honour or dishonour is determined by its previous merits or demerits. Its work in this world determines its place in the world which is to follow this. . .'

Origen Theologian 185-284 AD

`Confusion ? There are times when my mind is like a radio operators' convention - everyone on `transmit' and nobody on `receive' -'

Wilbur Wright 1919-199-

CONTENTS

1. The World View of Consciousness
2. The Brain
3. The Communication Process
4. Mind - the Great Enigma
5. The Conscious State
6. The Subconscious State
7. Communication Glitches
8. The Quantum Self
9. The Bose Einstein Condensate
10. Intelligence in Electromagnetic Fields
11. The Mind/Time Interface

GENERAL SUMMATION

8

MIND AND CONSCIOUSNESS

1. The World View of Consciousness.

Serious investigation into human personality and thought processes did not gain momentum until the 19th century, when consciousness was first recognised as a developed facility serving not only as a responsible channel for pain, inconvenience and discomfort, but also as a survival aid; as such, it was no less important than sight, smell and other senses. At an early evolutionary stage (within the last half-million years) man found that the exercise of his growing powers of concentration, contemplation and judgement was an end to itself. Mentation, which was hitherto a painful process, was now a self-rewarding form of activity requiring no artifacts, specific locations or stimulation, an activity in which he could indulge at any time, and more often than not resulted in a sense of inner achievement. But what *is* consciousness ?

Collins' English dictionary :

> `*Conscious - denoting or relating to a part of the human mind that is aware of a person's self, environment and mental activity. . .that determines his choices of action*'.

Well, at first sight that seems reasonable but somewhat incomplete : the dictionary gives us more :

`The conscious is only a small part of the mind'.

The mind ? Whatever is that ? Back to Collins :

`Mind is the entity in an individual responsible for thought, feelings and speech - Intelligence or the intellect - Recollection or remembrance - The faculty of original or creative thought - Imagination'.

But is mind an `entity' - or a process ? The problem intensifies : we are more confused than ever, faced with the task of identifying the Space 2 scanning entity. And we must be extremely careful in regard to definition. Stan Gooch [12] suggests that no definition is necessary : by our very awareness we know exactly what consciousness means to ourselves (even if we find it difficult to describe it to others). But this is misleading in context - ask anyone who has tried to describe colours to a colour-blind person. We know that a fruit cake is a solid confection eaten at tea time - but try explaining that to an alien who has landed on your front lawn ! Two complications arise in defining consciousness : first, there are almost as many definitions as researchers, and second, each aspect of consciousness requires scrupulous assessment and consideration. There is no way to simplify that situation and we must deal with each problem as it occurs, but let us assume temporarily that consciousness is a state of mind, leaving the definition of the `self' until it becomes necessary.

In this chapter, I quote extensively the work of Danah Zohar[15] who maintains that conscious human beings are the natural bridge between the everyday world and the world of quantum physics - that consciousness, like matter itself, emerges from the world of quantum events. Crucially, she suggests : *`the foundation of reality itself is an unfixed indeterminate maze of probabilities'* - which describes precisely the wave-function state ahead of the travelling Present Moment. Further, Danah asks, at what stage, and why, does one of Nature's manifold possibilities fix itself in the world of `real things' ?

I have shown that the transition occurs at the Present Moment discontinuity, when the Probability Field wave-function collapses (normally at random and in line with the Probability Geodesic). Zohar answers her question with an explanation of what happens when an electron makes a transition from one energy state to another (one of Planck's `lumps'). It does so in a completely random and spontaneous way - a matter of chance. *`Things can happen in any direction, offering a reason for the apparent time reversal sometimes seen at quantum level'.* Dealing with particle consciousness, Zohar writes : *`When an electron in the guise of a probability wave intends to move from one orbit to another. . .it displays a kind of eerie omnipresence in many orbits'.* Relating that statement to the Fixed Time Field, we can go a stage further : if the electron, as Zohar suggests, `decides' to shift orbits and thereby change the order of probability, I see no reason why the human mind/self (electromagnetic and electrochemical in nature) cannot trigger this change in orbit. This is a positive step towards explaining man's ability to influence future events. How may we define this mind/particle relationship ?

Zohar continues :

> `*Quantum physics promises to transform our notions of relationship. Both the concept of* "being" *as an indeterminate wave-function-particle dualism and a concept of* "movement" *which rests on virtual transitions* (tentative temporary explorations of different orbits by an electron. Auth.) *presage a revolution in our perception of how things relate. Things and events once conceived of as separate, parted in both space and time, are seen by the quantum theorist as so integrally linked that their bond mocks the reality of both space and time. They behave instead as multiple aspects of some larger whole, their "individual" existences deriving both their definition and their meaning from that whole'.*
>
> `*The new quantum mechanical notion of relationship follows as a direct consequence of the wave/particle dualism and the tendency of a* "matter-wave" (or probability wave - Auth.) *to behave as though it were smeared out all over space and time.* (i.e. ahead of the Present Moment - Auth.) *It follows. . .that the once ghostly notion of* `action at a distance', *where one body can influence another instantaneously, despite there being no apparent exchange of force or energy is, for the quantum scientist, a fact of everyday reality — a fact so alien to the whole framework of space and time that it remains one of the greatest conceptual challenges raised by quantum theory.'*

Quite clearly Danah Zohar has established a relationship between the human mind and the `wave/particle dualism' of subatomic particles, superliminal inter-particle communication and the Probability Field : it is in the mind/self itself that we will find our ultimate answers.

2. The Brain (Fig. 29)

The locus of all mentation, the human brain resembles nothing so much as a wrinkled cauliflower divided into two hemispheres by a deep central front-to-rear vent. They are connected by a bundle of nerves and tissue, the *corpus callosum* which we encountered in our discussion of dreams. Whilst there is no requirement to become involved in a detailed physiological description of the brain's structure, it is important to understand the main areas of brain activity and the locations of specific system-processes. The brain is also partitioned into front and rear halves, the four

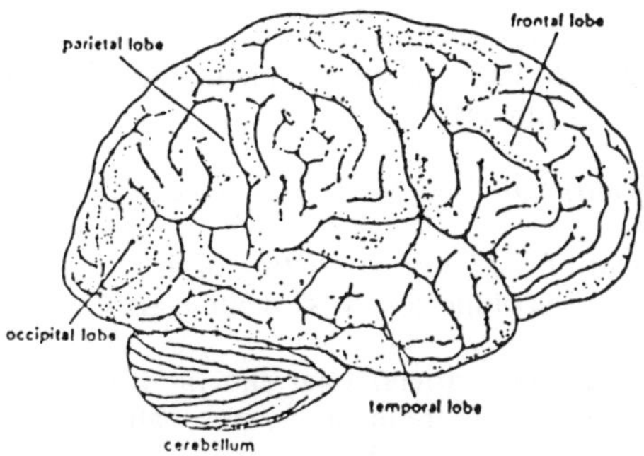

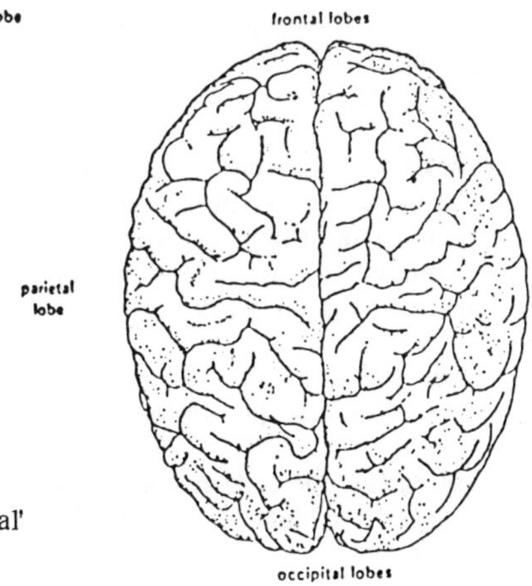

From Gooch : `The Paranormal'

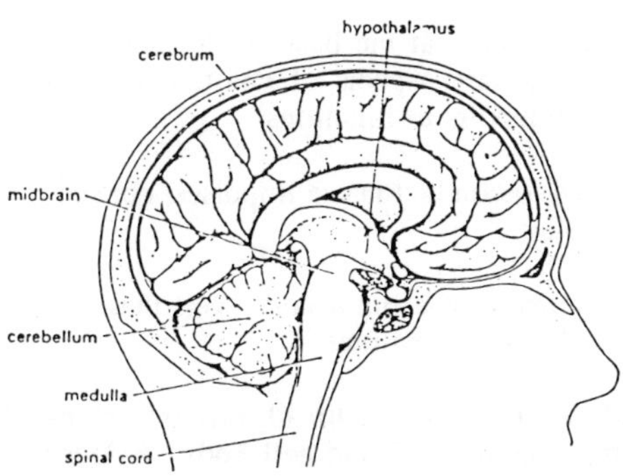

Fig. 29

The Human Brain

lobes being the frontal, temporal, occipital and parietal. Here are some definitions.

Brain Stem Links the spinal column to the thalamus/hypothalamus area - usually called the midbrain or `old brain', since it contains the primitive function controls : digestion, breathing etc.

Cerebrum The anterior (forward) part of the brain considered as a whole.

Cerebral Cortex The top layer of the brain, consisting of a 3 mm thick layer of `grey matter', whilst the rest of the cortex is `white matter'.

Temporal Lobe Lies underneath the parietal lobe and in front of the occipital lobe. Its main sensory functions are memory, personality, vision, hearing and social behaviour, but these are not limited to any specific area - there is a complex neural network linking all areas of the brain.

Frontal Lobe That area of the cortex located in front of the central sulcus, which is a deep groove in the folds of the cortex. It has little or no connection with the intelligence level of the brain : patients with their frontal lobes removed as a treatment for epilepsy suffer no deterioration in their IQ, but some personality defects commonly result.

Occipital Lobe The posterior or after-portion of each cerebral hemisphere, dealing with the interpretation of visual sensory inputs.

Parietal Lobe The side-portion of each cerebral hemisphere concerned with interpreting data input via touch, temperature, taste and muscular movement.

Hypothalamus A neural control centre at the base of the brain, dealing with various function including certain aspects of emotional behaviour, hunger, thirst, satiety and other autonomous functions.

Neuron A brain cell specialised to conduct nerve impulses, consisting of a cell body, an axon and dendrites.

Axon The long thread-like extension of a brain nerve cell that conducts nerve impulses *from* the cell body. A `transmitter'.

Dendrite Any of the multiple short branched thread-like extensions of a nerve cell, which conduct impulses *towards* the cell body. A `receiver'. See Fig.30.

Synapse The point at which a nerve impulse is relayed from the terminal point of an axon to the dendrites of an adjacent neuron.

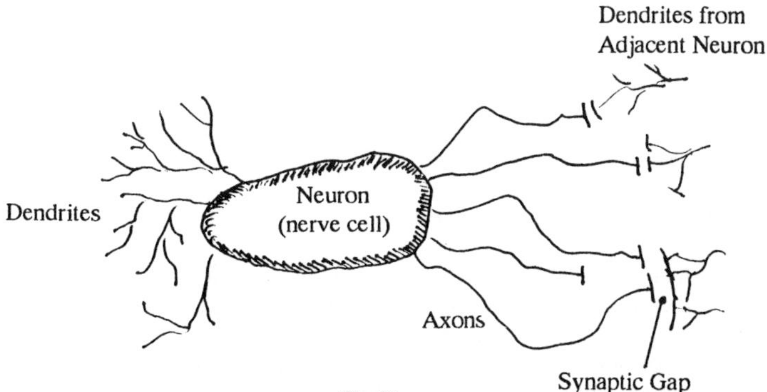

Fig. 30

A Neuron (diagrammatic only)

Midbrain or Mesencephalon Lies deep beneath the cortex between the forebrain and hindbrain, handling responses to sight and sound, plus some control of sleeping and waking. It includes the

Cerebellum Situated in human beings between the medulla oblongata and the cerebrum, it is in effect a second mini-brain with two lateral hemispheres joined by a thick band of fibres. It is the dominant part of the brain, associated with intellectual function, emotion and personality.

Medulla Oblongata The lower stalk-like section of the brain, continuous with the spinal column. It incorporates control centres for the heart and lungs.

The sheer magnitude of the neuron network of the brain is staggering. There are over ten billion neurons in the cortex alone - a hundred billion if one includes the interior of the brain. The network, which at birth is relatively small, simple and uncomplicated, grows and expands over the years, eventually resembling a map of an entire country depicting every type of communication system including roads, railways, canals, streets, alleyways, footpaths, telephone and telegraph wires, drains, sewers and water supplies. The number of alternative transmission routes is beyond computation, possibly approaching one of the larger prime numbers, such as the number of electrons in the universe. This degree of complexity has defeated all recent attempts to build a computer which thinks like a human being. Indeed, one would have to link together millions of the largest and fastest machines in order to simulate even one working system in the human brain.

Further, many brain functions are duplicated in various cortical regions, providing numerous alternate pathways by which impulses can travel from one point to another. This duplication provides a permanent defence against the continual loss of cells (some 100,000 brain cells die each day from about the age of 18 and are not replaced) ensuring that we remain capable of normal thought far into old age. If one pathway is lost, impulses can use alternative routes without interruption to the cerebral functions.

3. The Communication Process

Most cells have a single large axon extension, ending in terminal fibres, a clump of smaller branches rather like a sea anemone. The branch tips send out electrical impulses to other cells or neurons, and each cell has a set of dendrites, which receive incoming impulses; the transmitters and receivers are separated by synaptic clefts or gaps. The transmission process is extremely complicated : an impulse reaching the axon tip releases from surrounding tissue a burst of molecules from a range of 20 to 30 transmitter substances including norepinephrine and/or dopamine, which bridge the synaptic gap to the nearby dendrite and either dampen or excite activity in the second neuron - which then either fires its own impulse from its axons, or remains inactive, depending on the nature of the sum total of countless incoming signals at the synapses connecting it with other neurons. Not all synapses are chemically-operated, nor is the axon-dendrite/dendrite-axon rule inviolable. Some wholly electrical synapses have been found, as well as axon-to-axon and dendrite-to-dendrite connections.

After the linkage ceases to exist, microseconds after firing, the bridging chemicals are either absorbed by adjoining cells or chemically destroyed as the result of an automatic recycling process - and all this goes on hundreds of times each second ! Each of the millions of neurons involved in a particular transmission mode goes through this same cycle continuously, accounting in part for the speed of thought itself.

Now, this is a simple electrochemical manufacturing and recycling system. The operating power supply is produced by chemical processes or bled off from the electromagnetic fields in each particle of the brain tissue, but this does not tell us how the selectivity process itself works. How and from where comes the directives to individual axons and dendrites to either pass on or suppress a specific message impulse ? This is the basic fundamental thought-process which produces certain end-results : the assessment and analysis of data inputs from the senses.

I believe that the whole mentation system generates its own self-awareness - it becomes the conscious mind which, in the newly-born child, is rudimentary : confined to an awareness of light and darkness, noise and quiet, hunger and satiety. Some weeks pass before the child makes the vital link with the outside world, when sensory inputs are recognised and the eyes watch a swinging toy or react to a rattle. Initially there is only hunger and thirst, alternating light and dark, total concentration within the self. But soon the `I' is joined by `it' - something external is seen, heard or felt : learning begins, which is after all merely a process of incorporating the exterior environment into the interior memory.

There is as yet no `guiding spirit', no decision-making entity capable of assessing the images produced by the child's mind : it is ruled by instinct and gene/hormone based natural urges : thirst, hunger and sleep. But after a year, the personality begins to evolve, partly from inherited genes and partly from reaction to external events. This seems to coincide with the development of language and communication. From the moment a parent says "Don't do that !" and the import is understood, if not the language, the reasoning process begins, and the child perceives two options : to obey or refuse. It has no concept of causality - or what will happen if it refuses to obey - but a light slap on the wrist brings home the truth ! To obey seems good, to refuse brings pain. Typically, a child may not accept this logic at first, refusing or misbehaving repeatedly, pushing its luck too far in what a parent may see as wilful disobedience. Whilst there is much modern pressure and lobbying to make the corporal chastisement of children illegal, it seems to me that when a child is too young to understand logical argument or verbal admonition, only a slap will bring the lesson home. This is an absolute dictum in the animal world - and extremely effective, with no after-effects.

The thinking mind is initially a creature of impulse, governed by basic urges and reactions to outside stimuli : there is no controlling self or personality, and even body movements are erratic, uncontrollable. But somewhere along the line a decision-making entity gradually asserts itself, and cries out for identification. Is it merely a secondary stage of development in which the mind's reasoning powers gain control ? Is the mind merely an extension of the sensory systems, provided to analyse the input data ? Is the mind, in fact, another name for the `self' ?

The mind develops in stages, requiring a brain of sufficient complexity and size to generate the minimum neural network for survival and growth. The network is small and undeveloped in children, and in the mind of prehistoric man. The average human brain capacity developed as follows :

20 million BC	Dryopithecus/Ramapithecus	Monkey sized.
3 million BC	Australopithecine Hominids	500 cc
2 million BC	Homo Habilis	750 cc
1.5 million BC	Homo Erectus	1400 cc
40,000 BC	Homo Sapiens	1500 cc

The brain is only about 2% of total body weight but consumes more than 20% of the oxygen and glucose (a major energy source in human metabolism) carried by the blood. If the blood supply to the brain is interrupted for more than a minute or two, irreversible cell damage occurs, resulting in a stroke.

2. Memory

The precise mechanism of memory is far from being finally established. It is commonly believed to be based on a complex network of brain neurons storing information, accessed via associated semantic and comparative links working on category identification.

The memory operates fundamentally on comparisons. If the eye observes an apple on a dish, the mind is presented with a facsimile view on the thought background screen, based on incoming electrochemical signals from the optic nerve. The mind notes the `object/plate/food ?' connection, categorizes the object as food but not meat, fowl, fish or cereal : the remaining category is fruit. Next, it extracts from memory images of various fruits and compares : `Pear ?' No, wrong shape. `Orange ?' No, wrong colour. `Banana ?' No - wrong shape *and* colour ! Until the apple image matches with the observed object. All this, of course, in milliseconds. The comparison process depends wholly on the availability of and access to a similar object-image.

But consider the question of memory storage : with all memories including images stored permanently in the immutable solid-state `Past' of the human duration-extension, accessible to the self in Space 2 which is capable of instantaneous probing, there is a positive access channel to all stored information, connected directly to the mind : experiments under hypnosis show that memories are stored either shallowly for immediate fast access, or deeply if the mind considers them unimportant. But apparently, we never forget anything, and if at times our conscious mind fails to produce the image we want, the subconscious continues the search and the data eventually pops up in our minds unbidden. I see this as a further indication of a Space 2 deep-probe mechanism, perhaps as a back-up.

Brain size and intelligence are directly linked. As he developed, the mind of prehistoric man generated the minimum cortical capacity necessary for intelligence and self-awareness. There seems to be no single memory storage location in the brain. Instead, memories, logically, are distributed in all areas of the brain, for every fact, article or event will have connections with similar items. Certain functions occur within finite areas of the brain - for example, language-memory is stored in Broca's Area and Wernicke's Area. The distance between areas is irrelevant - given the number and complexity of synaptic connections there is instant availability and access to any stored memory. The human brain has an apparently inexhaustible reservoir of memories, stored data accessible to the mind in the comparing/analysing mode.

But who or what directs the conscious mind to carry out its tasks in the first place ? Francis Crick, co-discoverer of the double-helix DNA structure, wrote that `the *"fallacy of the homunculus"* is to be avoided at all costs, but it is easier to state the fallacy than to avoid slipping into it'.

The dichotomy is obvious : some psychologists think of the perceiving self as no more than the interaction process between various parts of the mind; others as a series of causally-triggered mental events. There are even those who suggest that the self is merely a feedback effect - the brain's reaction to its own processes. But the feeling is inescapable, when I analyse my own thought processes, that `I' am a unique and individual entity sitting behind my eyes surveying the outside world - the pilot of a mind/brain/body vehicle which will do my bidding. Further, it will function quite satisfactorily without any direct interference from `me', until I decide to undertake some particular action or individual thought process, which may be reading, writing, trying to recall something or trying to invent a better mousetrap. I can order my mind and brain to work on any task I devise, and I alone can decide when enough has been done and work can stop. It is `I', not my mind, that decides to go for a walk, pour a drink, ring a local friend : it is my *mind* that monitors my progress and sends the commands to my leg muscular systems. It is my mind that directs the pulling of the bottle cork, the guidance of the glass to my lips, and my mind that recalls, after prodding, my friend's number and guides the forefinger I wish to place on the first telephone studs. I know that the `I' riding in this body is the same entity whose first memory is one of repeatedly hurling a large teddy bear out of my cot - it has not aged, unlike my 72-year old body which has replaced its every cell at least seven times. I am a young entity riding in an obsolete vehicle.

A curious asymmetrical cross-connection exists between the cerebral lobes and the parts of the body they control : the left hemisphere usually controls the right side of the body and vice versa. In most right-handed people, the left hemisphere is dominant, controlling language and analysing logically situations passed to it by the sensory input channels. It is generally assumed to be the domain of the conscious mind, since most people think in words. The right hemisphere handles the side-processes of the thinking left lobe mind.: whilst the latter may hear musical input and through the cortical network identifies, for example, a tune by Gershwin, it is the right hemisphere that enjoys the music, assesses the quality of the performance etc. It functions more as a distiller of the quality of life involving many fields of the arts, such that a tone-deaf person (a by-product of distorted data transfer between the hemispheres) will not perceive accurately the sounds being received by the ears. If one suffers a stroke in the left hemisphere following the rupture of a blood vessel, it is extremely probable that the right-hand side of the body will suffer the major after-effects.

Many psychologists fear that the conscious mind may well become preoccupied, indeed obsessed, by the conscious assessment and analytical processes going on in the left hemisphere, and we find persons with no artistic appreciation, rarely experiencing creative thought. The sole remedy is to suppress left-lobe dominance and learn to think without words, according to Robert Ornstein (professor of psychology at University of Southern California) by means of eastern cultural methods such as meditation. In the hypnagogic state we experience a progressive eclipse of conscious left-lobe mentation in favour of the emotional/creative environment of the right lobe - movement towards a state of improving order.

This necessarily condensed discourse on brain physiology may provide a basic insight into the thinking process and the cortical neuron network. We are still some way from the problem of the mind/Time interface, but we can begin by considering the various mentational states in which the mind functions.

5. Mind - The Great Enigma

We identified and defined in a simplified fashion (Fig. 15) certain levels of consciousness associated with the left or right brain lobes : the `levels', more precisely, are states of mentation or `menzones' reigning in the appropriate lobe. The thinking process seems peculiar, to say the least, if we try to analyse what is going on. Whilst we appear outwardly to be a single entity - i.e. a moving thinking person - we perceive our mind as a the driver of an obedient body-vehicle, observing the material world as a car driver may peer through his wind-shield. We feel overwhelmingly that our `self' is both associated with and dissociated from our bodies, which develop, age and eventually wear out, despite regular replacement of redundant cells. But the `I' (the `passenger-in-charge' of the vehicle) remains as young and sprightly today as it was sixty years ago, making and imposing decisions on the mind. The self does not seem to age at all, whilst the mind deteriorates progressively due to the loss and nonreplacement of cells and degradation of the brain neural network, and this convinces us that our `self' is non-material and immortal. Whilst my brain may disintegrate and my body crumble into dust, I feel sure that `I' will in some way survive. But where and what is `I' ?

The problem is exacerbated when analysing our thought processes, because the mind and self appears to be separate entities. On the one hand we have the willing workhorse of the brain coping with day-to-day duties, guiding the body through the day's events, a mind/body duality operating for the most part in the cerebellum. On the other hand, we are aware that some decision-making mechanism receives the mind-processed sensory data input, and that entity seems to be more than just a part of the mind. It is the human personality - the self or psyche.

The apparent dualism of mind/self and mind/body has perplexed mankind since history began. The latter was described with great clarity by René Descartes (1596-1650) :

> *`I rightly conclude that my essence consists in this alone, that I am a thinking thing. . .And although perhaps I have a body with which I am closely conjoined, I have, on the other hand, a clear and distinct idea of myself as a* thinking non-extended thing *and, on the other hand, a distinct idea of my body as an* extended non-thinking thing; *it is therefore certain that I am truly distinct from my body, and can*

exist without it.'

Of all phenomena associated with human physiology, the mind is the most difficult to define or explain. It is located somewhere within the brain but no precise location has been established : most physiologists favour the cerebellum. It is a totally private and singular thing which we share with nothing except our dreams, and on the rare occasions when we experience telepathy or the strange voices heard in precognitive experiences. The mind encompasses all our emotions : we appear to think against an opaque background similar to that we see with eyes shut tight. The very thought process is difficult to describe : most of us think predominantly in words (when reading, writing, or calculating) and images when inactive mentally. Some people (including myself) can distinguish the active area of the cerebrum when thinking about a specific subject. In my own case, mental arithmetic is performed in the low left central area near the brain stem, whilst I enjoy music in the upper right area above the ear, about an inch under the skull. Most people can experience this if they concentrate sufficiently.

Closely associated with the mind is memory : we delve into storage banks at will, probing along endless mental tracks in search of an all-important link. I seem to think non-linearly : if I try to recall a fact or a name, without immediate success, a number of satellite images appear, which I examine closely but simultaneously for the connection I seek. For example, if I try to recall the name of the young aircraft apprentice who slept in the next bed on my training course 54 years ago, I develop a picture of a soccer team in which we both played, walks we took together, a memory of a football injury he sustained, a composite picture still recorded in memory, and I see his face - but not his name. At the same time another part of my mind reminds me that he had a typical R.A.F. nickname and I begin running through the more common examples : Harry Tate, Chalky White, Sweeney Todd. . .and yet another segment of my mind is working on my friend's home origin : London ? Liverpool ? Newcastle or Birmingham ? Suddenly it all comes together and I have it : square-jawed Dusty Rhodes from Bradford, who played right half beside me in the Squadron team. . .

Perhaps the most puzzling aspect of consciousness is sleep. While awake we are aware of the sensory data inputs, the environment, the tasks we direct our body to perform, and we are in complete control. Yet it is difficult to differentiate between mind and self, and it is impossible at times to maintain a steady state of mentation. When we order the brain to think of absolutely nothing, the self issues the order but the recalcitrant mind has other ideas : despite all efforts the thought-train continues, drifting desultorily into vague grey areas in which thoughts become incoherent, a state produced by a reduced level of concentration.

Taken to extremes, such incoherent thought-sequences result in day-dreaming; all external sensory data-input ceases, whilst the Dream Producer's scenarios pass before our mental eye. Stage Three is sleep, when the conscious mind severs contact with the material world, ceases to function : the subconscious mind takes over. Two minds ? Or one split mind ?

There are two alternatives here : two minds, conscious and subconscious functioning in left and right brain lobes respectively, or a single conscious mind working on two levels. In conscious mode, the self monitors and governs the mind, which processes and assesses incoming data - but the self makes the decisions based on that data. In sleep, however, conscious activity virtually ceases and the faithful `night-watchman' autonomous system takes over to monitor body processes and stand alert for possible danger. The crucial question is this : is the self an independent entity, or simply a facet of the mind ?

Consider what happens in sleep. The conscious mind is dormant : no mentation occurs in the left lobe. The subconscious mind, however, is deeply involved in the therapeutic `battery-charging' process - but it is essential that the `self' entity is also served. From this, we can safely assume that in sleep the self functions only in the subconscious mind. Clearly, the `self' entity is necessarily associated with both sectors of the mind at the same time, controlling the conscious mind in the waking state, and the subconscious during sleep. Most of us have experienced nightmares : the subconscious mind, totally dissociated with outside reality, is terrified, but the self suddenly intervenes to interrupt the nightmare, and the dream becomes lucid. There is no doubt in my view that mind and self are two totally different aspects of the personality.

In differentiating between mind and `self', we start with the two `menzones' (areas of mentation) located in right and left brain lobes. In each, certain autonomous systems function without supervision or interference in normal healthy subjects. For example, the left lobe `night watchman' and the right lobe `Dream Producer'. Others control physiological systems, ensuring that blood pressure, pulse and respiration rates are maintained within safe levels through a subsidiary structure of glands which produce and introduce specific chemicals according to need. A good example is adrenaline, a hormone secreted by the adrenal medulla of the adrenal gland located at the anterior end of each kidney, produced in response to stress. It increases the heart and pulse rates, and also blood pressure; it raises the levels of glucose and lipids in the blood.

The presence of the self in the conscious waking mind again gives the appearance of two levels of mentation : first, the background against which we think - the physical basis of conscious thought in the mind/brain, the blackboard upon which our thoughts are written. Second, the omnipotent decision-making self. We experience `self-awareness' precisely because that entity-system is present; in our conscious mind, we are self-aware - *aware of the self entity* - monitoring our thoughts.

These take the form of a seemingly-empty void in our brain within which thoughts condense in a semi-automatic fashion. When not thinking about a specific subject, our minds `tick over' in a continuous process of random mentation with unrestricted choice of subjects : images appear fleetingly and disappear almost at once, and the process has no apparent connection with the outside world. In bed in a dark and quiet room, with virtually no sensory input, the images continue, often in brilliant stark intensity. Whilst most are trivial, conjured up from memory and imagination by the Image Producer in our conscious mind, they become creative and inspirational in nature if, as sometimes happens, we slide into a hypnagogic state.

What seems to be happening here is that an interlobe interface is established between the waking conscious left-lobe mind and the right-lobe Dream Producer autonomous system, such that the dream images appear to be superimposed on the conscious observed field of reference, obliterating temporarily the real world. The Dream Producer, of course, manufactures scenarios round the clock.

But in conscious thinking mode, something extraordinary occurs. Against the background of continuous random trivial thought, there is intervention, usually in the form of an instruction to pursue a particular line of thought. A decision has been taken, a directive to change from non-productive contemplative mode to that of concentration. Somewhere within our brain, some entity has decided to act, issuing a command to the brain/mind duality which may take several forms.

For example, a person may find a well-filled wallet; his mind directs the body to pick it up. Contemplating the money, the subject's mind experiences an image montage of all the things the cash will buy, whilst wondering if it should take a chance. Without warning, a `voice' within the subject's brain warns that it would be criminal to keep the wallet : the intervening entity makes a decision to hand in the wallet at the police station, directs the mind to start the body walking in the right direction. This is clearly not a single thought process in which archetypal ethics emerge as a conscience : a separate something or entity has to make a decision, regardless of the effects of genes, upbringing, training and education. I hope to show that whilst the mind is an aspect of the electric and electrochemical thought processes in the brain, the self entity inhabits the electromagnetic field of the entire body.

6. The Conscious State

This is the mental state with which we are most familiar, the normal waking mode in which our minds handle constant sensory data input - analysing, storing, categorising, assessing. Our neural, nervous and muscular systems react automatically to external events : we close our eyes in a dust-storm, duck to avoid a hurtling projectile, cough to relieve a temporary discomfort. We react by body language, speech and behaviour patterns. But Tyrrell says that few as yet realise the full implication of the discovery that the conscious mind does not exhaust the human personality. We may not see much at first in the knowledge that there is more in us than we are conscious of; but reflection shows it to be more and more significant, until the perspective of the entire human being begins to change. I quote from his `*Personality of Man*':

> `*Watch a dancer : consider the incredible complexity of her movements. Each muscle is contracted at exactly the right moment and released after exactly the right interval : all are operated in perfect co-relation. Yet the dancer is unconscious of co-ordinating these movements in detail. She does not consciously issue to each muscle a separate order, yet something must do so. Something must control the nervous mechanism in detail. Purely mechanical reflexes are not the answer, for pure mechanism consists only of pushes and pulls exerted on pieces of matter. Something directive must be responsible for this perfect coordination of muscular movement, and it is not the conscious mind. There must be mental factors within us which are neither conscious nor purely mechanical*'.

Superficially, this seems to make sense. But I was disappointed that such a fine writer completely missed the vital clue, focussing on the purely-physical actions (which in dancing, as in many other occupations, become automatic after constant repetition and practice). What he described is the product of a conscious pre-programmed mind in a well-trained body : the dancer follows carefully-memorised routines, which her body performs without deliberate thought or concentration.

The true subconscious `self' element in the dancer's performance is quite different. All good performers know their routines, just as musicians learn to play orchestral pieces with only an occasional glance at the music sheet, watching for the most part the conductor who is striving to achieve the best aesthetic rendering of the composition. But the true perfectionist seeks the optimum artistic interpretation of the dance or role, and to this end (even whilst she is moving through the routine) she will try to visualise how the audience perceives her performance, and how she must modify and improve it to best effect. She draws heavily upon feedback from the crowd, and with an appreciative audience, will produce artistry far above her normal potential.

This is the true `unconscious' (subconscious) in operation : she is not consciously aware of the performer-audience interaction. Her subconscious mind is constantly assessing, analysing, directing special efforts and concentration in the areas she believes can be improved - and that is the real miracle. This seems to be a routine part and parcel of conscious mentation, except that it occurs on two different levels of consciousness, typifying the eternal enigma - the contradiction of a waking conscious mind and an apparently-independent second `self'.

Danah Zohar :

> `*Those who conclude that consciousness collapses the wave-func-*

tion (influencing future events beyond the PM discontinuity) *because its nature is essentially non-physical commit themselves to the old Cartesian view that mind and matter are separate entities. They view consciousness as something necessarily outside the physical world and thus as something alien to it - a* "ghost in the machine"... *What conscious being was here at the beginning of things to collapse the first wave function ?'*

The answer, of course, is `none'. The wave-function indeterminate future was there in position, ready for the first faint emanations of human consciousness. Yet Zohar has a different viewpoint, resorting to the strange paradox of Schrödinger's cat - a deservedly famous creature in philosophical circles, which has been incarcerated in a solid laboratory cage, so that to understand the meaning of the paradox, we must not see the cat until the end of the experiment and story. Inside the cage is placed radioactive material which has a 50% chance of emitting a deadly decay particle upwards or downwards. If the former, it strikes a particle detonator which triggers a switch to poison the cat. If, however, the particle is emitted downwards, food is released into the cage.

Now, this parallels the standard 50/50 decision-choice we encounter in everyday situations, but the set-up is critical for Schrödinger's quantum cat. According to current quantum theory, it is both alive and dead - precisely as an electron can be simultaneously both particle and/or wave. The existence of the cat is spread out through space and time in the form of a *Probability Wave* which fills the cage. The best we can do in pinning him down, Zohar suggests, is to describe all his possible states with a Schrödinger wave function - i.e. a mathematical equation which lists his many possibilities. Which of them really exists in the cage is a matter of probability.

The are two options : one, the cat has consumed the poison and died; two, that it has eaten well and survived. It is only when the wave function collapses (e.g. on opening the cage) that the possibilities condense into one fixed reality - in which we can either stroke or bury the cat. The paradox lies in the fact that Schrödinger's cat, alone amongst the millions of dead and alive cats on Earth, is neither dead nor alive whilst in the cage - until we take a look, and this is the vital point : the dilemma, the collapse of the wave-function, can only be resolved by human intervention. The cat may die simply because we opened the box, and this effect is of paramount importance in identifying the human mental process which collapses the wave function ahead of the Present Moment to transform a desired event version into reality.

7. The Subconscious State

This is the mind segment in control during hypnagogic states, sleep or other altered states of consciousness, which is monitored and directed by the self. The conscious mind is dormant and inactive, the self-entity is inoperative in the left hemisphere and control of body processes is left to the autonomous systems. A tenuous link exists between hemispheres (as Maury showed) via the *corpus callosum* such that the subconscious mind will react to external influences detected by the same autonomous systems. I believe that this same link may connect the dreaming mind and self in the right lobe with the dormant conscious mind in the left, as a result of which the latter may recall on waking details of dream sequences. In dreams, the subconscious mind is experiencing the scenarios, monitored by the self so that both benefit from the entertainment. The self (with the subconscious mind) may decide to enter the meditation menzone (Fig. 16) for the `battery-charging' process before entering the `dream theatre'.

8. Communication Glitches

Both conscious and subconscious minds cease to exist when physical death occurs, since they are ephemeral structures generated within the electric and electrochemical networks of the brain cortex. Indeed, the modern medical definition of total absence of life is `brain death' when no signs of electrical brain activity can be detected. The survival or death of the `self' is the most important question facing mankind.

In life, the system works reasonably well. The mind in both modes can operate in a number of mentation zones, loosely called `levels' : the self dictates which mode shall be operative, including cases of inspiration whilst asleep or in a hypnagogic state. If the conscious mind is faced by an intractable problem but continues work on other projects, the self puts the subconscious mind to work (in the waking state when the latter has full access to memory banks). The subconscious mind would not embark on such research in the absence of a specific directive; when the problem is solved or required information located, the data passes directly into the conscious mind, quite involuntarily.

Continuous communication between hemispheres in the waking state is confirmed - but what happens when these channels become defective or inoperative ? As many as 30 chemical substances are involved in bridging the synaptic `gap' : if only one is lacking, or in short supply, the resultant `message' may be distorted. Some of these substances prevent `feedback' between hemispheres, and since dream production goes on round the clock, chaos may reign in the conscious mind if a flow of brilliant visual images and audible transmissions of dream quality is suddenly experienced. Efficient working of the filtering and blocking process is absolutely essential, but what happens if that barrier breaks down ? This may be responsible for the `split personality' or schizophrenia syndrome, a group of psychotic disorders characterised by progressive deterioration of the personality, withdrawal from reality, hallucinations, delusions, social apathy and emotional instability (cf Collins English Dictionary).

Take `withdrawal from reality' - and open a real can of worms ! For a start, what precisely *is* reality ? We can say it is the state of things as they are or appear to be, rather than the way we would wish them to be, but this hardly applies when we consider abstract or ideal events : `realism' involves acceptance of the real universe and events as they are. But what about events which *may* happen ? All future events exist in potential and may achieve `realness'- but such events, like the death of Schrödinger's cat, are neither real nor unreal. Their `probability', however, is real, and this applies to all events which do not as yet exist !

The impression of reality constructed by the conscious mind is generated from external sensory data input. The panoramic frame of reference presented to the self may contain no immediate or implicit threat, and is filed without action. But suppose there is an additional source of data ? Suppose that a mental patient is suffering from a break-down of the `feedback-filter' system. His Dream Producer is creating continuous scenarios which begin infiltrating into the patient's conscious mind. The patient may `see' and `hear' (superimposed on the quiet vista of the medical ward) a terrifying jungle infested with carnivorous monsters such as the earth has never seen. He may `see' himself in a pit filled with poisonous snakes and scorpions, or slowly drowning in a sea of mud.

But the patient's self has been accustomed since birth to *accepting as real the environment presented by the mind* : horrified, overcome by terror, he will sever all contact, not only with the Dream Producer and his nightmare but with the real world surrounding him, unable to distinguish hallucination from reality. In other words, catatonic withdrawal and total dissociation of the self from the mind.

I am no psychoanalyst but this seems to match schizophrenic symptoms as I understand them. Could a cure be found by identifying as defective those substances or neural circuits responsible for isolating the subconscious mind from the conscious ? Further, this may explain the multiple-personality syndrome, such as the well-known case of a young 19th-century Irish girl named Bridie Murphy, who emerged in the mind of an American woman who had never been to Ireland. Some dream characters are startlingly real, even if we retain only minimal memories. It is just possible - I would put it no higher - that such multiple personalities are no more than characters from the subject's dreams. I know of no examples in which the actual existence (past or present) of a dream character has been confirmed, and in the case of delusions, it is again possible that a conscious patient's dreaming mind is participating in some dream scenario in which he is an intrepid airman, a world statesman or a military genius such as Napoleon. Given a defective feedback/filtration system, the patient cannot be blamed for believing the dream is reality and becoming convinced he is the real McCoy !

There is another possible explanation of multiple personalities. The patient's self in Space 2 may have extensive and constant contact with other self-entities waiting for a further cycle of existence, which may grasp the opportunity to enjoy some vicarious degree of existence in the mind of the patient. Who can say that Napoleon's spirit may not be still be alive in some deranged patient's mind ?

9. The Quantum Self

We come finally to the most important question of all : has the human mind the ability to select a specific variant of a future event, by collapsing the wave-function Probability Field ahead of the Present Moment ? If so, can we provide satisfactory proof that the phenomenon occurs ?

Whilst Danah Zohar points to the mind/body dualism, I take a step further by considering the self/mind duality : it is absolutely essential to maintain a clear distinction between the two. Zohar cites examples of severe epilepsy in which the two brain hemispheres have been separated by cutting the *corpus callosum* - with some remarkable after-effects. Most patients seemed to be unaffected - until subjected to laboratory tests, the end result of which appears to be the creation of two separate conscious minds ! This is predictable - each hemisphere performs specific functions (quite apart from the decision-making `self's activities). The right lobe controlling the left side of the body is the creative and aesthetic locale, the centre of imagination. The left lobe connected to the right side of the body is devoted to logic, calculation and specifically, the creation and monitoring of speech.

In normal mode there is a constant two-way flow of information via the *corpus callosum* - but after such an operation it becomes, quite literally, a case of the left hand not knowing what the right hand is doing. Yet remarkably, the self continues to exist in both hemispheres, controlling the left-lobe conscious mind as well as the subconscious in the right lobe. This is logical and predictable if, as I suggest, the self inhabits the EMF surrounding the body as a whole. For whilst the subject may be under great stress undergoing laboratory tests after the operation, in ordinary life-mode the two selves are reunited to form a single entity, using the alternative secondary communication links available via the brain stem. I see this as confirmation of the omnipresence of the self, not only in all parts of the body itself but in Space 2. But clear definition of the self is an extremely difficult problem, and the great breakthrough made by Danah Zohar is that the self conforms to quantum rules. She writes :

> `*Like the self, elementary particle systems are wholes within wholes, or* "individuals" *within* "individuals". *Because of the wave/particle duality, the constituent members of particle systems carry at all times the properties of both waves and particles. With their particle aspect they have the capacity to be something in particular which can be* "pinned down", *if only briefly and only somewhat. With their wave aspect they have the capacity to relate to other* "individuals"

through the partial overlapping of their wave functions. Through their relationships, some of their qualities merge in such a way that a new whole is formed'.

`The properties of the new "individual" *are influenced by those of the* "sub-individuals" *of whose relationships it consists. In every respect, however, it now behaves like a new entity in its own right, with its own wavy aspect and its own capacity for further relationship on its own terms. This is the notion of* "relational holism". . *.of the way our minds and bodies are. A whole created through quantum relationship is a new thing in itself, greater than the sum of its parts'.*

Here is our first real clue to the means by which the wave function state ahead of the Present Moment, which contains future events in potential, is collapsed : in wave function the subatomic structure is flexible, with the capability to relate to other nearby particles in wave mode, via their overlapping interference patterns, to provide multiple versions of any specific arrangement. But with the collapse of the wave function, as Zohar says, particles become something in particular which can be `pinned down' - in other words, reality. Danah expands on this :

`The process of quantum integration by which new and larger wholes are created is endless, to the extent that at its furthest extreme every particle in the universe can to some degree be related to every other particle, thus creating the quality of unbroken wholeness that can rightly be ascribed to physical reality'.

With this in mind, let us turn now to the basic thought mechanism itself.

10. The Bose Einstein Condensate.

For full understanding, we must define initially the `thought background' we first encountered on P. 228, and identify the mechanism which enables the mind to collapse the wave function of future events into a particular version of reality. This is, in fact, a quantum mechanical model of consciousness, and following Zohar's example I quote David Bohm[45] :

`We may well now ask whether the close analogy between quantum processes and our inner experiences and thought processes is mere coincidence. The remarkable point-by-point analogy between thought processes and quantum processes would suggest that a hypothesis relating these two may well turn out to be fruitful. If such a hypothesis could ever be verified, it would explain in a natural way a great many features of our thinking'.

But no reference to a Time mechanism, as yet . . . Bohm goes on :

'Thought processes and quantum systems are analogous in that they cannot be analysed too much in terms of distinct elements, because the "intrinsic" *nature of each element is not a property existing separately from and independent of other elements but is, instead, a property that arises partially from its relation with other elements'.*

There is a vital connection, Bohm suggests, between human thought processes and particles, i.e. between our selves and electrons. But it would not be easy to identify that connection and construct a model which would demonstrate that consciousness functions according to the laws of quantum mechanics. Attempts to construct computer and holographic models have been unsuccessful, because of their inability to solve the problem of the indivisibility of human consciousness. Roger Penrose[46] encapsulated the problem as follows :

'Quantum physics involves many highly intriguing and mysterious kinds of behaviour. Not the least of these are the (non-local) quantum correlations which can occur over widely-separated distances. It seems to me to be a definite possibility that such things could be playing a role in conscious thought modes. Perhaps it is not too fanciful to suggest that quantum correlations could be playing an operative role over large regions of the brain. Might there be any relation between a "state of awareness" *and a highly coherent quantum state in the brain ? Is the* "one-ness" *or* "globality" *that seems to be a feature of consciousness connected with this ? It is somewhat tempting to believe so'.*

I see here some corroboration of the evidence gained from studying cases of identical twins, but the first positive clues appeared in the Thirties and Forties, when biophysicists discovered that human brain nerve cells are sufficiently sensitive to register the absorption of a single photon (which signifies the transition of an individual electron from one subatomic energy level to another). The cells, accordingly, are sensitive enough to be influenced by the whole gamut of quantum-level particle behaviour involving non-local effects and indeterminism - i.e. particle interaction over great distances and in wave function mode, exemplified by the non-real future indeterminacy ahead of the travelling Present Moment discontinuity. Most important, it was found that this particle indeterminacy is built into the brain mentation process via random variations in the chemical composition of the synaptic bridge itself.

These chemical concentrations determine the rate at which neurons fire, and also the nature of the data impulse transmitted and received. In 1960 Ninian Marshall[47] was working on telepathy and memory, and suggested that current deterministic physical laws excluded the free play of thought processes, free will and intention (all of which we see as common features of consciousness).

Orlov[48] agreed : quantum indeterminism and superimposed probability states must be playing a role in the brain's openness to all the potentialities latent in consciousness. At the risk of being tautological : *the nature of creative thought processes is such that they can only function beyond the quantum discontinuity, where our known natural laws do not rule.*

My starting point, without doubt, had to be the `background' state upon which our creative thoughts are superimposed, the apparent void in our brain against which thoughts seem to condense into reality from the swirl of indeterminate ideas and images. Physicists call this a `steady state', uniform in space and persistent in time - the necessary qualities for consciousness to function. The nature of this background is at once extremely difficult to define, yet it contains the answer to our many besetting difficulties. Mentation would be almost impossible against a shifting changing background.

Danah Zohar writes :

> `*...this unusual orderly quality of our conscious attention considerably limits the choice of underlying physical explanations. . .it has the character of unbroken wholeness. It hangs together and allows our experience to do so. This mind of settled uniformity is rare amongst dynamic processes in Nature, but does occur in materials which exist in "condensed phases". The physics (and the physiology) of condensed states thus seems a candidate worth investigating further to see if it can suggest an explanation for how consciousness could arise in the brain'.*

A `phase' is a `state' within the general meaning, and in natural materials refers to the amount of order in a given system. Water has three phases : gaseous, liquid and solid, in increasing degrees of order appropriately, and other examples are ordinary magnets, superfluids, superconductors, laser light, electrical currents in metals and sound waves in crystals. (See Zohar, P.64). The common denominator is a certain degree of coherence such that the atoms and molecules of the subject suddenly behave as one, rather like a hologram in which an image exists holistically in every part of the structure. Zohar gives a fine example shown in Fig. 31.

The electromagnetic compass array is installed in a room shielded from the Earth's magnetic field, and with no current flowing, the needles assume random positions (left diagram). As power is applied and increased, the needles slowly assume a uniform pattern (right) as the induced electromagnetic field exceeds random external influences such as jiggling the table. The needles have entered a *condensed phase*. More importantly, by abandoning a non-random alignment they have created additional data which can be of use - indicating a specific direction by their coherency.

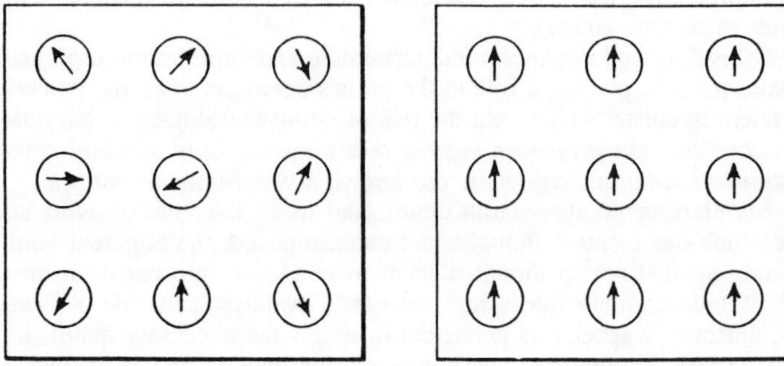

From Danah Zohar - `The Quantum Self'

Fig. 31

Induced Coherent State in Electromagnetic Compass Array

The problem is this : *How can we demonstrate that a similar condensed phase system may exist within the brain ?* Metal needles in no way resemble living cells, and it is difficult to envisage a mechanism which could `align' the neurons in the brain's network, in order to produce a higher state of coherency. The examples of superfluids and superconductors springs to mind, but these normally exist in very low temperatures. The brain, on the other hand, works at a relatively high body temperature. The requirement was for a mechanism which induced condensed phases at body temperatures, and the `pumped system' was first described some 20 years ago by Professor Herbert Fröhlich[49] of Liverpool University.

He proposed a simple system of vibrating electrically-charged molecules (dipoles - positive at one end and negative at the other) in the living tissue cell walls, into which energy is pumped. The dipoles emit electromagnetic vibrations (virtual protons, i.e. with a limited range of interaction). Fröhlich's great discovery was that beyond a certain threshold, any additional energy pumped into the system causes the molecules to vibrate in unison until they assume the most ordered form of condensed phase possible - a Bose Einstein condensate. The many parts forming an ordered system not only behave as a whole, but they *become* a whole. Their merging overlapping identities lose their individuality entirely to become a single entity - that is to say, *when the millions of cells in the cerebrum (which are performing routinely the mentation processes involved with daily life) achieve a sufficiently high energy level to form a Bose Einstein condensate, particle consciousness merges to form the background state of consciousness itself.* The condensate, incidentally, has been created in living tissues in the laboratory, using microwave techniques to induce the cell vibrations.

In the quantum mechanical model of consciousness proposed by Danah Zohar, the generated condensate accounts only for the ground state of awareness, the `blackboard' on which such things as perception, experience, thoughts, emotions etc. are written - in effect, routine mentation. Danah suggests that these, and many more, would appear individually or in combination as excitations of the underlying condensate. We can take the analogy of an bar-type electromagnet covered by a sheet of paper upon which iron filings or granules are scattered : as an applied electric current is increased, simulating the approach to a condensate state, we reach a threshold at which the iron filings suddenly arrange themselves in alignment with the magnetic field, from the positive end to the negative.

Remarkably, the mathematics describing the resultant patterns are those of the hologram, which we recognise as the familiar contents of consciousness. In this model, Zohar suggests, we find two interacting systems in the brain : the coherent consciousness condensate and the computer-like system of individual neurons in the cortex which form the `mind'. Experiments with electro-encephalographs suggest a link between the two : if either system is excited, it produces an electrical field which acts upon the other, resembling the effect of collapsing a low-voltage induced single-coil field within a double coil system to produce a larger induced voltage in a secondary coil. But because of the quantum factor, the excitations would always be coherent.

How does this work ? Bodies produce the electrical energy necessary to produce a BE condensate. Its coherency and quality is a function of the amount of extra `mental' energy pumped into the neuron cell network. Danah Zohar suggests we have a number of sub-selves which are preoccupied with personal problems such as traumatic childhood memories, immaturity and gene-generated personality defects which plague us from the moment of birth. These absorb a great deal of the available energy, leaving less for the generation of the BE condensate, which is logically less coherent and efficient than it would be in normally-functioning subjects. At the lower end of the scale, predictably, we find psychotic subjects who are `unable to get themselves together', with extensive personality defects which diminish the quality of the `self'. Indeed, it is relatively easy to recognise those people possessing high condensate coherence, in the well-educated people of above-average intelligence, able to absorb what they are taught - for example, barristers, physicists, engineers and medical researchers, potential Nobel prize-winners. Einstein, and others like him, were able to devote almost 100% of their generated electrical energy to constructing and improving their BE condensates, inducing a highly-productive conscious mind.

Interestingly, this may offer an explanation for the *idiot savants* - partially-retarded geniuses capable of extraordinary feats of mental calculation and artistic performance. If that part of their cortical neuron network responsible for such activities is powered up locally to become a

Bose Einstein condensate, they will have many times the conscious ability to think, count or create - but at the expense of the rest of the cerebral cortex, which will be starved of power to create a normal BE condensate.

But what of the self ? Take a long introspective look at your own thought processes : close the eyes and try to establish what is happening. We can sense the vague amorphous background of consciousness, and if we do not concentrate we experience the montage of random images generated by the mind, a product of the condensate. In deciding to concentrate on a problem, we initiate a process which the mind follows obediently - *but what or who makes the decision to concentrate and selects the subject ?*

There is a widely-held view that there is no sub-division here at all : that mind and self are identical, but I cannot support that idea. The quantum self is the `I' of Descartes but it remains undefined : it has substance and undoubtedly exists, and that existence is seemingly independent of the mind and body. I can say, like Descartes, `I am' - but not `*what I am'*. I can use the analogy of the computer, which is `dead' until a motivating power source is switched on. It receives external data (via the keyboard) which is stored in memory (floppy disks) which can be recalled when needed. It can be programmed to perform many of the human brain functions, such as calculation, writing (printing out) and designing. Depending on the designed RAM memory and operating speed, the computer develops a `thinking mode' to perform these tasks, which may be compared to the human mind, but is restricted by the inbuilt level of intelligence, ability and operating speed.

But somewhere outside the computer it is necessary to have a controlling directing entity - in the case of the computer, myself, and in the case of the mind, the self. The mind, a mentation mechanism processing data input to extract information, is a product of the BE condensate, but it is `I' to whom the results are presented, and `I' initiate each computation, directing the mind to a specific task. But when the computer is finally scrapped, the floppy disks erased, the current switched off permanently, `I' continue to function myself, outside the computer. Indeed, in the fullness of time I may find a new model, programme it according to my needs and begin another lifetime association with it. So where do we look for the elusive self ?

11. The Final Link - Intelligence in Electromagnetic Fields

All body cells live limited life spans in a continuous process of disintegration, being replaced with identical living cells manufactured from our input of food and liquids. Liver and serum proteins are renewed as frequently as every 10 days; the cells of lungs, skin, brain and principal muscles every 158 days. Our bodies are replicated *in toto* many times during life from the DNA `blueprint' - and our minds, distilled from the coherent BE condensate, will change progressively because some brain cells are not renewed : mental powers, memory etc. deteriorate progressively with age. Yet our personalities, our individual `selves' remain unchanged, unaffected by cell replication or time, in precisely the same form we experienced as children. As Walter de la Mare wrote :

`It's a very odd thing, as odd as can be
That whatever Miss T eats
Turns into Miss T. . .

Evidently the DNA* process of duplication is complex, each cell being replicated in the true image of the redundant cell, and since each bears the evidence of aging, the body produces a mature replacement cell exactly matching the original. Otherwise we would be truly immortal, if each new cell produced was unsullied by age or disease. The sole anomaly is the self : it is not subject to obsolescence and oblivion. Is there an explanation in the way the replication process works ?

First, it is fully-automated and controlled by the inbuilt blueprint in the double-helix DNA molecule containing all the necessary information to synthesise a replacement cell. However, the blueprint itself must be 100% accurate : even one tiny error in the composition of a single amino acid can change the hormones or antibodies upon which survival depends. Equally important is the bio-feedback which ensures that the DNA blueprint is constantly updated to produce identical replica cells. If ever a mechanism for immortality is developed, it will involve changing the DNA double-helix to reproduce the pristine, unsullied and untainted cells of our childhood again and again.

What triggers the replication process ? The innate difficulty is that human cells are, of necessity, so complex that they lack the inherent stability to remain in pristine condition. They cannot avoid disintegrating, in the process of which their constituents return to the general background material of the body. This is the fundamental cause of inherited disease transmission : any cell carrying the virus or disease bacteria will pass the contagion into the body as a whole, where it is absorbed into the sperm.

The DNA blueprint ensures that the new cell is replicated exactly - but how is it fitted into the body structure correctly ? The electromagnetic field of the body provides a template, a three-dimensional image created at the moment of conception which is present throughout life. These

---

* Chromosomes are microscopic rod-shaped structures that appear in a cell nucleus, consisting of nucleoprotein arranged into units with fixed positions on the chromosome called genes. The latter are units of heredity capable of replication and mutation, which are transmitted from parent to child during reproduction. DNA (deoxyribonucleic acid) is the main component of the chromosomes of all organisms except some viruses. It is self-replicating, playing a major part in protein synthesis (creation of new cells) and is a hereditary transmitter. Also in the DNA blueprint is the standard life expectancy of the subject, but where defective DNA, genes or chromosomes are replicated, resultant diseases may be inherited during reproduction.

EMFs (discovered by Dr. Harold Saxton Burr and Dr. F.S.C. Northrop of Yale University) may be measured accurately. But what exactly is an electromagnetic field ?

Where a spatial event occurs as a result of another spatial event elsewhere, with no visible means of interconnection, the two events are linked by a `field'. The most familiar example is the bar electromagnet already mentioned. Such EMFs always assume the same pattern regardless of locale and time of experiment, the person conducting the experiment and all other extraneous factors. The results are always the same and wholly predictable, and EMFs produced by electrochemical reactions of the type we find in human cells give rise to certain types of electrical activity in the cerebral cortex, including `alpha' and `beta' rhythms. The former is slower than normal, emitted by a drowsy or inactive person at a frequency of about 8 - 12 hertz. The latter is the normal emission encountered in alert and active subjects, from 13 - 30 hertz, both being measurable by encephalograph.

Electromagnetic fields exist even in the subatomic quantum level of particles, millions of such EMFs combining to form a resultant general field of higher complexity. The state existing in a confined area surrounding the human body is regarded as a primary field controlling all its secondary and extremely small components in every particle, molecule and cell of the body. Such human EMFs can be measured using any modern voltmeter registering at least 10 megohms, and are identified as DC potentials in no way associated with the alpha and beta rhythms.

The creation of the visible outline of the EMF surrounding a bar electromagnet using iron granules is a similar process to that of the replication of body cells : the cavity left by the disintegrated cell is delineated by the localised EMF, and when surrounding tissues and glands produce the required subatomic particles of various substances, the latter assemble themselves into molecules guided by the double-helix DNA matrix, which includes an instruction limiting the size of the new cell to fit the void. Where that instruction is defective, the new cell may be flawed or even cancerous.

Einstein wrote :

> `*The electromagnetic fields. . . are not states of a medium* (he was referring to the `ether' - Auth.) *and are not bound to any bearer, but they are independent realities which are not reducible to anything else'.*

And Zukav defines an EMF as :

`*The mutual exchange of virtual protons at the quantum level'.*

Collins English Dictionary states :

'An EMF is equivalent to an electrical field and a magnetic field at right angles to each other and to the direction of propagation.'

This is seen in the arrangement of magnetic force lines around an electromagnet : an electric current is always attended by magnetic force. Electric currents are constituted by movements of electrons : the moving electrons within an atom will give rise to their appropriate magnetic forces and this also applies in the atoms of a human body in Space 1. When the electrons in an atom are in wholly symmetrical arrangement, with no impulse to gain or lose energy by moving to another orbit, a closed magnetic system occurs with no resultant or detectable external effects.

With any markedly unsymmetrical arrangement (e.g. heat or the application of an electric current, which change the electron characteristics) we observe appreciable external magnetic effects throughout the subatomic structure, creating an EMF.

Professor G.D. Wassermann[50] postulated the existence of 'morphogenetic fields', existing in latent form in space ready to enter into a 'bound' state with specific cellular organisms such as an ovum. These 'fields' would appear to be 'self' entities which survive physical death of the body. The melding process, Professor Wasserman says, cannot commence until a sperm has changed the 'quantum state' of the ovum in such a way that the 'steering field' can begin organising the new entity. This idea seems to suggest an accurate explanation of reincarnation, provided our assumption that the self is a self-contained body EMF is true. Further, the duration-extension of the new individual commences at the moment the morphogenic field achieves the ovum quantum adjustment - that is to say, the EMF penetrates the subatomic quantum domain of symmetrical electrons and induces an electric 'spark' in the ovum. *Could this not be the very essence of life ?*

Research into the human EMF in 1911 by Walter J. Kilner of St.Thomas' Hospital, London resulted in the discovery of the aura, the existence of which had been widely rumoured and reported prior to that date, after work by Reichenbach. Kilner believed that observed changes in the colour and outline of the aura according to the health of the patient might be useful in diagnosis. Human survival, *per se*, is largely a function of health, and therefore of a healthy aura. If a decline in the strength of the aura is detected, the ultimate result is death, and this may explain why many seriously-ill patients become aware of their imminent death, without being told by doctors.

But is their aura actually diminishing in strength - or is it filtering away in some strange fashion, to some other place ? The aura, in my view, is a visual manifestation of the human EMF, itself is a vehicle for the self. If, as I suspect, the self survives death, the deterioration of the aura indicates that the self is leaving the body. This assumption is supported by many accounts of an ephemeral misty haze seen to be rising from the body at the time of death.

But what, in that event, happens to the aura itself ? W.E.Mann[51], writing about Kilner's work :

> '*If someone was placed against a dark background in twilight, a slightly-luminous mist, oval in form, was seen around the body. It has three distinct zones : the first was an edging about half a centimetre wide, surrounding the body. This was the* "etheric double" *(possibly the* "astral body" *observed in out-of-the-body experiences). Outside this was the interior aura, dense and streaked perpendicularly to the body : this was from 3 to 8 centimetres in width. Finally came the exterior aura which had no definite contour'.* (Other than the oval form mentioned above - Auth.).

If this is indeed the human self EMF, what exactly is it ?

First, any EMF generated as the sum total of billions of particle EMFs in the body would assume the approximate shape of the body, as seen in all auras, and the general outline of a bar electromagnetic field, i.e. an outline roughly oval or inverted pear-shaped, since the greater part of the human form is concentrated in mid-body, tapering off at the feet and the head, which contains the hundreds of millions of cell EMFs in the brain.

The human self, in my view, is located in the EMF surrounding the body, and concentrated almost exclusively within the cerebrum, but in assuming that the EMF survives physical death of the body, definitive proof is essential. One researcher, the Rev. Rosalyn Bruyere, describes the aura as an electromagnetic phenomenon akin to ionisation - the formation of visible ions as a result of an electrical discharge or radiation. (An ion is an electrically-charged atom or group of atoms formed by the loss or gain of one or more particles). Zukav, writing about EMFs, suggests they involve the exchange of particles at quantum level, and this seems to corroborate Dr. Bruyere's thesis.

In 1939 a Russian laboratory technician called Semyon Kirlian noted a tiny flash of light between the electrodes of an electro-therapy machine being used to treat a patient. Experimenting, he found that a photograph could be taken by inserting a photo-sensitive plate between the spark and his hand : the developed plate showed a glowing image of the hand ! From this fortuitous beginning he developed a machine by means of which the process could be observed without films, emulsion or developing.

More fascinating discoveries followed, the significance of which is only now being recognised. For example, every living creature produced the Kirlian aura patterns. Healthy living plant leaves showed a different pattern to diseased or dead specimens - and similar effects were observed in seriously-ill patients. But the most amazing result was obtained when part of a living leaf was removed and the aura checked. The characteristic Kirlian glowing outline showed the whole leaf *including the part just removed !*

I see this as clear proof that the aura not only encapsulates the life essence or self of the organism, but is a freely-existing EMF which will continue to exist after physical death of the body.

Lyall Watson suggests that the EMF waves of the human body are outside the spectrum of normal human sight (380 to 760 millimicrons), but some people can see the aura plainly. The shadowy entities leaving the body at the time of death could be the self EMF of the deceased person. Watson produces evidence to suggest that this energy matrix is a form of elementary plasma-like cloud of ionised particles (i.e. an EMF), suggesting significantly that it is not a `chaotic system' but a whole unified organism in itself. Such a biological plasma entity would be capable of exercising some form of organisational control over the body it embraces - I can see no other reason for its existence.

And so we come to the crux of our investigations - to identify the mechanism that enables human minds to influence the shape of future events.

12. The Mind/Time Interface

I was tempted here to enter into a lengthy and involved review of the ground covered thus far, but it is necessary only to demonstrate convincingly the connection between the self EMF and the Fixed Time Field in Space 2 and the self's omnipresence throughout its duration-extension.

Living organisms receive data input from three sources :

(a) Electromagnetic waves (light, sound, heat etc).
(b) Mechanical pressures (sound, touch etc).
(c) Chemical stimuli (taste, smell etc).

External receptors convert the data into electrical impulses, i.e. messages to the central nervous system. Nerve fibres and neurons convey the data via multiple routes to appropriate parts of the brain. (Faulty routing may produce a condition known as `synaesthesia' in which a sound may be `tasted' or a touch may be sensed as an odour). Stimulated neuron cells have two abilities which contribute to the creation of a Bose Einstein condensate :

(a) Generation of constant-value electrical charges.
(b) Chemical transmission of these charges at constant velocity.

The magnitude of the stimulus is irrelevant, except in so far as increased magnitude generates more charges : the frequency increases and the appropriate mind circuits assess this change. Each time an impulse passes, the nerve fibre absorbs a small quantity of oxygen and emits a comparable amount of carbon dioxide. As a result :

(a) The temperature rises slightly.
(b) A pulsation occurs along the nerve.
(c) The localised EMFs change their characteristics, modifying the total resultant EMF.

Factor (c) is important, demonstrating the connection between the routine mentation process and the higher-level freely-associated self EMF. Thus one link of the chain is forged.

In 1974 David Wechsler[52] wrote :

`Insight is the result of assessed external data input, and is the collective response of the elementary systems in the cortical cells in one or other region of the brain'.

Wechsler refers here to analytical assessment based on data input presented *by the mind to the self.* Further, he suggests that this response is not due to the transmission of impulses along the axons and dendrites, and across the synaptic gaps : it is rather a resonance phenomenon similar to that seen in a tuning fork. It is true that similar effects are found in reinforcement and impedance electrical sub-circuits, and in sub-atomic quantum mechanics. Further, we know that the Bose Einstein condensate is a product of the vibration of neuron cells in the brain : where such vibrations are synchronised, they are said to be in a state of resonance.

When two particle systems are in resonance by virtue of the wave emissions of sub-particles, the effect is greater than the sum of the interacting particles. In layman's terms, such wave interaction/resonance creates a new system, or produces meaningful resonance in an adjacent system, and this is a reasonable way to describe the connection between the thinking mind and the self.

Now, I see an important clue here. Bell's Theorem shows that when neon gas is excited by an electrical current, the neon atoms emit photons (light particles) in pairs. Identical twins, they fly off in different directions. But if one is polarised in a given direction the other follows suit instantaneously and without regard to spatial separation. This effect was predicted by the Einstein-Podolsky-Rosen experiments prior to Bell's work in 1964, but the principle is exactly the same.

Let us be quite clear about this vital statement. The meaning of Bell's Theorem is that one of a pair of twin particles is able to `sense' a change in its partner's characteristics with zero lapse of time - a form of resonance predicted by Wechsler. The vital conclusion is this : if both the mind/brain EMF and the self EMF are particle-related (they do occupy the same body and are generated by the same particles) and they function in both Space 1 and Space 2 by virtue of their duration-extensions, there is a direct resonating connection between :

(a) Unrealised wave-function events ahead of the Present Moment.

(b) Conscious and subconscious minds via the *corpus callosum* and

(c) The self EMF.

We can illustrate this phenomenon by taking the hypothetical situation of a subject in waking state faced with a two-way decision as described in the section on the *I Ching* (P.207). In conscious mode, he is anxious to obtain any clues he can on which decision will be the most beneficial. He may use any of a number of artifacts including the *I Ching* and tarot cards, crystal balls etc, but most people rely on what we call `hunches' or premonitions, as we saw in an earlier chapter. He may even be influenced by a precognitive dream involving a Time Shunt (Fig. 18) but the process is the same in all cases : his omnipresent self, within its duration-extension in Space 2, observes a range of potential future events linked to his present-time decision, and decides that one variant has particular merits. That information passes into the Present Moment subconscious mind as the best choice.

As with Schrödinger's famous cat, the Probability Wave of future events can be collapsed in two ways. Firstly by non-intervention, allowing a random event-version to achieve reality, within the limitations of the Probability Field. (The arrival of the Present Moment discontinuity collapses the wave-function Probability Field). Some versions will always remain low-grade probabilities (because no one `lifts the cage lid to check on Schrödinger's cat'). Secondly, as the subject's mind focuses on the desired identified event version, particle resonance between the mind in the `here/now' Present Moment and the wave-function indeterminacy of the future event will collapse the Probability Field and transform that one specific event version into reality.

Pause to take a deep breath. . .and read the foregoing again, for it encapsulates the entire thesis.

\+ + +

We are now approaching the final hurdle - to demonstrate beyond reasonable doubt the interaction/communication between the human self EMF and the wave function domain ahead of the Present Moment. By sheer chance I found the ultimate clues in the work of Dr. Robert O. Becker [53] from which he has given his kind permission to quote freely in the following explanation.

In examining the basis of data transmission within the human body, it had long been assumed that the electrochemical nerve cell synaptic interaction identified in 1921 by Otto Lowei was the only transmission channel between cells. It was, incidentally, discovered in strange way : Lowei dreamed one night of the exact way to perform an experiment confirming synaptic transmission, but he forgot virtually everything on waking, except the subject of the dream. The next night, the entire dream was repeated - and this time remembered ! This is not only a wonderful example of the Time Shunt but a logical explanation for repetitive dreams. Earlier, in 1871, Julius Bernstein had proposed a new explanation for the apparent paradoxes in the work of Emil DuBois-Reymond and Hermann von Helmholtz : the former found that the nerve impulse could be detected electrically, whilst the latter had measured the speed of the impulse along nerve fibres and found that it was much slower than electrical wire-transmission.

Bernstein believed that the ions (charged atoms of sodium, potassium or chloride) inside the nerve cell differed from the outside tissue fluid, resulting in the nerve-cell membrane being electrically charged or polarised. Lowei's contribution in 1921 was to confirm that data transmission across the synaptic gap between nerve cells is chemical-based.

The `current of injury' generated in the area of a wound, first noted by Galvani, is a Direct Current (DC), which always appears as a circuit (for example, a hand torch) in which one part of the system has a concentration of energy-carrying particles : these flow towards the lower-strength areas in an equalisation process, and depending on the direction of flow, the current is positive or negative. Current in a metal wire is composed of moving electrons and is called `electronic' or `metallic', whilst a current in a conducting solution is composed of moving ions, i.e. `ionic'. The moving particles are called `charge carriers'.

When Bernstein was working on his hypothesis, the only known types of electrical energy transmission were metallic and ionic conduction. In a third type - semiconduction - identified in solid materials, currents may be composed either of electrons or `holes' (i.e. the absence of electrons) and this forms an important feature in our approach. In 1941, Dr. Albert Szent-Gyorgyi proposed that semiconduction occurred in living cells. We can define semiconduction as a property of specific materials with atoms arranged in lattices - for example, in crystals - in which somewhat strange events occur. If one atom has an extra electron, the latter is free to move through the lattice by intercepting the orbital field of one atom and being propelled along to the next. Where an atom is short of an electron, a hole exists in the lattice - and that hole can move as freely as a real electron !

Further, semiconductor currents have very low strength voltages. Dr. Szent-Gyorgyi found that cell materials such as proteins have this organised lattice-characteristic. Now, when a bar-type permanent magnet is laid at right angles across a current-carrying wire or fibre, an electromagnetic field is created, but one with limitations : a steady-state (DC) field generated by a permanent magnet can affect only structures within the body which are themselves magnetic. (Certain creatures such as salamanders and homing pigeons possess internal magnetic `lumps' which react to the earth's magnetic field). Accordingly, we can eliminate such permanent-magnet DC fields as means of inter-cellular data transmission. Further, AC-type fields (whose strength fluctuates regularly on a time basis) induce currents too small to have any effectiveness as data carriers.

The Magic of Healing

Dr. Robert O. Becker next turned to the investigation of body data transmission, firstly in relation to injury repair systems (using frogs) and secondly, into the strange process of regeneration, exemplified by the salamander. If this mammal has a limb amputated, it has the unique capability to grow an identical and complete new limb, and Becker knew that simple chemical-based synapse-bridges and DC nerve impulses were incapable of carrying the huge amount of organisational information required. He suspected that there might well be another hidden channel of communication, because of the nature of the closed-loop healing process, as shown :

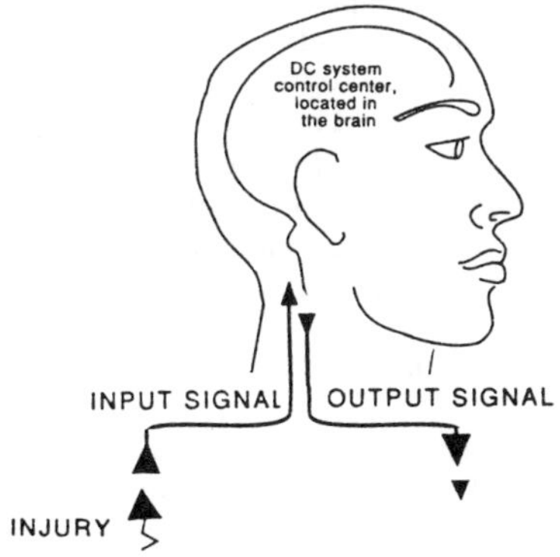

An injury causes bleeding, which forms a clot over the wound, followed by fibrosis, i.e the production of fibrous tissue called collagen. Blood platelets release a chemical called Platelet-Derived Growth Factor (PDGF) which activates the DNA in fibroblast cells, producing collagen fibres which draw the sides of the wound together. Meanwhile, skin cells at the injury `front' begin dividing, forming more new cells, which migrate over the fibrous tissue for complete healing. Later, the fibres are assimilated into the body background material.

But many questions arise : what started the healing process ? What tells the cells precisely what repair material to make, and what stops the process when healing is complete ? The cells are behaving in very odd fashion, seen to advantage in the case of a fertilised human embryo. This begins as a single apparently unorganised cell, but develops into an incredibly-complex organism composed of many types of cell. But how are these produced ?

The classic explanation is that the DNA in the original cell contains the blue-print for the end-product organism, and that where a specific type of cell is required, the rest of the blue-print unconnected with that type is somehow repressed and rendered inactive. Each part of the twin-helix DNA controls production of specific cells, e.g muscle, protein etc. in specific parts of body. This enables a human egg to produce the matured cells required for growth - `differentiation' - but we have not so far identified in DNA the blue-print for the *whole* design : we know a lot about the growth process, but little or nothing of the control system which tells the DNA what type of cell is needed in any specific part of the organism.

Clearly, the control system is not built into the synaptic-transmission design of nerve cells. Very early organisms had no neural network of cells but could heal themselves and rebuild. The basis of the human `healing' control system is an *input signal* from the injury area to brain, plus an *output* signal to the fibroblast cells around the affected area to make collagen fibres. Moreover, nerve fibres normally terminate in special sense organs - for example, touch or pressure receptors - and never terminate in the `dead ends' of simple skin cells. But skin and nerves have common cell characteristics (i.e. the exoderm) and Becker believed that a special electrical relationship could exist between skin and nerve. Was this part of the elusive control system ? To produce the differentiation effect in cells, it was essential not only to have an electrical power supply of the right polarity but the cells themselves should be sensitive to DC electrical currents - and not all cells fulfill that requirement.

The Miracle of Regeneration

Dr. Becker next turned to regeneration - the way in which a salamander can grow a complete replacement limb (Fig. 32). First, the skin grows quickly across the stump of the amputated limb and the nerves grow into it, making the `neuroepidermal junction' (NEJ). Thereafter, the negative DC `current of injury' alters the DNA of the mature red cells of muscle, bone etc causing them to differentiate, becoming a mass of primitive cells called the *blastema.* This is the raw material from which the new limb will grow : the new cells again differentiate and multiply, into the specific cells needed to make the new limb.

But the fundamental problem was unresolved : *what tells the blastema its precise location in the salamander's body, and what form it should eventually take ?* The search for the central control system went on.

More Clues along the Line -

Next, Dr Becker began an investigation into acupuncture, a system of points and meridians on the human skin developed by the Chinese. Quite extensive surgery can be performed under acupuncture. The points are pain-blockers with specific electrical parameters, and the meridians have the general characteristics of transmission lines which are lacking in

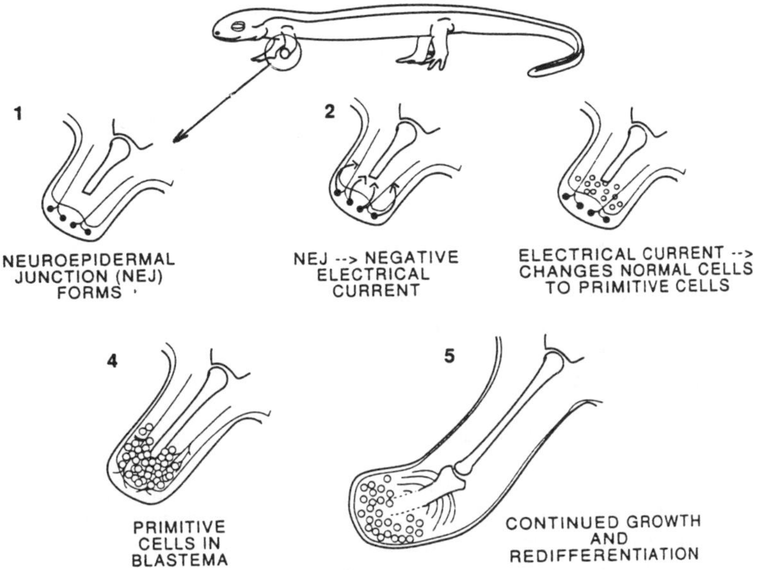

Fig. 32

Limb Regeneration in Salamanders

ordinary skin. But because DC currents flowing along conductors diminish in intensity because of resistance, the acupuncture points function as booster units. A metal needle inserted at such a point will cause electrical disturbance in that area, disrupting the transmission of pain input signals from the wound to the brain along the meridians. In other words, they open and deactivate a closed-loop input/output system.

This was encouraging : the alternate transmission control system was taking shape. Given that chemical/synaptic input injury signals and output healing signals are part of an established regeneration system, how is the new growth told what kind of tissue to become ? Becker's experiments showed that synaptic nerve cell transmission stopped at the end of an amputated stump, which still received external information, indicating the existence of a secondary *non-physical* channel of communication.

Morphogenetic Fields

The salamander's ability to regenerate amputated limbs is unique, although a severed earthworm will in time grow a new head and tail. For example, up to ten days after amputation, the blastema on a salamander's fore leg stump can be removed and re-attached near the animal's hind legs, where it will grow into a perfect *hind* leg, or perhaps a second tail. Dr. Becker saw this as confirmation of some directing mechanism within the animal which incorporates a total-body plan, including a directive to the blastema what member-tissue it should grow into. And remember, there is no identifiable physical nerve connection between body and blastema. The nerves in the *implantation* area will grow into the blastema and initiate regeneration, while those in the amputated stump remain uncommunicative.

The logical answer seemed to be the morphogenetic field postulated by Prof. G.D. Wassermann. He described them as `self entities' which are capable of surviving physical death, and develop in form and structure between embryonic form and adulthood; they surround and envelop the human body/brain entity. At this point we will benefit from reviewing what we know about electromagnetic fields.

Einstein tells us that EMFs are not bound to any bearer : they are independent realities which are not reducible to anything else. Even the simplest field has a high degree of organisational complexity, as Dr. Becker points out. He describes a field created by connecting to a battery two electrodes located in a dish containing a dilute salt solution. Electricity flows from one electrode to the other, but not as a linear current of charged particles : rather, we find a dispersed field of activity in which current, voltage strength and direction of flow at any one coordinate have particular values and can be used to represent information.

Dr. Becker saw this as a major breakthrough. If the elusive electronic control system proved to be a morphogenetic field as we have described, it represented a secondary nervous system so far undetected in the human body. The system appears to operate on an analog basis : early analog computers worked by means of DC currents in which data was encoded by current strength, flow direction and strength variation (precisely as happens in the morphogenetic field). It will be recalled that we described the body EMF as a resultant of the millions of small cell EMFs, sometimes seen as the aura, which extends outside the body. Becker suggested that such an analog data transmission system must be functioning in the DC injury repair system and in the regeneration process, using a semiconducting current; the vital point here is that the morphogenetic field, unlike the ordinary nerve-impulse data transmission system across the synaptic gap, can carry data to the blastema beyond the nerve fibre cut-off point. It is, in effect, an intelligence field, and the DC currents in the neural cell/fibre network are similarly semiconducting by nature.

How is this secondary transmission system powered ? Dr. Becker suggests that a likely source is the perineural cells - that is, all non-nerve cells in the brain. They are packed around the nervous system and include the glial cells in brain and spinal cord, and the Schwann cells encasing the peripheral nerves in the cortex. All have a common root, the ectoderm primary cell line. Only recently, it has been found that perineural cells can generate DC electric potentials and pass them from one to another, including the signals which cause fractures to heal, without involvement of the nerve impulse system.

We are now approaching the final stages of this exercise. Intensified research into body DC systems has shown that when a human subject is told to make a certain muscular movement when a signal is activated, there is an increase in negative DC after the signal - *but this occurs almost half a second before the muscular action is performed* ! What seems to be happening is that the DC current pre-organises the neurons for firing the command to move the muscles. It is a well-known phenomenon known as the `readiness-potential' and it has an even more startling characteristic discovered by Dr. Benjamin Libet of the University of California. In trying to establish which came first - the readiness-potential phenomenon, or the decision itself - Libet found firm indications that the RP *preceded* the decision. In his own words : `*The brain seemed to have a* "mind" *of its own'*. The DC system, in fact, appears to be a decision-making entity - the human self, generated and contained in a morphogenetic field centred around but independent of the body.

There is one further fascinating item. Dr. Becker predicted in the early 1960s that the DC current flow in the brain would produce a magnetic field that could be observed outside the head, given a suitable detection facility. That observation was greeted with hilarity, because no such device existed at that time. Today, the magnetoencephalogram (MCG) is easily detected using the SQUID magnetometer, at a distance of several feet from the subject's head. It is also known as the aura, and is an intelligent conscious field containing the `self' entity - and we know that entity has a duration-extension of its own in Space 2. Further, it is capable of interaction and interference with other fields (including the wave function Probability Field) at a considerable distance, providing a working mechanism for the human ability to collapse the wave function indeterminacy ahead of the Present Moment, and `realise' a particular event version.

\+ + +

This argument not only demonstrates the admittedly-limited ability of human beings to decide their own fates, but presents definitive evidence confirming the Fixed Time Field Theory. Further, it shows that whilst the human self functions in the body EMF in close association with the mind and brain, it is omnipresent in Space 2. After physical death, the self EMF, as an indistinct aura, may remain temporarily at least in Space 1 within the Present Moment discontinuity it experienced when alive : here, I refer to apparitions and ghosts. It is no surprise that the ghostly self EMF may register on camera film, in the same way that Kirlian photography can reveal the outline of a missing portion of a leaf. And in a remarkable way, all this evidence `seems to fit in', as I said at the beginning of this book. When we examine various paranormal phenomena (with the possible exception of astrology) we find an impressive degree of conformation to the thesis in precognition, telepathy, psychokinesis, déja vu, inspiration, magic, good luck and bad. Most important, the Fixed Time Field follows from simple basic precepts involving Time, motion and space : it contravenes no natural laws by co-existing with our own universe, and its very arrangement and configuration follows the principles of gravitation and curved Space-Time.

Most important for many readers, the theory suggests that the human self survives physical death since it already inhabits Space 2; there, it awaits the burgeoning of another universe from another Big Bang, a continuum in which the patterns of our lives are built-in, but always subject to improvement by the decisions we take. All this, with no religious connotations - except the one I accept in my own heart : that statistics indicate that this whole incredible arrangement could not have come into existence by chance. This is in no way confirmation of the existence of a Supreme Creator : if the great cavalcade of universes has always existed and will always continue to exist, there can be no moment of Creation and arguably no Creator. My own feeling is that there is such an entity, but of such dimensions and omnipotence that mere human beings are incapable of identifying it. Nor do I feel that we should try.

One point remains. The duration-extension containing a human self EMF in Space 2 begins at conception (the Space-Time location at which the self entity infiltrates itself into the newly-conceived embryo) and ends with physical death of the body and the start of a new cycle). Bearing in mind the indeterminacy of wave-function events ahead of the Present Moment, it is possible that a human time-track may not contain a physical-death event. In other words it is possible (within the limitations of the Probability Field) for a person to live forever - and the same applies to the salamander. But in real life, countless fatal diseases attack us and the future is filled with possible fatal accidents along the duration-extension. Whilst many a child dies during the birth process or is born dead, reason suggests that each had a long life - a duration-extension filled with potential events - ahead of it. And this goes some way to supporting the theory of reincarnation : during another cycle the child may survive the birth trauma to set out on that long journey into the indeterminate future.

Looking into that same future and measuring possibilities against recent progress in medical science, it may happen that all the major killing diseases may be exterminated, that we may learn to modify the DNA/chromosome/gene structure to reproduce young healthy cells, and perhaps even confirm (as I suspect) that aging itself is no more than a terminal disease for which a cure may be found. The secret of eternal life may rest in some undiscovered anti-agathic drug. Henry Stapp[44] wrote :

> `*The important thing about Bell's Theorem is that it puts the dilemma posed by quantum physics clearly into the realm of macroscopic* (universal) *phenomena. . . it shows that our ordinary ideas about the world are somehow profoundly deficient, even on the macroscopic*

level. Faster-than-light communication is impossible because no signal can travel faster than C - but because faster-than-light communication has been demonstrated, it must be by other means than signals.

`Quantum phenomena provide prima facie *evidence that information gets around in ways that do not conform to classical ideas. Thus the idea that information is transferred superliminally is,* a priori, *not unreasonable. Everything we know about nature is in accord with the fundamental idea that processes of nature lie outside Space-Time but generate events that can be located in Space-Time. The Theorem supports this view of nature by showing that subliminal transfer of information is necessary, barring certain alternatives that seem to be less reasonable. Indeed, the philosophical position of Nils Bohr* (a Danish physicist who applied quantum theory to Rutherford's model of the atom to explain spectrum lines of the hydrogen atom) *seems to lead to the rejection of the other possibilities, and hence by inference, to the conclusion that superliminal transfer of information is necessary.*

I rest my case.

\+ + +

GENERAL SUMMATION

1. In the conscious waking state the mind/brain in the left hemisphere handles real-world data input via the five senses, consciousness and self-awareness being products of the Bose Einstein condensate background.

2. The unconscious state is one of zero-mentation, e.g. under anaesthetic.

3. The subconscious in the right brain hemisphere is the corollary state to the conscious left-lobe mind.

4. The mind is a product of the total-order subatomic symmetry of a Bose Einstein condensate, existing as a composite electromagnetic field containing all the subatomic particle EMFs of the brain itself.

5. The BE condensate functions in conscious and subconscious states.

6. The self is literally a self-contained independent entity inhabiting the morphogenetic EMF of the whole body but concentrated in the cerebral area. It functions in both the conscious and subconscious states, is omnipresent in the body duration-extension and is the

supreme decision-making entity.

7. The subconscious incorporates a number of mentation zones including the meditation and dreaming levels, the unconscious mentation-free level and access to the numinous level.

8. On the subconscious level, an autonomous Dream Producer constructs dream scenarios on a continuous basis for the benefit of the self and the subconscious mind - a restorative therapeutic process which may be preceded by the mind/self spending a period in the meditational non-mentation level. The dreaming mind may be either spectator or participant.

9. The self receives continuous world-views of events from the scanning processing mind, and makes decisions accordingly. Where the input/analysis and data transmission systems are faulty, the self may receive a distorted world view causing personality problems.

10. Quantum particles possess a degree of consciousness and awareness within individual and larger resultant EMFs. When an additional energy input vibrates the cortical nerve cells to form a Bose Einstein condensate, full coherent consciousness is established, within the limitations of the developed neuron network of the brain.

11. Whilst the entire body and brain is replicated cell by cell many times during an average life span, the self EMF remains unaffected by Time or physical deterioration.

12. Electromagnetic fields including the morphogenetic human self may exist freely in space independent of any material body, possessing duration-extensions in Space 2 similar to those of solid bodies. The self EMF in Space 2 has access to all past and future events, remaining there after death of the physical body.

13. That transition may not occur immediately, and the self EMF may become visible to some sensitive observers as auras, ghosts or apparitions. In timeless Space 2 the self EMF is available again for injection into a newly-conceived foetus in the next cosmic cycle. Reincarnation is a natural function of the universe.

14. The Bell Theorem, the Bose Einstein condensate generating coherent thought and Dr Becker's work on the DC-powered secondary data transmission system, encapsulated in the morphogenetic field principle all demonstrate the link between the human mind and potential wave-function events ahead of the travelling Present Moment, by means of superliminal communication between particles at quantum

level. That link enables the human mind to collapse the wave function Probability Field ahead of the PM, to realise specific event-versions.

15. The Fixed Time Field concept presents a viable explanation for many aspects of the paranormal including precognition, inspiration, *déja vu*, telepathy and psychokinesis.

16. It removes to a great extent the uncertainty of the meaning of mankind's presence in the cosmos, showing that to a greater or smaller extent we have control of our own destinies, as long as they remain reasonably close to the Probability Geodesic.

17. Whilst the thesis contains no place for religion in the recognised sense, its very complexity suggests that the universe could not have come into existence by chance. The cosmic bottom line is this : if Time and the universe have always existed, there was never a creation and, *per se*, no Creator. Alternatively, mankind needed a crutch to lean on - a father-figure for reassurance, protection, love and a source of wisdom - and invented a Supreme Being to fit the bill. Your guess is as good as mine. . .

There is little more to say. In more educated and qualified hands, the FTF thesis could have been presented more clearly and authoritatively, perhaps with mathematical proofs. If the narrative is at times unsequential, repetitive and tautological, I can only point to the flow of additional information requiring evaluation, understanding and inclusion. Writing this book resembled being in a room with a dozen doors, each opening up on some new vista of this strange universe. In these domains, more often than not, I was a stranger - a tenderfoot armed only with the knowledge I could wring from some reference book. Reading the proof copy, I was confronted constantly with yawning omissions of material which, in the general context, was of vital importance to the story.

On a personal note, I find myself in a strange situation. If I am right (I have no personal doubts) I may be the only man alive to know precisely where I am going and what will happen, after I die. That time will soon arrive, since I am now 72 and suffering from multiple myeloma. Yet I have an unfair advantage over most of my friends : because of the implications of the thesis, I can face the future with enormous confidence. In my next incarnation I may have no recollection of this life, but I believe the next edition of this book will be suitably amended and corrected, with improved presentation and credibility. If so, it will be due wholly to my wife Joyce, who will be there, God willing, to answer the phone, open the mail and make the coffee.

Wilbur Wright
Southampton

BIBLIOGRAPHY

1. KUHN Thomas `The structure of Scientific Revolution' University of Chicago Press 1962
2. WILSON Colin `Beyond the Occult' Bantam 1988
3. BERGSON Henri `Time and Free Will' Allen/Unwin London 1959
4. GREENHOUSE Herbert B. `Premonitions - A Leap into the Future' Turnstone, London 1972
5. McKENZIE Andrew `Riddle of the Future' Arthur Barker London 1974
6. DUNNE John William `Experiment with Time' Faber London 1934
7. FRASER J.T. `The Voices of Time' Geo. Braziller Inc. 1968
8. GOUDSMIDT Samuel/CLAIBORNE Robert. From Life Science Library : `TIME' and Editors of LIFE (C) Time-Life Books New York 1966
10. ORNSTEIN R. `Right and Left-Handed Thinking' PSYCHOLOGY TODAY, May 1973
11. HAWKING Stephen/PENROSE Roger Space-Time Publications 1988. Extracted from `A Brief History of Time' Bantam Press. All rights reserved.
12. KOHLER Wolfgang `Gestalt Psychology' Liverwright New York 1929
13. OUSPENSKY P.D. `A New Model of the Universe' Routledge & Keegan New York 1929
14. PRIESTLEY J.B. `Over the Long High Wall' Heinemann London 1972
15. ZUKAV Gary `Nature of the Space-Time Continuum'
16. RANDALL John `Psyckokinesis' Souvenir Press London
17. BENTOV Itzhak `Stalking the Wild Pendulum' E.P.Dutton New York 1977
18. GOOCH Stan `The Paranormal' `Personality and Evolution' Wildwood House London
19. ZOHAR Danah `The Quantum Self' Bloomsbury 1990
20. ZOHAR Danah `Through the Time Barrier' Heinemann 1982
21. INGLIS Brian `Science and Parascience' Hodder & Stoughton 1984
22. GOWAN John C. `Operations of Increasing Order' Gowan 1980
23. BROAD Prof. C.E. `Philosophy' Vol.X No. 38
24. TYRRELL G.N.M. `The Personality of Man' Penguin 1947
25. RHINE Dr.J.B./Mrs. Luisa `The Reach of the Mind' Faber & Faber London
26. OSIS K./FAHLER J. `Space and Time Variables in ESP' ASPR 58 (1964)
27. WATSON Lyall `Beyond Supernature' Hodder & Stoughton London 1973
28. POLK V.A./KRYLOV N.S./KHALFIN L.A. Soviet Journal of E. & T. Physics 1947
29. OSBORN Arthur W. `The Future is Now' University Books New York 1961
30. STEVENSON Dr. (MD) Journal, ASPR 54, October 1950, 59 July 1965
31. LAMBERT G.W. SPR Journal June 1962
32. FREUD Sigmund `Interpretation of Dreams' 1899
33. JUNG Carl Gustav `Memories, Dreams, Reflections' Fontana London 1963
34. MYCROFT Charles `The Innocence of Dreams' Hogarth 1979
35. MACKENZIE Norman `Dreams and Dreaming' Bloomsbury 1989
36. HARDING Rosemary `An Anatomy of Inspirations' W.Heffer & Sons 1940
37. ZUKAV Gary `The Dancing Wu Li Masters' Hutchinson London 1979
38. GRIBBIN John `In Search of the Big Bang' Heinemann 1988
39. FOSTER David `The Intelligent Universe' Abelard London
40. WILSON Colin `Encyclopædia of Unsolved Mysteries' Harrap 1987
41. KOESTLER Arthur `Roots of Coincidence' Courtesy Peters Fraser & Dunlop Ltd
42. GOOCH Stan `Total Man' Abacus London
43. KANT Emmanuel `Critique of Pure Reason' Dutton New York 1972
44. HARRISON Michael `Vanishings' New English Library 1981
45. BOHM David `Quantum Theory' Constable 1951
46. PENROSE Roger in Blakemore/Greenfield `Mindwaves' Blackwell 1987
47. MARSHALL Ninian `ESP and Memory, a Physical Theory' British Journal for Philosophy of Science Vol.10 1960
48. ORLOV Yuri `The Wave Logic of Consciousness : a Hypothesis' International Journal of Theoretical Physics Vol.21 1982
49. FROLICH Prof. Herbert `Long-Range Coherence and Energy Storage in Biological Systems International Journal of Quantum Chemistry Vol.2 1968
50. WASSERMANN Prof. G.D.
51. MANN W.E.
52. WECHSLER D.
53. BECKER Dr. Robert O. `Cross Currents' Bloomsbury 1991

INDEX

Abercrombie, J. 106
Acceleration, 156, 199
Acupuncture, 255
Adrenaline, 232
Agostino, St. Thomas 212
Alpha rhythm, 123-4, 246
Amino acid, 245
Amnesia, 107
Anaesthesia, 10, 110, 122, 124
Andreyev, 180
Antimatter, 177
Apparitions, 15, 119, 126, 257, 260
Arc, Joan of 114
Archetypes, 105, 111
Arimathea, Joseph of 22
Aristotle, 7, 13, 16, 57-8, 60, 64, 156, 181, 201
Astral body, 248
Astrology, 23, 53, 202-3, 257
Atom, 163-5, 199, 241, 247-250, 259
Attenborough, Sir David 39
Auden W.H., 52
Audio-PCE, 45
Augustinius, Aurelius 56, 194
Aura, 40, 118, 247-9, 256-7, 260
Autosuggestion, 104, 130
Autonomous systems, 89, 95, 103, 108-10. 116,
- 128-9, 131,
- dream Production 103, 108-10,
- 116, 128, 131
- oneirolysis 112
- `night-watchman' 129
- self-preservation 129
Axon, 224-6, 250

Bacon, Friar 60
Background 125-6, 128, 157, 160, 179, 228, 231-3, 239, 241-2, 244-5, 253, 259
- consciousness 125-6, 128,
- thought 125-6, 128, 179, 228, 231-
- 233, 239, 241-2, 244-5, 253, 259
- thought screen 126
- imagery 119, 126
- light 157
- presentation 126
- radiation 160
Bang, Big - 64, 86-7, 159-60, 171-3, 178, 258
- before 64, 172-3, 182, 206
- date of 172
- location 178
- origin of 87
- preceding 159
- start of duration 86
- terminology 159-60
- universe 173
Barker, J.C. 35
Bathurst, Benjamin 212
Becker, Dr. Robert O. 251, 253-7, 260
Behe,George 29-31, 41-6
Bell Experiment, 70, 165-6, 168, 181, 203, 207,
- 250, 258, 260-1
Bentov, Itzhak 83-4, 177-8, Figs. 12-14
Bergson, Henri 52, 70
Berlioz, Hector 147
Bernadette, 147
Bernstein, Julius 252
Beta rhythm, 246
Blake, William 133, 143
Blastema, 254-6
Blyton, Enid 143
Bohm, David 239-240
Bohr, Nils 165, 259
Boson, 70, 166, 207
Brahms, Johannes 144
Brain, 8, 9, 26, 32, 69, 89, 111, 119, 122-3, 126,
- 161, 168-70, 179, 222-9, 230-3,236,
- 238, 240-243, 248-50, 254-7, 259-
- 261, Fig. 29
- and mind 119, 170, 233
- and self 229
- areas 228
- as superconductor 69
- axon 224-5
- Broca's Area 228, 231, 238
- capacity 227
- cell 161, 169, 226, 230, 240, 244,
- 256, 260
- cell loss 225
- cell vibration 250
- cerebellum, 225
- cerebrum, 224
- condensate state 242-3
- corpus callosum 222
- cortex 224, 236
- data transmission 122, 126, 250
- death 236
- DC currents, 257
- dendrite 224
- description 222 *et seq*
- development 227
- EMF 126, 168, 248, 250, 257, 259
- epilepsy 238
- frontal lobe 61, 224
- function duplication 225
- hyperthalamus 224
- image production 126, 161
- in dreams 106, 107
- input signals 254, 256
- interacting systems 243
- left lobe 61-2, 113, 117, 230, 232,
- 238, 259
- lobes 169, 224, 229-30, 232-3, 236
- location of mind 231
- medulla oblongata 225
- memory 105, 228
- mentation modes 110
- mentation process 233, 241

- mentation zones 111, 123
- midbrain 224-5
- neural dipoles 95
- neural network 89, 225, 242, 249,
- 260
- neuron 224, Fig. 30
- occipital lobe 117, 224
- operating temperature 242
- parietal lobe 224
- particle awareness 168
- perineural cells 257
- physiology 228, 230
- quantum state 240, 242
- research 61
- rhythms 212
- right lobe 61, 88-9, 95-6, 98, 103,
- 113, 116-7, 119, 123, 126, 230, 232
- 238, 259
- size 227-8
- stem 224, 231, 238
- sulcus 224
- synapse 224
- synaptic gap 226
- temperature 242
- temporal lobe 224
- thought process 179
- Time, perception of 61, 86-7, 89-91
- transmission systems 226
- weight 227-8
Breuer, Dr. Joseph 104
Broad, Prof.C.D. 16, 176
Broca's Area, 228
Bronte, Charlotte 142
Bruyere, Rev. Rosalyn 248
Buddhism, 8, 148, 169, 181
Bush, Pres. George 23
Burr, Dr. H.S. 246
Byron, Lord 136

Callosum, corpus 99, 123, 149, 222, 236, 238,
- 251
Carington, Whateley 19
Carroll, Lewis, 147
Cassandra, 26
Catatonia, 237
Causality, 8, 48, 53, 57, 69, 72, 98-9, 140, 147,
150-1, 198, 202, 213, 227, 205-6
- alternatives to 205
- beyond 203
- J.B. Priestley 68, 70
- Law of 57, 72, 98-9, 198, 202, 205,
- 206
- principle of 205
- root of 206
- Schopenhauer 205
- Time Shunt 140, 147, 150-1
- violation of 205
- world view 213
Cerebellum, 225, 230-1
Cerebrum, 224-5, 231, 242, 248
Chance, 97, 160, 165, 181, 185-6, 192
Cheetham, Erika 23
Ching, I 13, 21, 204, 213-5, 217, 251
- description 204
- Jung evaluation 204
- personal use 215
- modus operandi 213-5, 217
- text 213
Chopin, Frederic François 144
Chromosome, 245, 258
Claiborne, Robt. 58, 70
Clairvoyancy, 28, 44, 50, 53, 201
Claustrophobia, 41, 190, 188
Clytemnestra, 26
Cohen, John 70
Coincidence, 20, 22, 29, 37, 41, 55, 189-90, 192,
- 195, 202-5, 208, 214-5, 217, 239
Coleridge, Samuel Taylor 115
Collagen, 254
Concordski, 39
Condensate, Bose Einstein - 239, 242-4, 249-50,
- 259-60
Conduction, 253
Consciousness - 9, 10, 14, 16, 20, 24, 27, 36, 61-
- 63, 68-9,70, 76, 82, 84, 88, 92, 95-
- 96, 98, 120, 123-5, 129, 134, 137,
- 140, 144, 161, 165, 168, 181, 201,
- 203, 205, 207-8, 220-1, 230-1, 234-
- 235, 239-244, 254, 259, 260
- Altered States of 9, 10, 20, 24, 27,
- 36, 82, 84, 88, 92, 95-6, 98, 137,
- 140, 144, 161, 165, 168,
- 181, 201, 205, 208, 214-5, 217, 236
- and superconductivity 69
- background 95, 120, 242, 244,
- 259
- characteristics 241
- collapse, wave-function 235
- definition 219, 220-1
- discontinuity 92
- holographic model 243
- image generation 125 *et seq*
- levels 123, 230-1, 234, 254, Figs.
- 15-16
- models 239-240, 243
- nature of 10
- normal state 207
- `one-ness' 240
- origin 241, 260
- Ornstein thesis 61
- particle 203, 205, 221, 260
- quantum mechanics 240
- sleep 231
- Space 1 124
- stream of 129
- Time perception 61-3, 67-8, 70, 76
- Universal 88, 205, 240
- G.N.M.Tyrrell 134
- world view 218

Constable, John 133
Continuum, 57, 59, 67, 77, 81, 88, 92-3, 95, 98,
- 110, 127, 129, 140, 147, 258
Copernicus, 3, 156
Cosmology, 4, 5, 10, 63
Cortex, 224-5, 236, 243-4, 246, 256
Covenant, Ark of the 24
Creation, 43, 70, 88, 105, 117, 134, 140, 143,
- 147, 151-2, 159-61, 172-3, 180,218
- 238, 245-6, 249, 258, 261
Croesus, 25-6
Crook, William 47
Cross-section, duration-extension 203
Cyclic Universe, 169, 173, 178, 180

Darwin, Charles 117
Daudet, 140, 144, 146
Day-dream, 9, 20-1, 27, 61, 99, 110, 121, 123,
- 124, 137, 151
Death 3, 4, 7, 8, 14, 30, 41 *et seq*, 47, 53, 62-4, 66-7, 76, 89, 94-5, 148, 169, 173, 180, 182, 186, 236-7, 247-9, 256-260
- Abraham Lincoln 47
- awareness of imminent 247
- brain 236
- comparison with sleep 14
- Doug Worley 7,8, Frontispiece
- fear of 7
- future event 94-5
- in duration-extension 76, 186, 259
- inevitability 8, 53
- in *SS Titanic* 41 *et eq*
- in Time 62
- Ouspensky thesis 63, 66
- Robert Morris 30
- Schrödinger's Cat 237
- survival after 3, 4, 8, 63-4, 66-7,
- 89, 148, 169, 173, 180, 182, 236,
- 247-9, 256-258, 260
- W.T.Stead 44
Déja vu, 4, 64, 149, 151, 180, 182, 258, 261
Delphi, 13, 25-6
Delusions, 104
Dendrite, 224, 226, 250
Deoxyribonucleic acid, 245
Descartes, Réne 231, 244
Destiny, 3, 7, 8, 29, 33, 194, 196, 216-7
Determinism, 16, 31, 69, 73, 99
Dickens, Charles 143
Differentiation, 231, 254
Diffraction, 164, 165
Dimensions, 8, 16, 50, 55, 57, 59, 63, 65-7, 72,
- 74-9, 81-3, 87-8, 91, 93, 96-7, 148,
- 160, 171, 215
- additional 8
- 1st 75-9, 82, 97
- 2nd 77-9, 97
- 3rd 55, 57, 63, 67, 74-9, 81
- 4th 50, 65-6, 76, 79
- 5th 50, 63, 65-6, 79
- 6th 55, 65, 75, 79, 96
- curvature of 65, 76, 91
- Dunne 55, 71
- duration 66-7, 74, 76
- Euclidean 76
- Form 77
- in FTF 16, 72, 83, 88, 97
- in hyperspace 93
- in Space 2 : 75, 77, 87, 97, 148
- manifestation of 76, 78
- Mobius Strip 59, 63
- Ouspensky 65, 72
- perception of 76 *et seq*
- progression 79
- structure 76
- tesseract 77
- Time 55, 65, 74
Dipoles, 95, 243
Dirac, Paul Adrien Maurice 166
Discontinuity, 10, 68, 70, 76, 86, 158, 163-5,
- 168, 171, 178, 207-9, 217, 221, 235
- 240-1, 251, 257
Dizygotic Twins, 182, 185
DNA, 169, 181, 228, 244-6, 253-4, 258
Dobbs, H.A.C. 32
Dodds, Prof.E.R. 17
Dopamine, 226
Dream - 5-7, 9, 14, 16, 20, 23, 27-9, 30-40,
- 43, 46-8, 54-5, 61-2, 89, 94-96, 103
- 105-6, 109-10, 123, 126-132, 137,
- 139-42, 144-5, 149-51, 236-8, 232-
- 233, 251
- Abraham Lincoln 46-7, 62
- Brighton Case 34
- characters 237
- characteristics 237-8
- channel of communication 9, 129,
- 132
- construction 61, 107-9, 123, 131,
- 233
- content 28, 48, 94, 127
- 137, 140, 150
- delayed start 123
- deprivation 109, 132
- disasters 9
- Doug Worley 6, 7
- forgetting 20, 28, 96, 129, 131-2
- fulfilment 29, 46
- Horse racing 38-40
- imagery 126
- J.W.Dunne 20, 54 *et seq*
- Kubla Khan 140
- lucid 16, 38, 96, 232
- maker/producer 106, 110, 123, 127,
- 128, 140, 144-5
- meaning 105
- motion in 61
- nightmare 232
- Percy Bysshe Shelley 141-2, 145
- personal experiences 38

- precognitive 5, 9, 14, 16, 20, 23,
- 27-8, 32-7, 43, 46-7, 54-5, 89, 130-
- 132, 140, 145, 149-151, 251
- quality 237
- recalling 96, 103, 126, 139, 142,
- 149, 236
- Red airliner 39
- repetitive 47
- Robert Morris Case 30 *et seq*
- shared 128
- Sir Rider Haggard 141
- Sir Walter Scott 141
- Susan Anthony Case 33
- symbolism 39
- theatre 237
- therapeutic value 132
- Time in 61, 95
- *Titanic* Cases 41 *et seq*
- Van Gogh 140
- Victor Hugo 141
- warning 96, 131
- Williams Case 40
- Wolfgang Amadeus Mozart 142
Dreyfuss, Alfred 23
Duality, 10, 119, 138, 164, 230, 233, 238
Dunne, J.W. 5, 7, 10, 20, 54-7, 70-1, 76, 83, 94,
- 138, 161, Fig.1
- books 55
- confusion, Time and duration 55, 57
- PCG dream rejection 55
- duration definition 7
- duration-extension 71
- Experiment with Time 20, 138
- field of observation 76
- frame of reference 71
- PCG dreams 54
- perception of Time 55
- Present Moment 83
- Serial Time 10, 94
- Serial Universe 10, 94
- Time 1, Time 2 70
- Time flow 55-6
- world lines 71
Duration, 7, 8, 10, 43, 52-4, 56-8, 60-3, 65-6,
- 70-1, 73-9, 83-4, 86-7, 91-2, 94-7,
- 108, 137, 140, 156, 160-1, 169-70,
- 177, 205, 215
- and entropy 92
- and motion 178
- axis 75, 87
- Bentov thesis 178
- confusion with Time 56-8, 60, 65-6,
- 70-1, 91
- definition 58
- dimensions 66, 75, 78
- generation of 170
- in dreams 108
- infinite 63
- in Time Mechanism 66
- line 62, 75, 83-4
- measurement 53
- motion and 56-8, 61
- objective perception 57
- origin of 74, 77, 86-7, 91
- perception of 59, 61-3, 70, 73, 76,
- 79, 84, 86, 94-7
- Present Moment 53-4, 58, 87, 96
- rate of 91
- subjective perception 52, 56, 70
Duration-extension, 43, 61, 70-1, 73, 76, 87,
- 93-5, 109, 124, 127-8, 135, 150,
- 158, 163-5, 168-9, 173, 178-9, 181-
- 184, 186, 196, 199, 247-251, 257-9,
- Figs. 3, 4, 5, 27
- adjacent 183
- ahead of PM 70, 178
- behind PM 70
- on Probability Geodesic 184
- creation of 173
- cross-section 183, 186
- curvature 173
- Dunne, J.W. 71
- Earth's 73, 87, 95, 178, 196,
- Figs. 3, 4
- human 76, 179, 183, 186, 199, 247,
- Fig. 27
- identical twins 169, 184, 187
- matter in 158
- particle conciousness 179
- PM movement 96, 159
- Space 2 dimension 77, 88, 158, 178,
- 215, Fig. 5
- *SS Titanic* 43
- self 93-4, 109, 124, 135, 150, 165,
- 182, 186, 247-251, 257-259
- travel along 93, 247
Ecliptic, 74, 169
Ectoderm, 256
Eddington, Sir Arthur 50
Edison, Thomas Alva 134
Einstein, Albert 50, 57, 60, 68, 75, 155, 158-9,
- 162, 165, 170-1, 174-5, 178, 207,
- 239, 242-4, 246, 249-50, 256, 259-
- 260
- Bose Einstein statistics 166
- condensate 239, 242-4, 249-50, 259
- on EMFs 246, 256
- IQ 244
- light experiment 168
- light velocity 158-9, 163, 174, 176
- Nobel Prize 162
- Podolsky-Rosen experiment 247,
- 250
- Principle of Equivalence 175
- Space-Time curvature 159, 170
- Space-Time expansion 171
- Special Theory 159
Electron, 32-3, 50, 70, 162, 165-6, 199, 221-2,
- 235, 240, 247-8, 252, 255

- and Probability 165
- atomic model 165
- characteristics 235, 247
- in EMFs 247
- in electric currents 247, 252
- in thought process 240
- energy emission 162
- Pauli experiment 165
- paths 165
- Probability Wave 221
- quantum discontinuity 165
- symmetry 247-8
- virtual transitions 221-2, 240
- wave 165-6
Elgar, Sir Edward 143, 146
Eliot, George 133, 144
Energy, 32-3, 64, 73, 93, 161-5, 171, 177, 221-
- 222, 227-8, 240, 242-3, 247, 249,
- 252
- and mass 162
- black holes 177
- electrical 243-4, 247, 252
- electron emission 162, 221
- exchange 222
- in aura 249
- in BE condensate 242-3,
- proton streams 171
- pumped 242
- source 227
- in virtual transitions 228, 240, 247
Entropy, 92, 195, 207-8, 217
Epoch, 58, 71, 74, 77, 86-7
Equivalence, Principle of 174-5, 207-8
Eternity, 60, 63
Ether, 163, 246
Eudemus, 64
Event-horizon, 177
Exoderm, 254
Extension - dimension 66, 75, 77, 97
- Earth duration 74, 93
- of Time 63
Extrasensory perception, 16
Eye, 3, 14-15, 65, 67, 110, 117, 120-1, 125-6,
- 128, 143-4, 170, 212, 226-8, 229,
- 231-2, 235, 244
Fahler, J. 19
Fairley, Peter 35
Fatalism, 30
Fermi, Enrico 166, 207
Fermion, 70, 165, 207
Fibroblast, 253
Field, 50, 56, 76, 83, 94, 96, 117, 120, 124-7,
- 158-61, 163-6, 169-72, 175-79, 181
- 186, 189-90, 196, 208, 210-2, 216
- 217, 221-3, 233, 238, 241, 243,
- 248-9, 245-7, 251, 256-260
- Biogravitational 50
- Electromagnetic 117, 120, 124-5,
- 127, 208, 217, 245 (See EMF)
- Electromagnetic (brain) 126
- Gravity 94
- Morphogenetic 247, 256-257, 259-
- 260
- Of observation 56, 76
- Of presentation 120
- Of reference 83, 233
- Probability 96, 159, 163-5, 171, 173
- 179, 184-5, 187, 196, 210-2, 216,
- 221-2, 251, 258
Fixed Time Field, 61, 70, 72, 77-9, 81, 87, 98,
- 108, 130-1, 169, 175, 182-4, 189-
- 90, 221, 235, 245, 249, 252, 257,
- 261
- corroboration of 69, 116, 183, 184
- definition 72, 98, 131
- self in 61
- Space 2 92
- thesis 70, 72, 81, 87, 130
Flatland, 77-9, 82-3, 159
Flow - electric current, 251, 255-7
- Time 50, 55-8, 60-1, 69-70, 73, 81,
- 91, 97, 177, 237-8
Folk, V.A. 32
Forebrain, 225
Form - dimension, 75, 77, 98
Foster, David 205
Franz, M.L. von 70, 207
Fraser, J.T. 56
Frequency, 198, 246, 249
Fresnel, 162
Freud, Sigmund, 102-8, 110-2, 115
- analysis of dreams 103
- `condensation' 115
- history 102
- meaning of dreams 104, 107, 111-2
- sexual theories 106, 110
- theories 104, 110 *et seq*
- use of hypnosis 104
- use of symbolism 103-4, 106, 108
Friedmann-Gamov 173
Fröhlich, Prof. Herbert 242
Future, 10, 17, 28, 48, 54, 103, 109, 112, 122-3, 127, 130-1, 158, 161, 172, 178-9, 200, 203, 205, 214-6, 222, 235, 237, 240, 249, 251, 260-1
- clairvoyance 215
- duration-extension segment 178
- events 10, 17, 28, 48, 54, 103, 109,
- 112, 122-3, 127, 130-1, 158, 161,
- 172, 178-9, 200, 203, 205, 214, 216
- 222, 235, 237, 240, 249, 251, 260-1
- foreknowledge of 16, 19, 27-8, 48,
- 103, 109, 112, 122, 126, 201
- human interface with 132
- *I Ching* 21, 213-4
- indeterminate 179, 235
- intervention in 207, 217
- Maury's Dream 121-2
- multiple versions 21, 31, 36
- Nostradamus 22 *et seq*
- observable 7, 9, 10, 56, 216

- predetermined 8, 197
- predictable 20, 28
- probability 31, 173
- source of dream material 107, 123
- Space 2 205
- Time travel 5
- uncertain 199
- wave-function characteristic 216-7

Galaxy, 59, 62, 155-9, 196-7
Galileo, Galilei 2, 156, 181
Galton, Sir Francis 117
Galvani, Luigi 252
Gauss, Karl Friedrich 80
Ganglions, 27
Garrett, E. 16
Genes, 111, 169, 181, 227, 233, 245
Geodesic, Probability 165, 175-6, 178, 182, 184-
- 186, 188, 190, 199, 200, 210-1, 216
- 217, 221, 261
- adherence to 200
- evidence supporting 212
- human 199
- pressure on event-reality 200, 210,
- 211, 216-7
- return tendency 200
Geometry - Euclidean 79, Fig. 8
- 3-D 79
- non-Euclidean 80
- Riemannian 80, Fig. 9
Ghost, 15, 47, 235, 258, 261
Glial cells, 257
Goddard, AVM Sir Victor 36, 37
Gooch, Stan 88, 92, 209, 221
Goudsmit, Samuel 58, 70
Gowan, John C. 16, 25, 207-9
Gravitation, 7, 50, 165, 175, 258
Graviton, 166
Gravity, 32-3, 49, 76, 85, 93, 156, 170-3, 175,
- 177-8, 200-1, 216
- anti- 85
- strength 93
- template 93
- zero 76
Greenhouse, Herbert B. 36-7, 54, 113
Gribbin, John 70, 159-60, 170, 177
Gyroscope, 85, 99

Haggard, Sir Rider 118, 141
Hallucination, 21, 104, 126, 140, 148, 237
Halton, R.A.F. 2
Halyus, 25
Hamon, Count Louis 44
Harding, Rosamond 135, 138, 141, 144
Harrison, Michael 211
Harvey, William 3
Hauser, Kasper 212
Hawking, Stephen 62
Healing, 253-5
Heaven, 4, 8, 16, 60, 148
Heisenberg, Walter 32, 119, 165, 189, 208
Helmholtz, Hermann von 252
Heraclitus, 59, 107, 202
Herodatus, 25
Hexagram, 213-5
Hindbrain, 225
Hinduism, 8, 64, 148, 169, 180
Hippocrates, 202
Hitler Adolf, 23, 189, 191
Hole, Black 94
Hologram, 241
Horoscope, 53
Hoyle, Fred 159, 173
Hubble, Edwin Powell, 157, 171, 174
Hugo, Victor 141
Humperdinck, Engelbert 146
Huxley, T.H. 201
Hypersonic, 45
Hyperspace, 93
Hypnagogic state, 27, 96, 110, 123-4, 130, 137-
140, 169, 229, 235-6
Hypnosis, 9, 20, 27, 97-8, 104, 106, 112, 124,
- 140, 170
Hypothalamus, 224
Hysteria, 104, 147

Id, 61, 110
Image, 60, 86, 89, 102, 105, 107-13, 116-129,
- 137, 144, 147, 151, 161, 227-8, 231
- 233-4, 236, 240-9, Fig.17
- assessment 227
- construction 60, 86, 89, 102, 105,
- 116-8, 127-9, 137, 144, 147,
- 151, 161, 231, 233, 244
- holographic 241
- Kirlian 249
- memory 228
- Producer 233
- quality 233
- random 236, 244
Imagination, 138, 146
Immortality, 3, 4, 8, 148, 245
Indeterminacy, 241, 251, 257-8
Inertia, 87, 93, 98
Infinity, 158
Inglis, Brian 15
Inspiration, 3-5, 36, 104, 116, 123, 130-40,
- 142, 144-6, 148, 150-1, 157, 179-
- 180, 182-3, 186, 189-190, 210,
- 236, 257, 261
- and Time Shunt 130-40, Fig. 18
- and the paranormal 180
- categories 150
- connection with Time 135, 138, 150
- drying up 142
- Edison 134
- explanation 135
- in hypnagogic state 138
- involuntary 150-1
- mechanism 144

- proof of FTF thesis 5, 116
- reception of material 145-6, 148
- rejection as impossible 142
- secondary 135
- source of 134
- traumatic experience 134
Instantaneity, 73, 84-5, 92, 108, 128, 166, 168
Interval, 35, 46, 49, 53, 57-8, 62, 88, 92, 108,
- 124
Intuition, 5, 10, 27, 109, 115, 136, 147, 151
Ion, 131, 132, 137, 143, 156, 248, 252

Jago, Bishop 57
Jeans, Sir James 218
Jocasta, 25
Judaism, 22
Judas Iscariot, 145
Juladdin, 40
Jung, Carl Gustav 70, 88, 99, 105-7, 110 *et seq*,
112-4, 204-7, 209,
- archetypes 105, 110 *et seq*
- causality 205-6
- founder, analytical psychology 105-
- 106
- I Ching 204
- on dreams 112-4
- rejection of Freud's ideas 105, 107
- synchronicity 70, 99, 204, 206-7,
- 209
- the Id 110
- theories 107, 110 *et seq*
- Universal Consciousness 88, 205

Kant, Emmanuel 209
Keats, John 132, 143
Kennedy, Sen. Robert 113-4
Kepler, Johan 157
Kerlor, W,. de 44-5
Khalfin, L.A. 32
Khan, Kubla 136
Kilner, 248, 257
Kirlian, Semyon 248, 257
Koestler, Arthur 203-5
Kohler, Wolfgang 62
Korsakov, Rimsky 148
Krylov, N.S. 32
Kuhn, Thomas 3
Kummel, Friedrich 70

Laman, Ward Hill 46
Lambert, G.W. 35, 46
Lamon, 48
Levels, 110-1, 123-4, 126, 165-6, 168, 198, 207-8, 221, 230-4, 236, 240, 242, 248, 258, 260
- consciousness 110-1, 123-4, 165-6,
- 168, 198, 207-8, 230, 231, 234, 236
- energy 240, 242
- intelligence 224, 228, 244
- macroscopic 258
- mentation 111, 123, 126, 232-3,
- 236
- numinous 260
- quantum 166, 221, 240, 246, 248,
- 260
- subconscious 260
- unconscious 260
Levitation, 111
Libet, Benjamin 257
Life-wave, 183
Light, 27, 33, 47, 59, 64, 76-7, 83, 85, 157-0,
- 162-3, 165-72, 174, 176-7, 182, 186
- 199, 205,
- background 157
- black holes 177
- characteristics 162, 163
- cone 50
- Einstein 162
- ether 163
- Fitzgerald-Lorentz 163
- gravitational deflection 171
- in Space 2 170, 205
- photons 165, 169
- quanta 163
- red shift 157
- spectrum 77
- velocity of 59, 64, 76, 83, 157-9,
- 163, 166, 172, 174, 176-7, 182
- violet 163
- wavelength 77
- wave packet 199
- Young Experiment 167-8
- wave 85
Lincoln, Abraham 46-8
Lineworld, 79
Lorentz, Hendrik Antoon 163
Loye, David 61-2
Lowei, Otto 252

Macdonald, Colin 43
MacKenzie, Norman 106, 204
Mckenzie, Andrew 42, 54
Magic, 5, 13-4, 19, 29, 34, 36, 42, 44, 72, 85, 96
- 108, 111, 118, 132, 142, 165, 204,
- 207, 209, 212
Magnetoencephalogram, 257
Mann, W.E. 247
Marchant, J. 141
Marshall, Ninian 240
Mass, 5, 32-3, 61, 87, 90, 95, 158-9, 164-5, 170,
- 175, 182,
- General Relativity Theory 175
- gravitational distortion 170
- in Black Holes 182
- increase at high velocity 158
- infinite 159
- inertial 174-5
- link with energy 162
- particle 164-5
Matter, 33-4, 59, 62, 70, 77, 85, 92, 98, 156,
- 158-161, 163, 165, 173-7, 182, 188

- characteristics 77
- H.A.C. Dobbs 33
- in plenum 59
- motion of 62, 98, 178
- particle-function 70, 85, 92
- quantum discontinuity 34
- solidity 70, 92
- wave-function 70, 85
Maury, L.F. Alfred 122-3, 236
Maybus, 23
Mechanism - Data Transmission 112
- Decision-making 230
- Dream 106, 109, 119
- I Ching 215
- Image Generation, 102
- Immortality 245
- Memory 228
- Mentation 244
- Neuron alignment 242
- Thought 239
- Time 172-3,179-180, 199, 205,239
- dimensions of 96
- Dunne 54
- duration in 66, 74, 91
- human self in 95
- Isaac Newton 57
- J.B. Priestley 68
- Ouspensky P.D. 66
- perception of 76, 86
- search for 57, 71, 81
- Wave Function Collapse 239, 249
Medawar, J.P. 104
Meditation, 125, 128
Memory, 3, 9, 13, 28, 39, 109, 112-3, 139, 145,
- 147, 150-1, 201, 224, 227-9, 231,
- 235-6, 240, 245
- banks 109
- computer 3
- in dreams 9, 13, 39
- in PCG tests 201
- overload 28, 113
- retrieval 112
- Loop 140, 147, 151
Mentation, 10, 107, 110-11, 123, 125, 132, 220,
222, 226, 231-4, 236, 240-4, 250, 259-60
Menzones, 90, 123, 125, 131
Meridians, acupunture 256
Metaphysics, 2, 63
Michelson, A.A. 163
Milton, John 153
Mind - 3, 8-10, 13, 17-8, 20-1, 27, 29, 35-6, 46,
- 54, 61, 67, 73, 86, 88-9, 94-6, 103-
- 104, 110-12, 117-120, 123, 125-7,
- 129, 131, 133-5, 137-8, 143-4, 150-
- 151, 161, 166, 168-70, 173, 179,
- 201, 204, 208-9, 211-2, 214-5,
- 218-222, 226-239, 241-4, 249-51,
- 257-61
- and paranormal 179
- analytical function 96
- characteristics 209
- Collective Unconscious 111
- conscious 9, 10, 13, 17-8, 36, 54,
- 61, 73, 89, 226, 239
- control of 89, 239
- data transmission 73, 86, 88, 110,
- 123, 129, 131, 161, 169
- definition 10, 89, 117, 220-1, 243-
- 244, 259
- description 126
- deterioration 169
- duality 89, 111, 117, 119, 169, 230,
- 232-5, 238
- function 61, 110-11, 117
- I Ching 204, 214, 215
- image creation 118, 120, 125-7,
- 129, 237, 244
- interference, Probability Field 212
- hypnosis 170
- memory 231
- mind/particle relationship 232
- mind/Time interface 17, 249
- perception of duration 61
- psychokinesis 215
- quantum 21
- rejection of paranormal 20, 27, 54
- sleeping 9, 10, 27, 39-41, 47, 231-2
- source of inspiration 134
- subconscious 17-8, 29, 35-6, 46,
- 61, 67, 73, 89, 94-5, 133-5, 137-8,
- 143-4, 150-1, 209, 211, 214, 215,
- 232, 235-6, 259, 260
- states of 54, 70, 103-4, 112, 208
Miracle, 15, 19, 21
Mobius Strip, 60, 83, 159, Fig. 11
Molecule, 33, 94
Moment, Present 17, 53-7, 61, 67-8, 70-4, 76,
- 81, 83, 85-6, 91-7, 108, 125, 139,
- 151, 158-9, 163-4, 169, 178, 183-
- 186, 216-7, 221, 235, 238-40, 251
- 257-9, 261, Fig. 18
- adjacent PMs 61, 71, 95
- ahead of 164, 221, 235, 238-40,
- 250-1, 257-8
- and Time Shunt 151, Fig. 18
- at high velocities 76, 91
- behind PM 70, 159, 163, 178
- characteristics 86
- communal 108, 217
- Dunne 55-6, 76, 83
- duration-extension cross-section 97,
- 183-186
- duration of 53, 87, 96
- generates duration-extension 74
- identical twins, 188
- identification 53
- life-wave 68, 76, 85, 92, 96
- measurement of 53
- movement of 70, 81, 92-3, 96, 139,
- 158, 186, 216

- objective view 57
- perception 53-4, 68, 76, 86, 94, 125
- rate of motion 56, 70-1, 76, 81, 96
- shared 86, 96, 169
- Space-Time location 67, 73-4
- Specious Moment 54
- spread of 54
- stationary 72
- succession 54, 86, 96
- wave-function collapse 178, 217,
- 221, 251, 259, 261
Momentum, 87, 94, 97, 164-5, 198-9
Monads, 206
Monists, 59
Monozygotic twins, 183, 185, 188-9, 192
- characteristics 183
- corroboration of FTF thesis 183,
- 185, 189
- mirror-imaging 188
- one Probability Geodesic 183, 189
Morley, E.W. 163
Morphogenetic Field, 247, 255-7, 259-260
Morris, Robert 30 *et seq*
Motion, 55, 57-9, 61-2, 71, 74, 85-6, 92, 125,
- 156-8, 162-5, 169-70, 174, 176,
- 178
- absolute 157
- acceleration 156
- action quantum 165
- Aristotle 57, 156
- at high velocity 158, 174, 176
- connection with Time 156
- direction of 57, 62, 74, 92
- Dunne 55, 71
- generates duration 57, 62, 74, 169
- in FTF 85, 92
- in Space 1 170
- Michelson-Morley Experiment 163
- molecular 162
- objective 61
- of particles 86. 164
- origin of 59
- particle 162, 164
- perception of 125, 156
- relative 156
- relativity and 57
- relationship with Time 58
- wave 163, 164
- Zeno's Paradox 59
- zero acceleration 178
Mozart, Wolfgang Amadeus 142
Murphy, Gardner 16
Mycroft, Charles 105, 107, 116

Narcosis, 9
Nerve - 126-7, 249, 251-4, 256,
- cell characteristics 240, 252, 254
- circuits 126, 256
- DC impulses 253
- electric charge 252
- fibre 249, 252, 256
- impulse 253, 256
- synapse 251-4, 256
Neuroepidemal Junction, 254
Neuron, 89, 109, 126, 144, 205, 225-6, 230, 243, 249-50, 260, Fig. 30
- network 144, 205, 225-6, 230, 243,
- 249, 250, 260
Neuroses, 104
Neutron, 33, 70, 165, 174, 176
Newton, Sir Isaac 56-7, 80, 156-7, 181
Nietzsche, Friedrich Wilhelm 63
Nightmare, 34, 42, 89, 106, 113, 116, 121, 123,
- 232, 237,
Night-Watchman, 130
Nirvana, 148, 173
Nixon, Richard 113
Norepinephrine, 226
Nostradamus, Michel de 22, 28, 95
Nova, 158, 171
Nucleoprotein, 245
Nucleus, 33, 165, 177, 199, 245
Numinous, 8, 88-9, 124, 260

Oblongata, medulla, 225
Occam's Razor, 59
Occipital lobe, 224
Oedipus, 103
Olber's Paradox, 157
Omnipotence, 144, 181, 232, 258
Omnipresence, 10, 84, 88, 93-4, 124, 128, 131,
- 139-40, 151, 161, 165, 221, 238,
- 249, 257-259
Omniscience, 84, 88, 128, 161
Oneirolysis, 20, 96, 112, 128-130
One-ness, universal 205-6, 209, 214, 217, 240
Oracle, 13, 24-6
Order, 146-7, 168, 208, 211, 217, 230-1, 234,
- 241-2
Origen, 218
Orlov, Yuri 241
Ornstein, R. 61, 229
Osborn, Arthur W. 36
Osis, Karlis 19
Ouspensky, P.D. 4, 5, 63, 65-7, 72, 161, Fig.2
Out-of-the-body experience, 248

Paracelcus, 202
Paranormal, 3, 15-6, 20, 23, 25, 32, 53, 66, 68,
- 72, 91, 145, 155, 161, 164, 169,
- 179-80, 182, 198, 201-2, 215, 251-
- 252, 257, 261
- abilities 25, 28, 32
- and Time 16
- astrology 23, 53, 202-3, 252
- Church's attitude 15
- definition 198
- explained by FTF thesis 155, 169,
- 180, 182
- fear of 20

- *I Ching* 215
- machine-enhanced 201
- phenomena 179, 182
- psychokinesis 164
- Prof. C.D.Broad 16
- research 3
Parapsychology, 5, 68
Parmenides, 59
Particle, 10, 32-3, 70, 77, 83-6, 94, 96, 159-66
- 168-9, 173, 178-9, 183, 186-7, 199
- 203-5, 207-8, 221-2, 226, 235, 238
- 239-42, 246, 248-9, 250-2, 255-6,
- 259-60
- action quantum 165
- ahead of PM 183, 186
- behaviour 240
- Bell Experiment 166, 203
- boson 207
- categories 70
- characteristics 161-3, 165
- communication 203, 223, 260
- consciousness 179, 205, 207, 221,
- 242, 260
- Einstein experiments 168
- electrical charge 164-5
- EMFs 226, 246, 248, 251, 259
- EM radiation 199
- function 70, 77
- indeterminacy 240
- identification 199
- in electric currents 252, 256
- interaction 70, 241, 251
- ionisation 249
- light 162, 181
- location 203
- motion 86
- photon 70, 83
- Planck's Constant, 163
- quantum discontinuity 208, 239
- quantum theory 162
- resonance 250-1
- solidity 10
- space between 159
- spin 207
- tachyon 84, 169
- twin 166, 250
- universal relationship 204, 239
- wave-function 85, 94, 96, 163, 173,
- 178, 187, 222
- wave-function collapse 239, 255
- /wave dualism 222, 235, 238
- Young Experiment 166, 207
Past, 55-6, 60, 62, 67, 70, 83, 93, 103-4, 107,
- 111, 115, 122 126-8, 131, 150-1,
- 203, 205, 214, 216-7, Fig. 18
- association with memory 103-4, 107,
- 111, 115, 126-8, 131
- and déja vu 150
- and Time Shunt 151, Fig. 18
- Bentov thesis 83
- component of duration-extension 70
- division of Time 55
- events 62, 107, 122, 203, 214,216-7
- growth of 56
- in FTF 150, 205
- non-observable 56
- observation of 67
- St. Augustine thesis 60
- time travel 93
Pauli, Wolfgang 165, 199
PCG - see Precognition
Penfield, Wilder 61
Penrose, Roger 62, 240
Perineural cells, 256
Personality, 4, 8, 9, 13, 16, 19, 92, 95, 98, 103,
- 109-10, 124, 132, 143, 148, 173,
- 184, 220, 224-5, 227, 230, 232-4,
- 236, 243, 260
Photon, 70, 83, 162-3, 165-6, 168-9, 170-1, 173,
- 187, 240, 250
Planck, Max 33-4, 161-3, 165-6, 221
Plasma, 249
Plato, 59, 74
Plenum, 59, 60
Podmore, F. 16
Poincarré, Louis 142
Poinsot, Louis 56
Poltergeist, 112
Precognition, 5, 6 9, 14-21, 24, 27-9, 35 *et seq*,
- 44, 48-50, 66-7, 179, 180, 182-3,
- 186, 201, 203-4, 257, 261
- assessment of 35
- audio type 24, 44
- belief in 14-5
- characteristics of 16, 19
- confusion with prediction 17-9, 21
- connection with Time 54
- definition 17-8, 28, 49
- disbelief in 35
- dream type 36 *et seq*
- evidence of 19, 35, 48
- examples of 35 *et seq*
- explanation of 50
- J.B.Priestley 67
- of disasters 36
- origin of 9
- Ouspensky thesis 66
- proof of 5
- research 5, 6, 9, 19, 35
- source of 33
- theories about 17
- time scan 28
- types of 9 *et seq*, 20-1, 27, 29
- via Space 2 48
Prediction, 16-9, 21, 23, 28-9, 44, 48
Premonition - characteristics 113, 119 146, 179,
- 251
- imagery in 129
- in dreams 9
- of Titanic disaster 30, 40 *et seq*

- rejection of 27
- warning 129
Prescience, 130
Price, Prof. H.H. 16
Priestley, J.B. 36-7, 68, 70, 80-1
Probability - Fig. 28
- degrees of 30
- of future events 18
- quantum physics 8
- sub-atomic particles 10
Probability Field, 93, 95, 97, 159, 163-4, 170, 172, 178, 196, 210-2, 215, 217, 221, 235, 238
- 251-2, 257-8, 260
- ahead of PM 93, 95, 97
- collapse of 97, 221, 238, 252, 255
- Geodesic 165, 175-6, 182,
- 186-8, 192, 198-200, 211, 216-7,
- 221, 261
- limitations 252
- wave 221-2, 235
Prophesies, 14, 21-2, 53, 89, 201
Proton, 32, 70, 165, 242, 246
Psitrons, 32
Psyche, 230
Psychiatry, 35, 70, 102, 106, 108-9, 126
Psychoanalysis, 102, 104-5, 112
Psychokinesis, 112, 164, 179, 182, 215, 257,
- 261
Psychology, 70, 106, 110, 229
Pucchini, Giacomo 145
Pulsars, 158
Pyrrus, 25
Pythagoras, 63-4, 79

Quanta, 163
Quantum, 4, 5, 8, 21, 32-3, 69-70, 85, 92, 158,
- 161-2, 165-6, 168, 221-2, 235,
- 239-41, 243-4, 246, 248, 250, 258-
- 261
- consciousness model 243
- discontinuity 158, 241
- indeterminacy 241
- level 166, 248, 260
- mechanics 240, 246, 250
- mind 4
- physics, 4, 8, 33, 69-70, 85, 92,
- 158, 161-2, 165, 168, 221-2, 240,
- 248, 258-9, 261
- relationship 5, 21, 239
- Schrödinger's Cat 235
- self 69, 238-9, 244
- systems 240
- theory 32, 235, 259
Quarks, 33
Quasars, 158

Racecourse Dream, 116
Radiation, 10, 160-3, 169, 199, 240
Randall, J. 76 et seq
Readiness-Potential, 257
Reality, 10, 14-5, 19-21, 28-9, 33, 38, 43, 108,
- 110, 115-21, 140, 150, 158-9, 176-
- 181, 186-7, 198-9, 206-9, 216-8,
- 221-2, 232, 235-7, 239, 241, 251
Redgrave, Sir Michael 36
Regeneration, 253 *et seq*
Reincarnation, 3, 4, 8, 63, 169, 182, 247, 258,
- 260
Relativity, 55, 57, 93, 162, 171, 174
REM, 111, 122, 127-8
Resonance, 250-1
Retrocognition, 50
Rheingold, 143
Rhine, Dr. J.B. 18-19, 201, 209
- Mrs Louisa 18-19
Rhythms, brain 212
Ridley, B.K. 164
Riemann, Georg F. Bernhard 76, 80-1, 133
Rigidity, gyroscopic 85
RNA, 181
Robertson, Morgan 45-6
Rossetti, 64
Rousseau, Waldeck 23
Russell, Lord, 153, 175

Salamander, 253 *et seq.* Fig. 32
Saltmarsh, 32, 34, 54
Sand, George 132, 144, 146
Sandage, Dr. Alan 88, 173
Sapiens, homo 13, 20, 88-9, 216, 227
Scatcherd, Miss 45
Schizophrenia, 236-7
Schmeidler, Gertrude 19
Schopenhauer, Arthur 180, 203, 206
Schrödinger, Erwin, 164, 199, 235, 237, 251
Schwann cells, 256
Scott, Sir Walter 141
Seances, 82
Self - 2, 9, 10, 24, 28-9, 34, 36, 38, 40, 43, 48,
- 61-3, 67, 69, 88-9, 91-2, 94-7, 107,
- 134-5, 139-40, 148-9, 150-1, 164-5,
- 169, 173, 179, 182, 221-2, 229,234
- 236*et seq*, 238, 243-5, 247-251
- 257-60
- abilities 62
- aging process 230
- as dream-maker 40
- awareness 94-5, 107, 226, 228,240
- 243, 259
- characteristics of 9, 94
- definition 9, 89, 221, 227, 229,238
- 257
- duration-extension 179, 181
- EMF 233, 247-9, 250, 260
- function 232, 236 *et seq*
- /mind duality 10, 222, 231-2, 234,
- 238, 244, 251
- in FTF 10, 24, 28-9, 34, 36, 88, 92
- 94-6, 135, 149
- in sleep 38, 43, 48, 94-5

- in Time Shunt 140, Fig. 18
- location 236, 238, 245 *et seq*
- migratory 61, 67
- observer of future events 94
- omnipresence in Space 2, 94, 140,
- 151, 250-1
- origin of 63
- other selves in Space 2 : 97, 148-9,
- 237
- quality 243
- quantum 69, 238 *et seq*
- survival after death 67, 91, 173
- Time traveller 94
- world-view 88
Semiconduction, 252
Senses, 13-4, 18, 49, 57, 64, 73, 96, 120, 122,
- 124, 208-9, 216, 220, 226, 259
Serios, Ted 212
Shakespeare, William 3, 26, 50
Shelley, Percy Bysshe 141-2, 145, 153
Shipton, Old Mother 27, 95
Shunt, Time 36, 44, 138-40, 146, 149, 151-2,
- 201, 205, 210, 217, 251-2, Fig. 18
Simultaneity, 68, 148
Sleep, 61, 65, 98, 109-11, 116, 122-3, 125-31,
- 136, 139, 142-3, 227, 231-2, 235
Slither, 157
Smith, Flt.Lt 42
Snake dream, 39
Soal, Dr.S.G. 18-9
Socrates, 132
Somnabulism, 106
Soul, 60, 63, 89, 107, 194, 206, 218
Space, 3, 10, 16, 21, 24, 27-8, 31-2, 36, 43, 49,
- 107-11, 115-6, 119-20, 123-4,
- 127-8, 145, 149, 151-3, 159-60,
- 162-5, 168-71, 173-5, 177-9, 181,
- 206, 222, 228, 235, 237-8, 241,
- 247, 249-51, 257-8, 260
`1' - 28, 48-9, 108, 111, 115, 127-8,
- 159-60, 162-5, 168-71, 173-5,
- 177
- 179, 181, 206
`2' - 16, 21, 24, 31, 34-6, 43, 48-9,
- 88, 107, 109-110, 115-6, 119,
- 123-124, 127-8, 160, 163-4
- 168-9,
- 173, 178, 181, 196, 205, 207,
- 211, 214-5, 217, 228, 237-8,
- 250, 257-260, Figs. 5, 19
- 3-D 67, 74
- Absolute 157, 162
- and matter 196
- and Time 198, 209
- characteristics 158
- curvature 159
- definition 58, 69, 76
- Einstein 57
- Euclidian 159
- electromagnetic fields 182
- expansion 159, Fig. 26
- gravitational effects 174-5
- hyper- 93
- interface with mind 119
- less 16
- origin of 62
- quantum level 165
- ship 18
- Shuttle 27
Space-Time - 140, 149, 151, 183, 206
- bubbles 173
- curvature 75, 76, 91, 93, 176
- distortion 158-60, 170-1, 177, Fig.
- 24
- effects of entropy 208
- J.B.Priestley 69
- lattice 173
- matrix 173, 182
- normal 207
- orderliness 208
- origin 171
- paths in 173
- rupture of 158, 174
- Void 159, 172-3, 182
- Zukav thesis 175
Spin, particle 165-6
SPR, 34, 42, 46
SQUID, 258
Stapp, Henry 258
State (see Mind, Consciousness), 221, 230, 232-3, 235-6, 239-42, 243, 247, 251
- awareness 240, 243
- background 241, 243
- energy 221
- hypnagogic 230, 233, 236
- induced coherent Fig. 31
- mentative 230, 232
- morphogenetic 247
- probability 241
- quantum coherency 240, 242
- resonance 251
- steady 241
- unconscious 235
- waking 230, 236, 251
- wave-function 221, 239
Statistics, 165, 189, 192, 198, 201-2, 206-7, 209,
- 258
Stevenson, R.L. 142
Stoker, air gunner 14-5, 38
Subconscious - see mind
Sulcus, 224
Sun, 58-9, 62, 74-5, 86, 88, 155-7, 159, 170-1
Superconductor, 69, 241-2
Superfluid, 241-2
Superliminal, 166, 168
Supernatural, 24
Survival, 3, 4, 8, 13
Swinburne, Algernon Charles 142
Symbolism, 9, 25-6, 39, 48, 103-4, 106
Synapse, 128, 224-6, 228, 236, 240, 250-2, 255-

- 257
- bridge 253
- data transmission 254
Synaesthesia, 249
Synchronicity, 70, 99, 194-6, 202-6, 209, 217
System, Autonomous 139-40, 146, 149
Szent-Gyorgyi, Albert 252

Tachyon, 84, 166, 168
Tarot cards, 53, 201, 251
Tchaikovsky, Pyotr Ilyich 141, 146
Telepathy, 4, 5, 16, 18-9, 27, 36, 112, 121, 145,
- 149, 151, 169, 179, 182, 189, 192,
- 204, 231, 241, 258, 261
Teleportation, 85
Tesseract, 77
Thackeray, William Makepeace 132, 143, 147,
- 210
Thalamus, 98, 224
Theætetus, 59
Theophrastus, 202
Thought 53, 95, 120, 125-8, 131, 221, 226, 229-
- 33, 240-1, 243-4,
- background 95, 120, 125-8, 131,233
- 240, 243
- creativeness 221, 230, 241
- incoherency 232
- process 226, 229-31, 233, 239-41,
- 244
- spatialisation of 53
- speed of 226
- train of 232
Time - 3-4, 7-10, 16-17, 20, 32, 36, 41, 44, 49,
- 52-3, 57-9, 60-3, 65, 67, 69, 70-2,
- 76, 78, 83-6, 91-4, 97-8, 108, 116,
- 122, 130, 134, 137-41, 146, 148-9,
- 151, 153, 156-8, 160-6, 169, 170-3,
- 175-182, 186, 188, 202, 215, 219,
- 221-2, 230, 232, 235, 240-1, 244-7,
- 249-53, 255, 257-8, 260-1
- Absolute 157, 162
- and energy 32
- and I Ching 215
- and inspiration 134, 137-8, 146,
- 149, 151
- and motion 156, 178
- and relativity 57
- and synchronicity 202
- Aristotle 58
- at quantum level 10
- beginning of 172
- Bentov thesis 178
- Bergson thesis 52
- bibliography 3
- confusion with duration 61, 65
- David Lowe 62
- definition 7, 57-8
- dilation 91, 83, 97
- dimensions 65
- Dunne 71
- endless 160, 172
- Experiment with 20, 138
- flow 57, 69, 178
- identical twins 185-6, 188-9, 190-3
- in dreams 108, 116, 122
- infinite 160, 172
- in FTF 8-10, 49, 108, 116, 130, 148
- 169, 222,
- in static universe 78
- Isaac Newton 57
- less, 8, 10, 16
- linear 61
- loop 41, 139
- Kohler 62-3
- lapse 61, 69, 76, 84, 91-2
- machine 94
- measurement 53, 84, 91
- Mechanism 2, 4, 7, 17, 240
- objective perception 52
- perception of 57, 61, 67, 116
- research 7, 138
- reversal 221
- secret of 4
- Serial 10
- Shunt 36, 44, 98, 138-41, 146, 149
- 151, 251-2
- Sigmund Freud 61
- St. Augustine 60
- subjective perception 52, 84-5
- terminology 57
- /Time interface 219, 230, 249
- travel 92-3
- unidirectionality 57, 149
- warps 70
- world view 4, 58, 61, 63, 72, 86
- Zeno's Paradox 59
Tirewsias, 25
Titan, SS 45-6
Titanic, SS 29-31, 40-6, 53, 113, 138
Tolstoy, Alexis 64
Trance, 20, 26-7, 61, 92, 99, 137, 140, 144, 147
Twins, identical 5, 60, 72, 111, 166, 168-9, 182,
- 183, 185-90, 192-3, 240, 251
Tyrrell, G.N.M. 17-8, 40, 134, 144, 149, 233

UFO, 5, 93-4
Uncertainty, Principle of 7, 32-3, 35
Unconscious, 143, 148
Universe, 3, 4, 5, 8-9, 11, 16, 34, 50, 55, 58-60,
- 62-4, 67, 69, 70-72, 74-6, 77-80,
- 87-9, 92-94, 97-8, 151, 155, 157-8,
- 160-3, 170-4, 177-8, 180-182, 186,
- 196, 199, 203-7, 209, 214, 216-8,
- 225, 237, 239-40, 258-261
- 3-D 71, 74, 76, 78, 93
- adjacent 178
- and causality 206
- and FTF 151
- and reincarnation 259, 260
- and synchronicity 206

- and Time 72
- age 88, 89, 157, 172
- as a thought 218
- background light 157
- black holes 177
- co-existent 9-11, 64, 69, 74, 77, 93
- 158, 170, 173, 180, 182
- cyclic 8, 63-4
- creation 160-1, 181
- definition 72
- deterministic 16, 196, 199, 206
- development 158
- dimensions 55, 63, 75, 97
- disequilibrium 157
- dissolution of 67
- effects of entropy 207
- Einstein 162
- eternal 5, 60
- expansion 59, 64, 74, 157, 160, 171,
- 174
- functioning of 3, 34, 161
- in flux 60, 92
- intelligent 181
- layers 50
- macroscopic 177
- Mankind's place 4, 88, 155, 158,
- 180-1, 205, 216-7
- meaning of 181, 205
- microscopic 177
- models 158
- Mobius Strip model Fig. 11
- moving 58, 62, 163, 178
- multi-dimensional 79
- Newtonian 80, 157, 162
- one-ness 203-6, 205, 209, 214, 217,
- origin of 5, 87, 261
- parallel 94
- size 172
- static 70, 74, 76, 98, 170
- structure of 4, 16
- succession of 171, 258
- Timeless 8
- Void 174
- world view 209

Valhalla, 148
Virgil, 26
Vision, 14, 36, 111, 117, 125, 134, 136, 142,
- 145-7, 151, 208, 224
Voice, 9, 24, 26, 34, 41, 45, 110-11, 113-4, 128-
- 130
Void, 59-60, 77-8, 117, 157, 159-61, 170-6,
- 181, 206, 233, 241, 246

Wagner, Wilhelm Richard 143
Warning dream, 9, 27, 32, 35-6, 40, 42
- frequency of 35
- ignoring 32
- motivation of 35
- of disasters 36, 40, 42
- precognitive 27
- visual type 36
Wasserman, Prof. G.D. 247
Watson, Lyall 21, 249
Wave, 33, 43, 66, 70-1, 76-7, 83, 85, 95-7,
- 125, 158, 162-5, 168, 174, 178,
- 181, 221-2, 235, 238-40, 249-51,
- 257, 261
- characteristics 239
- definition 162
- description 164
- electromagnetic 249-50
- interaction 251
- function, 33, 43, 70, 85, 93-6,
- 163, 178-9, 183-4, 186-7, 216-7,
- 221-2, 235-6, 238-41, 250-1, 258,
- light 163
- matter 222
- packet 164
- /particle duality 222, 232, 235, 238,
- 239
- probability 221-2, 235, 238, 251,
- sound 242
Wavelength, 160, 162-3, 165
Wechsler, David 250
Wernicke's Area, 228
Wilkinson, D.H. 69
Williams, J.H. 40
Wilson, Colin 5, 40, 173, 180-1, 185, 188
- 192, 212
Wordsworth, William 142
World - 2-D 97
- 3-D 77, 82
- lines 55, 71
- Lineworld 79
- prehistoric 53
Worley, Doug 6-8, 31, 139, 161

X-rays, 77, 162

Yeats, W.B. 141
Yoga, 124
York, Susannah 94
Young, Thomas 162-3, 166-8, 180-1, 207, 227,
- Figs. 20-23
Zechariah, 22
Zohar, Danah - `Quantum Self' 27, 69, 221-2,
- 234-5, 238-241, 243
- `Through the Time Barrier' 34
Zukav, Gary 69, 162, 175, 246, 248